CULTURE OF ENCOUNTERS

SOUTH ASIA ACROSS THE DISCIPLINES

SOUTH ASIA ACROSS THE DISCIPLINES

EDITED BY MUZAFFAR ALAM, ROBERT GOLDMAN, AND GAURI VISWANATHAN

DIPESH CHAKRABARTY, SHELDON POLLOCK, AND SANJAY SUBRAHMANYAM, FOUNDING EDITORS

Funded by a grant from the Andrew W. Mellon Foundation and jointly published by the University of California Press, the University of Chicago Press, and Columbia University Press

South Asia Across the Disciplines is a series devoted to publishing first books across a wide range of South Asian studies, including art, history, philology or textual studies, philosophy, religion, and the interpretive social sciences. Series authors all share the goal of opening up new archives and suggesting new methods and approaches, while demonstrating that South Asian scholarship can be at once deep in expertise and broad in appeal.

For a list of books in the series, see page 363.

CULTURE OF ENCOUNTERS

SANSKRIT AT THE MUGHAL COURT

Audrey Truschke

COLUMBIA UNIVERSITY PRESS NEW YORK

Columbia University Press
Publishers Since 1893
New York Chichester, West Sussex
cup.columbia.edu

Paperback edition, 2019

Library of Congress Cataloging-in-Publication Data
Truschke, Audrey.
Culture of encounters : Sanskrit at the Mughal Court / Audrey Truschke.
pages cm. — (South Asia across the disciplines)
Includes bibliographical references and index.
ISBN 978-0-231-17362-9 (cloth)—ISBN 978-0-231-17363-6 (pbk.)—
ISBN 978-0-231-54097-1 (e-book)
1. Sanskrit language—History. 2. Sanskrit language—Usage.
3. Sanskrit language—Knowledge. 4. Sanskrit language—Etymology.
5. Mogul Empire—Intellectual life. 6. Mogul Empire—Court and courtiers.
I. Title.

PK423.T78 2015
491'.209—dc23
2015009585

COVER IMAGE: Arjuna slays Karna in *Razmnāmah*, 1616–1617

For Dad

CONTENTS

CONCLUSION: POWER, LITERATURE,
AND EARLY MODERNITY   229

PREFACE AND ACKNOWLEDGMENTS

THIS BOOK is about culture, literature, and power. More specifically, it is about how power works in relationship to literature, how poets and writers participate in politically fueled cross-cultural movements, and the elusive dynamics of cultural traditions. The case study is how and why the Mughals—one of the most impressive imperial powers of the precolonial world—engaged with Sanskrit texts, intellectuals, and ideas, and how Sanskrit intellectuals—some of the most sophisticated thinkers and poets of the precolonial world—responded to and participated in this demand for Indian stories, practices, and philosophies. This set of cross-cultural engagements did not merely constitute a handful of curiosities or intellectual experiments for either the Mughals or their Sanskrit interlocutors. For roughly one hundred years the Mughal elite poured immense energy into drawing Sanskrit thinkers to their courts, adopting and adapting Sanskrit-based practices, translating dozens of Sanskrit texts into Persian, and composing Persian accounts of Indian philosophy. Both Persian- and Sanskrit-medium authors blazed new paths within their respective literary cultures in response to this imperial agenda. When all was said and done, Mughal-Sanskrit engagements constituted one of the most extensive cross-cultural encounters in precolonial world history, rivaled by the likes of the Abbasid engagement with Greek thought in the eighth to tenth centuries and Chinese translations of Buddhist Sanskrit materials during the first millennium C.E.

Engaging with Sanskrit was not an obvious move for the Mughal dynasty. The Mughals came to India from Central Asia, were Muslims, and spoke Persian. India's vast learned traditions, written largely in Sanskrit, were no doubt intriguing, but the Mughals had several learned traditions (e.g., those in Persian, Arabic, and Turkish) that they could more seamlessly claim as their own. So why were the Mughals so interested in Sanskrit? I answer this question throughout the book. To put it succinctly, the Mughals understood power, in part, as an aesthetic practice, and they wanted to think about themselves as an Indian empire. They turned to Sanskrit to figure out what it meant for them to be sovereigns of the subcontinent. For their part, Sanskrit intellectuals did not merely assist the Mughals in their quest to learn about classical Indian knowledge systems; they also wrote about their imperial encounters and reimagined their literary and religious communities in light of Mughal rule. Indo-Persian thinkers, too, had many things to say about Mughal-Sanskrit engagements, and their reactions, in part, define what we mean today by the term "Indo-Persian." I narrate this story in its rich detail. Moreover, I pose and investigate queries concerning sovereignty, literary traditions, cultural dynamics, translation, and diversity that are pertinent far beyond the Mughal polity. For instance, I analyze political identity as a site for formulating ruling and cultural authority and suggest ways that we might think about large-scale shifts in literary traditions. Whether you are interested in empire, early modernity, Sanskrit, Indo-Persian, the relationship between politics and literature, or cross-cultural encounters, the story of Sanskrit at the Mughal court offers a wealth of invigorating resources.

◈ ◈ ◈

This book has been a decade in the making. In that time, it has undergone numerous changes and benefited from many avenues of support. Its first incarnation was as my dissertation at Columbia University, titled "Cosmopolitan Encounters: Sanskrit and Persian at the Mughal Court." In that form, I uncovered and tried to make sense of how members of two literary traditions, Sanskrit and Persian, decided to interact with each other (and each other's literary traditions) at the early modern courts of Akbar, Jahangir, and Shah Jahan. Few scholars of South Asia have been able to work in both Sanskrit and Persian. Analytically, this bifurcation has often replicated modern communal divisions between Hindus and Muslims (who are generally identified with specific linguistic traditions, Sanskrit/Hindi and Persian/Urdu, respectively). Practically, the language limits of most scholars meant that little prior work had been done to identify the archive of extant textual materials on Sanskrit-Persian encounters.

Accordingly, a large part of the work that went into my dissertation was identifying the relevant materials, working through key texts, and reconstructing what actually happened that involved both Sanskrit and Persian in the Mughal context from the mid-sixteenth until the mid-seventeenth centuries. Upon this foundation of laborious archival and textual work, I constructed this book. The period, major players, and scene remain the same. I have incorporated numerous new texts and encounters into the book. In contrast to my dissertation, the book engages more deeply with historical questions (although, I hope, without sacrificing literary analysis). The book also reframes the set of historical events I seek to investigate. I continue to be drawn to literary and linguistic categories (e.g., Sanskrit and Persian), but Mughal imperial power has emerged as the lynchpin of my narrative here.

◈ ◈ ◈

No book stands alone, and I am profoundly grateful to the many universities, institutions, archives, and individuals that have assisted with this project. I am honored to have received a Fulbright-Hays Doctoral Dissertation Research Abroad grant that funded one year of international research (2009–2010) in India, the United Kingdom, and France. Much of the manuscript work that undergirds this book stems from that opportunity. I thank the Andrew W. Mellon Foundation and the American Council of Learned Societies for a Dissertation Completion Fellowship (2011–2012). Gonville and Caius College at the University of Cambridge appointed me as a research fellow in the fall of 2012, which provided me with the time necessary to do the bulk of the heavy lifting crafting the first draft of this book. I completed this process at Stanford University, where I began as an Andrew W. Mellon Postdoctoral Fellow in Religious Studies in the fall of 2013. My warmhearted thanks go to both the Mellon Fellowship program and the Department of Religious Studies for enabling me to devote a significant amount of time to research and writing.

In terms of archives, many libraries, universities, and temples gave me access to their manuscript resources. Thanks are due in India to Acharya Shri Kailasasagarsuri Gyanmandir in Koba; Allahabad Municipal Museum; Anandasrama in Pune; Anup Sanskrit Library in Bikaner; Asiatic Society in Calcutta; Asiatic Society of Mumbai; Bhandarkar Oriental Research Institute in Pune; Bharat Itihas Sanshodhak Mandal in Pune; the Birla family in Calcutta; Deccan College in Pune; Digambara Jain Terapanth Bada Mandir in Jaipur; Hemacandra Jnana Mandir in Patan; Indira Gandhi National Centre for the Arts in Delhi; Iran Culture House in Delhi; Khuda Bakhsh Oriental Public Library in Patna; K. R. Cama Oriental Institute in Mumbai; LD Institute of Indology in Ahmedabad; Lucknow State Museum; Maharaja Man Singh Pustak Prakash in Jodhpur; Maulana Azad Library at Aligarh Muslim University; National Library in Calcutta; Oriental Institute in Baroda; Oriental Manuscript Library and Research Institute at Osmania University in Hyderabad; Rajasthan Oriental Research Institute in Jodhpur; Rampur Raza Library; Salar Jung Museum in Hyderabad; and the University of Mumbai. In Europe, I benefited from the resources and hospitality of the following archives: Bibliothèque nationale de France, Bodleian Library, British Library, Cambridge University Library, Royal Asiatic Society of Great Britain and Ireland in London, and Wellcome Library. I extend thanks to the Museum of Islamic Art in Doha, Qatar, and the Freer Gallery of Art in Washington, D.C., for providing access to key manuscripts. In addition to those mentioned in the preceding, I acknowledge the Art Institute of Chicago, the Cleveland Museum of Art, the Free Library of Philadelphia, and the Oriental Research Library in Srinagar for giving me permission to reproduce images from their collections. My sincere and heartfelt gratitude goes especially to those institutions that allowed me to photograph manuscripts or provided copies at a reasonable rate, a necessary privilege for enabling serious textual work.

I stand on the shoulders of many giants who have supported and shaped this book over the past decade. Special thanks go to Sheldon Pollock, who has challenged and supported me at every step of my work. I am profoundly grateful for his time, criticisms, and advice over the years. Allison Busch has likewise been formative to my research through countless enlightening conversations and her close attention to detail. Muzaffar Alam patiently taught me to read Persian manuscripts and has always been eager to push me further.

In addition, I thank the many scholars and colleagues who have helped at various stages of my research by providing valuable feedback, helpful questions, and encouragement. Key interlocutors and helpful critics include Janaki Bakhle, Shahzad Bashir, John Cort, Victor D'Avella, Debra Diamond, Arthur Dudney, Paul Dundas, Richard Eaton, Munis Faruqui, Supriya Gandhi, Najaf Haider, Walter Hakala, Jack Hawley, Abhishek Kaicker, Hossein Kamaly, Sudipta Kaviraj, Gulfishan Khan, Dipti Khera, Mana Kia, Anubhuti Maurya, Rachel McDermott, A. Azfar Moin, Francesca

Orsini, Frances Pritchett, Yael Rice, Sreeramula Rajeswara Sarma, Katherine Schofield, John Seyller, Sunil Sharma, Dan Sheffield, Hamsa Stainton, Somadeva Vasudeva, Anand Venkatkrishnan, Stacey Van Vleet, and Steven Vose. In addition, several colleagues assisted me with accessing manuscript collections at key points, including Krista Gulbransen, Jon Keune, and Pasha M. Khan.

Last, but never least, none of this would have been possible without my family, who have always encouraged me, often traveled to the subcontinent with me, and have graciously learned an incredible amount about India's past. I especially thank my husband for walking with me every step of this journey.

NOTE ON TRANSLITERATION AND OTHER SCHOLARLY CONVENTIONS

I HAVE AVOIDED diacritics for the names of kings, gods, places, characters, and languages. I use them for the names of intellectuals, texts, and technical terms. I follow standard Sanskrit transliteration and the Library of Congress (ALA-LC) system for Persian. At a few points I have reconstructed Sanskrit terms that are quoted (and, frequently, bungled) in Persian texts. I have flagged such occasions. I typically translate Persian terms, including names, that appear in Sanskrit texts without diacritics. Because of the high degree of transliteration in certain texts and my emphasis on translations, certain terms are spelled differently depending on whether they appear in Sanskrit or Persian (e.g., *Rāmāyaṇa* in Sanskrit but *Rāmāyan* in Persian).

All translations from Sanskrit, Persian, and Hindi are my own unless otherwise stated. I cite original language sources wherever possible. I transcribe quotes only if the original language is relevant to my argument or I am citing an unpublished manuscript and the language may be of interest to specialists. I do not hypercorrect either Sanskrit or Persian passages, and so some transliterated quotes contain grammatical and spelling variants.

CULTURE OF ENCOUNTERS

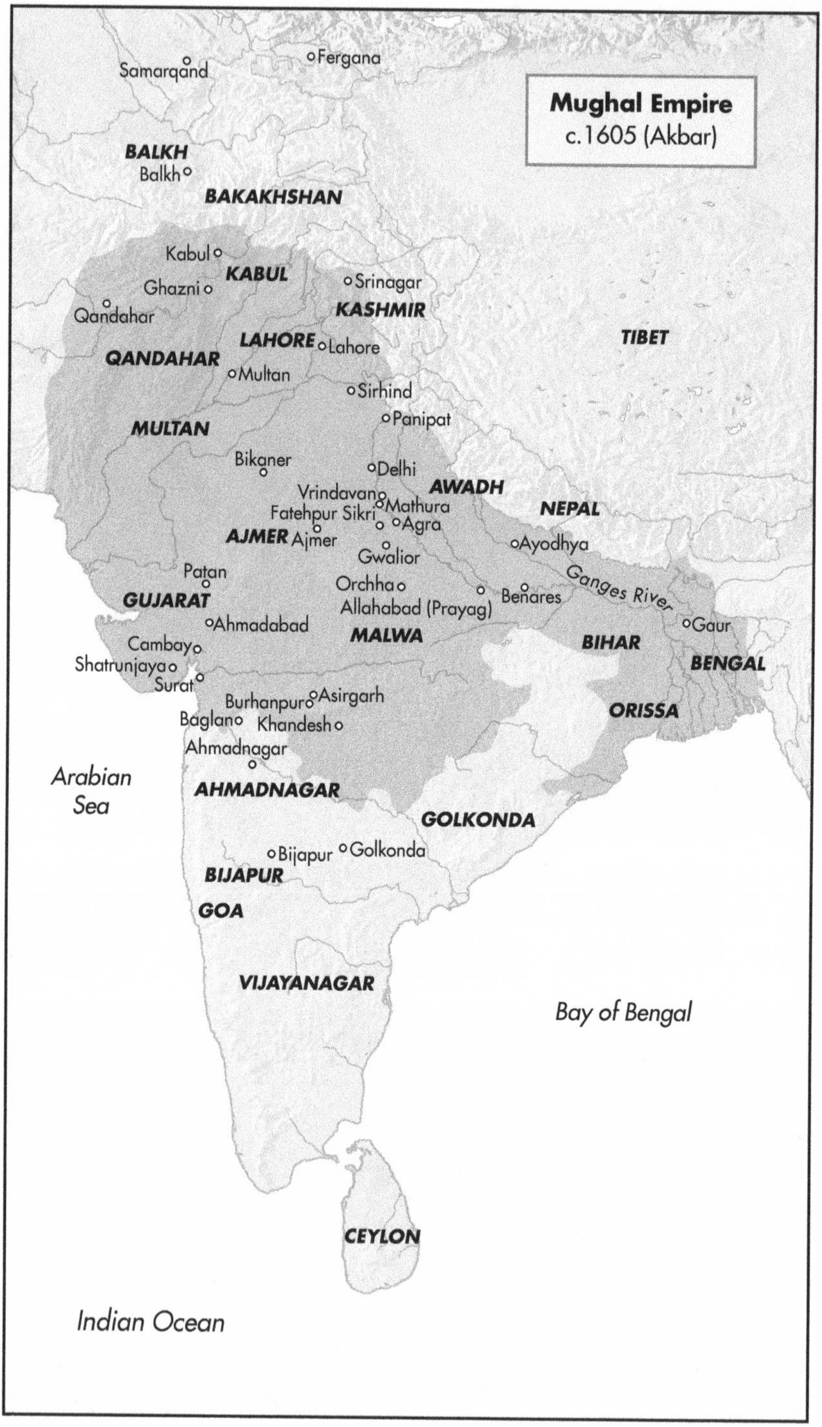

Mughal Empire
c.1605 (Akbar)
Samarqand
Fergana
BALKH
Balkh
BAKAKHSHAN
Kabul
KABUL
Ghazni
Qandahar
Srinagar
KASHMIR
TIBET
LAHORE
Lahore
QANDAHAR
Multan
Sirhind
Panipat
MULTAN
Bikaner
Delhi
AWADH
Vrindavan
Mathura
NEPAL
Fatehpur Sikri
Agra
AJMER
Ajmer
Ayodhya
Gwalior
Patan
Ganges River
Orchha
Benares
GUJARAT
Allahabad (Prayag)
Gaur
Ahmadabad
MALWA
BIHAR
Cambay
BENGAL
Shatrunjaya
Surat
Burhanpur
Asirgarh
ORISSA
Baglan
Khandesh
Ahmadnagar
Arabian
Sea
AHMADNAGAR
GOLKONDA
Bijapur
Golkonda
BIJAPUR
GOA
VIJAYANAGAR
Bay of Bengal
CEYLON
Indian Ocean

INTRODUCTION

THE MUGHAL CULTURE OF POWER

During the sixteenth and seventeenth centuries, the Mughals built one of the most powerful empires in the early modern world. Their wealth was unmatched in both the East and the West, they inspired writers across the world with their conquests and luxurious court culture, and at their height they ruled more people than any other political power of the time. Today, however, the Mughals are largely forgotten. The Indian state advertises Mughal palaces and mausoleums, above all the Taj Mahal, to attract tourism, and Mughal names are occasionally bandied about in charged political contexts on the subcontinent. Certain figures, such as Akbar and his Hindu minister, Birbal, feature in children's comic books in India. But, for most of the world, the Mughals are a dynasty lost to history, a relic of an unknown past that is buried deep below the far better studied British Raj and the modern nations of India and Pakistan. The Mughals certainly remain crucial in the historical study of South Asia. But the general assessment among scholars, indicated more by omission than argument, is that this early modern empire has little to contribute to our understanding of the world more broadly. In this book I argue that contrary to their undue neglect, the Mughals have a great deal to tell us about historical and contemporary issues, including the perils and possibilities of cultural diversity and the inner workings of political power.

Political authority is an unrelenting feature of human society, but we possess surprisingly inadequate tools for parsing the actions of governments beyond controlling and administering a set area of land. Politicians engage in all sorts of other activities, chief among them promoting and shaping culture and providing narratives of their own rise to power.

Too often scholars uncritically proclaim that such projects aim to justify a given king, president, or regime in the eyes of the masses. More recently scholars have begun to question whether this emphasis on legitimating one's rule to others, a theory to which I will return, enlightens or obscures our understanding of ruling dynamics.[1] As Rodney Barker has argued, following on Weber, rather than seeing legitimation as solely an instrumental activity directed outward, it is high time we also recognized the self-legitimation of rulers, the need to provide oneself with a distinctive political identity.[2] The Mughal Empire offers a prime case study in this regard. The Mughals cultivated a particular type of power, based on continually refining an image of themselves as Indian sovereigns, that can help us understand the actions of rulers and politicians far beyond South Asia, both in early modernity and today.

For the Mughals, power was often about the rulers first and foremost rather than the ruled. This plain fact has escaped many historians, and a cascade of other misunderstandings has followed. Chief among our modern oversights is a general failure to appreciate that the Mughal culture of power was inextricably linked with wide-ranging literary, aesthetic, and intellectual interests in Sanskrit traditions. Scholars have often neglected Mughal court culture in favor of emphasizing economic and administrative histories.[3] But even those interested in softer forms of authority have generally judged Mughal imperial culture too narrowly. In this book I argue that the Mughal imperium, particularly its central court, was defined largely by repeated engagements with Sanskrit thinkers, texts, and ideas. Select Indian communities that the Mughals ruled (primarily Brahmans and Jains) provided access to Sanskrit forms of knowledge and served as interlocutors for the imperial elite. However, these groups did not treat such encounters as a referendum on whether or not they were governed by a legitimate power. Indeed, Sanskrit thinkers seem to have had little interest in considering whether Mughal rule was legitimate or justified, which suggests that the contemporary focus on this question is anachronistic. Instead, Jains and Brahmans far more commonly viewed Sanskrit and Persian exchanges as an opportunity to participate in the imperial project and tried to adapt Mughal cross-cultural endeavors to the structures of their own literary, social, and religious networks. This largely unknown history has much to tell us about the diverse Sanskrit-language communities in Mughal India. Equally important, the Mughals and their Brahman and Jain interlocutors offer a notably rich set of insights into the complex relationship between power and culture, a dynamic that defined the lives of many early modern Indians no less than it shapes our own.

REWRITING THE HISTORY OF THE MUGHAL EMPIRE

The Mughals were a Persianate dynasty, meaning that they sponsored Persian as a major language of culture and administration. From the mid-sixteenth century onward, the Mughal kings extended lavish patronage to literature and the arts and fashioned their central court as a cultural mecca that attracted Persianate poets, thinkers, and artists from across much of Asia. Additionally, in an attempt to streamline government operations, Emperor Akbar (r. 1556–1605) declared Persian the official language of administration in 1582. Scholars have typically viewed these two processes as connected and generally declare that, after the 1580s, little space was left for Indian languages to flourish at the Mughal courts. Accordingly, Indologists have typically depicted Mughal imperial life as confined to the Persian-medium world, with occasional appearances from other Islamicate languages such as Arabic and Turkish. Scholars have almost uniformly ignored the role of Sanskrit, India's premier classical tongue, as a major component of Mughal political, intellectual, and literary activities.[4] This oversight has long obscured the close imperial relationship with the Sanskrit cultural world as well as the multicultural nature of Mughal power.

In fact, at the same time that the Mughals promoted Persian as a language of culture and administration, members of the ruling elite also aggressively formed ties with Sanskrit literati and engaged with Sanskrit texts. In the 1560s and 1570s, Sanskrit thinkers from across the subcontinent first entered the central court. By the 1580s, the Mughals hosted an array of Jain and Brahmanical intellectuals at court, bestowed titles on members of both communities, and supported a stunning range of Sanskrit textual production. Simultaneously, under royal orders, Mughal literati started to translate Sanskrit texts into Persian and compose their own expositions of Sanskrit knowledge systems. Seeking to capitalize on the court's interest in Sanskrit, regional rulers and communities commissioned Sanskrit praise poems for the consumption of the Mughal elite and also sent Sanskrit intellectuals to the central court. Most of these activities continued throughout the reigns of Jahangir (r. 1605–1627) and Shah Jahan (r. 1628–1658), coming to a close only in the mid-seventeenth century. In these ways Sanskrit literary culture flourished alongside Persian at the Mughal court. Moreover, these exchanges produced great effects within both cosmopolitan traditions, and Persianate and Sanskrit literati each responded in a myriad of written ways to Mughal cross-cultural engagements.

In this book, I reconstruct the forgotten history of Sanskrit at the central Mughal court from 1560 to 1660. Furthermore, I argue that these literary interactions and the networks in which they were embedded are not mere curiosities in the intellectual landscape of South Asia. Rather, these cross-cultural events are critical to understanding early modern literary dynamics and the construction of authority during Mughal rule. In terms of literary impacts, Mughal engagements with Sanskrit significantly affected the Sanskrit and Indo-Persian thought worlds, which both underwent massive changes during early modernity. Both traditions interacted with each other's ideas, idioms, and stories on unprecedented levels during the Mughal period. The Sanskrit tradition began to wane in the seventeenth and eighteenth centuries, ultimately collapsing almost entirely. We are still struggling to understand both the mechanisms behind its fall and the constitution of this classical tradition on the eve of its decline. The many crossroads that brought together Sanskrit and the Mughals speak to both sets of questions and constitute a neglected chapter in the history of India's longest-lived intellectual culture. The Indo-Persian tradition thrived as a literary and political force on the subcontinent well into the nineteenth century. As we shall see, the Mughals often strove to recalibrate this cultural tradition through their involvements with Sanskrit. They largely succeeded, and Indo-Persian culture during the seventeenth century and later was indelibly shaped by the earlier Mughal penchant for forming links with the Sanskrit tradition. More broadly, these dialogues across linguistic boundaries helped to solidify exchanges between different traditions as a prevailing mode of cultural growth and change in early modern India.

The Mughals articulated their political claims largely through interacting with the Sanskrit tradition. Recovering this key venue for developing and expressing Mughal imperial authority requires overturning a number of scholarly assumptions, including the presumed proper sources for accessing the Mughal past, the cultural framework of the central royal court, and the nature of power itself in early modern India. If the Mughals are approached with fresh eyes, their dynamic interweaving of politics and culture can be identified as the solid bedrock on which they built their empire. The Mughals cultivated a thoroughly multicultural and multilingual imperial image that involved repeated attention to Sanskrit texts, intellectuals, and knowledge systems. Monarchs and communities outside the ruling elite responded to this self-fashioning in many ways, and their reactions no doubt encouraged the Mughals to continue these dynamic encounters. Nonetheless, the Mughals did not pursue this set of exchanges for the benefit of their population but rather mainly for themselves. They sought to understand what it meant to become rulers of India. In the absence of an obvious answer, the Mughals set out to formulate a cluster of possibilities, many of which prominently featured Sanskrit, India's foremost premodern tongue of literature and learning. Reconstructing this complex set of encounters will undoubtedly change how Indologists understand Mughal history and also offers a fruitful case study for analyzing the culture of power in a non-Western, premodern setting. The Mughals may have declared Persian the medium of government, but activities at the royal court reveal a significantly more complex picture of how imperial claims actually worked on the early modern subcontinent.

SANSKRIT, INDO-PERSIAN, AND MULTILINGUALISM

The history of Sanskrit at the Mughal court involves interactions across the lines of culture, religion, and language. The best vocabulary for speaking about the participants in these exchanges is often elusive. Conventional discussions of cross-cultural activities in South Asia have prominently featured the categories of "Hindus" and "Muslims." Foregrounding religious identities is an old habit in Indological scholarship, but it has arguably done more harm than good. The religion-based dichotomy of Hindus and Muslims assumes conflict and difference where there was often cooperation and similarity.[5] In addition, the Hindu-Muslim division anachronistically projects two separate and broadly coherent, faith-based communities. In short, talking about Hindus and Muslims is largely a modern preoccupation that does not capture early modern religious diversity as well as other, more central configurations of identities. "Hindu" can be convenient shorthand for indicating the general cultural and religious background of a given individual, and I occasionally use the term thus. But we have too often clumsily labeled as either Hindu or Muslim individuals who elected to describe themselves and one another according to other geographic, religious, and ethnic classifications.[6] It should no longer surprise scholars that speaking about "religion" at all outside the modern Western world is a tricky business that, if done blithely, frequently obscures rather than elucidates cultural dynamics.[7]

In response to such criticisms, many scholars have adopted alternative dichotomies, the most useful of which is Islamicate and Indic. Marshall Hodgson introduced the term "Islamicate" in the 1970s in order to characterize aspects of Muslim civilizations that exceed the strictures of religion.[8] By this coinage, Hodgson wished to encourage scholars to investigate understudied aspects of Muslim societies that fall under the rubric of culture more easily than that of religion. "Indic" (or the more common "Indian") serves as a nice parallel to "Islamicate" and allows multiple Indian religious traditions to be grouped under a single loose umbrella of shared culture without positing a static, close-knit community. In the pages that follow, I frequently employ both terms and contribute to the ongoing scholarly project to highlight nonexplicitly religious materials in the study of South Asia. Nonetheless, these concepts also have their limits. At times, the juxtaposition of Islamicate and Indic seems to block the possibility of a Muslim tradition that is situated within the subcontinent and definably Indian. This concern is partly semantic (and I do not mean to suggest that Islamic things cannot also be Indian). But these broad and porous labels do not enable us to fully capture the distinct groups that met at the Mughal court.

Some Indologists have renounced altogether any divide that follows religious or civilizational boundaries in favor of emphasizing a joint syncretic or composite culture. This framework posits that early modern Indians participated in a common social milieu that incorporated both Indian and Perso-Islamic elements.[9] A hybrid sphere avoids the pitfall of assuming that cross-cultural meetings were characterized by fundamental incomprehension when in fact complex communications often took place.[10] I too wish to emphasize a shared space and a joint set of concerns that facilitated exchanges between members of different communities. But the notion of a single public realm fails to capture contacts as movements between discrete traditions. In this vein, Shahid Amin warns that the modern tendency to focus on syncretism may cause us "to miss out on the creation of India's vaunted composite culture as a *process*."[11] Moreover, as Thomas de Bruijn reminds us, while hybridity remains a popular metaphor in historical analyses of South Asia, this concept, especially in its idealistic forms, tells us more about our current preoccupations than the past.[12]

In many ways, the linguistic categories of Sanskrit and Persian most accurately describe the literary communities, textual materials, and power relations that I seek to analyze. In part, my emphasis on texts renders language a sensible mode of characterization, but these linguistic terms also connote larger cultural and political formations. Sanskrit and Persian were both cosmopolitan traditions in early modern India in the sense that they were expansive in time and space and cut across religious, ethnic, and regional boundaries.[13] Both were also strongly linked with sovereignty. Since the early first millennium of the Common Era, Indian kings had deemed Sanskrit literature a primary idiom for expressing their political ambitions. In part, I show here how Sanskrit continued to function as a cosmopolitan tradition under Mughal rule, particularly in offering appealing options for imagining and enacting imperial power. Persian was a newer tradition but had its own rich history as a courtly tongue for kings in the Middle East and India.[14] Under Mughal rule, Persian was inextricably linked with the state and had a complex and overlapping relationship with other vehicles for cultivating sovereign identity.

Sanskrit literati and intellectuals are people who wrote in Sanskrit or were renowned for their knowledge of that learned tradition. In Sanskrit, thinkers had long used the term "learned" (*śiṣṭa*) to describe an elite class defined by proper use of the Sanskrit language or residence on the subcontinent.[15] The Mughals frequently referred to these individuals with terms that are likewise predicated on cultural tradition and locale (e.g., *ahl-i hind*, *hindī*, and *hindū*) and are best translated as Indian or Sanskrit depending on the context. Sanskrit literati have always formed a fuzzy community in the sense that its members also possessed other identities that were tied to caste, region, trade, and so forth. Different markers of identity were more or less salient in different situations.[16] Those involved with the Mughals were a diverse crowd, particularly in their religious and geographic backgrounds. The group included Brahmans, the upper caste of Hinduism and the most numerous class of Sanskrit-using Indian elites, and also Jains, a religious minority who consistently participated in a larger Sanskrit cultural milieu. These literati came from across the Mughal imperium and beyond, including Gujarat, Bengal, the Deccan, Kashmir, and Rajasthan. Their layered identities often shaped how a given individual wrote in Sanskrit and acted in Mughal environs, and Jains in particular often pursued theological objectives through their imperial interactions. Nonetheless, a strong affiliation with Sanskrit and its conceptual categories remained a defining mark of these individuals and distinguished them within the more expansive categories of Brahmans, Jains, and Indians.[17]

Notably, Sanskrit intellectuals as I use the category in this book do not include Rajputs, Hindus, or other ethnic Indians who joined the Mughal administration and became absorbed into Persian-speaking communities. Such individuals proliferated from Akbar's reign forward. But they embody a story of cultural meetings and assimilation separate from the one I explore here. Unlike most Sanskrit literati, the Mughal Hindu elite learned Persian, and many even wrote Persian poetry, such as Chandar Bhān Brahman, who worked as an imperial secretary (*munshī*) under Shah Jahan.[18] Some Hindu members of the nobility, such as Todar Mal, Akbar's finance minister, maintained strong ties with the Sanskrit literary world as patrons but largely independently of their imperial responsibilities.[19] When such people appear in this book, they are classified as belonging to the Indo-Persian world because this is the linguistic milieu in which they operated within the Mughal court. In contrast, only a few Sanskrit intellectuals are known to have learned Persian.[20] Instead, their major contributions to Mughal court life generally involved opening up imperial linguistic and cultural boundaries to include Sanskrit.

Mughal political figures and Persianate intellectuals served as the primary interlocutors with Sanskrit literati at the royal court. The pairing of a political affiliation (Mughal) with a linguistic one (Sanskrit) reflects the uneven social groundings of these two communities. The Mughals were characterized largely by their ruling authority, which in turn significantly shaped the terms of their interactions with Sanskrit intellectuals and ideas. The Mughals also actively cultivated a court culture that featured Persian art and literature and is often called Persianate or Indo-Persian. Just as Islamicate divorces the cultures of Muslims from religious practices, so too does Persianate separate a cultural affiliation from the ethnic and geographical markers of Persia. The term Indo-Persian is often equally apt, however, because it foregrounds the Indian location of the Mughals while still emphasizing their chosen language of administration.[21] The Mughal Persianate elite incorporated people from an array of ethnic backgrounds, including Central Asians, Turks, Persians, and Indians.

Alongside their support for Persian-medium culture, the Mughals energetically shaped their court as a multilingual space. Even before they developed an interest in Sanskrit, the Mughals were never a monolingual dynasty. The founder of the empire, Babur, wrote in both Persian and Turkish and penned his memoirs in a dialect of the latter. Several generations of kings maintained some knowledge of the family tongue of Turkish.[22] By Akbar's rule, the royal library housed texts in both these languages as well as several others, including Arabic, Kashmiri, Hindi, Greek, European languages, and, of course, Sanskrit.[23] Select paintings from the royal atelier also brought together Islamicate and Indic tongues onto a single page.[24] The Mughals were not fluent in all these languages. Most notably, there is no evidence that members of the Mughal ruling class ever formally learned Sanskrit. Nonetheless, this did not prevent the Mughals from finding many roles for Sanskrit intellectuals, texts, and ideas in their court culture.

Among the plethora of tongues that thrived in the heart of Mughal power, Hindi deserves particular attention given my project here. Hindi was part of Mughal culture in two distinct incarnations: as an intellectual tradition through the literary dialect of Braj Bhasha and as a commonly spoken vernacular. Braj Bhasha spread rapidly as a favored poetic and learned register across northern India in the sixteenth and seventeenth centuries. Allison Busch has written extensively on this phenomenon and has underscored the prominence of Braj at the Mughal court.[25] In some ways, Braj and Sanskrit literati followed parallel journeys of pursuing connections with the Mughals, and comparing these two sets of cross-cultural exchanges is a promising avenue for future research. During the seventeenth century, Braj Bhasha also ultimately replaced Sanskrit in many ways as the premier Indian tradition to receive Mughal support. Additionally, spoken Hindi repeatedly served as a link language in Mughal attempts to access Sanskrit texts and knowledge systems. Indo-Persian court histories often obfuscate the importance of Hindi as a spoken vernacular in the Mughal imperium, and oral cultures are notoriously difficult to recover.[26] But plentiful evidence establishes that the Mughal kings from Akbar onward were fluent in Hindi.[27] The ruling elite frequently switched to Hindi in order to communicate with many in their kingdom, including Sanskrit intellectuals.

In this multilingual setting, Mughal connections with Sanskrit were encounters that occurred on a lively cultural frontier. Sanskrit and Persian existed in early modern India by and large as separate entities with their own genres, discourses, and conventions. The Mughals brought these traditions along with Hindi culture into a shared space in the imagined (and, in some respects, real) heart of their empire: the central royal court. The resulting cross-cultural engagements involved only a small portion of individuals who operated in either tradition. However, these meetings had far-reaching intellectual repercussions within each literary culture as well as weighty political consequences. In large part these aesthetic and imperial legacies are what make Mughal encounters with Sanskrit culture an important topic of study. In addition, this highly consequential history was part of several larger historical trends, foremost among them exchanges between Islamicate and Indian traditions.

A SELECTIVE HISTORY OF COURTLY CROSS-CULTURAL ENCOUNTERS

In cultivating a multicultural courtly environment, the Mughals inherited a substantial Perso-Islamic history of interactions with Indian traditions. Many of these encounters took place in courts, and exchanges were also frequent in nonroyal religious, intellectual, and social contexts. In the following chapters, I discuss specific antecedents for individual texts and types of interactions that provide an intellectual genealogy or an illuminating comparison. Here I provide a brief introduction to those kings and cultural achievements that the Mughals perceived as their forerunners, in both India and western and Central Asia, in order to highlight the enduring interest in Sanskrit traditions shown by Perso-Islamic rulers. The Mughals expanded upon this foundation in innovative ways, and yet their project was inconceivable without a long record of contacts across cultural lines.

Persianate kings evinced an interest in Sanskrit even before the advent of Islam and had a particular fondness for collections of Indian stories. In the sixth century, the Sassanian emperor Anushiravan sent his trusted vizier, Burzui, to India in order to find the Sanskrit storybook *Pañcatantra* (*Five Tales*) and translate the work into Middle Persian.[28] The rendition does not survive, but it enshrined the *Pañcatantra* as a central Persianate venue for engaging with Indian ideas. After its initial Sassanian treatment, the work was translated into Arabic, then into modern Persian, and subsequently reworked several times, including at the request of a senior adviser to a Timurid ruler in Herat in the late fifteenth century.[29] Pre-Mughal Indo-Persian rulers, such as the Lodis, copied and illustrated versions of the *Pañcatantra*, often under the title *Kalila wa Dimna*.[30] Akbar followed this custom and sponsored two new versions of the *Pañcatantra*.[31] This early history provided a solid precedent for the Mughals to devote resources to Sanskrit texts that grounded their activities in Persianate and even specifically Timurid cultural practices.

The Mughals' dual Timurid and Mongol heritages furnished additional precursors for incorporating Sanskrit-based knowledge into Persian histories. For example, Rashīd al-Dīn composed his *Jāmiʿ al-Tavārīkh* (*Collection of Histories*), an all-encompassing world history, for Mahmud Ghazan Khan, a Mongol Ilkhanid ruler who died in 1304. Since India was valued as one of the major intellectual centers of the premodern world, Rashīd al-Dīn narrates the basic plotline of both Sanskrit epics, tales from the life of the Buddha, and other Indian stories.[32] Rashīd al-Dīn used informants to access Indian traditions, a strategy the Mughals took up with fervor.[33] This world history was popular among the Mughal elites. An Arabic copy of Rashīd al-Dīn's *Jāmiʿ al-Tavārīkh* entered Mughal India during Akbar's reign, and Akbar's atelier also produced an illuminated Persian version in the 1590s that depicts, among other things, the birth of Ghazan Khan.[34] The work thus also supplied a precedent for connecting India's pre-Islamic history with Perso-Islamic claims of political sovereignty.

The Delhi Sultanate, a succession of kingdoms that ruled parts of northern India from 1206 to 1526, established numerous methods of integrating Sanskrit intellectuals and texts into an Indian-based Islamicate court. Already in the early fourteenth century, Persianate literati were highly cognizant of the Sanskrit tradition. Amīr Khusraw, who worked for several different rulers, discusses Indian languages in his *Nuh Sipihr* (*Nine Skies*, 1318) and therein proclaims Sanskrit superior to courtly Persian (*darī*) and inferior only to Arabic, the language of the Qurʾan.[35] Shortly thereafter, Muhammad bin Tughluq (r. 1325–1351) welcomed Jain scholars at his court in Delhi.[36] His successor, Firuz Shah Tughluq (d. 1388), underwrote Persian translations of several Sanskrit works, at least two of which are extant: a Persian *Bṛhatsaṃhitā* (*Great Compendium*) and an astronomical treatise titled *Dalāʾil-i Firūzshāhī* (*Firuz Shah's Proofs*).[37] The degree of Mughal awareness of these specific cross-cultural projects remains uncertain, but the Mughal kings were eager to link themselves with prior Indo-Persian dynasties more broadly.[38] For example, Jahangir ordered a Persian poet to fill in the missing pages of one of Amīr Khusraw's works in what one scholar has described as a Mughal attempt "to forge symbolic connections with the North Indian Muslim dynasties of the past."[39]

During the fifteenth century several regional rulers supported cross-cultural exchanges involving Sanskrit. Qutb al-Din Ahmad, a mid-fifteenth-century Gujarati ruler, sponsored the construction of a minar along with a celebratory bilingual inscription in Persian and Sanskrit.[40] Mahmud Begada (r. 1458–1511), another sultan in Gujarat, supported the poet Udayarāja, who authored a Sanskrit biography of the king titled *Rājavinoda* (*Play of the King*).[41] Zayn al-Abidin of Kashmir (r. 1420–1470) provides a particularly important precedent for Mughal-initiated encounters. Whereas many previous Sanskrit and Persian interactions occurred more piecemeal, Zayn al-Abidin undertook a sustained set of engagements. He instigated numerous Persian translations of Sanskrit works, including Kalhaṇa's *Rājataraṅgiṇī* (*River of Kings*), a chronicle of Kashmiri kings, and at least parts of the *Mahābhārata*, one of the two great Indian epics.[42] He also sponsored the *Rājataraṅgiṇī*s of Jonarāja and Śrīvara, which develop innovative types of historical consciousness in Sanskrit and provide detailed information about cross-cultural affairs.[43] Śrīvara would also later pen one of the rare translations of a Persian text into Sanskrit, the *Kathākautuka* (*Curiosity of a Story*), based on Jāmī's *Yūsuf va Zulaykhā* (*Joseph and Potiphar's Wife*).[44] The Mughals were familiar with most of these groundbreaking activities, and Akbar's court-sponsored work *Ā'īn-i Akbarī* (*Akbar's Institutes*) memorializes Zayn al-Abidin as a wise man who "had many works translated from Arabic, Persian, Kashmiri, and Sanskrit [*hindī*]."[45] The Mughals sought to foster a similar multicultural courtly environment, although on a much grander political stage.

During the sixteenth and seventeenth centuries, subimperial and non-Mughal Islamicate courts also formed patronage relationships and other types of connections with Sanskrit literati. For example, panegyrists composed Sanskrit encomia in praise of Burhan Nizam Shah of Ahmednagar (r. 1510–1553) and Sher Shah Suri (r. 1540–1545), who temporarily usurped the Mughal throne.[46] Some Deccani kingdoms backed Persian translations of Sanskrit texts or had such works dedicated to them, such as the Qutbshahi dynasty in Golconda.[47] Cross-cultural exchanges also flourished during the Delhi Sultanate and Mughal periods outside royal milieus, particularly in Sufi communities that were interested in yoga and other "Hindu" spiritual practices.[48] Sufi romances written in dialects of Hindavi mixed and melded Sanskrit and Persianate literary conventions.[49] The Mughal kings participated in this growing interest among much of elite Indian society in conversations across traditional boundaries and raised such exchanges to an unprecedented level.

ROYAL MUGHAL PATRONAGE 1560–1660

Beginning under Akbar, the Mughals developed an unmatched depth and diversity of links with the Sanskrit tradition that were concentrated around their central court. The royal court was defined first and foremost by the presence of the emperor. While the Mughals maintained a capital in Delhi, Agra, Fatehpur Sikri, or Lahore from 1560 to 1660, the true center of power moved with the king.[50] The Mughal emperors often personally instigated relations with Sanskrit literati, and Jains and Brahmans also sought out the support of the Mughal crown. In addition to the king, the central court also housed a variety of political figures and Persianate literati who introduced aspects of Sanskrit culture to court life. This cross-cultural patronage was an integral part of the public persona of individual kings and members of the Mughal ruling class. Imperial support of Sanskrit also intersected with numerous other courtly activities and underwent several changes in line with other political and cultural developments during the hundred years I consider here.

Akbar initiated most, although not all, types of Mughal engagements with the Sanskrit realm. He came to power at the age of thirteen in 1556 and spent the first five years of his reign under the charge of his regent, Bayram Khan. After coming of age Akbar expanded his territory and had carved out much of the heartland of the Mughal Empire by the close of the 1560s.[51] Sanskrit intellectuals first entered the Mughal court in the 1560s while Akbar was still charting out the core of his kingdom. Cross-cultural connections accelerated in the 1570s–1580s when Akbar had the leisure and resources to devote increasing attention to nonmilitary ambitions, and they reached their zenith during the 1580s–1590s. Akbar sponsored the translation of numerous Sanskrit texts into Persian, hosted dozens of Jain and Brahman Sanskrit intellectuals at court, hired Sanskrit-medium astronomers, and far more. Certain political changes encouraged specific Mughal interactions with Sanskrit intellectuals. For instance, the imperial takeover of Gujarat in 1572–1573 gave Jains incentives to seek out imperial support.

Within Akbar's court, several institutions facilitated intercultural interactions. Akbar established a house of religious debate (*ʿibādatkhānah*) in the mid-1570s.[52] Initially only Muslims were included, but soon Brahmans, Christians, and Jains also participated in a model that (whether intentionally or not) followed Mongol precedents from the thirteenth century.[53] Dialogues continued in the *ʿibādatkhānah* proper for only a few years, but religious discussions involving multiple communities persisted at least into Jahangir's reign.[54] Under Akbar, translation activity commenced and presumably took place largely in the writing bureau (*maktabkhānah*). Furthermore, Akbar's library held Sanskrit texts, which is occasionally mentioned in discussions between the emperor and Jain leaders.[55]

In addition to laying the groundwork for numerous types of contacts, Akbar also formulated a political ideology that served as the bedrock for Mughal ruling culture long after his death in 1605 and in which Sanskrit was a crucial element. Among his many policies, "universal peace" (*ṣulḥ-i kull*) was particularly critical to the Mughal vision of how to govern effectively over a diverse Indian population. This concept has long been loosely interpreted by modern academics as akin to modern, Protestant-based ideals of toleration.[56] My analysis of Mughal interactions with Sanskrit helps to clarify that *ṣulḥ-i kull* sought to ensure an atmosphere of civility not only by allowing for differences but more pointedly by enabling the emperor to use new sources of knowledge in order to condemn ideas he found distasteful. Akbar himself served as the judge of pleasing versus undesirable concepts. Thus, the Mughal kings mobilized their encounters with Sanskrit texts in order to promote a vision of strong royal authority.

While Akbar oversaw the commencement of Mughal engagements with Sanskrit, they were not indissolubly linked with a single ruler and are most fruitfully analyzed as part of Mughal sovereignty that stretched across the reigns of multiple kings. Mughal historians have often unduly focused on the personalities of individual emperors, most notably Akbar and Aurangzeb ʿAlamgir, and contrasted the former's supposed liberal inclinations with the latter's purported zealous bigotry. Such value judgments, cloaked in categories from our time, are unhelpful to historians. Methodologically, it remains mysterious how one would go about accessing the inner thoughts and opinions of long-dead kings. Sanskrit is an essential aspect of Mughal history because it was an integral part of courtly culture and imperial practices. In this sense, Akbar's sovereign persona is far more valuable (and accessible) than the king's personal interests for understanding and analyzing the Mughal imperium.[57] There is no doubt that imperial links with Sanskrit began and peaked under Akbar, and even in the early seventeenth century Persianate writers noted the unconventional multiculturalism of his reign.[58] Nonetheless, Jahangir and Shah Jahan each devised their own set of links to Sanskrit intellectuals and texts. We must account for specificity within each king's rule without recourse to speculation about personal preferences and also without losing sight of larger Mughal political and cultural dynamics.

Jahangir sponsored translations of Sanskrit texts into Persian even as a prince and continued his cross-cultural involvements when he ascended the throne in 1605.[59] He fostered both Jain and Brahmanical intellectuals at court and held Sanskrit works in the royal library.[60] Jahangir also read some of the translations of Sanskrit texts ordered by his father and even penned an annotation to one translation that offers insight into elite consumption of these works. He participated in several discussions with Jain leaders, although a disagreement led to the end of royal Mughal relations with Jain monks in the 1610s–1620s. His court also attracted intellectuals who sought to rework Sanskrit-based stories in Persian, and a few retellings of the *Rāmāyaṇa* epic are dedicated to Emperor Jahangir.

Shah Jahan's reign ultimately marked the fading of Sanskrit as a major literary, intellectual, and cultural tradition at the Mughal court, but it first witnessed a few especially high-profile encounters. Jagannātha Paṇḍitarāja and Kavīndrācārya Sarasvatī, two of the most well-known and influential Sanskrit intellectuals of the seventeenth century, had relations with Shah Jahan. Jagannātha was a long-term resident at court and spent several decades writing Sanskrit texts under Mughal support. The full extent of Kavīndra's relationship with Shah Jahan is less clear, but we know that he successfully negotiated the cancellation of a pilgrimage tax on Hindus and enjoyed a royal stipend. Both Jagannātha and Kavīndra also maintained strong ties with the vernacular world in addition to Sanskrit literary culture. This dual affiliation indicates one of the two main reasons for the lapse of ongoing Mughal encounters with Sanskrit texts and literati in the mid-seventeenth century.

Sanskrit ceased to be a major part of Mughal imperial life due to two discernible shifts, one linguistic and the other political. First, Hindi was on the ascent as a literary language in the seventeenth century and was increasingly occupying the cultural domain previously dominated by Sanskrit. Hindi was an active medium of literary and intellectual production at the Mughal court beginning under Akbar; it did not suddenly appear toward the end of Shah Jahan's reign. But, in the mid-seventeenth century, more and more Indian literati were affiliating with vernacular spheres, particularly in the Mughal context. Alongside this change, the Mughals increasingly looked to Hindi texts for classical Indian knowledge as opposed to seeking out Sanskrit works. Both the Mughal royal family and nobility sponsored Hindi poets and musicians throughout the second half of the seventeenth century, long after the Mughals ceased providing consistent support to Sanskrit intellectuals in the late 1650s.[61]

Additionally, when Aurangzeb ʿAlamgir came to power in 1658, he cut the few remaining ties between the Mughal court and Sanskrit literati. This decision may seem to fit easily into a commonly held and highly charged image of Aurangzeb as an intolerant Muslim oppressor, but it is more accurately characterized as a calculated political move. Aurangzeb was the third son of Shah Jahan and won the throne at the expense of his elder brother and the heir apparent, Dara Shikuh. In the 1640s and 1650s, Dara Shikuh oversaw a fascinating set of cross-cultural projects, including a translation of select Sanskrit *Upaniṣads* into Persian and a treatise on the unity of Hindu and Muslim ideas titled *Majmaʿ al-Baḥrayn* (*Confluence of Two Oceans*).[62] As I discuss in chapter 6, these activities were no doubt inspired by earlier and ongoing Mughal efforts, but they emerged out of a different set of impulses and are thus best considered separately from the larger royal Mughal interest in Sanskrit. From Aurangzeb's perspective, however, severing all imperial links with the Sanskrit world distinguished his cultural politics from those of his elder brother.

Nonetheless, Aurangzeb hardly instituted an irreparable break between the Mughals and the Sanskrit cultural realm. Aurangzeb periodically met with Jain leaders, for example. Given the poor state of historiography on his reign, he may have had further contacts with the Sanskrit sphere that we have not yet recovered.[63] Subimperial and princely courts continued to foster more sporadic interactions through at least the end of the seventeenth century. For example, in 1686–1687 Shaystah Khan, Aurangzeb's maternal uncle, asked a Hindu *munshī* to create a table of contents for Akbar's Persian *Mahābhārata*.[64] The scattered projects during Aurangzeb's rule, however, were a far cry from the continuous series of intense engagements in close association with political authority that marked the period from 1560 until nearly 1660.

FORMULATIONS AND IMAGINATIONS OF MUGHAL IMPERIAL POWER

Scholars have often ignored the many roles of Sanskrit intellectuals and texts in Mughal imperial life, particularly the political dimensions of these connections. In large part, this oversight is due to the persistent misreading of Persian court chronicles. With few exceptions, the Mughals penned their histories in Persian.[65] These works provide a valuable means of accessing much of the past, but they are carefully crafted political narratives that represent the Mughal imperium and courtly activities in highly selective ways. Following Indo-Persian precedents, Mughal histories only selectively recognize the presence of languages and cultures at the royal court beyond the Indo-Persian realm.[66] They also project an idealized image of strong, unwavering imperial authority that deliberately elides the consistently evolving and threatened quality of Mughal power.[67] In short, court chronicles must be read as limited, politically charged documents. Such works are tremendous resources for parsing the Mughal imperial image, and I rely heavily on Persianate histories here. However, they are best paired with materials from other traditions in order to produce a more historically accurate picture of the multifaceted nature of Mughal court culture and political power.

Several scholars have recently drawn attention to the many ways in which Mughal power operated that cannot be gleaned from official histories. For example, Azfar Moin has emphasized the importance of embodied kingship for the Mughals as expressed through performance and invocations of popular traditions.[68] Munis Faruqui has underscored the role of princely networks and competition in ensuring a vibrant dynasty.[69] Allison Busch has highlighted Hindi poets and literature in reconstructing the multicultural environment of the Mughal imperium.[70] These scholars have put to rest the old notion that written Indo-Persian histories alone tell us what was really important in premodern and early modern South Asia.[71] Nonetheless, scholars have been slow to look to Sanskrit texts in order to recover Mughal history, partially because few Mughal historians know Sanskrit and also because modern Indian language politics dictate the irrelevance of Sanskrit for understanding a Persianate empire.

Sanskrit texts present a nearly entirely neglected archive for understanding the venues and perceptions of Mughal imperial authority. In this book I draw on Sanskrit histories of the Mughals, Sanskrit praise poems for the ruling elite, and a wide range of Sanskrit poetry and intellectual treatises.[72] These works offer a myriad of insights, but no single work or genre of materials discusses the full spectrum of cross-cultural exchanges that took place under Mughal auspices. Accordingly, I also regularly draw on Persian courtly and noncourtly sources and, to a lesser extent, on Hindi and Gujarati texts. In this sense, my work exposes the flaws in monolingual analyses of early modern India when contacts between cultures were more often pivotal rather than peripheral. The precise political claims that the Mughals pursued through involvement with the Sanskrit realm are best understood by examining specific exchanges and texts, but a few aspects of this intersection of power and empire are helpful to elaborate at the outset.

First and foremost, Mughal engagements with Sanskrit were directed primarily toward a narrow band of ruling elites who were considered the true makers of empire. Individual texts repeatedly address a limited audience that was sometimes restricted to the Mughal emperor and other times included high-ranking members of the imperial administration. The Mughals rarely conducted cross-cultural exercises with an eye toward Jain or Brahmanical leaders and even more infrequently for the sake of the Indian population at large. Legitimation theory fails to capture this dynamic of Mughal imperial culture because it anachronistically assumes that the relationship between the government and the people was of paramount importance.[73] A legitimation framework posits that the Mughals incorporated Sanskrit literati into court life, became involved with the Sanskrit social sphere, and commissioned translations in order to justify their right to rule. However, I have uncovered little evidence that the Mughals, either intentionally or incidentally, won over any Indian communities through their interest in Sanskrit. This is not to say that the Mughals were uninterested in gaining the trust and loyalty of those they governed. On the contrary, Munis Faruqui has recently shown the careful and painstaking work that such attempts at integration generally entailed.[74] However, what Sanskrit offered the Mughals was a particularly potent way to imagine power and conceptualize themselves as righteous rulers.

Above all, encounters with Sanskrit reveal the centrality of literature in the Mughal effort to build an Indian empire. The relationship between aesthetics and politics was fluid for the Mughals and took different forms rather than being confined to a set framework. Here again legitimation theory offers a presumptive understanding of political power that automatically subordinates aesthetic events to political objectives and fails to accurately capture the multiple political and social dimensions of Mughal cross-cultural interests. Rather than mere tools of legitimation, the Mughals saw literary pursuits themselves as a crucial part of a successful imperial formation. Aesthetics was often deeply political in premodern India, a phenomenon that scholars have also noticed in other Asian societies, such as early modern Japan.[75] For the Mughals, encounters with the Sanskrit cultural world offered several promising possibilities in terms of advancing specific politico-aesthetic objectives.

In many instances, the Mughals sought to claim hitherto unavailable Sanskrit texts, stories, and knowledge systems as their own. By reinventing aspects of the Sanskrit tradition in Persian, the Mughals aligned themselves with a literary culture possessing the deep historical roots in India that Persian lacked. Persian linked the Mughal Empire with a larger early modern cultural world that included Safavid Iran, the Ottoman Empire, and much of Central Asia. But the Mughals also wished to see themselves as Indian kings and pursued this desire by appropriating a culture deeply grounded in South Asia's pre-Islamic past. The Mughals also adapted Sanskrit terms and ideas in order to develop new modes of expression. In this sense, they strove to recenter the Persophone world around the subcontinent and to create a distinctively Indo-Persian literary culture that prominently featured interactions with the Sanskrit sphere. In yet other cases, the Mughals encouraged textual production within the Sanskrit tradition and thus sought to participate in a long-standing custom of providing royal sponsorship to India's traditional elite. Without having a single unified agenda, the Mughals nonetheless consistently turned to the resources of the Sanskrit tradition as part of their multifaceted political interests.

Scholars have denied Sanskrit any substantive literary or historical, much less political, role in the Mughal Empire for so long that it may no doubt strike many readers as difficult to imagine that Sanskrit was a major component of Mughal imperial authority. But the forms and density of imperial interactions with Sanskrit demand that we rethink the very formulation of Mughal culture and power. The Mughals created (rather than merely vindicated) their claims to rule through their connections with the Sanskrit sphere, which we can best understand if we forgo the assumptions of much Western theory regarding the justification of power. They cultivated deep and diverse ties with Sanskrit thinkers and texts over the course of nearly one hundred years because they saw such activities as a central part of their political project. The opinions of the population at large were not at stake in these engagements. Rather, these cross-cultural exchanges were driven primarily by the cravings of political leaders to formulate their own locally flavored sovereign identities and narratives of power, above all for their own benefit. This hunger for a unique political self, dubbed the "inward-turning aspect of legitimation" by one theorist, is a phenomenon rampant across the premodern and the modern worlds.[76] By investigating the mechanisms of this political behavior during the height of the Mughal Empire, we stand to gain fresh insight into the actions of government figures both historically and today.

EARLY MODERN SANSKRIT TRADITIONS

In addition to serving as a significant archive for reconstructing the dense array of Jain and Brahmanical connections with the Mughal court, Sanskrit texts related to the Mughals also provide insight into key intellectual and literary developments in early modern India. Sanskrit intellectual production "on the eve of colonialism" has been a major topic of recent scholarly interest, particularly in the Sanskrit Knowledge-Systems Project, which my own work complements.[77] Classical Sanskrit had been a primary medium for literary, intellectual, and political pursuits on the subcontinent for roughly fifteen hundred years by the advent of Mughal rule. This broad tradition was one of the most complex, widespread intellectual and cultural formations of the premodern world. At its zenith, Sanskrit served as a shared language and culture for not only India but also large swaths of Southeast Asia and informed East Asian literary and religious practices. By the mid-sixteenth century, Sanskrit's boundaries had largely retracted to the subcontinent, but it was still an active tradition. Sanskrit literary culture collapsed largely in the century before the start of colonial rule, and vernaculars took over as the medium of choice for most Indian literary and intellectual pursuits. Scholars are still trying to recover the reasons undergirding Sanskrit's fall and even the basic story line and timing of its collapse.[78] Connections between Jain and Brahman thinkers and Mughal elites constitute an important part of the early modern Sanskrit tradition and a striking area of newness during its final centuries of vivacity. A careful study of the texts and ideas produced in these encounters may in turn influence how we understand Sanskrit's last flourishings and its demise.

Above all, links with the Mughals highlight that multiplicity rather than unity characterized Sanskrit literary culture in early modernity. Accordingly, we ought to disaggregate what is usually seen as a monolithic entity into multiple, often highly divergent Sanskrit traditions. Sanskrit scholars have already begun to tease out this idea when addressing regional differences among individual literati and texts that complicate any overarching theories about Sanskrit as a single cultural tradition.[79] I demonstrate here that religiously and regionally delineated communities also cultivated very different types of responses to similar circumstances. We will find the cultural complexities of early modern South Asia more comprehensible if we replace a model of orthodoxy and deviance with a series of parallel and overlapping Sanskrit cultures in which individuals made informed and competing choices.

Sanskrit intellectuals at the Mughal court fall into two broad religious categories, Jains and Brahmans, that often formulated distinct ways of negotiating their royal ties and acting within the Sanskrit thought world. The starkest difference between the two communities is that Jains wrote voraciously about their time at the Mughal court, producing numerous Sanskrit narratives and thousands of written pages on their imperial experiences. In contrast, Brahmans maintained a nearly complete narrative silence on their parallel activities. The omission of Sanskrit narratives about courtly happenings did not preclude Brahmans from accepting Mughal patronage, authoring Sanskrit texts for Mughal consumption, and participating in court life. However, Brahmans largely declined to produce any descriptive record of their imperial experiences in Sanskrit, and we possess no Brahman-authored body of Sanskrit materials that parallels the verbose Jain accounts of the Mughal court. It is difficult to surmise the reasons behind this Brahmanical reticence, but the presence of Jain Sanskrit narratives demonstrates that this silence was a real choice rather than a cultural inevitability.

Jains penned detailed, prolific records of the incorporation of Sanskrit into Mughal court culture. But they tended to discuss courtly events in genres that do not necessarily emphasize accurate reporting above literary and religious considerations (e.g., *kāvya*, *carita*, and *prabandha*). Scholars have generally neglected such "homeless texts" because they do not fit into modern groupings (in this case, fiction versus nonfiction).[80] Some academics have tried to draw a firm line between fantasy and reality in premodern Indian texts under the suspect assumption that current Western historical sensibilities are universal.[81] However, rather than rejecting such works or trying to slot them into a modern definition of "history," we are better served by examining how and why Sanskrit intellectuals privileged poetic remembrances and creative retellings of past events.[82] The cultivation of creative history offered a vehicle for Jains to think through the cultural implications of their close imperial ties. Moreover, quasi histories that openly discuss cross-cultural events, even making Persian cultural references and elaborating Islamic theology, attest to how some thinkers adapted the Sanskrit tradition to respond to and even benefit from rapid social and political changes associated with Mughal rule.

In outlining one set of literary choices, Jain works also remind us of a far more basic but oft-neglected point: namely, Jains were important participants in early modern Sanskrit literary culture. Modern scholars have often sidelined Jains and their texts as no more than footnotes to proper Sanskrit history. This marginalization rests upon an unexamined assumption that Brahmans defined a sort of Sanskrit orthodoxy from which others deviated. Ignoring Jain contributions to Sanskrit literature has prevented scholars from investigating some of the most dynamic approaches to writing about historical events in premodern India. Many scholars have written about the self-proclaimed "new" (*navya*) Sanskrit intellectuals of early modernity, some of whom developed unprecedented subjectivity and a "newness of style."[83] But, by and large, *navya* Sanskrit thinkers investigated the same philosophical and literary questions that had occupied their predecessors for hundreds of years. More appreciable innovation was cultivated elsewhere in early modern Sanskrit.[84] Jains manifested radical possibilities for how Mughal power could inform and even transform a community's sense of itself. Jains lacked the political force of the Mughal crown, but they nonetheless offer elite visions, largely inspired by their engagements with the ruling class, for how to reinvent themselves in early modern India.

Brahmans wrote far less about their imperial engagements, despite significantly outnumbering Jains at court, and they offer no cohesive Sanskrit narratives about their experiences with the Mughals. This inverse response is an important act of historical forgetting, although its motivations are far from clear. Brahmans seem to have suffered few negative social consequences for accepting patronage from an Islamic, Persianate dynasty. On the contrary, broad sections of the Brahmanical elite celebrated certain prominent individuals who visited the royal court, such as Kavīndrācārya Sarasvatī. Overall, however, the existence of cross-cultural ties likely struck Brahmans as unremarkable given that Sanskrit intellectuals had long accepted support from Indian kings of various religious leanings.[85] At the very least, we should not presume to read current religious tensions into a past silence and assume that it was controversial for Brahmans to accept Islamicate patronage. Instead, the omission of Sanskrit narratives likely indicates that Brahmans wished to maintain a community identity separate from the Mughal imperium, unlike their Jain counterparts, who sought to pair their religious values with an imperial mandate. Nonetheless, early modern Brahmans tried to make sense of Mughal power and the accompanying spread of Persian literary culture in other ways, such as by developing Sanskrit grammatical accounts of Persian and speaking to contemporary concerns through classical literary tropes. In these instances Brahmanical authors underscore that they were aware of historical and cultural changes taking place in Mughal India and tried to work through these shifts via traditional modes of thought.

INTERNAL FRONTIERS: TOWARD A NEW HISTORY OF THE MUGHALS

Over the past few decades, scholars have demonstrated the immense value of placing the Mughals within different connected histories. Many have elucidated aspects of the Mughal state by recovering political and intellectual links (often along with structural and cultural similarities) with the Safavid and Ottoman empires.[86] Others have productively explored Mughal ties with their Central Asian homelands, imperial treatments of their Timurid and Mongol heritages, and increasing Mughal links with Europe.[87] In such formulations, "connected history is directed toward recalibrating the received cartographies deemed meaningful for capturing historical reality."[88] I build upon such studies in making intersections the axis of my narrative. I stand apart, however, in introducing Sanskrit as a cultural tradition with which the Mughals were bound through networks, people, and texts. Mughal links with Sanskrit intellectuals overlapped with other imperial interests, including their ties with Central Asia and their perceived location within the wider Persianate world. But Sanskrit was also a significant frontier within India that stands on its own as a consistent component of imperial court life and a politically potent tradition for the Mughal rulers.

My initial concern in this book is to reconstruct the broad contours of relations between Sanskrit intellectuals and the Mughal elite. In chapter 1, I discuss how direct patronage ties and looser forms of affiliation drew Sanskrit intellectuals, both Jains and Brahmans, into the Mughal court beginning in the 1560s. Over the next hundred years, members of both communities served the Mughals in a variety of roles: as political actors, translators, authors, and far more. Mughal and Sanskrit leaders also jointly cultivated titling practices that spanned multiple political, religious, and linguistic traditions. This web of connections constitutes a nearly totally unknown dimension of the social history of the Mughal court. This multicultural imperial context also facilitated and prompted the diverse textual projects that occupy my attention in the next five chapters.

Chapters 2–4 explore different ways that Sanskrit texts, stories, and ideas entered the Mughal court and embodied political and aesthetic objectives. In chapter 2, I detail Sanskrit texts that were written either under Mughal support or intended for consumption by the imperial ruling class. These works offer compelling insights concerning the contours of Mughal political and literary cultures and how Sanskrit texts may have operated across linguistic boundaries. In chapter 3, I turn to Persian materials and offer an in-depth study of the translation and retranslations of the Sanskrit *Mahābhārata* under Akbar's sponsorship. I argue that the newly created Persian epic, called the *Razmnāmah* (*Book of War*), was the centerpiece of royal translation activity through which Mughal thinkers formulated some of Akbar's cardinal imperial ambitions. In chapter 4, I investigate Abū al-Faẓl's treatment of Sanskrit knowledge systems in his *Āʾīn-i Akbarī*, part of the major official history of Akbar's reign. This text, while much cited for numbers and dates, remains gravely underanalyzed in modern scholarship. I explicate the radical intellectual and political agendas that Abū al-Faẓl advances in importing specialized Sanskrit discourses into the domain of Persianate, Mughal-defined knowledge.

In chapters 5 and 6, I look beyond the royal court and examine responses within the Sanskrit and Indo-Persian realms, respectively, to the proliferation of Mughal ties with the Sanskrit cultural universe. In chapter 5, I investigate how Jain and Brahmanical communities thought and wrote in Sanskrit about links with the Mughals. Jains especially explored how Mughal authority had reshaped local communities and adapted imperial formulations to their own religious and cultural interests. Many early modern Sanskrit thinkers identified great value in working through the potential meanings and impacts of Mughal cross-cultural links. In chapter 6, I look at Persianate histories, literary retellings of Sanskrit stories, and manuscript notes in order to capture the wide-ranging Persianate receptions of Akbar's cross-cultural interests in particular. This history stretches from fierce condemnations to ringing endorsements and vividly illustrates how courtly and noncourtly actors understood (and, in some cases, reformulated) the imperial stakes of Mughal cross-cultural activities. In my conclusion, I detail the end of Sanskrit as a major tradition at the Mughal court and return to broad questions of imperial authority, literary traditions, and cross-cultural endeavors.

At the core of my concerns here is how power is constituted at moments of cultural contacts. Sanskrit and Persian exchanges demonstrate that we ought to privilege literary resources in such queries, particularly in early modern India. We need to correct the long-standing assumption that aesthetic interests were always subsidiary to political concerns and reevaluate how we parse imperial authority. The materials I discuss in the following chapters challenge any view that would restrict literature to supporting political ambitions and instead weave together culture and power in ways that show how this potent combination offered the Mughals (and their Indian interlocutors) the opportunity to act in truly imperial ways. Last, my work here exemplifies the value of historically minded philology that strives to conceptualize the meaning of texts in multiple contexts, including for us today. Repeated Sanskrit and Mughal interactions are a pivotal part of understanding imperial, religious, social, and literary facets of the early modern past. They also help us to articulate the larger implications of recovering, obscuring, and rewriting multicultural activities in South Asia and beyond.

[1] BRAHMAN AND JAIN SANSKRIT INTELLECTUALS AT THE MUGHAL COURT

JAIN AND Brahman Sanskrit intellectuals visited the courts of Akbar, Jahangir, and Shah Jahan in considerable numbers. A select few entered the royal court at the direct invitation of the crown, whereas others gained entrée through regional or subimperial patrons. Many championed political causes on behalf of their religious communities or local rulers. Above all, Sanskrit literati sought access to famed Mughal patronage, which drew individuals working in various languages from across much of Asia. Sanskrit authors crafted many works under imperial sponsorship and participated in numerous aspects of court life. They acted as intellectual informants, astrologers, religious guides, translators, and political negotiators for the Mughals.

This chapter provides the first scholarly attempt to comprehensively and chronologically reconstruct these social ties. Jain and Brahman Sanskrit intellectuals were first admitted to the Mughal court in the 1560s, and both groups flourished until Akbar's death in 1605. Jains' fortunes declined steeply under Jahangir, whereas Brahmans maintained a courtly presence through Shah Jahan's rule. In all, Sanskrit-knowing Jains populated the Mughal court for roughly fifty years (1560s–1610s; the 1580s–1610s witnessed a continuous Jain imperial presence), and their Brahman peers were members of imperial circles for a hundred-year period (1560–1660). These imperially situated networks provide context for the texts that I explore in the remainder of this book. Moreover, these cross-cultural links constitute an often overlooked part of social and intellectual dynamics in early modern India.

Connections between the royal court and Sanskrit intellectuals took forms that ranged from direct patronage to looser affiliations. In some cases, the Mughals extended support to writers to produce specific works. However, other sorts of links were far more common than direct literary sponsorship. Some Sanskrit intellectuals engaged with the Mughals on behalf of local communities or subsidiary rulers. In such cases, an individual worked primarily outside the central royal court but nonetheless engaged the Mughals in specific instances. Moreover, the Mughals supported Sanskrit intellectuals for an array of reasons other than generating literature. While in this regard the definition of a given individual as a Sanskrit literatus can become slippery, it is crucial to include those who did not author texts but were viewed by the Mughals as within the Sanskrit learned tradition.[1] This wider lens allows access to the polyglot nature of Mughal court life, including social practices that crisscrossed Sanskrit, Persian, and vernacular traditions.

Sanskrit intellectuals who attended the Mughal court formed a diverse lot. Both Jains and Brahmans enjoyed the Mughal imperial largesse, and many geographical and cultural differences fell along religious lines. The Jains came overwhelmingly from western India and were usually affiliated, often as ascetics, with one of two Shvetambara sects: the Tapa and Kharatara Gacchas.[2] Jains sought Mughal favor mainly of their own volition in order to pursue political concessions for their communities, which were largely under direct imperial administration after the Mughal takeover of Gujarat in 1572–1573. Brahmans at court hailed from a broader geographical area, stretching from Gujarat to Bengal and as far south as the Deccan, but they generally came from areas within the Mughal polity or threatened by imperial expansion. Brahmans also nurtured royal affiliations for more varied reasons than their Jain counterparts. Sometimes the Rajput elite who fostered Sanskrit (and Hindi) textual production in their own courts provided a gateway for Brahmans to access Mughal support. Both Jain and Brahman intellectuals freely entered and exited the Mughal court, and they often simultaneously preserved ties with subimperial and Rajput rulers.

While Jains and Brahmans both brought Sanskrit literary culture into the Mughal court, they would hardly have viewed their actions as a joint project. On the contrary, Jain texts often sneer at Brahmans and record conflicts between the two groups before an imperial audience. In addition, Jains were often divided along sectarian lines, and sects competed with one another for Mughal attention. Despite not acting cooperatively, multiple Jain and Brahmanical communities nonetheless developed an unprecedented diversity of roles for Sanskrit literati at a predominantly

Persianate court. Among the many cross-cultural practices that the Mughal emperors cultivated in conversation with Jain and Brahman intellectuals, I devote special attention to multilingual titling. Throughout their tenure at the Mughal court, Sanskrit intellectuals received official and honorary titles from the Mughal kings. Official titles were exclusively in Sanskrit and denoted ranks within Jain sects. The Mughal kings also decorated both Jains and Brahmans with honorary appellations in Sanskrit, Persian, and Hindi that marked some type of partiality or accomplishment. These two genres of titles provide sharp insight into the agencies exercised by different communities involved in multicultural practices.

Many sources provide information concerning cross-cultural connections, and I rely primarily on Sanskrit and Persian works with more sporadic references to Hindi, Gujarati, and European texts. Nonetheless, several difficulties arise in attempting to reconstruct this complex set of social relations. Above all, Persian chronicles often elide Sanskrit intellectuals' participation in royal court life. Many deservedly respected Mughal scholars have been misled by relying solely on Persian materials and mirror their sources in failing to mention that Sanskrit intellectuals were part of the Mughal court. For their part, Sanskritists have largely ignored the relevant Sanskrit materials. This oversight is due partly to the faulty (but so far ineradicable) assumption that Sanskrit thinkers were disinclined to write history.[3] Sanskrit materials that address Mughal relations furnish a detailed picture of cross-cultural activities and often include names of key figures, locations, dates, and narratives of specific episodes. When read in tandem, Sanskrit works underscore the brutal limits of relying exclusively on selective Persian court histories for reconstructing the Mughal past.

The literary quality of many Sanskrit (and vernacular) texts, however, introduces methodological challenges to relying on these works for recovering historical events. Many narratives follow preset formulas, and the details of some encounters seem implausible. When sources from two or more languages concur about a particular occurrence, I take its veracity as relatively firmly established. But many of the encounters I discuss in this chapter are based on attestations in the Sanskrit tradition alone, not infrequently in a single work. Given the limitations of Mughal court sources, lack of confirmation in the Persian tradition cannot serve as a responsible basis for condemning such ties as dubious reported history rather than reliable fact. Moreover, despite a few moments of obvious exaggeration, Sanskrit literati generally present credible stories of their interactions with Mughal figures.[4] Thus, while our knowledge of the imperial activities of Sanskrit literati remains tentative in some of its particulars, the overarching arc of this social history can be firmly established. These cross-cultural relations constituted a vibrant dimension of Mughal court culture that revolved around meetings between members of two cosmopolitan traditions in the center of a powerful, expanding empire.

BRAHMANS AND JAINS ENTER MUGHAL CIRCLES

Brahmans and Jains first formed ties with the Mughals in the 1560s. Early Brahman intellectuals often accompanied political embassies to or from the royal court and were associated with music, both legacies that endured through Shah Jahan's reign. Mahāpātra Kṛṣṇadāsa of Orissa is the first Mughal-sponsored Sanskrit intellectual whom we can reliably date. The *Akbarnāmah*, one of Akbar's official histories, describes Mahāpātra as "unrivaled in the arts of music and *hindī* [Sanskrit or Hindi?] poetry" and records that he joined an imperial envoy to Orissa in 1565.[5] Indeed Mahāpātra is most well known in Sanskrit circles for composing a treatise titled the *Gītaprakāśa* (*Light on Music*).[6] When Mahāpātra returned from Orissa a few years later, he led a second Sanskrit author, Narasiṃha, from the court of Gajapati Mukundadeva into the ambit of Akbar's patronage. We lack information about Narasiṃha's time at court, except that he claims to have "pleased the Lord of Delhi."[7] A series of Brahmans followed these two in entering the Mughal court, including at least one other musician, Puṇḍarīkaviṭṭhala, who visited in the latter half of Akbar's reign and wrote his *Nartananirṇaya* (*Ascertainment of Dance*) "to delight King Akbar."[8]

The initial Mughal enchantment with Sanskrit knowledge about music and dance dovetails well with Akbar's well-known enjoyment of Indian performance traditions. This imperial interest is exemplified by the longstanding relationship with the musician Tansen, who served Akbar from 1562 into the late 1580s.[9] The Mughals also encouraged the composition of Persian works on Indian music.[10] Sanskrit patronage connections attest that the Mughal kings, particularly Akbar, invested in a parallel effort to nurture the Sanskrit tradition of musical discourse. Some early modern Sanskrit musical treatises even evince Indo-Persian influences, including one of Puṇḍarīkaviṭṭhala's other works.[11] The multiple levels on which the Mughal court engaged with Indian performance traditions demonstrate that, from the beginning, support of Sanskrit intellectuals intersected with other courtly activities.

The initial Brahman recipients of Mughal sponsorship often moved from regional courts to the imperial center and thus mapped out a complex grid of overlapping political and patronage connections. As mentioned, Mahāpātra and Narasiṃha were first associated with rulers in eastern India who had political dealings with the Mughals from the 1560s onward. A bit later Kavi Karṇapūra also transitioned from Orissa to the Mughal court and penned a Sanskrit grammar of Persian for Jahangir (I discuss this text in chapter 2). Puṇḍarīkaviṭṭhala entered Akbar's court through the patronage of Man Singh and Madho Singh of the Rajasthani Kachhwaha lineage, one of the earliest Rajput backers of the Mughals.[12] Goviṇḍa Bhaṭṭa frequented the court of Ramacandra of Rewa in Madhya Pradesh before somehow gratifying Akbar and earning the title "Akbar's Kālidāsa" (*akbarīyakālidāsa*).[13] Taken together, these Sanskrit intellectuals outline some of the major eastern, western, and southern reaches of the growing Mughal Empire.[14] In addition, some Brahmans had previously worked under other Indo-Islamic patrons.[15] In accepting Akbar's sponsorship, they then embodied Mughal claims to be the legitimate successors to earlier Islamicate kingdoms on the subcontinent.

Padmasundara was likely the first Jain to meet Akbar and also inaugurated the composition of Sanskrit texts for Mughal consumption. We know nothing about why Padmasundara came to court, although, like his Brahman contemporaries, he had previously served a regional ruler (in his case, Maldeo of Jodhpur).[16] By 1569 he had crafted a treatise on Sanskrit aesthetic theory at the explicit request of Emperor Akbar titled *Akbarasāhiśṛṅgāradarpaṇa* (*Mirror of Erotic Passion for Shah Akbar*). Padmasundara invokes Akbar's name throughout his text in verses that exemplify the different aesthetic moods (*rasas*) and thus inserts the Mughal king into Sanskrit poetics. Whether or how the Mughal emperor may have understood such a work is a question that neither the Sanskrit nor Persian traditions directly address. I discuss possible means for a cross-linguistic reception in chapter 2, but it is entirely possible that the Mughals underwrote Sanskrit texts with no intention of reading (or hearing) them, as presumably countless Indian kings before them had done. Regardless of any potential reception, Padmasundara initiated the linked practices, shared by both Jains and Brahmans, of composing texts under Mughal patronage and dedicating Sanskrit works to Mughal figures.

The Jain tradition proffered several responses to the inauguration of relations with the Mughals, which sometimes signaled discomfort with the novelty of such ties. Padmasundara's intellectual descendants often tried to couch him within a lineage of Islamicate-Sanskrit patronage relationships rather than standing unabashed at the beginning of an unprecedented practice. For example, a younger contemporary of Padmasundara's added several verses to the end of the *Akbarasāhiśṛṅgāradarpaṇa* that name specific Jain thinkers, Jayarāj and Ānandarāya, who were allegedly patronized by Babur and Humayun, respectively.[17] Writing a few decades later, Harṣakīrti positioned Padmasundara as the penultimate figure in a sequence of eight Jains, seven of whom had links with Islamic rulers dating back to the early fourteenth century.[18] While the patronage connections (and indeed existence) of some of these earlier intellectuals remain highly doubtful, the search for precedents, whether actual or invented, telegraphs anxiety with Padmasundara's potentially acting outside any established tradition.[19]

The next major Jain intellectual who visited the Mughal court was Hīravijaya, who was invited by the emperor in 1582.[20] Akbar presumed that Padmasundara and Hīravijaya belonged to a single tradition and even bequeathed the former's library, which had fallen into Mughal hands upon Padmasundara's death, to Hīravijaya.[21] In reality the men belonged to related sects, the Nagapuriya Tapa Gaccha and the Tapa Gaccha, respectively.[22] These two Jain lineages pursued distinct paths regarding relations with the Mughals. After Padmasundara's death, the Nagapuriya do not appear to have forged any further imperial links. In contrast, members of the Tapa Gaccha called at the Mughal court well into Jahangir's reign. Later Tapa Gaccha authors often omit Padmasundara altogether and present Hīravijaya's arrival in Fatehpur Sikri in 1583 as the beginning of Jain contact with the Mughals.[23] From a Mughal perspective in the 1580s, Padmasundara certainly furnished an early model for Persianate associations with Jain intellectuals. But Hīravijaya marks the beginning of sustained Jain-Mughal relations.[24]

POLITICAL NEGOTIATIONS ACROSS CULTURAL LINES

A second wave of Jain and Brahmanical intellectuals began to populate Akbar's court in the 1580s and encountered a rather different political atmosphere than their counterparts a decade or two prior. Earlier intellectuals had entered the royal milieu ahead of the Mughals' major territorial

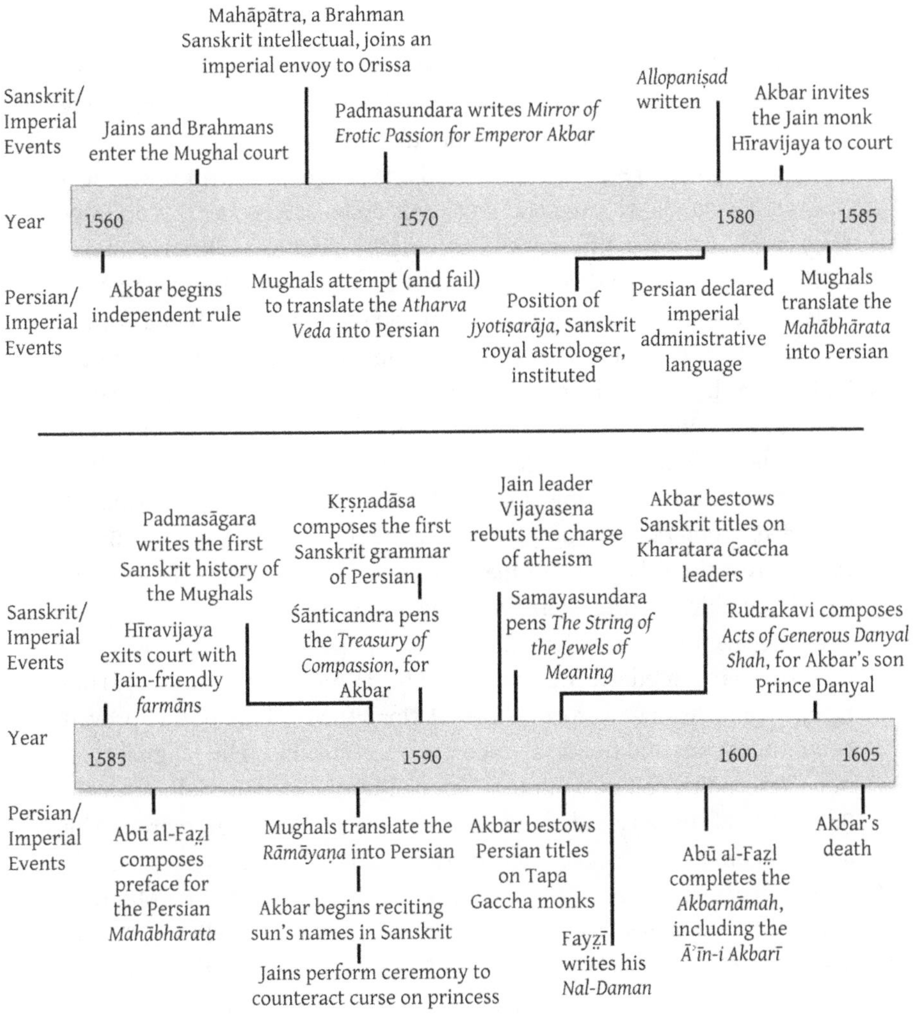

TIMELINE 1.1 Select engagements with Sanskrit at Akbar's court.

acquisitions of the 1570s–1580s and also well before the Mughals' wide-ranging interests in Indian ideas became manifest in a variety of forms. In contrast, by the 1580s Akbar had laid the foundation for an expansive empire. Around midway through his reign, Akbar and other key courtly figures also began evincing deep curiosity concerning Indian cultural traditions. Thus, while the next generation of Mughal-patronized Sanskrit thinkers built upon the links developed by their predecessors, they also forged political, intellectual, and religious connections that were newly available within the increasingly multicultural Mughal court.

Both Brahmans and Jains entreated the Mughal crown for political favors, although Jains gained far more concessions. Whether this discrepancy resulted from a difference in accomplishment or ambition remains unclear, and there is evidence to support both readings. Sources in multiple traditions confirm that Jains often had the ear of the Mughal king.[25] Persian texts from Akbar's court acclaim Jain monks as holy men who are "intent on the contemplation of the Deity," whereas Brahmans are cast as ignorant, willful deceivers of their own followers and "entrenched in false beliefs."[26] Alternatively, Jains may have sought Mughal concessions more than their Brahmanical rivals. Direct control of much of Gujarat provided strong reasons for Jains to solicit imperial favor, whereas Brahmans across the subcontinent may very well have entreated local rulers for comparable benefits. Moreover, Jains from different sects often asked the Mughals for royal orders in order to compete with one another. In contrast, early modern Brahmans resolved conflicts through internal mechanisms. Brahmans formed associations that relied upon improved communications and financial opportunities introduced by Mughal rule, but these nonetheless operated independently of imperial control.[27] Regardless of the reasons behind their success, Jains were extraordinarily adept at convincing the Mughals to grant them royal orders (*farmāns*).

Hīravijaya commenced Jain political negotiations with the Mughals during his first stay at the royal milieu from 1583 to 1585. Hīravijaya, the leader of the Tapa Gaccha, walked to Fatehpur Sikri over the course of several months at the entreaty of Akbar, who had heard of the monk's reputed wisdom and integrity.[28] A local Tapa Gaccha convert known as Sthānasiṃha announced Hīravijaya's arrival to the court and reappears in later stories as a liaison between Gujarat-based Jain monks and the Mughal elite.[29] Over the next few years, Hīravijaya solicited several imperial concessions that benefited his regional and religious interests. The major *farmān* he procured prohibited animal slaughter during twelve days each year, including the eight-day Jain festival of Paryushan.[30] Hīravijaya had been attending the Mughal court for nearly two years when the *farmān* was issued and sent to provinces across the empire. Sanskrit texts laud this achievement as promoting the central Jain value of nonviolence. However, the Persian *farmān* justifies the concession by emphasizing that Jain monks focused spiritual attention on a single deity and possessed "extraordinary holiness."[31] In such ways, Jain-solicited *farmāns* often worked as cross-cultural exercises by having distinct meanings for the different communities involved.

Sanskrit sources also celebrate several other concessions that Hīravijaya extracted on his initial imperial sojourn. He ensured the release of prisoners captured during the Mughal invasion of Gujarat, which benefited the region widely.[32] Akbar also granted Hīravijaya's wish that fishing be prohibited in Damara pond (also known as Dabara), which was located not far from the imperial capital of Fatehpur Sikri.[33] While this request accords with the Jain commitment to avoid harming all creatures, it is not immediately clear why Hīravijaya singled out this body of water. Perhaps he wished to visibly display Jain values in the very heart of the Mughal Empire, near the city of red sandstone that Akbar had personally commissioned. One of Hīravijaya's Sanskrit biographers, Devavimala, notes that Akbar personally ordered Damara excavated.[34] Additionally, Padmasāgara, another biographer, celebrates the effective enforcement that the Mughals supplied for this particular order: "Having banned the slaying of any living beings in the waters of the glorious lake Dabara, Glorious Padshah Akbar ordered servants to sound drums throughout the city in order to inform all people and secretly appointed spies to arrest those who violated the rule."[35]

Hīravijaya brought several members of the Tapa Gaccha with him to court and also paved the way, perhaps unintentionally, for members of the rival Kharatara Gaccha to penetrate Mughal circles.[36] Over the next several decades, monks and, less commonly, lay Jains from both sects petitioned Akbar, and later Jahangir, for assorted political concessions. Sanskrit and Gujarati texts and inscriptions all celebrate the resulting Mughal *farmāns*, and several are also extant in the original Persian or in translation.[37] Sometimes monks lobbied for imperial policies popular across sectarian lines. For example, numerous sources record *farmāns* against killing animals that were effective for varying lengths of time and for assurances of freedom of movement, an important concern for peripatetic Jain monks. However, the Tapa and Kharatara Gacchas also regularly competed for Mughal attention and obtained royal orders directed against each other. One particularly contentious issue was which group controlled Shatrunjaya, a popular pilgrimage destination in Saurashtra, Gujarat. Both sects secured *farmāns* ensuring their administration of the site on different occasions.[38]

In general, local communities joyfully heralded Mughal *farmāns* and lauded their solicitors. For example, in 1610, Vijayasena, the leader of the Tapa Gaccha after Hīravijaya's death in 1596, acquired an order from Jahangir that barred animal slaughter during Paryushan (the similar *farmān* solicited by Hīravijaya twenty-five years earlier was presumably no longer in effect). That same year, the Jain community of Agra sent a formal invitation (*vijñaptipatra*) to Vijayasena informing him about the good news. The letter was accompanied by a lavish scroll illustration executed by the celebrated Mughal painter Shalivahana and depicts an energetic scene at the Mughal court that includes Jain monks.[39] Here a Jain community reveled in its close imperial links, even hiring an artist in the royal atelier to visually depict the sect's political position. In written texts, authors regularly applauded Jain leaders for "promoting the Jain teaching" through procuring imperial concessions. For example, the lay Kharatara and Bikaner politician Karmacandra elicited many favors from Akbar, including the return of Jain idols that had been looted during Mughal campaigns in Rajasthan.[40] Karmacandra is remembered even today in popular Jain histories for his involvement with the Mughals.[41]

Brahmans and others also entreated the Mughal crown for political favors, although often these figures had only tenuous connections with the Sanskrit cultural realm. During Akbar's reign, Rajputs who had entered Mughal service procured *farmāns* protecting cows and temples near Mathura.[42] As Cynthia Talbot has pointed out, Hindu members of the imperial elite often contended with one another for the local honor attached to funding temples in the region.[43] François Bernier, a French traveler in the mid-seventeenth century, records that Jahangir prohibited animal slaughter at the request of Brahmans.[44] Members of the Mughal administration under Akbar and Shah Jahan issued *farmāns* concerning the management of temples in Mathura and Vrindavan, respectively.[45] Several Mughal rulers, from Akbar through Muhammad Shah (r. 1719–1748), adjudicated issues of land ownership and use in Benares among the Jangam, a Shaivite community.[46] Nonetheless, it is unknown whether Sanskrit intellectuals mediated any of these imperial orders. In terms of *farmāns* obtained specifically by Brahmanical Sanskrit literati, few cases are known in the reigns of Akbar and Jahangir.[47]

During Shah Jahan's rule Kavīndrācārya Sarasvatī successfully convinced the Mughal king to rescind a tax on Hindu pilgrims to Benares and Prayag (Allahabad). Kavīndra notes this achievement in his writings, and his fellow scholars collected two sets of poems lauding Kavīndra's political victory.[48] These parallel encomia were composed in Sanskrit and Hindi, respectively, which appropriately mirrors Kavīndra's own bifurcated literary production.[49] We possess no known linear narrative of Kavīndra's interactions with the Mughal king, but the dual encomia testify to the importance of gaining this imperial concession for Kavīndra's contemporaries.

SANSKRIT LITERATI AS INTELLECTUALS AND RELIGIOUS GUIDES

Sanskrit figures also acted as intellectual and religious informants under the Mughals, particularly at Akbar's court. The Mughal kings treated both Brahmans and Jains as cultural ambassadors of the larger Sanskrit tradition and often called upon individuals to provide access to Indian texts, knowledge systems, and practices beyond their sectarian affiliations. In this vein, Shaykh Bhāvan, a Brahman convert to Islam, was a particularly colorful character. Shaykh Bhāvan resided at Akbar's court in the 1570s and 1580s and was often requested, despite his conversion, to explain Brahmanical ideas. However, Shaykh Bhāvan frequently characterized Sanskrit texts in ways that disconcerted Hindus and Muslims alike. For example, he reported that the *Atharva Veda* permitted Hindus to eat beef in certain circumstances and prescribed burial of the dead rather than cremation.[50] The Mughals quickly ascertained that Shaykh Bhāvan's interpretations fell outside mainstream Brahmanical beliefs, and the confusion he created partially prompted Akbar's desire for direct translations of Sanskrit texts. Indeed, translations from Sanskrit under Akbar began with the *Atharva Veda.*

Other Brahmans also assisted with Mughal renderings of Sanskrit texts into Persian. More than one dozen Sanskrit works were translated under the direct orders of Akbar or Jahangir. All these projects required Sanskrit intellectuals to verbally communicate the text in Hindi to the Mughal translators, who invariably lacked working knowledge of Sanskrit. Most Persian works do not bear the names of their Indian informants; however, the few that do record Brahman aides.[51] Jains provided Sanskrit texts to the Mughals for translation on occasion but are not listed as translators in any known works.[52] Notably, the Sanskrit tradition is completely silent about Brahmans serving as cotranslators under Mughal orders. Brahmans are reticent in general to describe their imperial experiences in much depth. But while they occasionally refer to other courtly activities, translating Sanskrit texts was something they chose never to write about.

Brahmans also served as astrologers for the royal family, which was a thoroughly political role in the Mughal context. Speaking of Perso-Islamic sovereigns generally, Azfar Moin has compared astronomy to history in terms of its political import.[53] The Mughals relied on Islamic-based versions of this art, and Akbar even fashioned his own solar calendar beginning on the date of his ascension (the *tārīkh-i ilāhī*, "divine era"). The Mughals also incorporated Sanskrit astrology into courtly practices. Beginning under Humayun, royal horoscopes were cast according to both Indian and Persian systems. Akbar instituted the position of *jyotiṣarāja* (or *jotik rai*, "royal astrologer") in order to have a scholar versed in Indian astrology formally recognized at court, and several Brahmans successively held this office into Shah Jahan's reign.[54] Some of these astrologers also wrote texts for the Mughals, such as Paramānanda, who composed a Sanskrit work on Indian astrology for Jahangir on the orders of Iʿtibār Khān.[55] More frequently, these Brahmans cast horoscopes and were handsomely rewarded for their work, often receiving their weight in silver or gold. Other cross-cultural astrological activities also thrived at the imperial court during this period. A bilingual Sanskrit-Arabic astrolabe was crafted by a Brahman pupil of an Islamic astrologer at Jahangir's court.[56] In the 1630s Asaf Khan even commissioned Nityānanda to translate a hefty work of Persian astrology, the *Zīj-i Shāh Jahānī*, into Sanskrit, which is one of the rare Persian-to-Sanskrit translations known today.[57]

In contrast to their muteness about working as translators, the Brahmanical community evinced considerable pride in being royal astrologers for an Islamicate court. Akbar's *jyotiṣarāja*, Nīlakaṇṭha, is commended in Sanskrit texts authored by his son and grandson as an honored member of Akbar's entourage.[58] One of Jahangir's court astrologers, Paramānanda, proclaimed that he was revered by the Brahmanical community after receiving the title *jyotiṣarāja*.[59] This positive reception may be due partly to the cross-cultural nature of Sanskrit-based astrology for several hundred years preceding Mughal rule and the long association of Islamicate patrons with this science.[60]

Brahmans outside the royal court also acknowledged the important connection between Sanskrit astrology and the Mughals. For example, in 1583, Sūryadāsa fashioned a short Sanskrit-Persian lexicon of astrological items within a chapter titled "Mlecchamatanirūpaṇa" (Investigation into

Views of Foreigners).[61] At the beginning of his lexicon he specifies, "Now I will give the technical terms used in the science of the foreigners [*yavana*] for things such as the constellations, etc. The meanings of these terms will be useful in royal courts and for astrologers."[62] Several decades later, Shah Jahan's Indian astrologer, Malājit Vedāṅgarāya, authored a more expansive bilingual lexicon (*Pārasīprakāśa* [*Light on Persian*]) that also explains date conversion between the Islamic and Indian (*śaka*) systems.[63] But Brahmans were not immune from criticism for crafting such innovative works. For example, in 1639, Nityānanda composed a text titled *Sarvasiddhāntarāja* (*King of All Siddhāntas*) that David Pingree has characterized as "an elaborate apology" for his earlier use of Muslim astronomy.[64]

The Mughals also turned to Sanskrit intellectuals for information concerning other Indian practices and ideas that could inform an imperial agenda, including the notion that Akbar was an incarnation of the Hindu god Vishnu. Badā'ūnī unhappily attests that Brahmans introduced Sanskrit works that predicted Akbar's rise to power as Vishnu's avatar:

> [Cheating imposter Brahmans] told [the king] repeatedly that he had descended to earth, like Ram, Krishan, and other infidel rulers, who, although lords of the world, had taken on human form to act on earth. For the sake of flattery, they presented Sanskrit poetry [*shiʿr-hā-yi hindī*] allegedly uttered by tongues of sages that predicted a world-conquering padshah would arise in India. He would honor Brahmans, protect cows, and justly rule the earth. They wrote such nonsense on old papers and presented it to [the emperor]. He believed every word.[65]

Some Sanskrit works written under Akbar's support mirror these claims rather precisely. For example, in his bilingual grammar from the late sixteenth century, Kṛṣṇadāsa praises Akbar as Vishnu embodied:

> Since Brahma was described by the Veda
> as changeless and beyond this world,
> therefore Akbar, great ruler of the earth, was born
> in order to protect cows and Brahmans.
> His virtuous name is celebrated throughout the ocean of *śāstras*
> and among scriptures [*smṛti*], histories [*itihāsa*], and the like.
> It is established forever in the three worlds, and
> therefore with his name this work is composed.
> It is no surprise that cows were protected by Lord Krishna, son of Gopala,

and the best of the twice born guarded
by the Ramas, gods of the Brahmans.
But it is truly amazing that the lord Vishnu
descended [*avatīrṇa*] in a family of
foreigners that loves to harm cows and Brahmans.
Akbar protects cows and Brahmans![66]

How Akbar might have linguistically understood these Sanskrit lines remains unclear, but Badā'ūnī attests that the royal court was familiar with the claim that Vishnu was Akbar's divine identity. Similar inclinations toward religious-based expressions of political authority also led to the production of other Sanskrit texts for explicit Mughal use, such as the *Allopaniṣad* (*Allah's Upanishad*).

Probably around the year 1580, an anonymous author, likely a Brahman, composed a strange but noteworthy Sanskrit text at Akbar's request titled *Allopaniṣad*.[67] Imitating a Vedic style, this short work of ten verses identifies Allah as equipollent with all Hindu deities. The author also plays heavily on the multivalence of "Akbar," which may mean "great," particularly in reference to God, and is also the regnal name of the Mughal king.[68] Twice the *Allopaniṣad* invokes the phrase *allāhu akbar*, which sometimes appears on coins and at the start of Akbar-period texts with the intentional double meaning of "God is great" and "Akbar is God."[69] Akbar also used the exclamation as a greeting among members of his inner imperial circle with the equally duplicitous response of *jalla jalāluhu* ("May his [God's or Akbar's] glory be ever glorious").[70]

The *Allopaniṣad* also twice declares, "The God of the messenger Muhammad Akbar is the God of gods."[71] In identifying Akbar as God's prophet (*rasūla* in Sanskrit, from the Arabic *rasūl*), the *Allopaniṣad* echoes the *kalima*, the Islamic statement of faith: "There is no god but God, and Muhammad is his messenger [*rasūl*]." The *kalima* was an important site of Muslim identity that Akbar also sought to recode on other occasions.[72] For instance, he unsuccessfully tried to emend the statement of faith in 1579–1580 to read, "There is no god but God, and Akbar is his representative [*khalīfat*]."[73] Even after he backed down from this explosive attempt, Akbar sometimes ordered Persian authors to eschew praise of Muhammad in their texts.[74]

Precisely how (or whether) Akbar's court used the *Allopaniṣad* remains unclear, but it was likely part of his effort to cultivate a claim to semidivine kingship. Many similar attempts to proclaim Akbar's near divinity marked the year 1582 (990 A.H.), an important year for millennial claims, and provoked significant outrage.[75] Akbar quickly abandoned some of the experiments (such as rewriting the *kalima*). He restricted other programs, such as his imperial discipleship program (*tawhīd-i ilāhī*), to a select group of followers.[76] The *Allopaniṣad* likely fell into the discarded category and lapsed into disuse soon after it was written. Quite apart from its Mughal reception, the *Allopaniṣad* became absorbed into some Sanskrit copies of the *Atharva Veda*, and independent manuscripts have also been found across the subcontinent.[77] The text caused a bit of a stir in the nineteenth century when Hindus split on whether the *Allopaniṣad* was valid or fraudulent.[78] In its original Mughal context, the text demonstrates how some Sanskrit intellectuals participated in millennial attempts to formulate Akbar's claims to divinity by mixing Sanskrit, particularly Vedic, and Islamic idioms.

Jains also provided Akbar access to certain Sanskrit-based practices that would prove politically potent, such as sun veneration. Bhānucandra, a Tapa Gaccha ascetic whom Hīravijaya sent to the Mughal court in Lahore in 1587, taught Akbar how to recite a Sanskrit text titled *Sūryasahasranāma* (*Thousand Names of the Sun*). Siddhicandra, Bhānucandra's Sanskrit biographer, tells the tale thus:

> One time, the ruler of the earth repeatedly asked the Brahmans for the *Thousand Names of the Sun*, but they could not find it anywhere. By a stroke of luck they located some wise man. He gave [the text] to them, and they presented it to the glorious shah [*śrīśāha*]. Having seen it, the glorious shah said to them excitedly, "Tell me who among good people can teach me this?" They replied, "Only one who has subdued all the senses, sleeps on the ground, and possesses sacred knowledge is qualified in this matter." When he heard this, the shah said, "Only you [Bhānucandra] possess such qualities here. You alone, venerable one, will teach me this every morning."[79]

Later in his work, Siddhicandra portrays Akbar as devoted to honoring the sun to the exclusion of other religious activities:

> The glorious shah diligently learned the *Thousand Names of the Sun*. He forgot any other taste and recited the names there. He devoted his mind, stood in the correct direction facing the sun, and learned from Bhānucandra with his folded hands pressed against his forehead.[80]

Siddhicandra does not explain further this "other taste" (*anyarasa*) for which sun veneration eliminated any need on the part of the Mughal emperor. But it is likely a covert reference to Islam, especially given that Siddhicandra carefully mentions that Akbar faced the correct direction in venerating the sun and used his head and hands properly, which are both important concerns in Islamic prayer as well. Furthermore, Badāʾūnī, a notorious critic of Akbar in his unofficial history of the era, testifies that this ritual occurred up to four times daily, including at times for Islamic prayers such as sunrise.[81] Jerome Xavier, a European traveler, even noted Akbar's predilection for sun worship as one reason why he was best not considered a Muslim.[82] Most likely, rather than indicating his personal religious inclinations, Akbar designed this royal custom to promote his absolute sovereignty.

In distinction to most of his engagements with the Sanskrit tradition, Akbar used sun veneration as a public ritual whereby he communicated his prestige and authority to many communities across his empire. Indeed, while many contemporaries viewed Akbar's exaltation of the sun as emerging unequivocally from Brahmanical practices, it also resonated with many other traditions alive in Mughal India, including prior royal activities. Humayun, Akbar's father, had appeared to his people daily at sunrise, and courtly texts compare Humayun's face to the dawning sun.[83] Akbar's recitation of the names of the sun also overlapped with his interest in illumination philosophy, connections with Shattari and Nuqtavi Sufis, and engagements with Zoroastrians.[84] Reverence for the sun arises in imperially sponsored paintings by artists such as Basawan and in Persian literature, such as in the quatrains of Fayẕī, Akbar's poet laureate.[85] In this sense, Mughal sun veneration was an attractive imperial activity precisely because it intersected with numerous traditions. Perhaps because this practice spoke powerfully to many audiences, it was also contentious. Jahangir, like his father, repeated litanies to the sun daily. But thinkers a generation later found it necessary to argue that this practice strove to control rather than exalt the sun.[86]

Tapa and Kharatara Jains also succeeded in bringing their perspectives into Mughal circles under Akbar. For example, one text tells how Jinacandra, the leader of the Kharatara Gaccha, spent a monsoon season in Lahore instructing Akbar in Jain theology (*darśana*).[87] Tapa Gaccha texts describe similar encounters, even portraying Abū al-Faẕl, Akbar's vizier, as "acting like a student" and bowing to Hīravijaya.[88] The historical accuracy of the Mughal elite humbly acquiescing to Jain teachers seems doubtful, although certain types of behavior were perhaps misunderstood across cultural lines. Europeans at Akbar's court frequently misread the emperor's interest in Western culture (particularly art) as willingness to adopt Christian theological precepts.[89]

Certainly the Mughals were highly curious about Jain thought, as is evidenced by including Jains in interreligious discussions in the *ʿibādatkhānah* (house of religious debate) and elsewhere and the extensive section on Jainism in the *Āʾīn-i Akbarī*. One of Akbar's official Persian court histories even lists three Jains (Hīravijaya, Vijayasena, and Bhānucandra) as among the learned men of the age.[90] A painting by Basawan, an artist in the imperial atelier, also survives that depicts a Jain monk, probably either Bhānucandra or Śānticandra (figure 1.1). The Mughals also appreciated Jain intellectual displays. On one occasion, Nandivijaya, a Tapa Gaccha monk, demonstrated *avadhāna*, a difficult mental feat of focusing on multiple (often eight, but sometimes as many as a hundred or even a thousand) things at once, before the Mughals. This achievement greatly impressed Akbar and his poet laureate, Fayẓī.[91] On a few occasions, Jains convinced the Mughal emperors to alter their personal behavior regarding animals. Most notably, Akbar abstained from meat on particular days of the week, and Jahangir refrained from hunting and consuming meat for approximately four years of his reign, likely due to Jain influences.[92]

In one notable case, Kharatara Gaccha members conducted an elaborate religious ceremony on Akbar's behalf that involved both Akbar and Prince Salim (later, Emperor Jahangir) presenting offerings to Jain idols. The most reliable record of this event was penned in Sanskrit in 1594 and is worth quoting in full:

> One time a daughter bound by the curse of the *mūla* constellation was born in the house of glorious Sultan Salim that was already blessed with a son. Glorious Shah [Akbar] called upon wise men such as Shaykh [Abū al-Faẓl] to counteract that curse. Then the king summoned minister [Karmacandra] and ordered him thus, "Perform whatever is the purifying rite in the Jain philosophy!" Honoring the shah's request, [Karmacandra] directed the purifying bathing with pots made of silver and gold with perfect injunctions. At the time of lighting the auspicious lamp, Shaykhū jī (Jahangir), the son of the shah, came and was hospitably received after giving ten thousand silver gifts. [The minister] placed water from the purifying bathing on the two eyes of the glorious king, surrounded by his harem, to alleviate [the curse].[93]

FIGURE 1.1 Mughal image of a Jain ascetic, Basawan, ca. 1600.

CLEVELAND MUSEUM OF ART, SEVERANCE AND GRETA MILLIKIN COLLECTION 1967.244

This event features a startling case of imperial participation in a Jain ceremony. Persianate historians, including Akbar's fiercest critics, do not discuss or even allude to such in-depth engagements with Jain practices.[94] Nonetheless, this narrative is likely authentic. It is attested in both Sanskrit and vernacular texts that emerged from competing groups.[95] Moreover, the Mughals were generally invested in Sanskrit astrological calculations, and so the story fits with known imperial concerns.

Despite often appreciating and enlisting Jain ideas and practices, however, the Mughals occasionally grew suspicious of Jains, suspecting them of being atheists. Being an atheist (*nāstika*) was outside the pale of acceptability in Mughal circles. Thus, Jains answered Mughal questions as to who constituted God (usually referred to as *parameśvara* or *paramātma* in Sanskrit texts) in their theological system in order to protect their position in royal esteem. These accusations of atheism frequently arose at the instigation of Brahmans who sought to have their rivals exiled from court and often stated this goal explicitly.[96] Several such clashes are recorded in Tapa Gaccha works, generally featuring Hīravijaya or his successor, Vijayasena, although Jain-Brahman conflicts before the Mughal elite dated back to Padmasundara's presence at court in the 1560s.[97] As I discuss in chapter 5, the content of these debates is recorded primarily in Sanskrit texts directed toward a Jain audience and often contains specialized terminology that may not accurately reflect the precise course of a given discussion (at the very least, the debates were certainly conducted in either Persian or Hindi rather than Sanskrit). Nonetheless, these exchanges point up atheism as one nonnegotiable limit of Mughal toleration of cultural and religious differences.

The celebrated Gujarati poet Samayasundara, a Kharatara Gaccha affiliate, combines the religious, intellectual, and political activities of Mughal-affiliated Sanskrit intellectuals in a text he presented to Akbar in 1592 titled *Artharatnāvalī* (*The String of Jewels of Meaning*).[98] In this work, Samayasundara interprets an eight-syllable Sanskrit sentence (*rājāno dadate saukhyam*, "Kings bestow happiness") to have eight hundred thousand separate, linguistically viable meanings.[99] Partly he devised this work to demonstrate to Muslim and Brahman challengers at the Mughal court how the Jain tradition allows multiple interpretations of its scriptures (including theistic understandings). Samayasundara also creatively provides readings that would have spoken to Akbar's diverse cross-cultural practices. For example, the first alternative meaning he offers is "The glorious sun grants us happiness," which he notes would be uttered by sun worshippers.[100]

Samayasundara attests that he unveiled his work in Kashmir before the Mughal king and learned Brahmans. Akbar was so pleased that,

> With complete mental astonishment born from an overflowing, novel joy arising from hearing these meanings, glorious Shah [Akbar] offered high praise and said, "Let [this book] be read, taught, and brought everywhere." He grasped this book with his own hands and, having placed it in my hand, held this text to be authoritative [*pramāṇīkṛto*].[101]

To further ensure Akbar's favor, Samayasundara ended his work by incorporating the Mughal king within the Jain Sanskrit tradition and pronounced the final reading of his sentence to mean, "King Akbar gives us happiness."[102] He also embeds a further claim of Akbar's greatness with this proclamation. He equates the final letters of the word *rājā* to three different Hindu (largely Vedic) deities who have alternative names that match the last three syllables of Akbar's Sanskritized name (*akavara*). Thus Akbar, an Indian *rāja*, is also identified with Brahma (*ka*), Vayu (*va*), and Agni (*ra*).[103] In these ways Samayasundara exhibits the ability of Sanskrit texts, especially in Jain hands, to express Mughal imperial claims.

DIVERGENT PATHS: JAIN CLASHES WITH JAHANGIR

Timeline 1.2 Jahangir's Relations with Jain Ascetics

Year	*Event*
1605	Jinasiṃha, Kharatara Gaccha leader, predicted Jahangir's rule would end in less than two years.
1608–1610	Vijayasena and other Tapa Gaccha monks gained royal orders from Jahangir. Mughal painter Shalivahana illustrated celebratory letter to Vijayasena.
1611–1612	Jahangir argued with Siddhicandra and banished Tapa Gaccha ascetics (possibly all Jain monks?) from the Mughal court.
ca. 1613–1615	Jahangir rescinded banishment order and monks, including Siddhicandra, returned to court.
1616–1618	Tapa Gaccha ascetics procured several beneficial imperial orders.
1617	Jahangir called Jinasiṃha to court, and the monk died en route.
1618	Jahangir again expelled Jain monks from his court.

Jain monks populated the Mughal court through Akbar's death in 1605 and into the early years of Jahangir's reign. But Jain Sanskrit thinkers fluctuated in royal favor and lost any presence at court by roughly 1620. Even before he ascended the throne, Jahangir upset Jain leaders by allowing his ministers to revive animal slaughter and taxes on non-Muslims in Gujarat before Akbar reined in such excesses.[104] Despite Jahangir's youthful indiscretions, several Tapa Gaccha ascetics patronized by Akbar, most prominently Bhānucandra and his pupil Siddhicandra, continued as active figures at court when Jahangir took power. In 1608, Jahangir issued a *farmān* that confirmed bans on pilgrimage taxes and animal slaughter instituted under his father and also permitted the Tapa Gaccha to rebuild certain temples.[105] In 1610, Vijayasena, the Tapa Gaccha leader, secured another royal *farmān* that forbade butchering animals. The Kharatara Gaccha was on shakier ground from the inauguration of Jahangir's reign. When Jahangir first became king, Jinasiṃha (also known as Mānasiṃha), the Kharatara leader, predicted that he would fall from power in less than two years. In his memoirs, Jahangir attributes Rai Singh of Bikaner's rebellion to this false prophecy and maligns Jinasiṃha as "black-tongued."[106] Despite this rocky start, however, Sanskrit and vernacular texts testify that Kharatara Jains visited the imperial court and enjoyed favor with Jahangir.[107]

In the 1610s, Jahangir banished nearly all Jains from his court and also barred Jain ascetics from entering populated centers across the entire Mughal Empire. He issued this severe proclamation because Siddhicandra, a young monk at the time, disobeyed an imperial order to take a wife.[108] This injunction, however, did not spell the end of Jain-Mughal relations. Jahangir allowed Bhānucandra to remain at court, likely because he was viewed as a broad-ranging Sanskrit-based intellectual rather than primarily a Jain monk. Moreover, Jahangir eventually rescinded his harsh order and authorized Jains to move freely once again about the Mughal kingdom. Both the Kharatara and Tapa Gacchas claim responsibility for securing this reversal.[109] For a few years, normal relations resumed. Jahangir issued a *farmān* in 1616 that promised Tapa Gaccha followers freedom to worship and praised Jains as "singularly devoted to worshipping God."[110] Sir Thomas Roe, an Englishman who visited Jahangir's court in 1616–1618, notes that Jains often procured royal bans on animal slaughter.[111] But Jahangir's animosity toward the Kharatara Gaccha soon resurfaced. He wrote in his memoirs that in 1617 he suddenly remembered Jinasiṃha's erroneous forecast that his rule would be short-lived and summoned the monk to court. Jinasiṃha died before reaching Agra (probably because of poor health), and Jahangir trumpets that the ascetic poisoned himself rather than face imperial wrath.[112]

Jahangir exiled all Jain ascetics again in 1618 and says nothing positive about them after that date. He writes in his memoirs, "There is no shame or modesty [among the Shvetambaras], and they enact all sorts of perversities and lewdness. Therefore, I issued an order expelling the Shvetambaras, and decrees were sent in all directions that wherever Shvetambaras reside they should be thrown out of my empire."[113] The *Majālis-i Jahāngīrī* (*Jahangir's Assemblies*) confirms that "it was also ordered that no *sīvarah* [Shvetambara] be allowed to enter the city [of Cambay] and that the governor of that district be told that if a *sīvarah* other than an elderly person appeared in the city, he will be guilty of perversions."[114] In fact this second prohibition also did not remain in force for any length of time.[115] But 1618 nonetheless marks the last known direct communication between Jain intellectuals and Jahangir. Even Bhānucandra either left the court or was not particularly prominent in later years, since Jahangir referred to him in the 1620s as someone "whom I used to know."[116]

No Mughal links with Jain ascetics during Shah Jahan's reign have been uncovered, and only sporadic contact is known under Aurangzeb. In 1645, then Prince Aurangzeb desecrated a Jain temple in Gujarat that had been financed by Śāntidās of Ahmedabad, an affluent Jain businessman.[117] Nonetheless, as king he periodically granted land and *farmāns* to Tapa Gaccha representatives.[118] Interestingly, Jain vernacular texts offer a positive picture of Aurangzeb as promoting religious tolerance across the Mughal Empire.[119] Given these occasional later encounters, we ought to be careful about proclaiming a definitive end date for Mughal interactions for Jain ascetics. Moreover, Jain merchants maintained more consistent imperial connections throughout this period and even financed Mughal state activities.[120] Close ties frequently bound together Jain commercial and ascetic communities in the seventeenth century. Prominent Jain merchants, such as Śāntidās, no doubt benefited in their imperial dealings from earlier Mughal familiarity with Jain monks.[121] Nonetheless, Jains steeped in the Sanskrit tradition never regained the variety of roles at the royal court that they had enjoyed under Akbar and, more intermittently, under Jahangir.

BRAHMANS DURING THE REIGNS OF JAHANGIR AND SHAH JAHAN

Brahmans overall experienced no imperial condemnations or vicissitudes in royal favor akin to those that plagued Jains during Jahangir's rule. We lack evidence that Jahangir sought relations with Brahmanical intellectuals with the same vigor as his father, but he still participated in cross-cultural meetings. For example, Jahangir reports in his memoirs at least six separate encounters from 1617 to 1620 with Gosain Jadrup, a Brahman ascetic whom Jahangir describes as "well learned in the science of Vedanta, which is the science of Sufism."[122] The Mughals knew Jadrup at least by name even during the late years of Akbar's rule, and Jahangir attests that his father visited Jadrup once.[123] The content of most of Jahangir's conversations with Jadrup remains unknown, but enough has trickled down for us to know that the two covered a range of topics. For instance, Jahangir attests in his memoirs that Jadrup convinced him to recalibrate a Mughal weight measurement so that it was in accordance with Vedic thought.[124] This might strike modern audiences as a mundane administrative point, but the Mughals considered weights a serious knowledge system and even detail Indian opinions on the topic in the *Āʾīn-i Akbarī*.[125] Another Persian source of the period, the *Iqbālnāmah*, attests that other Mughal elites, such as Mirza Aziz Koka, also met with Jadrup and even persuaded the yogi to secure Prince Khusraw's release from confinement (which resulted from his earlier rebellion).[126]

Interestingly, both Jahangir and Akbar personally traveled to visit Jadrup instead of following the more standard method of calling Sanskrit intellectuals to court. Paintings survive of both emperors meeting with Jadrup where the two parties are seated on the ground in or near a cave.[127] A Mughal painting from Shah Jahan's period further underscores Jadrup's separation from court-affiliated Sanskrit intellectuals by depicting him alongside Indian poets and *bhakti* figures commonly associated with vernacular traditions, most of whom had no connection with the Mughals, such as Ravidas, Namdev, and Kabir.[128] Jahangir also periodically hosted Brahman intellectuals at court, such as a Brahman from Gujarat who accompanied Ramdas Kachhwaha and spoke with Jahangir about the sanctity of cows and the mythology surrounding Dadhici, a Brahman who generously gave his bones to the Hindu gods.[129]

Jahangir also engaged with Sanskrit poets, although it is difficult to reconstruct the precise nature of these relationships. As I discuss later in this chapter, Jagannātha Paṇḍitarāja crafted a verse extolling Jahangir, which suggests he may have entered the Mughal court during the early to mid-1620s. The *Padyaveṇī*, a collection of Sanskrit verses assembled by Veṇīdatta in the mid-seventeenth century, contains a verse by Cintāmaṇi on Jahangir's battle prowess.[130] The same author also penned a verse lauding Parvez, a son of Jahangir's, for frightening enemies.[131] Whether Cintāmaṇi was present at the Mughal court, however, remains unconfirmed. A member of the ruling family of Mithila, Harideva Miśra, authored a work in the first half of the seventeenth century praising Jahangir (*Jahāṅgīravirudāvalī*).[132]

Under Shah Jahan the Brahmanical profile at the Mughal court became more pronounced with the entry of Kavīndrācārya Sarasvatī and Jagannātha Paṇḍitarāja. These two figures built on the tradition of earlier imperial patronage of Sanskrit literati but also revealed important changes in the Indian intellectual world and the Mughal court in the seventeenth century. Kavīndrācārya Sarasvatī was a major leader in the Brahmanical community based in Benares. He initially approached Shah Jahan in order to negotiate the relinquishment of taxes on Hindu pilgrimage sites. While no narrative accounts of Kavīndra's time at Shah Jahan's court are known, Sanskrit and Hindi verses praising Kavīndra attest that he spent time in Mughal company teaching Sanskrit texts to both Shah Jahan and his son and heir apparent, Dara Shikuh. He instructed them in Sanskrit philosophy, poetry, and likely the *Yogavāsiṣṭha*.[133] Deploying the same strategies previously honed by Jains, Kavīndra mobilized his ability to provide the Mughals access to Sanskrit knowledge for political gain. He successfully persuaded Shah Jahan to rescind a tax on Hindu pilgrims to Benares and Prayag, which delighted the Brahmanical community.[134]

Kavīndra's encounter with the Mughals also marks shifts in the identities and roles of seventeenth-century Sanskrit intellectuals. First, Kavīndra served the Mughals as a Hindi author and singer in addition to being a Sanskrit pandit. He composed several works in Hindi, including a shortened version of the *Yogavāsiṣṭha*.[135] This likely functioned as an aid for tutoring Shah Jahan and Dara Shikuh or was the product of those sessions. Kavīndra also wrote the vernacular *Kavīndrakalpalatā* (*Wish-Fulfilling Vine of Kavindra*), in which more than half the verses are dedicated to Shah Jahan.[136] These verses also incorporate *dhrupad* songs (a musical tradition based in Hindi texts) that celebrate Shah Jahan.[137]

The Persian tradition remembers Kavīndra for his talents as a singer of *dhrupad* and even records that Kavīndra accepted monetary rewards at the Mughal court in his capacity as a musician.[138] Even Sanskrit thinkers of the time recognized that Kavīndra was a renowned singer in addition to a learned scholar.[139] However, multiple perceptions were at work in Kavīndra's ties to the Mughals. The French traveler François Bernier explains that Kavīndra received an imperial stipend because he was "eminent for knowledge" and to "gratify the *Rajas*."[140]

In a sense, Kavīndra expanded upon a mode of cosmopolitanism established by Bhānucandra of being an Indian intellectual conversant in many fields. But Kavīndra's emphasis on Hindi in addition to Sanskrit in the Mughal context is a noticeable change that is also found in the case of Jagannātha. The rising profile of the vernaculars in imperial culture was likely linked to more widespread changes in early modern India. Scholars have established no drop-off in the volume of Sanskrit textual production during this period, although intellectual thought in certain fields may have stagnated.[141] Undoubtedly, however, vernaculars were on the ascent as mediums for expressing literary and intellectual ideas.[142] At the Mughal court, royal interests likewise gradually shifted to support Hindi above Sanskrit in the mid-seventeenth century.

In the late 1650s to early 1660s Kavīndra moved outside the central royal court and joined the retinue of a Mughal noble, Danishmand Khan, and later of the European François Bernier.[143] In Kavīndra's case, Aurangzeb severed his imperial stipend upon ascending the throne, which prompted Kavīndra to seek alternative avenues of support.[144] Nonetheless, even before Aurangzeb took power, many Sanskrit intellectuals had gravitated to the princely household of Dara Shikuh.[145] Previously, the flow had often worked in the opposite direction as Sanskrit intellectuals moved from local and subimperial centers into the royal Mughal court. Kavīndra's later association with a European also reflects wider changes in India's cultural landscape. Europeans had traveled in India since well before the establishment of Mughal rule, but the early seventeenth century witnessed expansions of their numbers and interests on the subcontinent.[146] Kavīndra's ties with a Frenchman are part of this larger process whereby India became ever more integrated into global networks of knowledge.

Jagannātha Paṇḍitarāja is the other major Sanskrit intellectual to have spent significant time at Shah Jahan's court, and his imperial career displays similar shifts in cultural affiliations. Jagannātha professes to have "passed the prime of youth" at the Mughal court and therein authored a number of works considered masterpieces in the Sanskrit tradition.[147] But he scarcely mentions his Indo-Persian patrons in his Sanskrit writings.[148] The handful of verses that refer to Mughal figures admit no contemporary context. Rather, Jagannātha fully incorporates the Mughals into the Sanskrit cultural world, such as in this praise of Jahangir:

> Why is your sacred thread black? From touching black powder? From where has it come? How did the water of the Narmada River become laced with collyrium? It became so because of the confluence of rivers born from the showers of tears of the hundred thousand beautiful-eyed ladies of kings who are enemies of angry Nuruddin [*nūradīna*, i.e., Jahangir].[149]

Scholars have suggested that the personal tone of some of Jagannātha's poetry may reflect Perso-Islamic poetic practices.[150] But, except for the names of his patrons, he offers little overt recognition of his Mughal location in his extensive oeuvre. His own chosen context is entirely Sanskrit based, and Jagannātha often carefully positioned himself with reference to the Sanskrit tradition and its more influential contributors.[151]

His Sanskrit works aside, however, Jagannātha Paṇḍitarāja was a highly regarded vernacular singer at the Mughal court, which drew him into Indian vernacular culture. The *Bādshāhnāmah*, an official history of Shah Jahan's reign, contains three references to Jagannāth *kabrāy* (King of Poets) and later *mahākabrāy* (Great King of Poets) and praises his skills as a singer (*kalāvant*) of vernacular *dhrupad*.[152] The work's author, Mullā ʿAbd al-Ḥamīd Lāhawrī, describes Jagannātha as "the best of composers of this time, who is filled with pleasure and decorated with joy" and testifies that his talent was handsomely rewarded, to the tune of forty-five hundred rupees on one occasion.[153] A second Persian history of Shah Jahan's reign, Amīn Qazvīnī's *Bādshāhnāmah*, also notes the singer Jagannāth *mahākabrāy*.[154] There are fourteen *dhrupads* in a collection from the late seventeenth century attributed to Jagannāth *kabrāy*, and a collection of his *bhajan* songs survives in a single manuscript in Baroda.[155] A Braj Bhasha work that details Jagannātha Paṇḍitarāja's life confirms that the Hindi singer and the Sanskrit poet were indeed the same person.[156] The earliest Brahman Sanskrit thinkers who visited Akbar's court wrote Sanskrit discourses on music. But not until Kavīndrācārya and Jagannātha does clear evidence surface that Sanskrit literati doubled as performers in the royal assembly.

Jagannātha also forged a personal connection within the Indo-Islamic world by pursuing a love affair with a Muslim woman known in Sanskrit texts as Lavaṅgī. Jagannātha refers to this woman in several Sanskrit verses and confirms that she was Muslim (*yavanī*).[157] The Braj Bhasha work on Jagannātha's life specifies that the couple married.[158] Whereas most connections between Brahmans and Muslims passed without comment within Brahmanical circles, Jagannātha's contemporaries strenuously objected to this affair. R. B. Athavale argues that Kavīndrācārya condemned the relationship in a verse that plays on the meaning of *lavaṅgī* as a clove plant.[159] There is an unconfirmed report that Bhaṭṭoji Dīkṣita, a seventeenth-century Sanskrit grammarian, denounced Jagannātha as a *mleccha* (barbarian) for taking a Muslim wife.[160] A Sanskrit legend also relays that Appayya Dīkṣita, a major Sanskrit poetician, once chastised Jagannātha after catching him with his Muslim lover.[161] This story is historically implausible because a century separated the two men.[162] But it captures the deep discomfort of the Sanskrit Brahmanical community with one of their own becoming too fully immersed in Indo-Islamic culture.

Jagannātha's marriage pressed the limits of tolerance among Sanskrit intellectuals for involvement in the Mughal world. Earlier and later Sanskrit intellectuals who wed Muslim women and even wrote about their romantic feelings received less push back from their communities, and so even this line was negotiable.[163] Perhaps Jagannātha's prominence in Brahmanical scholarly circles attracted scrutiny to his love life. However, Jagannātha drew ire only for his personal relationship with a Muslim woman and seems to have received little or no reproach from his contemporaries for accepting Mughal patronage. In Sanskrit philosophical works of the seventeenth century, some Brahmans argue that learning a foreign (*mleccha*) tongue such as Persian is illicit and warn that bilingual people (*dvaibhāṣika*) may break the prohibition on teaching Sanskrit to non-Brahmans.[164] Nonetheless, such philosophical positions seem to have rarely been applied to individuals.

In a sense, Jagannātha Paṇḍitarāja represents the height of Mughal support of Sanskrit authors, because he was the most highly regarded intellectual in Sanskrit literary culture to work under imperial sponsorship. However, he was also one of the last Sanskrit literati known to be present at the central Mughal court. Beyond Kavīndra and Jagannātha, Shah Jahan sponsored only a few other Sanskrit authors, including a Sanskrit astrologer.[165] Shah Jahan has often been depicted by scholars as instituting a more strictly Islamic political culture than his predecessors, and there is some evidence for this shift.[166] But the waning imperial interest in Sanskrit is more directly explained by rising attention to Hindi. Shah Jahan's court increasingly employed Hindi intellectuals, who filled similarly varied roles as their Sanskrit predecessors. For example, Sundar of Gwalior composed original Hindi texts and Hindi translations for Shah Jahan. Sundar also participated in diplomatic negotiations with Rajput rulers.[167]

By the time Aurangzeb took power in the late 1650s, Mughal associations with Sanskrit intellectuals had already largely ceased, and Sanskrit literati themselves were increasingly drawn to vernacular traditions. Like Shah Jahan, Aurangzeb supported Hindi poets.[168] Under Aurangzeb's rule, Indian vernacular music also thrived in imperial and subimperial courts, both in performance and textual production.[169] For their part, Jain and Brahmanical authors alike continued to write favorable Sanskrit verses about the current Mughal king and often dated their works by his reign, both common practices from Akbar's time forward.[170] They also served subimperial Mughal figures.[171] However, sustained relations between Sanskrit intellectuals and the central Mughal court had more or less faded away by the end of Shah Jahan's tenure on the throne.

Timeline 1.3 Select Encounters with Brahman Sanskrit Intellectuals at Shah Jahan's Court

Year	*Event*
1628–1641	Jagannātha Paṇḍitarāja composed Sanskrit poem *Play of Asaf Khan*.
ca. 1630s–1640s	Asaf Khan commissioned Nityānanda to translate the *Zīj-i Shāh Jahānī* into Sanskrit. Kavīndrācārya Sarasvatī convinced Shah Jahan to relinquish tax on Hindu pilgrims to Benares and Prayag (Allahabad). Jagannātha received titles *kabrāy* and *mahākabrāy* from Shah Jahan. Jagannātha wrote Sanskrit works and composed and performed vernacular songs under Mughal support.
ca. 1640s–1650s	Kavīndrācārya read Sanskrit texts with Shah Jahan and Dara Shikuh and was also a courtly vernacular singer.
1657–1659	Aurangzeb ʿAlamgir seized power and halted royal stipend to Kavīndrācārya.

OFFICIAL TITLES AND THE PERFORMANCE OF MUGHAL POWER

Throughout the period of sustained Mughal connections with Sanskrit literati (ca. 1560–1660), Jain and Brahman intellectuals received official and honorary titles from their royal benefactors. Akbar, Jahangir, and Shah Jahan all granted titles to Sanskrit figures alongside numerous other engagements, as I have detailed in my discussion of cross-cultural events during each king's reign. But the practice of imperial titling merits additional discussion because it highlights the types of agency exercised by different communities in Mughal encounters with Sanskrit literati. To date, no scholar has compiled the information available about this diverse cultural activity, much less analyzed titles as a social and imperial practice. Here I offer the first comprehensive account of multilingual titling at the Mughal court, including official titles given to Jain leaders and honorary appellations granted to Jain and Brahman Sanskrit intellectuals.

Sanskrit and vernacular traditions provide the overwhelming majority of existing data on cross-cultural imperial titling, which highlights a noteworthy case of Mughal silence. Mughal Persian sources offer precious little information about any appellations bestowed on Jain and Brahman thinkers, and they mention nothing whatsoever about official raises in Jain religious ranks. These omissions likely communicate little about the value the Mughals placed on titling Sanskrit intellectuals but rather signal that they conceptualized such activities as outside the Persianate sphere. Indeed, aside from naming astrologers *jyotiṣarāja* (royal astrologer), titles given to Sanskrit intellectuals appear to have never been associated with formal Mughal court hierarchies and so are discussed primarily in Sanskrit, the cultural realm in which they operated. This context did not dissuade the Mughal kings, however, from participating in various forms of titling as part of their project to perform imperial authority in multiple religious and literary venues.

Akbar and Jahangir repeatedly meted out formal titles that advanced individuals' standings within either the Tapa Gaccha or Kharatara Gaccha. Earlier kings had tried to interfere with internal Jain hierarchies to some degree, but Jain communities often rebuffed these intrusions.[172] In contrast, Jains accepted Mughal changes in religious ranks within certain boundaries. Akbar vigorously pursued this sort of interaction. Even upon the initial Jain-Mughal contact in the 1560s, Akbar intervened in Jain affairs by refusing to give Padmasundara's books to his disciples, whom the king deemed unworthy.[173] When Akbar began bestowing formal Jain titles, he introduced unprecedented levels of imperial Persianate authority into the Jain religious sphere but nonetheless found himself restrained by preexisting protocols.

Akbar was often compelled to consult with Jain leaders and perform joint rituals to successfully raise a given individual's status. For example, within the Tapa Gaccha, Akbar awarded the Sanskrit title of *upādhyāya* (Instructor) to Bhānucandra through an involved series of negotiations. Siddhicandra relays this story, beginning with Akbar's asking Bhānucandra one morning, "In your tradition what is the most illustrious title for a person who possesses all virtues, like my title of Universal Ruler [*sārvabhauma*]?"[174] Bhānucandra replied, "*Ācārya* [Teacher] is predominant and then *upādhyāya*."[175] Akbar inquired which grade Bhānucandra held, and the answer was neither, since such positions were accorded only by the leader of the Tapa Gaccha, Hīravijaya, who was currently far away.[176] Akbar initially tried to circumvent Hīravijaya's authority: "Having heard that response, the King of the Earth said over and over, very determinedly, 'Then let me bestow upon you the title *ācārya*.' "[177] But Bhānucandra steadfastly refused to accept this honor without Hīravijaya's approval, and Akbar closed the discussion for the moment, being more impressed than ever with the monk's virtue.[178]

A while later, Abū al-Faẕl took over as negotiator on behalf of the king and orchestrated the successful promotion of Bhānucandra through a melding of Mughal and Jain authority. First, he convinced Akbar to bestow the lesser title of *upādhyāya* on the Jain teacher. Here the Mughals conceded limits to their power in the Jain realm by following the standard advancement through the Tapa Gaccha hierarchy. Next Abū al-Faẕl announced the royal decision to the Jain community, at which point a Jain leader again protested that titles ought to be affirmed by the head of the Tapa Gaccha. Abū al-Faẕl duly penned a *farmān* on the matter to Hīravijaya. In response Hīravijaya wrote a letter granting permission and sent the appropriate physical accoutrements needed to assume the new position.[179] The consecration ceremony for Bhānucandra's ascension to *upādhyāya* was performed sometime later when Hīravijaya was in town. Crucially, Siddhicandra notes that while Akbar initiated the ritual, Hīravijaya personally instituted the new rank: "One time glorious King Akbar affectionately summoned the chief of Sūris and said joyfully, 'Let glorious Hīra [vijaya] Sūri bestow the title of *upādhyāya* on honorable

Bhānucandra in accordance with my prior speech.' "[180] Subsequent verses describe the ceremony and attest to the presence of both Jain and Mughal forms of authority. For example, Hīravijaya taught Bhānucandra a secret mantra, and Abū al-Faẓl distributed horses to members of the gathered crowds.[181]

Akbar also changed formal ranks for Kharatara leaders in similarly joint exercises of Jain and Mughal agencies. In 1593, Akbar simultaneously named Mānasiṃha *ācārya* and *jinasiṃha* (Lion of Jinas), the name by which he is often known. According to the *Mantrikarmacandravaṃśāvalīprabandha* (*Account of the Genealogy of Minister Karmacandra*, 1594), Akbar requested approval to raise Mānasiṃha's status to *ācārya* from Jinacandra, the head of the Kharatara Gaccha.[182] But for the renaming as Jinasiṃha, Akbar relied on his own authority and said, "The name [*nāma*] Jinasiṃha Sūri is to be given to Mānasiṃha, because he possesses power equivalent to that of a lion in every way."[183] Next, "The circle of regional rulers and the minister [Karmacandra] accepted the king's speech with the *taslīm*, like a flower garland on the head."[184] The *taslīm* was a common form of bowing in Akbar's court that signified acceptance of the king's authority.[185] The Sanskrit commentary on the text defines *taslīm* (*tasalīma* in Sanskrit) as "a sign of humility preceded by placing the right hand on the head with foreign speech."[186] Thus, Jain and Muslim leaders alike affirmed Jinasiṃha's new name according to Mughal norms. However, the Kharatara community later orchestrated the appropriate rites to celebrate both titles and announced them to the Jain community.[187]

Akbar and Jahangir also bestowed the designation *yugapradhāna* (Primary Man of the Age) on successive leaders of the Kharatara Gaccha. Akbar gave the appellation to Jinacandra, and later Jahangir conferred it on Jinasiṃha.[188] This title did not signal a rise in rank, but it affirmed the lofty position of the Kharatara leader. Later records of the Kharatara spiritual lineage (*paṭṭāvalī*s) laud this honorific and often mention it in tandem with *farmān*s obtained from the Mughal kings.[189] Inscriptions in Rajasthan suggest that the Mughal kings may also have granted the title *yugapradhāna* to other Jain monks.[190]

Thus, even while Jains typically affirmed formal positions, they also admitted Mughal imperial power and its associated prestige into their religious hierarchies. For the Mughals, such titlings and their accompanying ceremonies offered an opportunity to imagine and perform their kingship on an Indian stage. The Mughals seem to have targeted primarily an audience of ruling and Jain elites, rather than any larger community, through these titlings. Azfar Moin has recently spoken about "multiple scripts of sovereignty" and the importance of performance in Mughal idioms of rule.[191] Formal titlings offered Akbar and Jahangir an unprecedented opportunity to enact sovereign power through the framework of Jain religious practices.

HONORARY TITLES FOR COSMOPOLITAN INTELLECTUALS

The Mughal kings granted honorary Sanskrit, Persian, and vernacular appellations to both Jain and Brahmanical figures. Each emperor developed a slightly different emphasis for his honorary titles, but Akbar, Jahangir, and Shah Jahan all participated in this diverse practice.[192] Moreover, Sanskrit intellectuals who received appellations from Mughal rulers frequently trumpeted this distinction in their writings. Religious and genealogical descendants of these individuals also proclaimed Mughal-bestowed honorifics as a noteworthy heritage. While Sanskrit intellectuals sometimes indicated tensions in being marked by Perso-Islamic kings, they generally celebrated the particular prestige associated with Mughal-granted titles.

Akbar bestowed several honorary Sanskrit titles that all carried significant imperial cachet but also triggered certain cultural anxieties. Most prominently, after meeting Hīravijaya in the 1580s, Akbar labeled him *jagadguru* (Teacher of the World). This name appears prominently in the title of the first of two Sanskrit hagiographies of Hīravijaya (*Jagadgurukāvya* [*Poem on the Teacher of the World*]). Devavimala, Hīravijaya's second Sanskrit biographer, also mentions the appellation. But he hints at some reservations by placing the honorific in a long line of titles given to Jains by kings and Islamicate figures:

> Just as "Pious Ascetic" [*tapā*] was given
> by the ruler of Aghata to Jagaccandra, the lord of ascetics
> who performed particular austerities for twelve years;
> just as "Skilled Among Orators" [*vādigokulasaṅkata*] was joyfully given
> by Zafar Khan at Sthambhatirtha to Munisundara, the moon of Sūris;
> so the title [*biruda*] "Teacher of the World" [*jagadguru*]
> was given by [Akbar] to glorious Lord Hīravijaya,
> an ocean of jewels that are good qualities.[193]

In interpreting this passage, Phyllis Granoff has convincingly argued that Devavimala refers to a series of monks who became involved with governing figures in order to justify Hīravijaya's controversial relationship with Akbar.[194] Many Jain communities, including the Tapa Gaccha, were uncomfortable with monks' frequenting opulent courts. Devavimala thus names precedents for Jains receiving titles from rulers, including the Indo-Persian figure of Zafar Khan, in order to position Hīravijaya as continuing an acceptable ascetic tradition rather than forging brazen imperial relations. Despite inciting some suspicions, being titled by Akbar held significant cultural power. Members of the rival Kharatara Gaccha tried to undermine Hīravijaya by spreading the rumor that *jagadguru* was conferred by Tapa Gaccha followers instead of the Mughal king.[195]

The other honorary Sanskrit titles given by Akbar are likewise commemorated by Sanskrit literati, although not by their recipients. Again this suggests the coexisting anxiety and value associated with this imperial practice. For instance, Akbar conferred on Nṛsiṃha, a Brahman, the descriptor *jyotirvitsarasa* (Elegant among Astronomers) in 1600–1601, which we know through Nṛsiṃha's son.[196] In a slightly unusual case, Akbar issued a Sanskrit-derived title to Abū al-Faẕl, his royal vizier. In 1599, Akbar sent Abū al-Faẕl south to assist Prince Murad, who became ill while championing Mughal military interests in the Deccan.[197] Siddhicandra was at the royal court when Abū al-Faẕl returned and reported his successes in the Deccan campaigns. Siddhicandra attests, "Having heard that news, the king's eyes gleamed with joy, and he named [Abū al-Faẕl] Pillar of the Army [*dalathambhana*]."[198] Abū al-Faẕl never claims this title (*ākhyā*) in his Persian writings, but awareness of it survived within the Sanskrit cultural realm. Curiously, Siddhicandra mentions no other titles given to non-Jains, which suggests that he viewed Abū al-Faẕl's Sanskrit title as both rare and noteworthy.

Akbar accorded at least one Persian title, *khūshfahm* (Wise Man), to two Jain intellectuals, Nandivijaya and Siddhicandra, for performing intellectual feats. Neither occasion is mentioned in Persian courtly works, but both are celebrated in Sanskrit accounts of Jain-Mughal relations.[199] Siddhicandra and his teacher, Bhānucandra, also proclaim Siddhicandra's Persian title using identical verses in separate Sanskrit commentaries, and Siddhicandra uses it in colophons throughout his *Kāvyaprakāśakhaṇḍana*, a commentary on Mammaṭa's eleventh-century work of literary theory.[200] Moreover, a Persian seal dating to 1599 has been found on two of Siddhicandra's Sanskrit works that reads in Nastaliq script, "Khūshfahm, pupil of Bhānucandra, 1008.[201] These repeated invocations attest that Persian titles and even the Hijri calendar held significant power within the Sanskrit intellectual tradition.

Akbar also honored a Sanskrit intellectual with a vernacular title, which further indicates the fluid lines between linguistic traditions in Mughal environs. He fashioned Vijayasena as *savāī* (One and One-Quarter), a vernacular honorific later common in Rajput circles to mark those superior to any single man. Devavimala describes the occasion thus: "Shah [Akbar] gave the title [*biruda*] *savāī* to the moon of sadhus, Vijayasena, just as he did 'Teacher of the World' to Hīra[vijaya] Sūri."[202] Here Devavimala juxtaposes Vijayasena's vernacular appellation with Hīravijaya's Sanskrit one, indicating that he viewed these as part of the same multilingual practice.

Jahangir succeeded his father in issuing honorary titles to Sanskrit figures, although he was partial to titles that included his regnal name. First, he fashioned Vijayadeva Sūri, Vijayasena's successor as leader of the Tapa Gaccha, *jahāṅgīramahātapā* (Jahangir's Great Ascetic), after hearing his views on the benefits of austerities.[203] In part this title cleverly plays on the appellation of *tapā* given to Jagaccandra centuries earlier that eventually became the namesake of his entire community. As Vijayadeva's biographer reports, "[Jahangir] said, 'before you always held the title [*biruda*] of Ascetic [*tapā*]. Therefore you are now always to be known to me as Jahangir's Great Ascetic [*jahāṅgīramahātapāḥ*].' "[204] Jahangir also bestowed two full Persian titles, both on Siddhicandra: *nadīrah-i zamān* (Wonder of the Age) and *jahāngīr-pasand* (Jahangir's Favorite). Siddhicandra claims these honors in Sanskrit commentaries on two texts, curiously avoiding them in his account of Jains at the Mughal court.[205] The inclusion of Jahangir's regnal name in titles foregrounds Mughal royal authority in cross-cultural interactions.

Shah Jahan returned to Sanskrit titles for the major Sanskrit intellectuals who graced his court. He declared Jagannātha *paṇḍitarāja* (King of the Learned), the name by which he is often known today.[206] He named Kavīndrācārya Sarasvatī *vidyānidhāna* (Treasure House of Knowledge). Numerous contemporaries of Kavīndra's record this title in the Sanskrit anthology *Kavīndracandrodaya* (*Moonrise of Kavīndra*), and one author even proclaims the slightly greater designation *sarvavidyānidhāna* (Treasure House of All Knowledge).[207] However, other authors omit any mention of the Mughal king's involvement in this title.[208] Since the *Kavīndracandrodaya* was compiled explicitly to commemorate Kavīndra's gaining imperial tax relief, it seems unlikely that the authors were trying to evade references to events involving the Mughals. Instead, we might postulate that knowledge of this title's source was widespread enough to not merit a reminder. Alternatively, even given the prestige associated with harnessing Mughal power in Sanskrit, some Brahmanical discomfort may have lingered regarding imperial sway over Sanskrit cultural practices.

Alongside titling Sanskrit intellectuals, the Mughals also participated in other multilingual titling practices. Allison Busch has drawn attention to several instances in which the Mughal emperors, beginning with Akbar, bestowed honorifics on Hindi poets.[209] In some cases, Sanskrit thinkers who doubled as vernacular intellectuals also received titles in the latter capacity. For example, Jagannātha Paṇḍitarāja secured the titles *kabrāy* (*kavirāja*, "King of Poets") and later *mahākabrāy* (*mahākavirāja*, "Great King of Poets") in thanks for serving as a vernacular singer under Shah Jahan.[210] In addition, the Mughal kings granted titles to Indian members of the imperial administration, such as Birbal, Man Singh, and Ramdas Kachhwaha.[211] For their part, Sanskrit literati also received appellations from subimperial figures.[212] These diverse connections indicate a broader cultural practice that operated along many vectors beyond Mughal relations with Jain and Brahman Sanskrit thinkers. Within this larger milieu, Mughal titlings of Sanskrit intellectuals brought into being a particular configuration of cultural, religious, and imperial authorities in the multilingual and multicultural royal court.

CONCLUSION: MULTICULTURAL MUGHALS

The wide-ranging social connections between Sanskrit intellectuals and the imperial elite belie the dominant scholarly perception of a Persianate Mughal court and suggest instead a multicultural imperial context. Persian was the administrative language of the Mughals from the 1580s onward, but the evidence presented here emphasizes anew that Persian did not exclusively define Mughal culture. On the contrary, Sanskrit had a vibrant presence in Mughal circles in terms of cultural, religious, and intellectual practices. Moreover, imperial interest in the Sanskrit tradition permeated the highest levels of courtly life. Top nobles and even the Mughal kings themselves actively forged cross-cultural connections. Given this, we must abandon the age-old conception, guided by Indo-Persian court histories, that the Mughal court was a space dominated by Persianate culture and in which all other languages were outliers. Instead, it is more accurate to describe the royal Mughal court as a multicultural environment where Sanskrit literati held vital and prominent positions. Within this revised view of the multicultural Mughal court, a few points are worth emphasizing concerning the dynamics of political power and intellectual traditions.

First, Mughal links with Sanskrit intellectuals did not grow out of apolitical curiosity but rather were fueled by a desire to pair Sanskrit intellectual and cultural resources with imperial authority. The Mughals viewed both Jains and Brahmans as able to provide access to wider Sanskrit learning and identified much of this tradition as relevant to ruling India. Alongside this cross-cultural agenda, the majority of Mughal support was devoted to Persianate artists, painters, historians, and the like. One might suppose, then, that Mughal ties with Sanskrit elites hardly mattered to the much larger group of court-sponsored Persianate thinkers and artists. But the evidence suggests otherwise. Some of the most esteemed members of the Mughal inner circle, including Abū al-Faẕl, Fayẕī, and Asaf Khan, were interlocutors with Sanskrit intellectuals. In some cases, we can trace the impact of multicultural meetings within an individual's Persian writings or artistic production. Additionally, we must recognize that Mughal power and sovereign imagination often operated entirely outside Islamicate culture and Persian literary production.

Despite the depth and diversity of links between Sanskrit and Mughal elites, relatively few such cross-cultural ties are mentioned in Persian court texts. Particularly imperially sanctioned histories either portray Sanskrit intellectuals as marginal figures at court or, more commonly, elide their presence altogether.[213] This textual silence has several major implications for future work on social and imperial aspects of the Mughal state, and I highlight two here. First, any account of the royal court that makes a legitimate attempt at being comprehensive must be multilingual. Persian court histories are partial records, often deliberately so, and they need to be supplemented with and weighed against works from other linguistic traditions. Second, Mughal court histories ought to be treated less as documents that communicate unquestionable records of the past and analyzed more critically for their commentaries on the Mughal imperial image. In this sense, highlighting the biases, omissions, and inaccuracies in court-sponsored histories does not lessen their value but rather opens up underexplored questions about the differences between historiographical traditions and the value of representation in early modern India.

Last, imperial connections with Jain and Brahman Sanskrit intellectuals prompt reconsideration of the nature of Mughal kingship. These cultural links indicate that Mughal authority claims often crisscrossed multiple traditions, an intersection that infused certain practices with layers of ambiguity and overlapping meanings. These porous connections often increased the potency of a particular act. In the case of Akbar's sun veneration, for example, the king performed a ritual that could be interpreted, above all by the king himself, as based in multiple traditions. In official titles granted to Jains, the fusion of Mughal and Jain hierarchies undergirded imperial interests. In other cases, the Mughals drew on the specific cultural resources of the Sanskrit tradition by integrating Sanskrit thinkers and ideas into the fabric of Indo-Islamic court life. These complex interactions cannot be accurately characterized as Mughal attempts to legitimize their rule to passive audiences of Jain and Brahmanical communities. Rather, the Mughals sought to formulate a multicultural imperial culture largely to introduce fresh ideas into their own enactment of Perso-Islamic rule. Jains and Brahmans reacted with both suspicion and eagerness to Mughal cross-cultural exchanges, although their concerns too stayed far away from questions about whether their imperial interlocutors were justified rulers. Instead, Sanskrit intellectuals were far more concerned with how Mughal multicultural engagements might inform and change their own literary, social, and religious spheres.

[2] SANSKRIT TEXTUAL PRODUCTION FOR THE MUGHALS

SANSKRIT LITERATI composed a wide variety of texts for the Mughals under direct imperial orders. Additional writers addressed Sanskrit texts to imperial figures on behalf of local political and religious leaders who sought to improve relations with the Mughal crown. Both the sponsored and dedicated works crisscross numerous Sanskrit genres, but two provide particular insight into Mughal cross-cultural interests: literature and grammar. One of the first Sanskrit works that claims a Mughal audience explicates aesthetic theory, and literati subsequently authored many poems for the enjoyment of imperial figures. Particularly enlightening is a little-known group of seven Sanskrit panegyrics sent to members of the ruling elite under Akbar, Jahangir, and Shah Jahan (table 2.1).[1] As for language analysis, intellectuals crafted two full Sanskrit grammars of Persian under the respective instructions of Akbar and Jahangir that probe the relationship between languages of power in the Mughal dispensation. Poetics and language had long served as fundamental discourses for expressing royal authority in the Sanskrit thought world and also constituted central topics in the Mughal cultural order. These subjects provided prime territory for carving out the aesthetic and political roles of Sanskrit in the Mughal imperium.

In writing texts for the Mughals, Sanskrit authors built upon a substantial history of fashioning works for Indo-Islamic courts. Since the fourteenth century, Sanskrit-medium literati from across the subcontinent had labored under the support of Muslim rulers. Often the details of these ties remain hard to pin down, both because Persian documents rarely mention Sanskrit writers and Sanskrit texts frequently obscure the historical circumstances of their production. Nonetheless, certain

TABLE 2.1 Sanskrit Praise Poems for Mughal Figures

Author	Year	Patron	Text	Dedicatee
Śānticandra	ca. 1587	N/A	*Kṛpārasakośa (Treasury of Compassion)*	Akbar
Rudrakavi	1603	Pratap Shah of Baglan	*Dānaśāhacarita (Acts of Generous Danyal Shah)*	Prince Danyal, Akbar's son
Rudrakavi	1609	Pratap Shah of Baglan	*Khānakhānācarita (Acts of Khan-i Khanan)*	ʿAbd al-Raḥīm Khān-i Khānān
Rudrakavi	ca. 1610–1620	Pratap Shah of Baglan	*Jahāṅgīracarita (Acts of Jahangir)*	Jahangir
Rudrakavi	ca. 1610–1620	Pratap Shah of Baglan	*Kīrtisamullāsa (Brilliance of Fame)*	Prince Khurram, future Shah Jahan
Harideva Miśra of Mithila	ca. 1605–1627	Self	*Jahāṅgīravirudāvalī (String of Praises for Jahangir)*	Jahangir
Jagannātha Paṇḍitarāja	ca. 1628–1641	Mukunda Raya of Kashmir	*Āsaphavilāsa (Play of Asaf Khan)*	Asaf Khan

There are several additional purported Sanskrit praise poems for Mughal elites that I discount for reasons explained in this chapter, including Raghudeva Miśra's *Virudāvalī*, *Jahāṅgīrakāvya* (surviving in a single manuscript at the Bodleian Library), and the *Jagadvijayacchandas* attributed to Kavīndrācārya Sarasvatī.

relationships are firmly established, such as Zayn al-Abidin's support of Śrīvara and Jonarāja (authors of successive Sanskrit *Rājataraṅgiṇīs*) in fifteenth-century Kashmir.[2] Salakṣa produced the first known bilingual lexicon of Sanskrit and Persian words under an Islamic Gujarati ruler in the fourteenth century.[3] Also in fourteenth-century Gujarat, a copy of Cāṇḍupaṇḍita's commentary on the *Naiṣadhīyacarita* (*Adventures of the King of Nishada*) was copied for the study of a local governor, Farḥat al-Mulk.[4] Bhānudatta, author of highly influential works on aesthetics, thrived under the support of the Nizam Shahi dynasty in fifteenth-century Ahmednagar.[5]

Sanskrit authors also inherited an extensive tradition of writing about Perso-Islamic figures. Indians came into contact with Muslims almost as soon as there were Muslims, beginning in the late seventh century during the incursions in and around Sindh. Sanskrit literati mentioned Muslims in inscriptions beginning in the eighth century and featured them in full-length texts as early as the late twelfth century.[6] Nearly all authors showed a decided predilection for eliding religious or ethnic characteristics that would have set Muslims apart as a new community. Instead, writers repurposed Sanskrit categories previously used to describe other foreign groups (e.g., *mleccha*, *yavana*).[7] Sanskrit literati portrayed Islamicate kings both positively and negatively but always with time-honored frameworks (praising them as virtuous rulers or condemning them as destructive raiders, respectively).[8] Even when select Indo-Persian concepts were imported into Sanskrit, writers preferred to craft "Sanskritized" versions of foreign terms. For example, a Persian *sulṭān* becomes *sūtratrāṇa* or *sūratrāṇa* in Sanskrit, which retains both its original reference, a particular type of king, and is also endowed with a new meaning, "chief protector" or "protector of the gods." Similarly a royal decree (*farmān*) becomes *sphuramāna*, "a thing that goes forth."

Sanskrit literati who wrote for the Mughals built upon these received practices. Most of the time, they followed their predecessors in relying upon conventional Sanskrit norms, and only the inclusion of Arabic and Persian names betrayed any trace of a contemporary context. But occasionally writers fashioned more creative mixings of the Sanskrit and Perso-Islamic worlds that highlight how they perceived the expansive boundaries of Mughal imperial culture. The poets offer compelling and sometimes surprising descriptions of Mughal elites, royal genealogies, imperial achievements, and court life. The grammarians provide lively commentaries on imperial language politics, especially the relevance of both Sanskrit and Persian to Mughal kingship. Taken together, these literary works and bilingual grammars constitute some of the most potent cultural contributions of Sanskrit thinkers to the growing Mughal Empire.

WRITING SANSKRIT LITERARY WORKS FOR THE IMPERIAL ELITE

The Sanskrit literary works I discuss in this chapter all envision an imperial reception, which raises the complicated question of what it meant to write a Sanskrit text for Mughal consumption. Through their active patronage of the Sanskrit tradition, the Mughals constructed their court as a multicultural space. Nonetheless, the Mughal elite generally did not study Sanskrit. Even Mughal translators and those engaged in other cross-cultural projects depended on native informants rather than learning Sanskrit themselves. In the mid-seventeenth century, a small number of Indians began to gain competency in both Persian and Sanskrit, however such bilingualism remained largely restricted to Hindus and Jains. Those who came from Iran or Central Asia and even Indian Muslims, including the Mughal royal family, almost never learned both tongues. As a result, the question remains open of how the Mughals could have meaningfully received Sanskrit texts. In addition to the issue of linguistic comprehension, Sanskrit literature presupposes familiarity with aesthetic and cultural conventions that have traditionally been considered outside the Mughal experience.

Sanskrit literature addressed to the Mughals furnishes compelling evidence that these works' sponsors intended them to be accepted and understood by members of the ruling elite. While this viewpoint is difficult to square with what we know about the Mughal court, the Sanskrit materials are too substantial and persuasive to be casually dismissed. Persian works from Akbar's period corroborate that Sanskrit texts were indeed presented to the emperor.[9] Some of the Sanskrit praise poems were also directed, in part, toward Sanskrit literati, as I discuss later in this chapter. However, this second audience does not justify blithely ignoring the claims of these materials that they were designed primarily for imperial consumption. Different texts suggest several possible means for a cross-linguistic, Mughal comprehension, and it is helpful to outline the major ideas at the outset.

Some Sanskrit texts may have been verbally translated into Hindi for Mughal listeners. Francesca Orsini reminds us of the importance of foregrounding orality in studies of multilingual environments.[10] The Sanskrit tradition furnishes precedents for verbal vernacular explanations of certain works, such as *purāṇas*, for the sake of a non-Sanskrit-knowing audience. Additionally, verbal recitation of texts was a common feature of early modern Islamic societies (and often remains so today). Ronit Ricci has suggested that we speak of "audiences" instead of "readers" for texts in order to capture this prevalent oral dynamic.[11] Akbar frequently enjoyed hearing texts read aloud and was unable to read in any language.[12] The verbal third party in Sanskrit and Persian exchanges was typically Hindi, which served as the default intermediary language for translation activities. No Mughal-directed Sanskrit texts explicitly profess to have been rendered into Hindi, but some of their authors were prized in the Mughal milieu for their skills in oral vernacular traditions.

In addition to oral translation, select Mughal nobles may have grasped a limited amount of spoken Sanskrit. Sudipta Kaviraj has argued that educated Bangla speakers could comprehend significant portions of some recited Sanskrit works.[13] This type of transverse understanding worked because of shared Sanskrit-Bangla vocabulary and a minimal use of verbs. Many members of the imperial elite, including the Mughal kings starting with Akbar, were fluent in conversational Hindi and enjoyed Hindi poetry.[14] Given this background, Mughal kings and nobles might well have possessed a degree of cross-language facility that enabled them to appreciate aspects of recited Sanskrit works.

Last, there may have been Mughal modes of reception that did not require linguistic understanding. Imperial addressees may have accepted Sanskrit works as objects more than readable materials and identified their value in being gifted. Certain features, such as the use of alliteration, could have been pleasing even absent understanding the content.[15] While this suggestion is the least upsetting to accepted historiography, we ought to be wary of assuming it uncritically. Persian texts form the exclusive basis for rejecting Sanskrit as an intelligible (or semi-intelligible) language at the royal Mughal court. Sanskrit and vernacular sources offer an altogether different picture of the Mughals as seriously engaging with Sanskrit literature that is only surprising given our long-standing ignorance of these texts.

While the question of reception is important, it ought not to obscure that numerous contemporaries of the Mughals viewed them as suitable addressees for Sanskrit poems and prose. Perception is itself a historical phenomenon, and there was widespread agreement that Sanskrit was an effective medium for petitioning the Mughal ruling class. As we shall see, some works engaged with live political issues and so posit that Sanskrit was a felicitous language for intervening in current imperial affairs. Other texts brought the Mughals into a Sanskrit-defined world and explore the implications of that literary act. In both cases Jain and Brahman literati and their patrons advanced Sanskrit as an imperial and aesthetic language of consequence in response to cues from the central Mughal court. Here I reconstruct the contours of the overlapping realities and imaginations regarding Sanskrit literary culture in the Mughal imperium.

Recovering the contemporary valence of Sanskrit praise poems for the Mughals is beset by an additional methodological challenge that it is helpful to name at the outset. Early modern Sanskrit authors inherited a strong penchant for conventions. This banal observation is true across many genres of Sanskrit works, but it is perhaps nowhere more evident than in praise poetry. Authors frequently recycled lines and verses for different subjects. Original contributions often followed predictable patterns and set formulas. These conventions did not render Sanskrit praises devoid of meaning or prohibit specificity, but they made novelty a subtle art. The writers I discuss in this chapter embedded many politically and culturally salient ideas within conventions, and in order to recover their artful innovations we must read sensitively with an eye to how seventeenth-century readers would have understood seemingly generic formulations in rather specific ways. Through time-honored Sanskrit tropes, Brahman and Jain authors simultaneously appealed to aspects of Mughal court culture and recast Mughal figures within Sanskrit literary thought. Their praise poems testify to both the malleability of Sanskrit and the perceived porous borders of Mughal court culture.

A MUGHAL HANDBOOK ON SANSKRIT AESTHETIC THEORY

In 1569 Padmasundara, an early Jain visitor to the imperial court, authored one of the first Sanskrit works commissioned by the Mughals, titled *Akbarasāhiśṛṅgāradarpaṇa* (*Mirror of Erotic Passion for Shah Akbar*).[16] Padmasundara predated the explosion of Mughal connections with Sanskrit intellectuals in the 1580s. Nonetheless, he inaugurated a tradition of writing literary texts under Mughal sponsorship that continued through Shah Jahan's reign. The majority of these works mention little about their Persianate patrons other than their names.[17] But literati faced a choice of whether or not to emphasize their social ties, and Padmasundara stood at the beginning of a handful of authors who elected to more openly reflect upon their cross-cultural milieu. Padmasundara invokes a Mughal production and reception context throughout his treatise by situating Akbar at the center of Sanskrit aesthetics.

In the *Akbarasāhiśṛṅgāradarpaṇa*, Padmasundara treats the nine standard aesthetic moods (*rasas*) in four chapters. Padmasundara devotes the bulk of his attention to the erotic (*śṛṅgāra*) mood and its accompanying typology of heroines (*nāyikā-bheda*). During the early modern period, Sanskrit literati became enamored with elaborating the system of heroines. Although Padmasundara could not have known at the time, *nāyikā-bheda* would also later become a popular topic among seventeenth- and eighteenth-century Mughal readers, who consumed treatises on the subject in Hindi, Arabic, and Persian.[18] In his comparatively early text, Padmasundara explores how to integrate aspects of the Mughal world within this classificatory scheme. He also closely models his work, including many individual verses, on Rudrabhaṭṭa's eleventh-century *Śṛṅgāratilaka* (*Ornament of Erotic Passion*), and later critics have positively compared Padmasundara's reworking to its predecessor.[19] Within the expectations of his subject matter and model text, Padmasundara treats Sanskrit literature as malleable enough to accommodate some Perso-Islamic ideas while forcefully arguing that Akbar's kingship would benefit from familiarity with the Sanskrit aesthetic tradition.

Padmasundara opens with ten verses that contain significant Perso-Islamic resonances. His initial praise verse is perhaps the most arresting in calling upon Allah:

> The entire world shines with his splendor such that it blinds the eyes.
> Our welfare rests in him like a genuine jewel, always and forever.
> He stands beyond the darkness and is called Rahman, the highest point.
> O Akbar, Crown Jewel of Shahs! May that light always protect you.[20]

Here Padmasundara threads several Perso-Arabic words, including Akbar (*akabara*) and Shah (*sāhi*, used in the compound *sāhi-śiromaṇe*) into what is otherwise a standard Sanskrit verse. Especially eye-catching is his use of *raḥmān* (*rahamān* in Sanskrit), a Qur'anic name for God meaning "Gracious" that is commonly invoked at the beginning of Islamicate texts, whether secular or religious. While Padmasundara stays well within Sanskrit conventions in praying for his king and patron, he follows Islamic practices in entrusting Akbar's protection to Allah. Earlier Sanskrit literati rarely appealed to the Islamic God by any name and stringently avoided using Perso-Arabic terms.[21] Moreover, Sanskrit intellectuals virtually never recognized Islam as a religious tradition with which they could engage on similar terms as with Brahmanical, Jain, and Buddhist schools of thought. Against this staunch rejection of Islam, Padmasundara stands out as a fresh voice that identifies Islam as providing a theological basis with which to begin a Sanskrit literary work.

In his subsequent acclaim of the Mughals, Padmasundara transitions into a more customary mode of treating nontraditional figures with Sanskrit literary conventions. He lauds Akbar's ancestor, Babur, with accepted tropes.

> That lofty lineage known as Chaghatai is famous
> among all noble families,
> pure as the celestial Ganges, and the jewel of all earthly kings.
> In that line Padshah Babur was born
> who defeated many enemies as he approached the prize of Delhi.
> His steps should be worshipped by all worldly rulers.[22]

In this praise, Padmasundara adds some contemporary context by mentioning Babur's victory over Delhi (*ḍillī*). He also introduces further Perso-Arabic vocabulary, such as Chaghatai (*cagatta*) and padshah (*pādisāhi*). Nonetheless, Padmasundara remains well within established Sanskrit norms for praising Indian kings. In the next verse, he employs Sanskrit vocabulary (and light alliteration) in commending Humayun's military successes from Gujarat (*gaurjara*) to western Bengal (*gauḍa*).[23] In the several following verses that extol Akbar, Padmasundara draws an idealized picture of a wise, just Indian ruler.[24]

Even while conforming to typical Sanskrit practices, however, one verse eulogizing Akbar offers more specific insights into the social and intellectual frameworks that informed this treatise. Padmasundara describes his patron as embodying each of the nine Sanskrit aesthetic moods in contexts that also highlight Akbar's virtues:

> He is the lover [*śṛṅgārī*] of young women, a soldier in battle, compassionate [*kṛpālu*] toward the world, and smiles at curious sights. He has astonishing [*adbhuta*] fame, fears [*bhīru*] the violation of order, is disgusted [*bībhatsa*] by hunting, fierce [*raudra*] in destroying enemies, and tranquil [*śamī*] in power. Glorious Shah Akbar was duly created even now with all the aesthetic *rasas*.[25]

In the construction of this verse, Padmasundara closely follows his work's model, Rudrabhaṭṭa's *Śṛṅgāratilaka*, which commences with a similar eulogy of Shiva:

> He is the lover [*śṛṅgārī*] of the mountain's daughter, compassionate [*sakaruṇa*] toward Rati, a warrior to Kama, revolting [*bībhatsa*] with his bones, causing fear [*bhayakṛt*] with his snakes, wondrous [*adbhuta*] with height, fierce [*raudra*] in slaying Daksha, prompting laughter [*hasakṛt*] when naked, and meditative [*praśānta*] for a long time. May Shiva, the abode of all *rasas*, give good people success.[26]

Here Rudrabhaṭṭa relies on Shiva's known mythology, and several later poets also used a similar framework to glorify other deities. For example, in his fifteenth-century *Rasataraṅgiṇī* (*River of Rasa*), Bhānudatta acclaims Vishnu as displaying one *rasa* in each of his incarnations.[27] Padmasundara analogously alludes to known details of Akbar's life in his experience of specific *rasas*. The poet evokes Akbar's penchant for marvels (*ʿajāʾib*) in portraying the king as amused by curiosities (*kautukavīkṣaṇa*). He also depicts Akbar as loathing hunting, which no doubt reflects the Jain value of nonviolence but also corresponds to a known incident in Akbar's life where he temporarily gave up the hunt.[28]

Padmasundara also introduces a few major innovations in his verse. He applies Rudrabhaṭṭa's pattern of praising a Hindu deity to an earthly Islamicate patron. In so doing, Padmasundara maps categories of the Sanskrit aesthetic experience onto a Perso-Islamic king and brings together two distinct cultural worlds. Moreover, he implicitly puts Akbar on a par with a Hindu god. Most crucially, Padmasundara conceives of Akbar as personally experiencing eight of the nine emotions, whereas Rudrabhaṭṭa imagines Shiva to prompt others to feel several of the *rasas*.[29] This subtle shift elevates Akbar as the central aesthete (*rasika*) in Padmasundara's vision of the Sanskrit literary experience. Indeed, in colophons to each of his four chapters, Padmasundara characterizes Akbar as a *rasika* who is "learned in all arts" (*sakalakalāpārīṇa*).[30] In framing Akbar as directly engaging with and appreciating Sanskrit literature, he posits that Sanskrit aesthetics is integral to Mughal kingship.

Padmasundara also addresses Akbar throughout his text, typically in verses that aver that the Mughal emperor displays a certain sentiment. For example, at the end of his lengthy discussion of heroines (*nāyikās*), Padmasundara asserts,

> Who always enjoys uninterrupted pleasure with his own beautiful women,

is renowned for his talents in scratching
with nails and biting with teeth.
He forgoes making love with others' wives.
He is beloved and famous for his true justice.
May that just Akbar, a golden vessel
of erotic passion [*śṛṅgāra*], be pleased![31]

In other verses, Padmasundara speaks directly to his patron in the second person and the vocative, which underscores Akbar as his primary audience.[32] These lines are both lovely and highly complimentary. For example, in one verse Padmasundara asks his patron how he can possibly be described since he is like the sea, too vast for words to encompass and never sating the thirst of those who seek him.[33] In another, he marvels that Akbar's fame whitens the three worlds but blackens the faces of his enemies.[34] Many verses are closely modeled on lines in Rudrabhaṭṭa's work.[35] Particularly against this earlier blueprint, however, Padmasundara makes a rather conspicuous move by invoking Akbar as a named, Indo-Persian king within the constellation of Sanskrit aesthetics.

Padmasundara does not elaborate on how Akbar might have linguistically or culturally understood these Sanskrit verses, but he unequivocally projects his text as designed for a royal Mughal reception. In addition to addressing Akbar throughout the treatise and repeatedly casting the Mughal king as an aesthete, Padmasundara also offers this penultimate verse:

With this composition on the radiating beauty of the nine *rasa*s
that are displayed in the definitions of heroines [*nāyikā*]
illustrated by clever verses,
may Lord Akbar spend his days and nights
propitiating a beautiful woman
who has the sign of fame that concurs with Kama's *rasa*.[36]

Padmasundara thus advocates the almost practical relevance for Akbar of Sanskrit literary theory, as shown through his work. In these ways, Padmasundara moves beyond merely dedicating his work to the reigning king and declares that Akbar enacts Sanskrit aesthetics. Moreover, Padmasundara was not alone in suggesting that the Mughals actively used Sanskrit knowledge systems. Several later texts, particularly praise poems directed toward imperial figures, suggest further ways that a Mughal audience might have interacted with Sanskrit texts.

ENLIGHTENING AKBAR WITH ŚĀNTICANDRA'S *TREASURY OF COMPASSION*

Śānticandra composed the first full Sanskrit encomium for a Mughal figure, Akbar, during the height of Jain relations with the central court. Śānticandra was a monk in the Tapa Gaccha branch of Jainism, whose leader, Hīravijaya, established a solid rapport with the Mughals in the early 1580s. Śānticandra remained at court after Hīravijaya's departure in 1585 and returned to Gujarat himself two years later bearing several new Mughal *farmāns* that benefited the Tapa Gaccha. Śānticandra claimed that Akbar granted these Jain-friendly orders after being enlightened (*pratibodha*) by his *Kṛpārasakośa* (*Treasury of Compassion*), a poem of 128 verses that details the Mughal king's life and lineage. I will return to the question of whether it is historically plausible that Akbar received this Sanskrit text (not to mention that the panegyric was politically exigent). But first it is worthwhile to examine the work's contents and see how Śānticandra constructs the relationship between Jain political motives, Sanskrit royal praises, and the Mughal ruler.

In the first half of his text, Śānticandra describes Akbar's ancestors, birth, and childhood. He treats the emperor's ancestral lands and lineage within standard Sanskrit literary practices while also indicating a contemporary Mughal environment in subtle ways. For example, he characterizes the urban landscape of Kabul according to accepted tropes for describing cities (*nagaravarṇana*), noting that beautiful women live in the harem, flowers burst into bloom during the rainy season, and the city shines with its sovereign's splendor.[37] But he explicitly locates the land of Khurasan outside India (*viṣayāntare*) and overflowing with things associated with that foreign region, such as walnuts, dates, and horses.[38] He extols Akbar's family in a conventional manner, portraying Babur as formidable on the battlefield and dwelling on Humayun's beauty in his youth.[39] When Humayun assumes the throne, the poet favorably compares him to Rama, the archetype Indian sovereign, and proclaims that Akbar's mother (here called by her common nickname, Coli Begum[40]) "receives the riches of love. She is to the king as Lakshmi is to Vishnu."[41]

As Akbar enters the narrative, Śānticandra increasingly portrays events that align with specifically Jain sensibilities. During her pregnancy, Akbar's mother experienced intense pregnancy cravings (*dohadas*) that incited her to play with a lion on her lap and mount a mad elephant without reins.[42] Such irrational actions, done without fear on the part of an expectant mother, frequently augur the birth of a great hero in Jain stories.[43] Śānticandra also marvels at Coli Begum's increased compassion during her pregnancy that compelled her to forgo courtly pleasures harmful to living beings.

Surely musk, obtained only by slaying a deer,
is not pleasing to decorate limbs.
Pearls found by breaking open oysters
are not thought appropriate ornaments.
A good-hearted woman does not desire to wear silk clothes.
When pregnant with a son,
a mother is in Hari's ocean of great compassion.[44]

After Akbar's birth, Śānticandra further incorporates him into the Sanskrit literary realm in his recounting of the naming ceremony. Śānticandra explains the king's name as if it were a Sanskrit word that proclaims his predominance above Hindu deities.

a means the Supreme Lord, *k* Brahman, *a* the Soul,
and *vara* best, so that he [*akabara*] is the best of these [three].[45]

Śānticandra next details Akbar's education and military training. After Akbar ascends the throne, Śānticandra devotes a dozen verses to describing the teenage ruler's youthful good looks and famed benevolence.

Until this point, more than halfway through the text, Śānticandra has not discussed any Mughal land acquisitions, leaving his readers with the impression that the kingdom is still based in Babur's Kabul. He identifies Babur as "king of the Mughals" (*mudgalādhipa*) and gives no indication that either he or Humayun moved into the subcontinent.[46] This treatment stands in stark contrast to contemporary Sanskrit writers, such as the Jain author Rājamalla (also known as Rāyamalla), who wrote in 1575 about how Babur had defeated his enemies to become "lord of Delhi" (*dillīśa*).[47] For Śānticandra, leaving Babur and Humayun outside India allowed him to promote Akbar as singularly responsible for the Mughal subjugation of the subcontinent.

Even though enjoying his father's kingdom,
[Akbar] desired greater victory in all directions.
There was no restraint in that yearning
since the son has exceeded the father in fame.[48]

Over the next twenty verses, Śānticandra reports the methodical extension of Mughal control. He paints a vivid picture of the royal army and their battles but mentions no historical opponents or kingdoms. Notably, contemporary Jain texts generally portray Akbar's martial feats in fairly concrete terms. Nearly all name specific conflicts, such as his takeover of Gujarat in the early 1570s, and many proffer details about favored military strategies and key combatants.[49] But Śānticandra elected to define the growth of the Mughal imperium exclusively through the conventions of Sanskrit poetry.

Śānticandra frames the Mughal conquest as a "conquering of the four directions" (*digvijaya*), a central ritual of traditional Indian kingship. Akbar's army first advanced east, where even the landscape submitted to his rule and facilitated his progress:

> A skillful tree on the banks of the Tapi River
> revived his horses and elephants with shade,
> delighted the infantry with fruit,
> and served him with blossoms while he reclined.[50]

Trees lining the Kaveri River likewise fanned the toiling Mughal troops until they turned south and conquered the Malaya Mountains, known from the Indian epics.[51] Then Akbar moved west, appearing like a sun that never sets.[52] Last, the Mughal king headed north to the Himalayas:

> Like Kubera himself, that lord of wealth
> pursued the direction of Kubera's dwellings.
> The all-destroying, intensely fierce lord of the earth
> broke the pride of the northern kings.[53]

In this depiction, Akbar does not dominate sixteenth-century India but rather maps the Mughal Empire onto the topography of a timeless, idealized subcontinent demarcated by mountains, myths, and rivers. Here Akbar's power is expressed in purely Sanskrit terms that, at least temporarily, erase any comparable Indo-Persian political framework.[54]

Śānticandra does not leave India's geography completely untouched by Mughal rule, however. He invokes the contemporary political context with several verses that celebrate the establishment of Fatehpur Sikri, Akbar's city of victory. In contrast to his earlier treatment of Akbar's name according to Sanskrit etymology, the poet explains "Fatehpur" according to its meaning in Persian as "city of victory":

> Thinking, *I who live in this city have conquered*
> *the full circle of the earth with my own two arms,*
> [Akbar] entered the city called "Fatehpur,"
> a name given according to the sounds of his own language.[55]

Here the multifaceted power of the Mughal Empire altered the Indian urban landscape and called for the introduction of Persian, even in a limited way, into a Sanskrit poem. Śānticandra still declines to name the specific victory over Gujarat for which Fatehpur Sikri became known as such, but nonetheless the Mughals made their mark on India's geography.

Śānticandra next commits a few verses to highlighting identifiably Mughal practices in the newly formed empire. He mentions Akbar's strategy of ensuring Rajput loyalty by marrying the daughters of local rulers.[56] He also hints at Akbar's status in religious matters, saying, "Khan-i Khanan and the other khans took a vow of firm devotion [*ūrdhvadīkṣāvrata*] / and turned toward that king like pupils to a teacher."[57] This verse likely refers to the *dīn-i ilāhī* (also called *tawhīd-i ilāhī*), Akbar's discipleship program that enjoined his inner circle to a code of ethical conduct.[58] From Śānticandra's perspective, Akbar's position as a quasi-religious leader was likely an important precedent since he next discusses royal actions that promoted Jain values.

Śānticandra devotes most of his remaining thirty verses to lauding Akbar's rule and frames him as a Jain king in two senses. First, he portrays Akbar as extending benefits to Jains within his kingdom. Second, he claims that the Mughal sovereign personally evinced Jain religious inclinations. Both strategies were well-practiced Jain methods of praising kings.[59] For instance, in one verse Śānticandra allays the concerns of compassion personified (*kṛpā*) by assuring her that Akbar is just like Kumārapāla, a twelfth-century Chaulukya ruler who converted to Jainism and quickly became the poster child in the Jain community for a personally devout and publicly generous ruler.[60]

> Lady, who are you?
> *I am Compassion.*
> Why are you troubled?

King Kumāra[pāla] is gone.
What of it?
I am banished now day after day by hostile, violent men. I desire to be reinstated.
Then, O Pure Compassion, go to the one who possesses the earth.
Now, after a long time, Akbar is the sole king;
he will cause you no distress.[61]

Śānticandra also offers verses that cast certain concessions to the Jain community as ethically motivated on the part of Akbar. For example, he hyperbolizes that even the cranes were compelled to obey an imperial ban on fishing in a particular lake because of the king's personal devotion:

In consideration of the virtue [*puṇya*] of Akbar, great moon of the earth,
cruel cranes that have captured fish with their beaks
sympathize, and their hearts fill with wonder.
Even though fish are their only food, the cranes abandon them at once.[62]

While Śānticandra endorses Akbar as a Jain-friendly sovereign, he does not shy away from hailing Mughal rule as promoting the values of multiple religious traditions. Even the verse about vegetarian cranes concurs with Persianate ideas about how the Mughals, like King Solomon, extended authority over all the animals of creation.[63] In other lines, Śānticandra explicitly avers that Akbar's cancellation of certain taxes and compassion toward cows benefited Hindus and Jains:

Surely this joyful wishing tree [Akbar]
enacted a measure surpassing even his nature
by relinquishing taxes
for the sake of all Indians [*hindūbhyaḥ sakalebhya eva*].
Thinking, *how can I become the crown jewel*
at the head of all shahs, that wise man,
in whom overflowing compassion [*kṛpā*] arises, grants life to cows.[64]

In the late sixteenth century, the Perso-Arabic word *hindū* was used in multiple languages to denote Indians as a vague ethnic or spatially defined group.[65] Even when this term carried a religious meaning, it was generally quite broad. For example, the fourteenth-century Jain writer Vidyātilaka used *hindū* in Prakrit to describe non-Muslim Indian rulers.[66] In his early seventeenth-century bilingual lexicon, Kavi Karṇapūra defines *hindū* as a Persian word for "theistic Indians."[67] Śānticandra likely intended a similar meaning in extolling measures that pleased many non-Muslim Indian groups. Śānticandra also celebrates Akbar's admirable moral sensibilities more generally as exemplified by bans on gambling, liquor, and prostitution.[68]

Śānticandra identifies Akbar as the chief recipient of his *Kṛpārasakośa* and indicates several times that the Mughal king heard and understood the Sanskrit text. In addition to addressing Akbar throughout the work, he frames his *Kṛpārasakośa* at both the outset and close as composed "for the sake of enlightening [*pratibodha*] glorious Padshah Akbar."[69] Some manuscript copies have additional closing verses that elaborate on the results of this awakening.

> He removed the jizya tax.
> He rescued temples from Mughals who were difficult to restrain.
> He who is compassion embodied [*kṛpāṅga*] broke the chains of prisoners.
> Even base kings hospitably receive the Jains, lords of ascetics.
> For six months of the year, beings are born without fear.
> Large groups of cows were born unafraid.
> Among the causes of the arising of such decrees,
> this book was the primarily reason [*paraṃ nimittaṃ*].[70]

Here and elsewhere in his work, Śānticandra venerates Akbar as full of compassion (*kṛpā*). Jain writers often use the term *kṛpā* to refer to an explicitly Jain inclination toward preserving all life. The word also appears in Brahman-authored Sanskrit works that celebrate Mughal generosity regarding their non-Muslim subjects.[71]

Other Jain writers bolster Śānticandra's bold claims about his work spurring Mughal actions. One of Śānticandra's pupils echoes his teacher in recording that Śānticandra taught (*prabodha*) Akbar.[72] Another contemporary Sanskrit text on Hīravijaya's life attests,

> Then Śānticandra, the best of the Jains—who bears royal messages, whose hand delivers *farmāns* regarding the jizya and nonviolence, and who is skilled in continually reciting the *Treasury of Compassion* [to the shah] on the order of [Hīravijaya] Sūri—was joyfully sent from his own side to the guru by the king.[73]

This verse unambiguously declares that Śānticandra verbalized his Sanskrit text before the Mughal court and that this activity resulted in

Jain-friendly imperial commands. But this narrative leaves us with the thorny question, how did Akbar understand praises and solicitations in a language he did not know? Here we must interrogate our preconceptions regarding recitation, textual reception, and linguistic comprehension. Taking into account the larger cultural context of early modern India, several possibilities arise that take seriously the claims of Sanskrit materials and advance our knowledge of literary culture in Mughal circles.

Śānticandra may have verbally translated his verses into a language more commonly understood among the Mughal elite, most likely Hindi. Śānticandra was renowned for his oratory skills and publicly debated in other royal contexts, which makes verbal transmission in a vernacular a plausible option.[74] Another real possibility is that Akbar understood portions of Śānticandra's recited Sanskrit verses. As I mentioned, knowledge of an Indian vernacular often enabled early modern listeners to comprehend Sanskrit to a surprising degree. The *Kṛpārasakośa* is written in relatively simple Sanskrit, and it would certainly have helped that Śānticandra was narrating Akbar's personal history. Nonetheless, in a transverse reception many subtle points and cultural references would have been lost.

In addition to claiming an imperial reception, Śānticandra also outlines a second, more local audience for his text. He says in his final verse, "The *Treasury of Compassion* is to be examined, recited, followed, and cherished by those who have abandoned malice and know good conduct."[75] Here "those who know good conduct" are certainly Śānticandra's fellow Jains, most likely Tapa Gaccha affiliates in particular, and one can easily imagine them welcoming a text that celebrates recent Jain successes at the Mughal court. This verse is missing in some manuscript copies and so may have been a later addition (perhaps along with imagining an alternative audience).[76] Although Śānticandra's work also opens with verses praising Jina that appear to be directed toward a Jain readership.[77]

It is tempting, then, to postulate that it was more important for Śānticandra to represent himself to his own community as writing a text for Akbar than to actually speak to the Mughal emperor in Sanskrit. This explanation would place Śānticandra's work within a sizable body of contemporary Jain Sanskrit texts that detail experiences at the Mughal court and are explicitly addressed to a Jain readership. Nonetheless, it would be uncritical to flatly reject Śānticandra's assertion that Akbar received this encomium merely because it seems unusual to address a Persianate court in Sanskrit. Sanskrit has been written out of Mughal history for so long that it may seem absurd to even consider that this language was part of imperial court culture. However, if we simply accept centuries of accreted scholarly biases that blindly condemn Sanskrit materials as peripheral to Mughal history, then we place artificial limits on our ability to understand the diversity and complexity of Mughal court culture. Additionally, Śānticandra's work is not an anomaly. Many Sanskrit texts followed in directly appealing to members of the Mughal ruling class. Rudrakavi's panegyrics in particular advance even bolder claims regarding how they were intended to be received, understood, and acted upon by Mughal figures.

RUDRAKAVI PLAYS POLITICS IN JAHANGIR'S EMPIRE

Rudrakavi composed four Sanskrit panegyrics for Mughal elites at the instruction of Pratap Shah, who headed the small kingdom of Baglan near Nashik (in modern-day Maharashtra). Baglan was traversed by several trade routes and was also well cultivated by Akbar's time.[78] The region had come under Mughal control in the 1570s but maintained a degree of autonomy until the 1630s.[79] Rudrakavi became a court poet during the reign of Pratap Shah's father, Narayan Shah, and is best known for his literary history of the Baglan dynasty, completed in 1596.[80] He subsequently produced four Sanskrit encomia for Mughal figures, beginning with the *Dānaśāhacarita* (*Acts of Generous Danyal Shah*), in praise of Akbar's son Danyal, in 1603.[81] In 1609, Rudrakavi wrote the *Khānakhānācarita* (*Acts of Khan-i Khanan*) for ʿAbd al-Raḥīm, an important literary and political figure often known by his title, the Khan of Khans.[82] Sometime later, likely before 1620, he authored two undated panegyrics: the *Jahāṅgīracarita* (*Acts of Jahangir*) for Jahangir and the *Kīrtisamullāsa* (*Brilliance of Fame*) in honor of Prince Khurram, the future Shah Jahan.[83]

Of this rich collection of praise poems, two texts command particular attention. First, the *Khānakhānācarita* puts forth a specific request for military action on the part of its recipient that forces us to reconsider the potential of Sanskrit poetry as a communicative medium in a Mughal context. Second, the *Jahāṅgīracarita*, which survives in a single, fragmentary manuscript and has never been explored by modern scholars, exhibits a vivid, nuanced treatment of the Mughal king that rewards a comparative reading against Rudrakavi's other works.

Rudrakavi's *Khānakhānācarita* entreats ʿAbd al-Raḥīm Khān-i Khānān, a powerful Mughal general, to intervene in an armed dispute between Pratap Shah and the imperial army. The political backstory is that Jahangir attempted to take the Baglan kingdom (or at least parts thereof) by siege in 1609.[84] While holding off Mughal forces, Pratap Shah called upon Rudrakavi to pursue diplomatic channels. The resulting *Khānakhānācarita* mixes Sanskrit poetry and prose in four chapters and pursues a twofold approach to enlisting the general's assistance.[85] First, Rudrakavi heavily flatters Khān-i Khānān in terms that fancy the general as no less than a king himself. Second, in the final chapter, Rudrakavi describes the current military situation and directly implores Raḥīm's mediation. This second tactic strongly indicates that Pratap Shah intended Raḥīm to comprehend the panegyric's contents. Especially in light of this projected reception, the *Khānakhānācarita* evinces strikingly complex linguistic constructions and expects its Mughal recipient to possess detailed Sanskrit literary knowledge. Whereas Śānticandra wrote his *Kṛpārasakośa* in relatively short and easily understandable verses, Rudrakavi is a much more sophisticated poet who introduces long strings of compounds, complex imagery, and a myriad of cultural references. It seems that Rudrakavi not only expected Raḥīm to grasp a basic cry for help in Sanskrit but also anticipated that he would appreciate a nuanced display of Sanskrit poetic skills.

In the first three chapters of the text, Rudrakavi eulogizes Raḥīm with standard Sanskrit conventions. He repeatedly exaggerates the general as the one true sovereign who holds sway over the earth. But the lesser rulers who bow down to Raḥīm's authority are not the kings of Gujarat and Mewar, the true subsidiaries of the Mughal Empire. Rather, the Hindu gods of the eight traditional directions serve the Khan of Khans, here called simply "Navab":[86]

> Indra with power, Fire with rage,
> Death with a sword, Destruction with brutality in battle,
> Varuna with waters of destruction,
> Wind with the speed of his steed,
> Kubera with his cache of wealth,
> Shiva with his cruel eye set on an adversary,
> the lords of all directions, who rule everywhere, serve glorious Navab.[87]

Rudrakavi also rhapsodizes on Raḥīm's prowess in battle and his resulting fame with more complex Sanskrit metaphors. For example,

> From seeds that are pearls sliding down
> the bursting temples of elephants

abandoned on battlefields soaked with enemies' blood
and torn up by beasts,
the lovely creeper of the khan's fame is blooming.
Its roots strangle Shesha, it gives rise to stars,
and bears the fruit of the moon as it oozes Ganges nectar.[88]

In prose, Rudrakavi marshals the cataloguing tendencies of Sanskrit thinkers to introduce an array of culturally specific information. He often nearly loses sight of his Mughal addressee in a haze of comparisons to Indra, Kamadeva, Arjuna, Bhagiratha, and the like.[89] In one creative section, he says that when King Khān-i Khānān rules the earth, a series of things flourish that are negative in general life but positive in respect to specific intellectual and literary standards.[90] He lists around seventy items in this vein, of which I offer a sampling here:

Debate [*vivāda*] among the six philosophies,
atheism [*nāstikatā*] among atheists,
imagination and censure [*utprekṣākṣepau*] among poetic ornaments,
deceptive war in the *Mahābhārata*,
deceit in the crooked glances of southern Gujarati [*lāṭa*] women,
languidness in the charming movements of Mathura women,
despair among women separated from their lovers,
rashness among women going to meet their lovers,
[all these things] flourish when King Khan-i Khanan rules over the earth.[91]

Even in this short excerpt, Rudrakavi touches upon an impressive range of Sanskrit learning, including philosophy, poetics, regional characteristics of women, and the types of heroines (*nāyikā-bheda*). Without some grounding in these traditions, the praise would make little sense to a reader or listener. Moreover, some items depend upon the concept of double entendre (*śleṣa*) in Sanskrit where a word or set of phonemes intentionally possesses multiple meanings. Thus, Rudrakavi esteems "the mixing of colors [*varṇa*s] in paintings," while the intermingling of castes (*varṇa*s) is undesirable.[92] Far beyond the issue of linguistic intelligibility, such formulations suggest that Rudrakavi viewed Raḥīm as conversant with Sanskrit learning and conventions.

ʿAbd al-Raḥīm Khān-i Khānān was reputed to be a connoisseur of Indian traditions, and Rudrakavi likely appeals to these skills when soliciting him in Sanskrit. Raḥīm's patronage to several languages, including Persian,

Arabic, and Hindi, was well documented during his lifetime, and he also personally wrote in Hindi.[93] Whether he had command of Sanskrit is more dubious, although there are Sanskrit verses attributed to him as well as a Sanskrit astrological treatise laden with heavy Persian vocabulary.[94] Even Persian texts remember Raḥīm as a poetically gifted polymath, such as the eighteenth-century *Ma'āṣir al-Umarā*, which attests, "Khān-i Khānān had unique skills in his age. He was fluent in Arabic, Persian, Turkish, and *hindī* [Hindi or Sanskrit?]. He understood and wrote good poetry."[95] Thus, Rudrakavi may have used Sanskrit not only because of its general valence in Mughal culture but more pointedly as a tailored appeal to a lover of Indian literature.

Raḥīm was also widely renowned for his military prowess, which no doubt informed Pratap Shah's decision to entreat this general regarding a dispute with Jahangir's army. Raḥīm enjoyed a fair amount of autonomy from his Deccan-based court and exercised his resources against the royal center on several occasions.[96] Rudrakavi hints at the geography and extent of Raḥīm's power throughout his work. He also celebrates Khān-i Khānān's protection as more certain than even the most basic features of the world.

> Even the ocean might transgress the shore,
> the moon could burn, and golden Mount Meru may move.
> But we all know that a promise of security,
> furnished by Khan-i Khanan, will never falter.[97]

Rudrakavi emphasizes the safety provided by Raḥīm in other verses and only rarely notes his subservience to Jahangir. Instead, our poet prefers to cast Raḥīm as an independent ruler and, particularly in his closing chapter, as a maker of kings.

In the fourth and final section of the panegyric, Rudrakavi launches his poem into the constellation of Mughal politics to solicit Khān-i Khānān's direct intercession. This closing chapter, made up of five verses, soundly demonstrates that Rudrakavi intended his text to be linguistically and poetically understood by Khān-i Khānān. First Rudrakavi stresses Pratap Shah's high opinion of Raḥīm.

> Depending on the power of your stafflike arms, I ask you alone.
> I experience the joy of hearing about the tradition of your good fortune.
> Even though far away I speak your praises based on others.

How am I, Pratap, not worthy of your affection, O Khan-i Khanan?[98]

Next, Rudrakavi outlines Pratap Shah's historically good relations with Akbar and again extols Raḥīm.

Previously, O hero, the Glorious One gave me the title of son,
and I enjoyed the food of Shah Akbar, jewel of kings.
This Pratap was thoroughly delighted at the feet of the Navab.
Therefore, O King Khan-i Khanan, do the right thing now!

The sole standard for judging all virtues,
the single home of speech fit for the royal assembly,
may Navab Khan-i Khanan, King of Girivana,
conquer the world! His name be praised![99]

Here Rudrakavi perhaps alludes to Pratap Shah's participation in Akbar's 1595–1596 campaign against Ahmednagar that was overseen by Khān-i Khānān (while glossing over seven years of military hostilities between Akbar and Pratap Shah).[100] In mentioning Girivana, a hill in the Deccan, Rudrakavi further highlights Raḥīm's authority in central India and thereby indicates one of Pratap Shah's reasons for imploring this particular individual.

In his final two lines, Rudrakavi outlines his patron's wishes and makes a political play through the language of Sanskrit poetry.

Like Vishnu with Bali, victorious Khan-i Khanan checks powerful kings.
His two sons, Mirza Iraj and Darab, are two Kamadevas fighting the
Shambara-like demon [Malik] Ambar [*ambaraśambaramadanau*].

Heroic Shah Jahangir has become attached to union with the deer-eyed lady
of the south who is agitated by the fierce glory of his rising passion.
If Khan-i Khanan, ruler of the entire earth, extends his hand
to touch her garments, she will be pleased.[101]

In the penultimate verse, Rudrakavi invokes both classical and contemporary references to promote Khān-i Khānān as a kingmaker. First, he exalts Raḥīm as able to quell the maniacal tendencies of rulers, just like Vishnu in his dwarf incarnation rescued the heavens and earth from the grip of the demon Bali (*balinṛpabandhanaviṇṇur*).[102] Next Rudrakavi names Raḥīm's sons, Mirza Īraj (better known as Shāhnavāz Khān) and Dārāb.[103] Both sons often performed well on military campaigns, particularly in the Deccan, and are remembered in the Indo-Persian tradition as fierce warriors.[104] Mirza Īraj was particularly renowned for successfully repelling Malik Ambar, a powerful Ahmednagar minister, in a battle at Telangana in 1602.[105] Rudrakavi compares this feat to the legendary cosmic battle between Kamadeva (Pradyumna) and the demon Shambara.[106] The parallel between Raḥīm's sons and Kamadeva also further identifies Raḥīm with Vishnu (Kamadeva is sometimes said to be Vishnu's son). After this extended metaphor, Rudrakavi suggests that Pratap Shah desires Raḥīm, perhaps with his sons, to intervene on behalf of the Baglan ruler. Poetically put, Raḥīm should touch the garment of Pratap's kingdom that is being threatened by Jahangir's looming army.

Notably, Pratap Shah's plea is articulated through Sanskrit poetry. The penultimate verse invokes Indian mythology, and the final line displays heavy compounding. Rudrakavi imagined that Raḥīm would not only grasp such complexities but also that he would value the expression of current concerns through a classical literary medium. We possess no account of whether Raḥīm received this text or its impact on the military situation. However, at the very least, Pratap Shah treated Sanskrit poetry as a communicative language through which he could initiate political negotiations and even subvert Mughal imperial objectives. One way or another, Pratap Shah successfully warded off Jahangir's forces at this time and was later received amicably at the royal court.[107]

While Rudrakavi intended for Raḥīm to linguistically and literarily comprehend the *Khānakhānācarita*, he did not pursue a similar approach in his other Sanskrit encomia. Neither the *Dānaśāhacarita* nor the *Kīrtisamullāsa* (for Akbar's son Danyal and Jahangir's son Khurram, respectively) requests its recipient to take specific actions. Danyal was a connoisseur of Indian music and poetry and even composed Hindi verses, as Jahangir notes in his memoirs.[108] This cultural affinity may partially explain Danyal's being the addressee of a Sanskrit work. Nonetheless, it is unclear what (if anything in particular) Rudrakavi and Pratap Shah hoped to gain by praising Danyal and Khurram in Sanskrit.

The *Jahāṅgīracarita* is Rudrakavi's most enigmatic praise poem, not least because it is available only in a single incomplete manuscript today. In this copy, the first three chapters (*ullāsas*) are missing, save the third chapter's final two verses and colophon.[109] The text continues for one and a half more chapters before breaking off in the middle of a prose section in chapter 5 (additionally, folio 70 is missing). Because of its partial state, conclusions about the *Jahāṅgīracarita* remain tentative. Nonetheless, in its original form, the *Jahāṅgīracarita* was substantially longer than the *Khānakhānācarita* and, as Rudrakavi's only panegyric addressed to a reigning Mughal sovereign, promises insight regarding the perceived power of Sanskrit in the imperial center.[110] When read against Rudrakavi's other works and contemporary texts, the *Jahāṅgīracarita*'s preserved portions exhibit several remarkable literary and historical features that underscore the possibilities and limits of Sanskrit at the Mughal court.

Rudrakavi relies heavily on reused verses and prose across his four panegyrics, which is most striking in the *Jahāṅgīracarita*. Approximately 60 percent of the extant portion of the *Jahāṅgīracarita* is recycled material.[111] For example, Rudrakavi offers the following verse in three of his four praise poems, substituting the appropriate name (here given as it appears in the *Jahāṅgīracarita*):

> When swords flash in glorious Jahangir's army,
> like streaks of lightning in a cloud,
> they release showers of arrows and burn the glory of hidden enemies.
> A river of blood rises, the passion of celestial women is calmed,
> and enemy women cease to part their hair.[112]

Such sentiments are broad enough to extol any military figure, and in fact this verse also appears in Rudrakavi's Sanskrit history of the Baglan dynasty that predates the encomia written for Mughal consumption.[113] Sanskrit (and Indo-Persian) poets frequently repeated verses in commissioned panegyrics, although most commonly to different courts.[114] In this sense, duplication in Khān-i Khānān's praise poem is less awkward than Rudrakavi's exaltations of successive princes and a king within the same imperial family. Jahangir would certainly not have appreciated being lauded with verses identical to those once used to exalt Danyal, his brother and onetime rival for the throne.[115] The Mughal king might also have been displeased with similar verses being applied to his son Khurram in light of the earlier rebellion of Jahangir's oldest son, Khusraw, and the general tension between sons and fathers in the Mughal dispensation.[116] In order for the *Jahāṅgīracarita* to dispose

Jahangir favorably to Pratap Shah, the Mughal emperor would need to read it independently of Rudrakavi's earlier poems or not comprehend the text at all.

His repeated verses notwithstanding, Rudrakavi also composed fresh contributions for his *Jahāṅgīracarita* that sometimes lend more specificity to the work. For instance, at the end of chapter 4 several verses glorify Jahangir as the "lord of Delhi" and acclaim the wealth of the Mughal Empire.[117] In chapter 5, he describes the king's harem as full of beautiful women and marvels at Jahangir's urban development. In an overt admission of his historical circumstance, he mentions that *faqīrs* (dervishes; *phagira* in Sanskrit) are revered in Agra.[118] Such allusions add a contemporary framework but nonetheless rarely diverge from accepted Sanskrit literary practices, such as describing cities (*nagaravarṇana*), and none seem to refer to specific political situations.

In the prose of the *Jahāṅgīracarita*, Rudrakavi praises the Mughal emperor even more conventionally. For example, he compares Jahangir to Hindu gods and ancient kings, lauding the Mughal king as "a great scourge to all enemies just like Prithu" and one who has "conquered Love like Shiva."[119] Nonetheless, the use of stock tropes hardly renders these similes meaningless. On the contrary, Jahangir quite possibly would have understood such cultural references based on familiarity with Akbar-period translations of the epics and other Sanskrit texts into Persian.[120] Jahangir lacked Raḥīm's reputation as a connoisseur of Indian learning, but there is significant evidence that, like his father, he was familiar with a high register of Hindi poetry.[121]

It remains unclear what Pratap Shah hoped to gain by sending a Sanskrit poem to Jahangir as opposed to a Persian or Hindi message. In this case and indeed for his two panegyrics for Mughal princes, Rudrakavi and his patron may have intended the encomia to be received as gifts in court rather than be parsed linguistically. A member of another local ruling family, Harideva Miśra of Mithila, also authored a praise poem for Jahangir that appears to take a similar tack. In Harideva's case, his use of heavy alliteration and rhyme suggests that he may have anticipated Jahangir would appreciate the sounds of his praise even absent full understanding. For example, Harideva lauds Jahangir in quick succession as *kīrakara*, *vīravara*, and *hīraśara*.[122] But, even if Jahangir grasped only certain words and allusions or accepted the poem as an aesthetic feat, regional courts perceived Sanskrit as a fruitful language for flattering the Mughals.[123]

JAGANNĀTHA PAṆḌITARĀJA'S HIGH LITERATURE FOR ASAF KHAN

Jagannātha Paṇḍitarāja followed Rudrakavi in directing an encomium to a member of the Mughal court at the petition of a regional ruler. Between 1628 and 1641, a local chieftain in Kashmir named Mukunda Raya commissioned Jagannātha to compose a Sanskrit panegyric for Asaf Khan, the royal vizier. The text, titled *Āsaphavilāsa* (*Play of Asaf* [*Khan*]), is a short work primarily in prose that commemorates a visit Asaf Khan paid to Kashmir in the company of Shah Jahan.[124] In a sense, Jagannātha wrote from within the central Mughal court. By his own admission he spent his youth therein, but he admits notably few traces of this social context into his Sanskrit oeuvre.[125] His *Āsaphavilāsa* proves no exception and evades direct contemporary references aside from the names of Shah Jahan, Asaf Khan, and Mukunda Raya. Jagannātha dedicates the majority of his attention to the beauty and mythology typically associated with Kashmir in Sanskrit. Nonetheless, within this largely conventional treatment, Jagannātha exhibits several ways of writing cross-culturally in Sanskrit about Mughal India.

Jagannātha opens by commending Shah Jahan and even directly addresses the Mughal king at times. Unlike in Rudrakavi's praise of Khān-i Khānān as able to challenge Jahangir, the reader senses no tension between Asaf Khan, a major power broker in the empire, and Shah Jahan, who owed his coronation to his vizier's stratagems.[126] Instead, Jagannātha vociferously exalts the emperor in lines replete with dense Sanskrit imagery.

> Many kings—resplendent with bows that buzz with lines of bees swarming
> to meet the liberal rivers of juices oozing from the lobes of dense legions
> of elephants that are blind with madness and shaking the city gates—
> rely upon your eye, shining, intoxicated, lovely, and brilliant as a lotus.
> [Shah Jahan] is the sun that pierces the darkness of destitution.[127]

Jagannātha transitions to a loose prose narrative for the remainder of his text. He relates that Shah Jahan once came to Kashmir accompanied by his stunning cavalry. He vividly depicts the lush, dramatic landscape of Kashmir, which loomed large in the Mughal imagination and frequently appears in Indo-Persian works.[128] In this respect, while Jagannātha drew on Sanskrit norms to describe Kashmir, his Mughal audience would have heard resonances with their own literary tradition.

Jagannātha introduces Asaf Khan near the middle of his panegyric and characterizes the vizier as powerful using Sanskrit standards of comparison. He likens Asaf Khan's fame, a virtue associated with whiteness in Sanskrit, to the waves of the Ganges and the snowcapped peaks of Kashmir's Himalayas. He extols the vizier as beneficial for all people, "helpful as a sacrifice for the twice born" and "pleasing to the mind like the cool-rayed moon to women."[129] Perhaps the most interesting passage in the *Āsaphavilāsa* occurs at the end of this prose section where Jagannātha places Asaf Khan within numerous hierarchies of Sanskrit aesthetic theory.

> [Asaf Khan] is respected in battle and honored by the gods. Among all neighboring rulers who are related to the world conqueror, he is like literature [*kāvya*] is to speech, like poetic suggestion [*dhvani*] is to literature, like aesthetic emotion [*rasa*] is to poetic suggestion, and like erotic love [*śṛṅgāra*] is to aesthetic emotion. Navab Asaf Khan, who bathes in the essence of all *śāstras*, is esteemed thus because of his sweetness and greatness that stir the hearts of all sensitive critics.[130]

Here Jagannātha invokes a technical Sanskrit vocabulary to pay tribute to the Mughal vizier. This reliance on classical Sanskrit knowledge harks back to the approaches of earlier Sanskrit panegyrists of the Mughals but deserves fresh consideration in respect to Asaf Khan.

Asaf Khan falls short of Raḥīm's renown as well versed in Indian traditions. Nonetheless, he had a history of engaging with Sanskrit learning, such as ordering an astronomer named Nityānanda to translate a Persian astrological treatise into Sanskrit. This connection hardly demonstrates that Asaf Khan personally desired (or was able) to access Sanskrit texts, but it establishes that cross-cultural patronage links permeated Mughal cosmopolitanism rather broadly. Moreover, regional figures often interpreted such prolific ties as an invitation to address influential imperial actors in Sanskrit.

In the quoted passage, Jagannātha further inscribes the hierarchy of Sanskrit poetics onto the Mughal vizier. This literary act parallels Padmasundara's glorification of Akbar as embodying specific aesthetic moods. But whereas Sanskrit aesthetic vocabulary would have been new to the Mughals in the 1560s, by Asaf Khan's time the basics of *rasa* theory were available in multiple Persian and Hindi sources.[131] If Asaf Khan was informed in such matters, however, then awareness of traditional Sanskrit learning was far more common among Indo-Persian elites than modern scholars have generally acknowledged. Even if we assume that the *Āsaphavilāsa* was translated in order for Asaf Khan to understand it, only someone already familiar with Indian poetic conventions could understand the compliment of "[You are to all other kings] as *śṛṅgāra* is to *rasa*."

After his succinct treatment of Asaf Khan, Jagannātha dedicates the remainder of his *Āsaphavilāsa* to retelling old stories set in Kashmir, parts of which also had contemporary resonances. He begins with the adventures of Kamadeva, who uses Kashmir as his playground for dalliances. He also narrates how Indra came to Kashmir and became ashamed of himself after meeting Shiva, a truly illustrious deity. Within these tales, Jagannātha frequently lingers on generally appreciable points, such as the allure of Kamadeva's female companions and Kashmir's verdant scenery, including its famed gardens. He concludes by declaring that Indra "does not think highly of his own heavenly gardens, which bring no joy to his eyes because their beauty was robbed by the lovely pleasure gardens [of Kashmir]."[132]

In the seventeenth century, the Indo-Persian tradition strongly associated Kashmir with both manicured grounds and Hindu mythology. Asaf Khan personally sponsored the construction of a Kashmiri pleasure garden known as the Nishāt Bāgh (Garden of Delight) in the 1630s.[133] There is even a legend that Shah Jahan wished Asaf Khan to gift him the Nishāt Bāgh, but the vizier risked the king's wrath and declined in order to avoid parting with such lovely grounds.[134] Mughal texts frequently dwelled more generally on Kashmir's beauty.[135] Additionally, court histories, such as the *Āʾīn-i Akbarī*, depicted Kashmir as a sacred space, saturated with Hindu stories and spiritual energy.[136] Given these social and literary factors, Asaf Khan may well have understood Jagannātha's poetic portrayal of Kashmir's god-filled gardens to echo his interests in the region more than is made explicit in the Sanskrit text.

Jagannātha offers a final paragraph that contains the most overt historical information in his succinct work. Here he mentions his sponsor Mukunda Raya, whose precise identity and connection with the Mughals is uncertain, and prides himself on pleasing the mind of Asaf Khan.[137] Returning to Shah Jahan, Jagannātha celebrates that the Mughal ruler honored him with the title *paṇḍitarāja* (King of the Learned). Jagannātha's *Āsaphavilāsa* remains puzzling in many respects, and some scholars have even postulated that the brief extant text is incomplete.[138] Even as we have the panegyric, however, *Āsaphavilāsa* adds an important layer to how different patrons and authors made Sanskrit relevant within the Mughal imperium. In threading Kashmir's landscape throughout his work, Jagannātha exploits the overlapping interests of Sanskrit poetics and Mughal court culture. He wrote within his tradition but nonetheless produced a text that reverberated with the Mughal imagination and experience of Kashmir.

As with other Sanskrit panegyrics addressed to Mughal figures, we have no evidence of whether or how Asaf Khan received the *Āsaphavilāsa*. The encomium makes no direct call for action and thus may have been designed as a gift to please a high political official instead of a means of imparting specific information. Perhaps precisely because he wished this panegyric to be recognized as a gift, Mukunda Raya engaged a known Mughal court poet as its author. Jagannātha's name would certainly have been recognizable to the imperial elite, although his other Sanskrit works were not read within Persianate circles (so far as we know). But far more concrete than any possible Mughal reception is Jagannātha's literary strategy of simultaneously writing specifically and transversely about Kashmir. This dual approach goes against the still popular and derogatory view that a Sanskrit panegyrist was a mere mimicking "talking house-bird" who desperately said whatever he thought his patrons wanted to hear about a limited set of topics.[139] On the contrary, Jagannātha crafted a work that was culturally compelling for the Mughals and poetically pleasing in Sanskrit. He provides a remarkable exemplar of how Sanskrit literati could effectively speak across cultural lines without stepping outside their traditional conventions.

DEFINING BILINGUALISM IN SANSKRIT GRAMMARS OF PERSIAN

At the same time that poets across the subcontinent were writing Sanskrit panegyrics to the Mughal elite, the imperial court explored another type of Sanskrit discourse by sponsoring bilingual language analyses. Akbar and Jahangir each ordered the production of a full Sanskrit grammar of Persian, both of which were accompanied by a bilingual lexicon. These technical treatises were intensely political. Sanskrit intellectuals had long capitalized on the deep link between philology and power in India, where grammatical correctness was integral to royal authority.[140] Moreover, a body of roughly one dozen Sanskrit-Persian lexicons that date from the fourteenth to the eighteenth centuries sought to make sense of the spread of Indo-Persian dynasties and culture through the tools of Sanskrit language analysis.[141] The two bilingual Mughal grammars drew upon both traditions and deployed the intellectual resources of Sanskrit to advance Mughal imperial ambitions and comment on the rapidly expanding Indo-Persian cultural order.

Vihāri Kṛṣṇadāsa composed his *Pārasīprakāśa* (*Light on Persian*) at Akbar's request in the late sixteenth century and emphasizes his imperial Mughal sponsorship throughout both the lexicon and grammar portions of his work.[142] He proclaims early on that he designed his text to serve as a resource for teaching Persian:

> A collection of some Persian speech is produced by me
> so that those who understand Sanskrit can enlighten themselves.
> For those who desire to plunge into the great ocean of the Persian language,
> Kṛṣṇadāsa makes this life raft of words [*nibadhnāti vacaḥplavam*].[143]

Kṛṣṇadāsa thus promises to explain Persian to Sanskrit intellectuals. His lexicon is a list of common words in the two languages modeled on the *Amarakośa* (ca. seventh century?), a popular Sanskrit thesaurus, and is relatively easy to follow. But the style of his grammar in addition to the social context of late sixteenth-century northern India prompts serious doubt about whether straightforward language instruction was truly his primary goal.

Kṛṣṇadāsa explains Persian grammar according to fairly technical and elliptical Sanskrit conventions. At the start, he openly proclaims that he assumes readers already have a firm grasp of Sanskrit technical vocabulary: "Here there is no collection of [Persian] grammatical terms because the accomplishment of grammatical operations will be expressed through Sanskrit technical terms alone in reference to given things."[144] Kṛṣṇadāsa then provides a full linguistic account of Persian by outlining different Sanskrit grammatical formations in terse aphorisms (*sūtras*) and slotting in the equivalent Persian constructions. He generally employs the well-established method of substitution (indicated by use of the genitive) to graft Persian grammar onto Sanskrit, along the way noting the many forms that Sanskrit possesses but Persian lacks.[145] For example, using the common verb "to be," he explains the stem for the simple past as follows: "there is *śud* [*shud*] in place of *bhū* for the past tense."[146] He draws primarily on the Sārasvata system of grammatical analysis, which was popular in northern India during this period and would have been intelligible to those trained in Sanskrit grammatical discourse.[147]

However, while Indians began learning Persian in substantial numbers during the late sixteenth century, we lack evidence that they typically studied Sanskrit first. On the contrary, Indians gained fluency in Persian primarily through the *madrasa* system of Islamicate education, which was reformed during Akbar's reign.[148] Moreover, while Kṛṣṇadāsa's grammar could have imparted basic grammatical knowledge, it would hardly have cultivated any ability to speak or read Persian and contains no discussion of pronunciation or the Perso-Arabic script.[149] Perhaps a teacher was imagined to fill these gaps, but we possess little evidence of many bilingual individuals that could have fulfilled this role. Such people seem to have been largely unknown in Akbar's court (aside from Kṛṣṇadāsa himself and, toward the end of Akbar's rule, Siddhicandra).[150] Even during Jahangir's rule, only a few individuals are known to have been capable in both languages.[151]

Rather than enable practical language instruction, it seems more plausible that Kṛṣṇadāsa sought to configure the relationship between Sanskrit, Persian, and the Mughal Empire. Intellectuals had produced Sanskrit-Persian lexicons since the mid-fourteenth century in order to make sense of the spread of Indo-Persian rule and culture.[152] Kṛṣṇadāsa took the significant step of adding a full bilingual grammar to his lexicon, an innovation perhaps impelled by the unprecedented extent of Mughal authority. While his project spoke poignantly to those steeped in the Sanskrit thought world,[153] Akbar's support of this text remains to be explained. The Mughals had only recently articulated a formal relationship with Persian when Akbar commissioned Kṛṣṇadāsa's *Pārasīprakāśa*.[154] Akbar's ancestors spoke Turkish, and earlier Indo-Islamic kingdoms typically operated in a combination of Persian and Indian vernaculars. Kṛṣṇadāsa's treatise spoke to the evolving status of Persian as a principal political and literary language of the Mughal Empire and examines the possible places of Sanskrit in this dawning cultural order.

Kṛṣṇadāsa most directly addresses the place of Sanskrit in the Mughal imperium in a set of bilingual example sentences that feature the reigning Mughal king. These phrases, given in Sanskrit and Persian, exemplify different cases and often reflect official court proceedings (for a full list, see appendix 1). They include expressions such as "Long live glorious Shah Akbar!" and "Shah Akbar's fierce rule reduces a forest of enemies to ash."[155] Several expressions place cross-cultural endeavors at the heart of imperial court life. In an example of the accusative case, Kṛṣṇadāsa celebrates that "Glorious Akbar made the Kali Age into the Era of Truth [*satyayuga*] by his own justice."[156] The four Indian ages (*yugas*) were a common trope in Persian retellings of Indian stories during and after Akbar's reign.[157] In the Sanskrit version of this sentence, Kṛṣṇadāsa adds that Akbar is "very ethical" (*atīvadhārmmikaḥ*), which frames the Mughal ruler as a righteous Indian monarch. Kṛṣṇadāsa refers to the extensive imperial practice of multicultural titling with one sense of the dative: "Great Akbar Shah gives titles [*khiṭāb*, *padavīm*] to important people."[158] In this view, the Mughal court is the site of cross-cultural activities that are also embodied in Kṛṣṇadāsa's bilingual work.

Moreover, embedded in Kṛṣṇadāsa's project is something so basic in terms of Mughal interests that it is easy to overlook: he penned one of the earliest known grammars of Persian in any language. Persian intellectuals had long devoted sustained attention to explaining the grammatical structure of Arabic.[159] But there are only a few references to Persian grammars written in Arabic and Turkish beginning in the fourteenth century, and texts are extant only from the mid-sixteenth century.[160] Therefore, in underwriting Kṛṣṇadāsa's work, Akbar sought to innovate within not only the Sanskrit realm but the Persian one as well. We lack information regarding the imperial reception of Kṛṣṇadāsa's text, but the existence of this treatise shows that the Mughals viewed the intellectual resources of Sanskrit as relevant to their emerging imperial relationship with Persian.

After Kṛṣṇadāsa, the central Mughal court sponsored one additional bilingual grammar: Kavi Karṇapūra's *Saṃskṛtapārasīkapadaprakāśa* (*Light on Sanskrit and Persian Words*). Kavi Karṇapūra came into the ambit of Mughal patronage from Orissa in the early seventeenth century.[161] He attests to receiving Jahangir's support for his treatise: "Having taken the blessing of Jahangir, great king of the earth, in the form of a command, poet Karṇapūra composes this *Light on Sanskrit and Persian Words*."[162] Karṇapūra's text is structurally quite similar to Kṛṣṇadāsa's work in that it is comprised of discrete lexicon and grammar portions, and the lexicon defines a similar set of vocabulary.[163] But Karṇapūra's grammar lacks the technical terminology that pervades Kṛṣṇadāsa's work. Karṇapūra uses far simpler language that relies on basic knowledge of Sanskrit words and case endings rather than formal grammatical discourse.[164] This approach does not seem to have appealed to any audience, and the *Saṃskṛtapārasīkapadaprakāśa* survives in far fewer manuscript copies than Kṛṣṇadāsa's *Pārasīprakāśa*.[165] But Kavi Karṇapūra nonetheless outlines a strikingly different vision for how Sanskrit knowledge might speak to the interests of the Mughal state.

Karṇapūra projects his work as able to teach Persian and Sanskrit alike. At the beginning of his lexicon, he announces,

> Knowledge of Persian will come for those who know Sanskrit,
> knowledge of Sanskrit for those who know Persian,
> and knowledge of both for those who know both.
> Thus this book is to be studied.[166]

After noting a few details of his text he reiterates, "From knowing one, the other will be understood. From knowing both, both will be understood."[167] In these lines, Karṇapūra acknowledges the existence of people who know both Sanskrit and Persian and, more important, expresses a keen interest in generating more such cross-cosmopolitan intellectuals. A few verses later, Karṇapūra again heralds the value of his work for Persian literati who wish to learn Sanskrit: "For *yavana* cows that are drowning in the mud of lack of treatises, glorious Karṇapūra will pull them up with the rope that is this composition."[168]

Particularly given the numerous Sanskrit panegyrics addressed to Mughal figures, one can imagine that courtly Persian speakers might want to understand a bit of Sanskrit. At the very least, Kavi Karṇapūra was in good company in supposing that Sanskrit could be a linguistically meaningful medium to some degree among the imperial elite and accordingly provides a relatively simple presentation of the language. It is doubtful that endeavors to become bilingual in Sanskrit and Persian ever became widespread, especially among those who learned Persian first. But Karṇapūra projects Sanskrit as a desirable tongue to be acquired by Mughal Persianate intellectuals. In this perspective, the Mughal endorsement of Persian did not limit their interest in other languages but rather was part of an imperial agenda to engage with literary cultures more broadly.

Indeed, in comparison with earlier Indo-Islamic kingdoms, the Mughals exhibited an unusually robust dedication to promoting Sanskrit as well as Persian. The world of words had always mattered deeply in both the Sanskrit and Islamicate worlds, which overlapped to a new degree of density in early modern northern India. The two authors of bilingual grammars developed distinct visions for the possibilities of Sanskrit in this thoroughly multicultural context. Kṛṣṇadāsa deploys the intellectual resources of Sanskrit to affirm the prominent status of Persian. Karṇapūra proclaims an affinity between the cultural worth of Sanskrit and Persian for the Mughal elite. Both intellectuals promote cross-cultural knowledge as essential to intellectual and cultural dimensions of the increasingly multicultural Mughal court.

CONCLUSION: MULTILINGUAL MUGHALS

Sanskrit literary and grammatical texts carve out diverse possibilities for how the classical language of India could participate in the Mughal imperial project. Literary works often claim a Mughal reception, beginning with Padmasundara's 1569 treatment of Sanskrit aesthetic theory. Regional political and religious leaders turned to Sanskrit panegyrics to solicit and negotiate with Mughal kings, princes, and nobles. These works invoke Sanskrit poetry and cultural norms to both explain and resist Mughal power. Sanskrit grammars of Persian emerged from direct royal patronage and locate much of their audience among Sanskrit intellectuals. Nonetheless, Akbar and Jahangir ordered these language analyses in order to unearth the potential contributions of Sanskrit traditions to the Mughal cultural order. Taken together, these wide-ranging texts enable us to reconstruct the vitality of Sanskrit in the Mughal Empire as a literary and intellectual tradition that repeatedly intersected with contemporary interests. More broadly, these Sanskrit materials offer key insights regarding Mughal knowledge, cultural politics, and textual reception.

The texts surveyed here testify that Sanskrit was an integral and complex part of Mughal knowledge systems. The praise poems of Śānticandra, Rudrakavi, and Jagannātha Paṇḍitarāja demonstrate that people from diverse communities, geographies, and times perceived Mughal imperial culture as open and able to engage with Sanskrit. Moreover, numerous contemporaries of the Mughals felt that the idiom of Sanskrit poetics in particular was well suited to serve as a political vehicle in Mughal India. Equally important, the Mughals were deemed worthy to be incorporated into the Sanskrit literary tradition. The Mughals appear to have largely concurred with the perceptions of Sanskrit intellectuals and their regional patrons regarding the potential dynamism of Sanskrit ideas and texts in an imperial context. Padmasundara's *Akbarasāhiśṛṅgāradarpaṇa* encodes a similar expectation of aesthetic knowledge from within Mughal patronage networks. The Sanskrit grammars and lexicons of Persian express a slightly different but complementary claim that Sanskrit intellectual discourses were pertinent to Mughal imperial ambitions.

In addition to claiming an imperial context, the panegyrics addressed to members of the imperial elite further anticipate a Mughal reception. However, we still lack a solid understanding of how the Mughals apprehended Sanskrit texts, and thus the historical implications of these praise poems remain murky. We might conclude that the Sanskrit panegyrics were simply insignificant works, failed attempts that were in fact never consumed in a royal context and circulated only outside courtly circles if at all. All the encomia survive in relatively few manuscripts today. However, the paucity of copies may not reflect anything more than their increasing irrelevance as their recipients faded into history. Moreover, if the court so blatantly rejected Sanskrit praise poems, then one wonders why regional figures kept asking literati to produce them.

Several possibilities allow us to take seriously the Mughal reception claims of these Sanskrit panegyrics. I suggested earlier that encomia may have been verbally translated into Hindi for their addressees. Additionally, many members of the Mughal nobility could likely understand portions of recited Sanskrit by virtue of their familiarity with Hindi. A lively Hindi vernacular culture at the Mughal court also helps to contextualize the literary allusions and conventions in these Sanskrit praise poems. Alternatively, certain Sanskrit praise poems may have been designed more as gifts than as meaningful texts. Whatever else the Mughals did or did not know about Sanskrit, they were certainly aware that it was a time-honored language associated with Indian royalty. The Mughal court frequently invoked imperial idioms from a variety of traditions, including Sanskrit in their sponsorship of bilingual grammars. In some instances, the royal court relied on nonverbal mediums of expressing authority such as robes of honor (*khilʿat*).[169] Combining these two trends, Sanskrit literature could have signified power to the Mughal elite, either absent of or alongside any communicative function.

Despite their significant interest in Sanskrit, the Mughals never studied this language in any systematic way. Particularly in light of the hefty presence of Sanskrit literati and texts in the imperial milieu, this omission warrants further reflection. Muzaffar Alam has previously suggested that the Mughals did not choose Sanskrit as the language of empire because it was "too sacred, too divine."[170] On the contrary, like so many Asian rulers before them, the Mughals understood Sanskrit primarily as a language of literature, learning, and politics rather than a mode of theological expression. We will likely never know how the Mughals received specific Sanskrit praise poems. But none of the panegyric writers or patrons perceived lack of language training to be a barrier to addressing the Mughals in Sanskrit. The Mughals also did not recognize linguistic ignorance to impede serious engagement with Sanskrit intellectual culture. On the contrary, they projected an affinity with this tradition by sponsoring diverse Sanskrit textual production, including works on aesthetics and grammar. Given this seeming gap between comprehension and interest, we might label the Mughals as more multicultural than multilingual when it came to Sanskrit. Sanskrit was an undeniable part of Mughal court culture, and yet the language itself remained grammatically inaccessible.

However, rather than condemning Sanskrit as unimportant in Mughal culture based on its limited linguistic reach, it is more fruitful to consider multilingual Mughal court culture as open to including languages in various configurations. Sanskrit grammars of Persian declared that Sanskrit was a pertinent part of the Mughal imperium and tried to engage those inside and outside the court in thinking through the associated cultural and political implications. Praise poems injected Sanskrit into the Mughal courts and invoked Sanskrit aesthetic tropes and conventions to comment on contemporary affairs. Some panegyrists treated Sanskrit literature as a legitimate means of advancing military objectives. Moreover, the Mughals supported Sanskrit intellectuals, commissioned Sanskrit texts, received Sanskrit works, and, as we shall see, translated Sanskrit stories. According to many definitions, perhaps including those current in early modern India, Mughal multilingualism indeed included Sanskrit.

There is little evidence that the Sanskrit texts addressed to the Mughals justified imperial rule to Brahman, Hindu, or Jain populations. Their goals were far more complex and often located within the Mughal court. The Mughals were formulating the contours and boundaries of their imperial culture, and Sanskrit was a significant part of that process. Those outside royal circles played crucial roles in these negotiations as well, through their perceptions of the Mughal elite and subsequent claims on the court by sending Sanskrit texts to imperial figures. It bears reminding that the Mughal Empire began to be firmly established only in the 1560s, the same decade that serious Mughal engagements with the Sanskrit thought world were inaugurated. From the very beginning, an interest in Sanskrit texts and at least some familiarity with Sanskrit literary concepts were an integral part of what it meant to be a Mughal emperor or a member of the Mughal elite.

Mughal control expanded rapidly in the later sixteenth and seventeenth centuries and quickly exceeded any other political force in living

Indian memory. But empire is never a finished product. Like any vibrant state, the Mughal imperial dispensation continually evolved. Sanskrit thinkers, texts, and knowledge systems participated in the ongoing project of defining and redefining Mughal power, particularly its cultural politics. The Mughals never sought a single answer to what it meant to rule India, and, accordingly, there was never a rigid set of ways that Sanskrit thinkers and texts played into Mughal sovereignty. However, we cannot hope to accurately understand Mughal court culture or political interests without taking into account the Sanskrit works and ideas that permeated imperial circles.

[3] MANY PERSIAN *MAHĀBHĀRATAS* FOR AKBAR

IN THE 1580s, Emperor Akbar ordered the translation of the Sanskrit *Mahābhārata* into Persian. The newly minted Mughal epic, called the *Razmnāmah* (*Book of War*), would prove a seminal work in imperial circles for decades. In the twenty years following the initial translation, Mughal literati composed a highly political preface for the *Razmnāmah* and reworked portions of the text several times.[1] The translation was even incorporated into the education of royal princes.[2] While scholars have long been aware of Mughal engagements with the *Mahābhārata* and the epic's visibility at the imperial court, few have tried to parse the impacts of the translation on Mughal political and literary culture.[3] Nobody has provided substantial textual analysis of the *Razmnāmah*, and its two major subsequent rewritings remain unpublished altogether. As modern theorists remind us, translation is always an act embedded in larger cultural, social, and political networks.[4] Through repeated encounters with the *Mahābhārata*, the Akbari elite remade a Sanskrit epic into an imperially potent part of the Indo-Persian tradition.

The Mughals took up the *Mahābhārata* as part of a larger translation movement that Akbar had inaugurated in the mid-1570s. Scholars have spilled much ink in repeatedly listing the known translations, but a brief recap is helpful here.[5] In 1575, three successive translators failed to produce a Persian *Atharva Veda*, an enigmatic Brahmanical religious text.[6] Around the same time literati authored two Persian retellings of the *Siṃhāsana-dvātriṃśikā* (*Thirty-Two Tales of the Throne*), a popular collection of Sanskrit stories.[7] A team of translators produced the *Razmnāmah* in the mid-1580s and tackled the *Rāmāyaṇa* a few years later. Thereafter imperial support abounded for translations of all sorts. Akbar liberally patronized

Persian adaptations of astronomical and mathematical treatises, the most renowned of which was Fayẕī's poetic rendering of Bhāskara's *Līlāvatī*.[8] He underwrote Persian versions of several narrative texts, including story collections such as the *Pañcatantra* (*Five Tales*) and historical chronicles like the *Rājataraṅgiṇī* (*River of Kings*).[9] Another noteworthy Sanskrit-based narrative sponsored by Akbar is Fayẕī's *Nal-Daman*, a *maṣnavī* retelling of the love story of Nala and Damayanti. The imperial atelier lavishly illustrated many of these works, and art historians have produced some of the most insightful analyses to date on Mughal translation projects.[10]

Akbar's successors also supported translations, although to a lesser degree. As a prince, Jahangir commissioned a Persian *Yogavāsiṣṭha* (*Vasishtha's Treatise on Yoga*), a philosophical work, and the Persian rendering was later brought into Safavid intellectual circles.[11] Also, beginning during Jahangir's reign, translations did not merely come out of the royal court but also entered into it as individual authors generated Persian renderings of Indian texts of their own accord and dedicated these works to the reigning Mughal king. This practice engendered two poetic re-creations of the *Rāmāyaṇa* addressed to Jahangir and a new Persian *Siṃhāsana-dvātriṃśikā*.[12] Shah Jahan evinced less interest in translating Sanskrit materials, although he did back another Persian *Siṃhāsana-dvātriṃśikā*.[13] Shah Jahan is also credited with supporting Hindi versions of Sanskrit materials, such as Sundar Das's *Siṃhāsanbattīsī*.[14]

Among this wider group of texts, the *Mahābhārata* was a consistent focal point, especially in Akbar's court. Akbar employed some of the chief literary stars of his time to participate in the translation and retranslation processes. For example, Fayẕī, Akbar's poet laureate, and Abū al-Faẕl, the head vizier and a master of *inshā*ʾ (Persian literary prose), were both involved at different points. Additionally, Persian histories situate the *Mahābhārata* in the center of court life by depicting Akbar as consulting with the *Razmnāmah* translators regularly and even challenging parts of the Persian text.[15] The accuracy of these stories matters less than the fact that official court histories project the *Mahābhārata* as closely connected with the Mughal sovereign, who embodied imperial authority. Akbar also poured immense resources into illuminating manuscripts of the initial translation, and the master copy of the *Razmnāmah* numbers among the finest, most highly valued specimens of Mughal art that survive today.[16] Akbar never devoted equivalent resources to another translation and rarely to other manuscripts (the Akbari *Rāmāyan* being a notable exception). Even after Jahangir came to power, the *Razmnāmah* continued to be shown and read at court regularly for decades.[17]

The Mughals treated the *Mahābhārata* as a crucial component of their multifaceted project to make the Sanskrit tradition a living part of Indo-Persian culture. Moreover, Mughal literati repeatedly reframed and reworked the *Razmnāmah* to participate in multiple imperial interests, including political disputes, poetry, and history. Often these visions developed the potential of the epic in ways that far exceed the scope of the initial translation. In the late 1580s Abū al-Faẓl penned an extensive preface that outlines a much more direct political application of the epic than can be gleaned from the translated text. Several years later, Fayẓī liberally mixed his own poetic verses into the first two books of the *Razmnāmah*. Last, Ṭāhir Muḥammad Sabzavārī, a historian in Akbar's court, abridged the *Razmnāmah* within his larger world history in 1602. He explores the value of the *Mahābhārata* as reported history that provides a politically charged account of India's pre-Islamic past. These writers do not share a unified vision of what the *Mahābhārata* meant for Mughal claims over India. But each one revisited the epic as an important aesthetic or political work.

Scholars have typically paid little attention to translation in South Asia overall, and Mughal translations are particularly neglected. This overarching lack of interest is due in part to prevailing Western attitudes about the derivative nature of moving texts between languages.[18] Indologists sometimes seize upon translation as an apt metaphor to talk about cross-cultural exchanges in medieval and early modern India.[19] As I noted, scholars have occasionally provided lists of known Mughal translations. But few academics value (or find the time to pursue) the painstaking work of reading a translated text, alongside its original where possible.[20] This neglect is unwarranted. Translation was a nuanced practice in Mughal India, and authors frequently displayed close attention to previously unknown sources, for both Western and Sanskrit works.[21] The Indian epics were especially important in Mughal culture, standing on a par with works such as the *Shāhnāmah*, the major Persian-language epic.[22] Careful comparative reading of the *Razmnāmah* and its reworkings is a promising and unexploited tool for recovering Mughal imperial culture. Mughal elites redefined the *Mahābhārata* as an Indo-Persian epic that spoke to the concerns of their expanding polity and had direct implications for Akbar's sovereignty.

In and of itself, it is perhaps unsurprising that the *Mahābhārata* was an important text in Mughal eyes. This epic was "premodern India's most sustained and profound discourse on power" as well as one of its most beloved stories.[23] What makes Mughal engagements with the *Mahābhārata* worthy of close philological analysis are the choices that were made in transforming this martial, kingly tale across cultural lines. The Persian texts that resulted offer much needed insight into Mughal self-conceptions of power in particular and the tense, productive relationship between political and literary cultures in general. Here the clear line fades away that so many theorists have tried to draw between reducing texts to being instruments of power versus divorcing literary endeavors from politics.[24] The *Razmnāmah* and its later adaptations transcend such artificial dichotomies and reveal how the Mughals understood their evolving imperial identity as cutting across literary and political realms.

COLLABORATION IN VERBALLY TRANSMITTING THE EPIC STORY

The initial Mughal version of the *Mahābhārata* was a collaborative effort that drew Sanskrit and Persian intellectuals into a common task. Nobody involved in the project knew both languages, and as a result two teams of translators were assembled. On the Persian side, Naqīb Khān led the effort and was assisted by Mullā Shīrī, Sultan Thānīsarī, and Badāʾūnī.[25] These men served Akbar's court in various capacities: Naqīb Khān was a court historian, Mullā Shīrī a poet, and Sultan Thānīsarī a fiscal administrator.[26] Badāʾūnī is often called a secretary, but he is more fittingly described as Akbar's most prolific translator and is mostly remembered for having composed a critical, clandestine history of the period (*Muntakhab al-Tavārīkh*). The Persianate translators collaborated with Brahmans in order to access the Sanskrit *Mahābhārata*, which Naqīb Khān notes in his colophon to the translation that appears on several copies (the earliest dated 1599):

> Naqīb Khān, son of ʿAbd al-Laṭīf al-Ḥusaynī, translated [this work] from Sanskrit into Persian in one and a half years. Several learned Brahmans—such as Deva Miśra, Śatāvadhāna, Madhusūdana Miśra, Caturbhuja, and Shaykh Bhāvan, who embraced Islam because of the attention of His Blessed Majesty, who has replaced Sulayman—read this book and explained it in Hindi to me, a poor wretched man, who wrote it in Persian.[27]

Mughal histories attest that collaboration was the standard method of translation at court, and Badāʾūnī even uses separate terms for Sanskrit interpreters (*muʿabbirān*) and Persianate translators (*mutarjimān*).[28] Of the named Brahman translators of the *Razmnāmah*, several assisted with other Mughal translations, but little additional information about these individuals is available.[29]

The Brahmans communicated the text orally to the Mughals via a common vernacular, which Naqīb Khān calls *hindī*, in this case certainly a form of Old Hindi (Hindavi). This verbal transmission is reflected in phonetic changes in transliterated Sanskrit words in the *Razmnāmah* as well as a line of Old Hindi.[30] An oral Hindi culture often facilitated Mughal encounters with Sanskrit texts and provided the shared language for most imperial contacts with Brahman and Jain communities. Later Persian retellings of Indian tales also often cite verbal sources, such as Fayẓī's *Nal-Daman*, which he heard from an Indian storyteller (*fasānah-pardāz*).[31] In the case of the *Razmnāmah*, this method of communication occasionally allowed folk stories not present in the Sanskrit original to enter the Persian text.[32]

This oral transfer also shaped the overarching structure of the new imperial epic. The Mughal translators wrote the Brahman narrators into the *Razmnāmah* and thereby framed the entire Persian text as a story being told across a cultural divide. The *Razmnāmah* consistently repeats expressions such as "then the narrators of the story said" and "then the Indian storytellers relayed." Such formulations launch most of the epic's eighteen books and recur persistently throughout the tale. The *Razmnāmah* also preserves the numerous other narrative layers of the *Mahābhārata*, in which a bard tells the story as he heard it at the snake sacrifice of Janamejaya and so forth. The late sixteenth-century Brahman pandits are grafted onto this series of frameworks as the final set of storytellers who made this epic come alive for a Mughal audience. In an illustrated manuscript from 1598–1599, a painting also visually captures this verbal storytelling and depicts the two groups of translators working together (figure 3.1). In emphasizing their collaboration, the Mughal translators and artists alike foreground the *Mahābhārata*'s foreignness and underscore that this tale originated outside the Persianate tradition.[33] Simultaneously, the translators and artists provide a historical context for how this work entered Akbar's court and thus initiate an endeavor that the translators continue to pursue through various written strategies in the text: namely, reinventing the *Mahābhārata* as a work that belongs in an Indo-Persian imperial context.

FIGURE 3.1 Akbar's translation bureau with Sanskrit and Mughal translators collaborating, preface to the *Razmnāmah*, 1598–1599.

FREE LIBRARY OF PHILADELPHIA, LEWIS M18

MULTIPLE SANSKRIT SOURCES FOR THE STRANGE TALE

Despite the attention they paid to hearing the epic tale, Mughal records do not name which Sanskrit texts they used as the basis for their translation. By the late sixteenth century, there were at least a dozen different Sanskrit versions of the *Mahābhārata* that were typically defined by discrete scripts and associated with particular regions.[34] Thus, the Kashmiri *Mahābhārata* is written in Sharada, the Tamil version in Grantha, and so forth. The regional versions can be loosely grouped into two grand recensions, the northern and the southern, that differ from each other by including or excluding episodes and altering the order of stories. Within the northern and southern recensions, each regional version is defined by its own variant readings and textual additions.[35] We must identify which rendition of the Sanskrit *Mahābhārata* was used to produce the Persian translation in order to proceed with serious comparative analysis.[36] Additionally, the specific Sanskrit source texts used for the *Razmnāmah* indicate some of the reasons the Mughals were captivated by this Indian tale.

The Sanskrit informants generally communicated the text accurately and in detail to the Mughal translators. The *Razmnāmah* contains all eighteen books of the Sanskrit *Mahābhārata*, plus the *Harivaṃśa* appendix, and the plotline is largely unchanged, complete with many of the side stories and digressions.[37] In fact, the episodes selected for illustration in the master imperial manuscript frequently focus on the epic's side stories rather than its main narrative.[38] The Persian translation is not a line by line rendering of the Sanskrit original, and some sections are abridged or significantly altered. But, contrary to the assumptions of scholars over the past few centuries, Akbar's translators provided a near-literal rendering of many passages.[39] A nineteenth-century manuscript of the *Razmnāmah* contains a series of verses from the Sanskrit *Mahābhārata* written in the margins intermittently throughout the initial part of the *Ādi Parvan* (*Book of Beginnings*), the first book of the epic (figure 3.2).[40] These Sanskrit citations correspond to the Persian text and deliver a vivid attestation that the translation was so close that a later reader who was familiar with both traditions could match the Persian and Sanskrit.

The collation of the stories and selection of episodes attest that the majority of the *Razmnāmah* follows the northern recension of the *Mahābhārata*.[41] The *Razmnāmah* furnishes further evidence of its regional source version by faithfully reproducing the *Mahābhārata*'s long lists of genealogies and names of sages and gods. Such lists vary substantially

FIGURE 3.2 Folio from book 1 of the *Razmnāmah* with Sanskrit verses filling the margins.

SRINAGAR ORIENTAL RESEARCH LIBRARY 188, FOLS. 12B–13A

among regional *Mahābhāratas* and thus hold decisive clues to which version was in front of the Sanskrit pandits who read the names to the Mughal translators.[42] An evaluation of several lists of names reveals that the *Razmnāmah* consistently corresponds most closely with the Devanagari version of the *Mahābhārata*.[43] In and of itself, this is unsurprising. The Devanagari version had gained widespread currency across northern and central India by the late sixteenth century. Thus, the Mughals found the most easily available redaction of the story to render into Persian.

However, the *Razmnāmah* deviates from its overall reliance on the Devanagari version in one case that provides deeper insight into Mughal interests in this Sanskrit epic: the fourteenth book. This book, the *Aśvamedha Parvan* (*Horse Sacrifice Book*), is based on the *Jaiminīyāśvamedha*, a starkly different Sanskrit retelling of this section of the epic.[44] The *Jaiminīyāśvamedha* is an anonymous work, likely composed in the twelfth century, which proved wildly popular in Sanskrit and vernacular translations.[45] The *Jaiminīyāśvamedha* is marked by several key features, including an emphasis on devotion to Krishna.[46] Most crucially for the Mughals, the *Jaiminīyāśvamedha* tells a far more exciting tale than its canonical counterpart.

The *Mahābhārata*'s fourteenth book focuses on Yudhishthira's decision to perform the horse sacrifice as a newly (re)established king. However, in the canonical version the sacrifice gets postponed when Krishna embarks on a tediously long philosophical monologue, often characterized as a rehashing of the *Bhagavadgītā*. In brief, there is a lot of talk and no action. In contrast, the *Jaiminīyāśvamedha* skips Krishna's speech and instead revels in Arjuna's wild adventures as he follows the sacrificial horse about India. He stumbles upon a kingdom inhabited solely by women, visits a place where all men are born and die within a single day, and has his head cut off and reattached. Arjuna also faces his own son in a heated battle, and the middle of the book detours into the drama of the *Rāmāyaṇa*.[47] In Persian, these lively and sometimes bizarre narratives fall easily into the category of marvels (*ʿajāʾib*).

Islamicate literature had long cataloged curious aspects of the world that stretch the limits of human imagination. Several authors penned entire treatises on the wondrous, often pairing marvels (*ʿajāʾib*) with the related category of rarities (*gharāʾib*).[48] Generally, Muslims understood *ʿajāʾib* as real and celebrated these astonishing things because they provoked awe at God's magnificent creation.[49] Although, as Travis Zadeh has argued, Islamicate audiences often found heightened pleasure in seemingly impossible stories precisely because of their uncertain veracity.[50] The genre of marvels had been "reinscribed" in Indian contexts, to use Aditya Behl's word, before the Mughal period through Hindavi Sufi romances.[51] Crucially for my purposes here, the Mughals understood *mirabilia* as the prerogative of kings. Azfar Moin has recently pointed out that both Babur and Jahangir devote substantial attention to rarities (*gharāʾib*) in their respective memoirs.[52] Akbar's court was likewise attracted to fantastical occurrences, particularly as a way of interpreting Sanskrit tales.

Akbar's court perceived Sanskrit texts as full of oddities from their first attempted translation,[53] and many Mughal elites commented on the jaw-dropping anecdotes of the *Mahābhārata* in particular. For example, in a letter to Prince Murad, Akbar describes the *Mahābhārata* as "containing strange stories."[54] Many members of the imperial court went further and judged the epic as so stupefying that it went beyond the normal Islamicate definition of *ʿajāʾib* as real wonders and encroached on the realm of the imaginary. Mullā Shīrī, one of the translators, reportedly characterized the epic as containing "rambling, extravagant stories that are like the dreams of a feverish, hallucinating man."[55] In his preface, Abū al-Faẓl is almost beside himself, exclaiming, "I see such agitation in myself from hearing these stories that what can I write?" and, "In this book, such extraordinary things are on every page, in every section, in every chapter."[56] Abū al-Faẓl even compares the *Razmnāmah* to the *Ḥamzanāmah* (*Tales of Amir Hamza*), a notoriously fabulistic text, and exclaims how the former is even more amazing than the latter, bordering on unbelievable.[57] At one point in the Persian translation of the *Aśvamedha Parvan*, a character even bursts out upon hearing about the shape-shifting sacrificial horse: "This speech is full of strange things [*ʿajāʾib*]!"[58]

The cultural interest in *ʿajāʾib* is likely what drew the Mughals to the *Jaiminīyāśvamedha* instead of its Devanagari counterpart and also helps explain the Mughal engagements with the *Mahābhārata* as a whole. We lack concrete evidence that the Mughal translators were aware of the multiplicity of Sanskrit *Mahābhāratas*, and thus they may not have consciously chosen one version of the fourteenth book over another. The translation flows seamlessly from the earlier thirteen books based on the Devanagari version into the *Jaiminīyāśvamedha*, and to my knowledge no Mughal work ever identifies book 14 as different from the rest of the *Razmnāmah* as a single, outlandish tale.[59] Nonetheless, if not the Mughals themselves, then perhaps the Sanskrit informants elected to present the *Jaiminīyāśvamedha* for translation, because they thought the Mughals would appreciate its captivating narrative. Regardless of the agency involved, reliance on the *Jaiminīyāśvamedha* indicates that *ʿajāʾib* elements were a decisive factor in selecting appealing texts for Mughal translation. Indeed, Mughal artists celebrated the marvelous quality of the *Aśvamedha Parvan* by disproportionately illustrating this book in the first illuminated manuscript.[60]

RE-CREATING THE *MAHĀBHĀRATA* AS AN INDO-PERSIAN EPIC

The Mughals transcreated the *Mahābhārata* in Persian using multiple techniques that made the epic simultaneously foreign and familiar for an Indo-Islamic audience. Three practices point up the continuum of Mughal approaches to translation. First, the translators preserve hundreds of Sanskrit words, transliterated into Perso-Arabic script. This high degree of transliteration foregrounds the Indian origins of the *Mahābhārata* and introduces Persianate readers to a significant amount of Sanskrit vocabulary. Second, the translators incorporate Islamic religious notions, most prominently a monotheistic God, into the *Razmnāmah* while simultaneously retaining many Indian gods and spiritual suppositions. This mottled approach results in an uneven religious landscape that lightly acculturates the story for an Islamicate audience while still introducing the Sanskrit epic's religious scaffolding. Last, the translators sprinkle Persian poetry throughout the prose text. These poetic verses express the sentiments of the *Mahābhārata* in terms culturally relevant to Persophone readers, but a dispute over one interpolated line highlights the limits of transculturation for the Mughals. Through these variegated strategies, the translators craft an Indo-Persian text that spoke to the literary and political needs of Akbar's multicultural court.

The *Razmnāmah* translators use Sanskrit words and phrases to spin a web of associations between the epic and Indian knowledge systems. Often they retain terms for culturally specific concepts, such as *gandharb* (*gandharva* in Sanskrit), a class of mythical beings; *narak* (*naraka*), the underworld; and *pūrān* (*purāṇa*), a genre of ancient tales. Other times, the translators invoke Sanskrit terms even when Persian equivalents are readily available, for things such as "discus," "constellation," and "father." Certain words, such as *Veda* (*bīd* in Persian), might seem untranslatable because of their specific cultural resonances, but the Mughals could have used approximate terms far more frequently. *Naraka* could be reframed as *dūzakh* (hell) and *purāṇa* transformed into *tārīkh* (history). Such loose translations would change the resonances of the *Mahābhārata*, but so too did designing a Sanskrit-inflected Persian register that featured thousands of new transliterated terms that readers were expected to learn.

In addition to a strong Indic tone, the *Razmnāmah*'s Sanskrit terms also cultivate a body of Sanskrit knowledge in the text's audience. Some passages introduce information about classical Indian learning and society, such as genres of Sanskrit texts, caste system divisions, and names of different communities. On certain occasions, the Mughal translators even elaborate beyond the source text. For example, a passage early in book 12 refers to six types of forts, but only the Persian translation fills in their proper Sanskrit names, presumably based on knowledge solicited from the Sanskrit informants.[61] The Mughals also occasionally updated Sanskrit knowledge. For example, a list of ethnic and tribal groups retains the original *Mahābhārata* classifications, such as *uśīnara* and *kāmboja*, but also adds Sikhs, a new religious sect in early modern India.[62] In such instances, the Mughals viewed Sanskrit knowledge as pertinent enough to current concerns to merit contemporary revision.

In addition to individual words, the *Razmnāmah* also contains at least one extended quotation of Sanskrit that operates more as a literary signal than linguistically meaningful text. The translators insert several full Sanskrit verses in the *Ādi Parvan* during a scene replete with *ʿajāʾib* features. In this section, the sage Astika halts Janamejaya's snake sacrifice, thus rescuing the snakes from death. The relieved snakes offer Astika a boon in thanks, and he requests a spell (*afsūn*) against venomous bites. The snakes graciously oblige, reciting several Sanskrit verses that the *Razmnāmah* gives in transliteration without any further gloss.[63] The linguistic meaning of these Sanskrit lines was apparently irrelevant to the Persian translators. Rather, the Mughals were interested in the magical force contained in the Sanskrit sounds, a translation phenomenon that Ronit Ricci has described as a "certain power associated with the incomprehensible."[64] Later Persianate translators cite occasional Sanskrit verses in order to prove that they relied on Indian texts or to capture the aesthetic beauty of Sanskrit poetry.[65] In contrast, the *Razmnāmah*'s Sanskrit lines serve as an incantation whose very syllables ensure protection. The transliterated verses quickly became corrupt in later manuscripts, but the Sanskrit spelling was never cut or translated. Sometimes scribes even drew attention to the lines, such as by writing them in red ink.[66] At least three later manuscripts contain marginal annotations by later readers (or scribes) that reconstruct these lines in Devanagari script, but still no translation (see figures 3.3 and 3.4).[67] Some Sanskrit expressions cannot be put into Persian words.

Last, the *Razmnāmah* contains numerous lengthy lists of Sanskrit names and titles. Most books of the Persian translation have several such lists, whether epithets of Surya (the sun god), names of gods and sages, or the hundred sons of Dhritarashtra.[68] Such catalogue-style information accurately reflects the Sanskrit *Mahābhārata*, but it had also long been privileged in Islamicate encounters with India. Al-Bīrūnī carefully transcribed

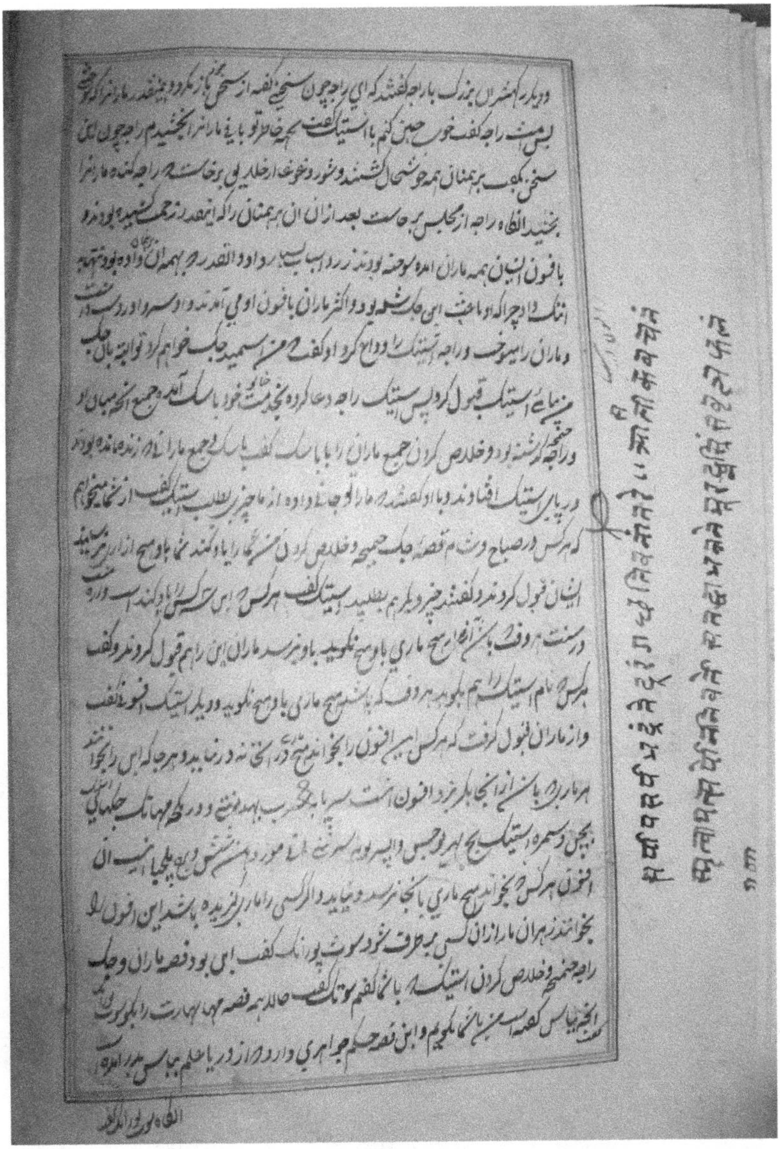

FIGURE 3.3 Folio from book 1 of the *Razmnāmah* with the Sanskrit spell against snakes reconstructed in Devanagari.

MS. PATNA, KHUDA BAKHSH LIBRARY, PERSIAN 2714, FOL. 29B

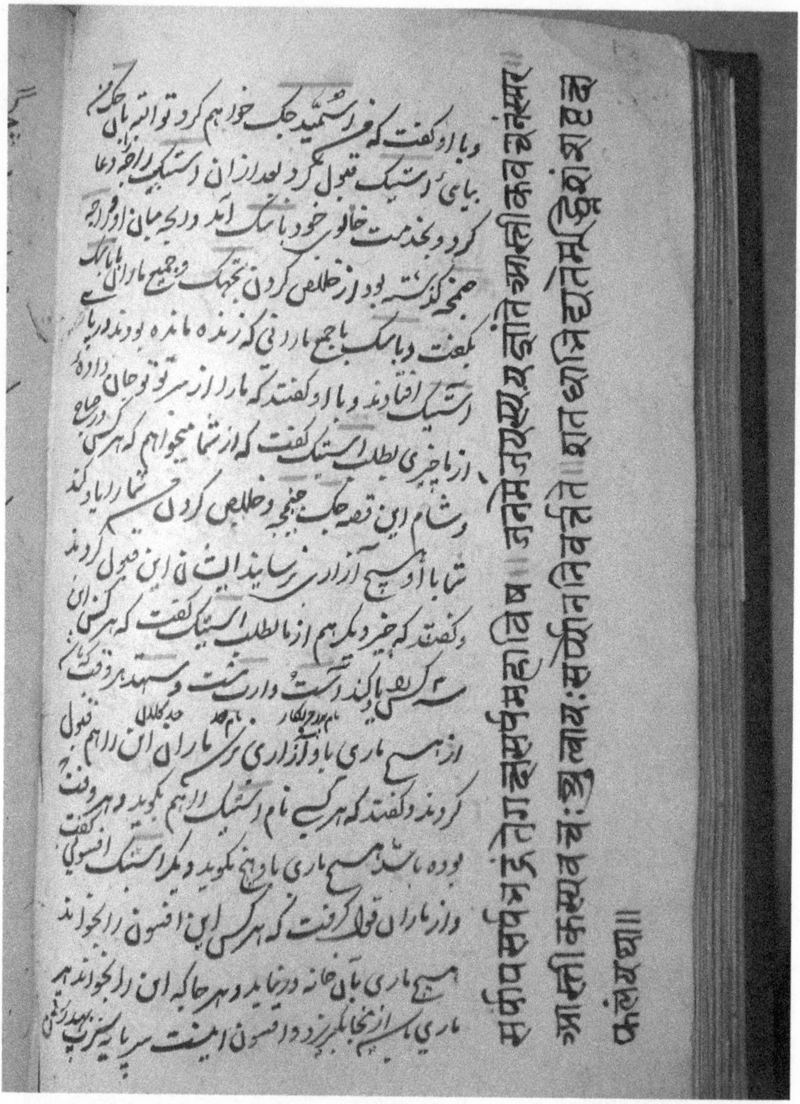

FIGURE 3.4 Folio from book 1 of the *Razmnāmah* with the Sanskrit spell against snakes reconstructed in Devanagari.

MS. OXFORD, BODLEIAN LIBRARY, OUSELEY 239, FOL. 31B

place-names from the *purāṇas* in his eleventh-century Arabic account of the subcontinent.[69] In the early sixteenth century Babur, founder of the Mughal dynasty, inventoried local names of Indian animals, flora, and fauna in his Turkish memoirs.[70] The *Razmnāmah* expands on this trend in its sheer number of Sanskrit lists. Moreover, in the early manuscript tradition, *Razmnāmah* scribes were often careful to write out diacritic marks for the Sanskrit words so that their pronunciation was clear in the Persian script (which does not normally indicate short vowels).[71] Later scribes frequently dropped the diacritics and bungled the words, but all copied the lists nonetheless. Some even emphasized their importance by overlining or numbering the names.[72] Even when intelligibility ceased, the idea remained current that foregrounding the epic's foreign, Sanskrit origins was an essential aspect of the Mughal *Mahābhārata*.

Whereas the Mughals preserved many Sanskrit words, they took more liberties with religious elements of the plot. To be sure, the Persian text reproduces much of the *Mahābhārata*'s theological framework intact, including the concept of *avatāras* (incarnations of gods), Sanskrit terms for "god," and many specific deities and their stories.[73] At the same time, however, the translators overlay the entire story line with a monotheistic Islamic deity. For example, at the opening of the *Razmnāmah*, Brahma is replaced by the Islamic God (*khudāvand*): "When the *sūtapūrānik* [narrator, *sūtapaurāṇika* in Sanskrit] knew that Shaunaka and the others desired to hear this story, he began the tale. He first invoked the name of God, Great Be His Glory and Magnificent His Bounty [*jalla jalālahu wa ʿamma nawālahu*]."[74]

This monotheistic God who prompts Arabic praises appears frequently throughout the *Razmnāmah*, but not always at the expense of Hindu gods. The translators commonly place Allah alongside his Hindu counterparts in haphazard ways. For instance, during the Great War Duryodhana boasts about venerating an Islamic deity described as Creator (*āfarīdgār*) and God (*khudāvand*). After Duryodhana reminds the cosmos of his virtuous rule and monotheistic piety, the heavens rain down flowers and *gandharva* songs, which are both typically associated with Hindu deities.[75] Elsewhere in the story, in an apparent theological innovation, Hindu gods are even recast as intermediaries between humans and Allah. During a digression into the saga of the *Rāmāyaṇa*, for instance, Rama's son Lava praises the sun god Surya by marveling, "Whatever people ask of *khudā* [the Islamic God], you serve as the mediator and petition *khudā*."[76]

The story of Nala and Damayanti presents a striking case study for the blended religious landscape of Akbar's *Mahābhārata*. In the tale,

Nala attends the self-choice ceremony (*svayaṃvara*) where Damayanti will select her husband. Damayanti desires Nala, but four Hindi gods take on Nala's appearance to dupe her into picking one of them as her bridegroom. In the Sanskrit text, Damayanti beseeches the scheming gods to desist from their deceit.[77] But, in Persian, in the midst of Hindu deities who all look like Nala, Damayanti prays to "God, the Exalted and Glorified" (*khudā-yi ʿazz wa jall*).[78] She then calls upon God as "O Solver of Obstacles and Guide for the Lost."[79] Here the Islamic reference is unmistakable as Solver (*gushāyandah*) and Guide (*rāhnumā*) correspond to two Qurʾanic names for God.[80]

The Islamic notion of a single nonincarnate God stands in stark contrast to the legions of physically present, often devious Hindu deities in the *Mahābhārata*. Nonetheless, even the periodic incorporation of an all-powerful God likely rendered the *Mahābhārata* more understandable and palatable to Islamicate readers. The pairing of Allah with Indian gods also placed the *Razmnāmah* within a known lineage of Indo-Islamic works. Beginning in the fourteenth century Hindavi Sufi romances had mixed these two religious traditions, often starting out with a strong Islamic framework and then featuring Indian deities throughout the story.[81]

While for the most part Islamic and Hindu traditions comfortably coexist in the *Razmnāmah*, the Mughals indicate discomfort with the perceived Hindu message of the *Bhagavadgītā* by drastically shortening and altering this section. In roughly the middle of the *Mahābhārata*, the *Bhagavadgītā* constitutes the final attempt to address the moral ambiguities of war before the devastating slaughter ensues. Time seems to stand still with armies arrayed on both sides of the battlefield as Krishna, an incarnation of the Hindu god Vishnu, lobbies the reluctant warrior Arjuna to fight by way of a philosophically dense discourse about the nature of the universe, dharma, and human action. In comparison with seven hundred or so verses in Sanskrit, the *Bhagavadgītā* occupies a mere few pages of the *Razmnāmah*.[82] The Persian version gives a bare-bones sketch of the conversation, including Krishna's contention that Arjuna is not morally culpable for killing his kinsmen and should join in the impending carnage. But it eliminates most of the source version's abstract reflections on the different types of yoga and other philosophical concepts so that the focus remains on the battle itself rather than providing an ethical climax of the epic.

The abridged *Bhagavadgītā* stands in stark contrast to more expansive sections of the *Razmnāmah*. Most notably, the translators elaborate Bhishma's political advice in the *Śānti Parvan* (*Book of Peace*) even beyond the Sanskrit original, as I discuss in the next section. However, Akbar's translators also truncate other religiously tinted portions of the text, such as a segment on pilgrimage locations in book 9.[83] Thus, it seems that the Mughals wished to avoid the theological content of the *Mahābhārata* where possible.[84] This choice is especially noteworthy in light of the Mughals' enthusiastic explication of Indian religious ideas in other works. For instance, in his *Āʾīn-i Akbarī*, Abū al-Faẕl details the tenets of nine Indian philosophical schools as well as Hindu, Jain, and Buddhist religious practices. A Persian work on Indian philosophy attributed to Fayẓī lists the *Bhagavadgītā* as one of its sources, along with the *Yogavāsiṣtha* and the *Bhāgavata Purāṇa*.[85] The *Bhagavadgītā* itself was rendered into Persian as a freestanding text several times during Mughal rule, and the first translation may have been in Akbar's court.[86] But the Mughals decided that such topics were outside the bounds of the *Book of War*.

The Mughal translators confirm their understanding of the *Bhagavadgītā* as theologically awkward by adding a much stronger Islamic framework to this section than is present in the *Razmnāmah* overall. The Persian *Bhagavadgītā* opens like the Sanskrit with Arjuna instructing Krishna to position their chariot between the two armies ready for war.[87] When Arjuna has his crisis of conscience, however, the Persian Krishna speaks to him as a wise teacher but not as a divine incarnation.[88] The *Razmnāmah* Krishna articulates the distinction between himself as a messenger and God at the close of the *Bhagavadgītā*:

> So long as I am ignorant of what God Exalted [*khudāvand-i taʿālá*] has ordained, I do not interfere. If I had not known the state of the Kauravas and the wrath of God Exalted toward them, I would never have come to the battlefield and encouraged you in this matter. But I know that they all must be killed and that therein is the happiness of God Exalted.[89]

While the religious content of the *Bhagavadgītā* compelled the Mughals to thoroughly rework this section of the epic, they were not consistent in their vision of a prophetlike Krishna. Elsewhere in the *Razmnāmah* Krishna is portrayed as an Indian *deva* and alternatively equated to *khudā*, the Islamic God.[90]

In light of this variable approach, we can most fruitfully understand the treatment of religious elements in the *Razmnāmah* as reaching toward cultural accommodation for a predominantly Islamic audience rather than tied to any calculated theological objectives. The translators themselves may have had no other way of understanding the text than by some rough parity with their own religious thinking. Thus, they reframe an overly Hindu *Bhagavadgītā* within a monotheistic framework while truncating the text to avoid devoting too much time to either Hindu or Islamic theology. Earlier translations frequently elided Hindu religious ideas to a much greater degree. For example, the fourteenth-century adaptation of Varāhamihira's *Bṛhatsaṃhitā* (*Great Compendium*) omits eight chapters dealing with Hindu idols and religious practices "because of the heresy" (*sabab-i kufr*) contained therein.[91] In contrast, Mughal translators appear unconcerned with transmitting potentially blasphemous ideas and at one point in the *Razmnāmah* even detail the origins of idol worship.[92] The Mughals adopted some religious elements in order to make a foreign work intelligible to a new readership while still striving toward some conception of faithfulness to the text. Thus, in sections such as Damayanti's *svayaṃvara*, God and the gods share the stage.

The Mughal translators added a decidedly Persianate, courtly context to the *Razmnāmah* by quoting Persian poetry. The majority of the *Razmnāmah* is written in prose, but the translators also insert sporadic verses, taken largely from the great masters of Persian literature, including Niẓāmī, Ḥāfiẓ, Saʿdī, Sanāʾī, Anvarī, and Rūdakī.[93] The poems are unattributed in the translation, but an educated reader would have been expected to recognize such verses and their literary resonances.[94] By inlaying the *Razmnāmah* with a rich grid of intertextual literary associations, the Mughal translators participated in a long-standing Persianate method of using quoted poetry to enhance the weight and appeal of a new prose work.[95] This strategy is also pursued in a more limited way in other Persian translations of Sanskrit texts sponsored by Akbar, such as the *Panchākhyānah* (*Five Stories*), which quotes Ḥāfiẓ and Saʿdī.[96] Additionally, interpolating intertextual references was a common assimilation strategy in premodern translation projects more broadly, such as Chinese translations of Sanskrit texts between the third and fifth centuries C.E.[97]

In the *Razmnāmah*, poetry quotations often serve to reformulate core narrative and emotional moments according to Persianate aesthetic sensibilities. For example, Arjuna's son, Abhimanyu, knew how to penetrate the Kauravas' superb lines of defense but sadly not how to exit and so sacrificed his own life in order to advance the Pandavas' military position. In meditation on his untimely death, the *Razmnāmah* poignantly summarizes, "If an old man of ninety years dies it is not strange. / What is tragic is when they say a young man has passed."[98] Faced with the distressing fall of Bhishma, the Kaurava patriarch, the soldiers similarly recite a series of verses by Sanāʾī lamenting the dismal state of the world.[99]

The translators also insert verses into the mouths of the epic heroes, who then speak the language of Persian poetics. For instance, after the war is over, Yudhishthira mourns the loss of many relatives. He especially grieves for Karna, the Pandavas' elder half brother, who nonetheless fought on the side of the Kauravas:

> Now I have regained the places that my ancestors held. But one thing that deeply saddens and distresses me is that Bhishma, our lord and benefactor, Dronacarya, everyone's teacher, and Karna, our elder brother, have passed away. Without them I will gain no enjoyment or pleasure from this kingdom and rulership. I see Karna's houses—where learned men always used to recite the Vedas and where religious men and scholars always used to gather and where great alms used to be found—now those houses are empty. The place where, if a needy person came, he found so many alms that he would cry out of pure happiness . . .[100]

In order to capture the emptiness of Karna's house and his own overwhelming grief, the *Razmnāmah* Yudhishthira next utters the following famous lines by Muʿizzī:

> I see a land devoid of the face of my beloved.
> I see a meadow empty of the stature of that upright cypress.
> That place where that beloved used to wander in the garden with friends
> Is now the dwelling of the wolf and fox, the domain of wild asses and vultures.[101]

These four lines invoke the Persian trope of a lost love, expressed through her now deserted camp after the caravan has departed. Persian literature possesses extensive imagery associated with the beloved and abandoned places that has no connection to Sanskrit. Yet these lines poignantly express the *Razmnāmah* Yudhishthira's pain as an aestheticized, Persianate emotion.

While the Mughals embrace the use of poetry in the *Razmnāmah*, this type of cultural overlay also proved problematic at times, particularly when combined with possible theological references. One of the few-recorded incidents concerning the translation process brings to the fore Mughal anxiety about how poetry might covertly impose Islamic ideas on the Indian epic. Badāʾūnī, one of the translators of the text, describes Akbar's vehement accusation against him in this vein:

> [Akbar] called me forth from the *jharoka* in the public and private audience hall and said to Shaykh Abū al-Faẕl, "We imagined that this person [Badāʾūnī] was a young, unworldly adherent of Sufism, but he has turned out to be such a bigoted follower of Islamic law that no sword can slice the jugular vein of his bigotry."[102]

Here the king couched his complaint within a view of the strict application of religious law as opposed to Sufism, an oft-cited conflict that dates back to the early days of Islam.[103] Akbar next specified that the text prompting his outburst was the *Razmnāmah* and that Naqīb Khān had personally testified on the matter. Badāʾūnī assured his king, "I am no more than a servant, a translator. Whatever the Indian wise men have explained, I have translated precisely."[104] Islamicate writers often claimed to be merely repeating others' stories in order to deny culpability for the content of their narratives.[105] Only after proclaiming his innocence does Badāʾūnī cite the verse that had stirred up so much trouble, namely a half line authored by Ḥāfiẓ and inserted in the fifth book of the *Razmnāmah*: "Every action has its reward and every deed its recompense."[106]

According to Badāʾūnī, Akbar recoiled from the use of this verse because of its alleged allusion to the Islamic Day of Judgment, complete with Munkir and Nakir, two angels who judge the dead. As I noted earlier, the *Razmnāmah* is full of references to an Islamic God, both as a replacement for Hindu deities and alongside them. If we consider the translation along with Abū al-Faẕl's preface to the text, which is replete with praise of Allah, the Islamic context becomes even more apparent. In light of all this, Akbar is unlikely to have been upset merely because a single line of poetry contained an indirect religious reference. Rather, it seems that the emperor was concerned that specific Islamic theological ideas, such as the Day of Judgment and its accompanying angels, might have crept into what was supposed to be a pre-Islamic Indian tale.[107]

Badāʾūnī defended himself by recourse to the *Mahābhārata*'s internal religious framework. He argued that the epic teaches the ideas of reward and punishment, because everybody spends time in both heaven and hell after death.[108] In the end, Badāʾūnī successfully convinced Akbar of his faithfulness to the text, and Ḥāfiẓ's half line remained in the *Razmnāmah*.[109] Nonetheless, this episode indicates the thorny problems of cultural comprehension that the Mughal translators faced in translating a text across literary traditions. By inserting an Islamicate proverb into the *Mahābhārata*, Badāʾūnī was potentially unfaithful to the original Sanskrit meaning, at least in the eyes of one (especially important) reader. The project of integrating Sanskrit knowledge into Indo-Persian culture was an intricate process and could give rise to multiple interpretations and even volatile reactions among Mughal readers.

POLITICAL ADVICE FOR AKBAR

In addition to their literary interests, the Mughals understood bringing the *Mahābhārata* into Persian as a thoroughly political project that was intimately connected to Akbar's kingship. In his preface to the *Razmnāmah*, composed a few years after the translation itself, Abū al-Faẕl categorizes the entire text as history (*tārīkh*), a genre that had long dovetailed with imperial objectives. Moreover, he names royal advice as a core motivating factor for the translation:

> Likewise, the minds of most people, particularly great kings, yearn to listen to histories [*tavārīkh*]. All-encompassing, divine wisdom has made the science of history, which offers examples to the wise, dear to their hearts so that having taken advice from past events and counted it advantageous for the present, they pass their cherished time in things pleasing to God. Thus rulers need above all others to listen to the tales of their predecessors.[110]

Later in his preface, Abū al-Faẕl reiterates the *Mahābhārata*'s royal relevance when he describes the work as consisting of "advice, guidance, stories, and descriptions of war and feasting," or, more concisely, kingship.[111]

The Mughals treated book 12, called the *Śānti Parvan* in Sanskrit, as the crux of the *Mahābhārata*'s political commentary, which they indicate in several ways. The translators rendered the *Śānti Parvan* into Persian at disproportionate length to the rest of the text so that the book constitutes nearly 25 percent of the Persian *Razmnāmah*.[112] Moreover, they quote poetry extensively in the first two of three sections of the *Śānti Parvan*, which address kingly ethics (*rājadharma*) and ethics in times of emergency (*āpaddharma*).[113] The only other comparable concentration of poetry quotations in the *Razmnāmah* occurs in the *Udyoga Parvan* (*Book of Effort*), which focuses on negotiations to avoid civil war.[114] Indeed, a later retranslator of the *Mahābhārata* in Akbar's court singles out the *Udyoga* and *Śānti parvans* as books of "guidance and instruction" (*mashvarat ū maṣlaḥat*) and "advice and counsels" (*pand ū naṣāʾiḥ*), respectively.[115] In his preface, Abū al-Faẕl also characterizes Bhishma's advice to Yudhishthira, contained in the *Śānti* and *Anuśāsana parvans*, as particularly pertinent to sovereigns.[116] The translators also changed the framing and content of book 12 so that it became a definitively Mughal mirror for kings that spoke directly to Akbar.

The Mughals began refashioning the *Śānti Parvan* by opening the Persian rendering of the book with the martial story of Barbarik. In the Sanskrit *Mahābhārata*, the *Śānti Parvan* commences with Yudhishthira lamenting the dead.[117] In contrast, Barbarik's tale showcases Yudhishthira taking pride in the recent military triumph and thereby reframes the entire book with a positive view of war.[118] The story starts with the Pandavas fighting among themselves regarding who had ensured victory. After much bickering, they posed the question to the head of Barbarik, which had been lopped off by Krishna and positioned above the field of Kurukshetra for the entire war.[119] After hearing Barbarik describe celebrated battle motifs and events, including Krishna's all-destroying *cakra* and the defeat of the elephant-mounted Bhagadatta, the Pandavas fell at Krishna's feet. Krishna then ordered Barbarik's head removed and burned with the rest of his body. The Mughals' penchant for *ʿajāʾib* aspects of Sanskrit stories largely explains the allure of this bizarre episode, which was illustrated in the master imperial copy of the translation.[120] But the story also allows for a victorious reprise of central combat moments, which was perhaps more attractive to Akbar, who was constantly expanding his kingdom, than King Yudhishthira's mourning a costly victory.

After the odd tale of Barbarik, the Persian *Book of Peace* next turns to the story of Karna, which is recounted in significant detail and with a notably positive spin, often beyond the parallel portion of the Sanskrit text.[121] Perhaps Akbar had a soft spot for Karna's position as an exiled half brother owing to his own clashes with Mirza Hakim, his half brother based in Kabul.[122] Additionally, Akbar's fascination with illumination theory likely undergirded the Mughal interest in Karna, the son of Surya. Akbar repeatedly turned to light imagery in his imperial self-fashioning. For example, in the opening of the *Akbarnāmah*, Abū al-Faẕl narrates that Alanquva, a Mongol ancestor of the Mughals, conceived triplet sons through a beam of divine light. According to Abū al-Faẕl, the divine light was passed on in a latent form through the generations until it manifested itself visibly in Akbar.[123] The *Razmnāmah* echoes this Mughal legend by modifying the story of Karna's conception in book 1 so that his mother was impregnated by Surya, the sun god, via a ray of light (in Sanskrit, the conception occurs the old-fashioned way).[124] The Mughal translators do not maintain a parallel between Akbar and Karna throughout the text, but they dwell on Karna, especially his association with light, wherever possible. Playing on his origins, for example, when Karna was decapitated in battle, several *Razmnāmah* manuscripts depict a ray of light emerging from his body and winding upward toward the sun (figure 3.5).[125]

After expanding upon the stories of Barbarik and Karna, the Persian translators reduce the twenty-seven-chapter Sanskrit debate over whether Yudhishthira will ascend the throne, the final framing section of the *Śānti Parvan*, to a mere two pages.[126] The Sanskrit epic describes Yudhishthira's disinclination to rule at length. In the end he relents to the arguments of sages and family members but not before putting forth some of the weightiest criticisms of kingly rule in the *Mahābhārata*.[127] In contrast, the Persian Yudhishthira quickly becomes convinced by Arjuna's argument that "if you want to worship, there is no worship equivalent to the justice of padshahs" and undertakes preparations for his coronation.[128] Here Yudhishthira's brief hesitation merely moves the story line forward as opposed to being a formidable part of the *Mahābhārata*'s larger commentary on the grave harms of royal ambitions.

Throughout the remainder of book 12, the Mughal translators reformulate the content of Bhishma's wisdom in order to speak to Akbar's interests as a Mughal sovereign. In some cases, the changes are subtle. For instance, where the Sanskrit text narrates the establishment of dharma in the world, the Persian elaborates on the virtues of a padshah, a Perso-Islamic ruler.[129] The story of Manu offers a compelling example of a significant rewriting where the Mughal translators openly invoke Akbar's name. The *Razmnāmah* translates Manu's story with its own Perso-Islamic slant, which ends,

> Raja [Manu] showed compassion and mercy to the entire world and spoke to everyone with visible joy. Day by day, his majesty and pomp increased, and many years passed on earth in his rule and good fortune. Because of his virtuous conduct, God Exalted granted him a long, generous life. It is hoped, according to the magnificence of God, Praised and Exalted, that the shadow of the justice and compassion of his most exalted majesty, Akbar Shah—under whose justice, compassion, and grace all people in the world rest—would be perpetual and everlasting so long as the world exists.[130]

FIGURE 3.5 Arjuna slays Karna in the *Razmnāmah*, 1616–1617.

ART INSTITUTE OF CHICAGO, RESTRICTED GIFT OF THE JOSEPH & HELEN REGENSTEIN FOUNDATION, 1980.277

Here the translators draw upon an earlier teaching in Manu's story that "the first responsibility of subjects is to pray for their king" and apply it to their own political situation.[131] They furthermore laud Manu and Akbar with nearly the same breath, which connects Akbar with a paradigmatic Indian monarch. The passage concludes with verses quoted from Saʿdī:

> O God! This king, a friend to those in need,
> in whose shadow lies the refuge of the world,
> may you grant him long life on this earth.
> May you enliven his heart through obedience to God.
> So long as there is day and night, may the king be on the throne,
> and may prosperity reach the zenith of the sky.[132]

The voice that articulates these good wishes remains tantalizingly ambiguous. The speaker is either Bhishma, who praises Akbar across the reaches of time, or the Mughal translators, who step outside the narrative framework of the text to offer a few kind words to their patron. Either way, temporal and narrative boundaries are breached to celebrate Akbar's eminence and to immortalize him through inclusion in one of India's great epics.

Given the stress on kingship in the *Razmnāmah* and particularly Akbar's cameo appearance in the ancient Indian world, it seems accurate to conclude that the translation was designed largely to promote Mughal political objectives.[133] However, the precise relationship between Emperor Akbar and the *Mahābhārata* remains unexamined. Legitimation theory proves unhelpful, because it assumes that the Mughals needed to validate their rule through the discourses of Sanskrit (and Persian) aesthetics without specifying the impetus, means, or audience for such a justification. Moreover, while political objectives are important, so too are literary and rhetorical aspects of the *Razmnāmah*, such as its Sanskrit vocabulary, religious amalgamation, and Persian poetry. In many ways, we are best served by abandoning the modern fantasy that there is a split between literary and political worlds. On the contrary, the Mughals understood aesthetic and cultural concerns to fall within the purview of the imperial project. Nonetheless, texts were not reducible to being instruments of power for the Mughals. Instead, exerting influence within literary and cultural realms was itself a valid and vital royal activity in early modern India. The *Mahābhārata*'s heritage of mixing Sanskrit political and aesthetic modes of discourse is largely what made this epic an appealing work to translate for Akbar's court.

POWER POLITICS IN ABŪ AL-FAẒL'S PREFACE

After its initial rendering, the Mughals continued to see unexplored potential in the *Mahābhārata* and returned to their Persian translation several times to supplement and adapt the text. The first addition was made in 1587 when Akbar requested his vizier, Abū al-Faẓl, to compose a preface that thereafter accompanied the translated epic.[134] I have referenced this work several times already, but a brief overview of its contents is helpful here. Abū al-Faẓl's preface comprises three discrete sections: an elaborate encomium of Akbar, an exegesis of the imperial motivations for sponsoring the *Razmnāmah*, and a synopsis of Brahmanical beliefs (including the *Mahābhārata* story). The panegyric and plot summary constitute the overwhelming majority of the work, but the most revealing segment is the succinct central passage on why Akbar supported the project.[135] Here Abū al-Faẓl provides the most direct contemporary exposition available of the intellectual framework that sustained translation activity under Akbar. Abū al-Faẓl places the *Razmnāmah* at the center of current political disputes about the nature of Indo-Persian knowledge and the extent of Akbar's authority.

Abū al-Faẓl articulates several overlapping reasons for royal support of the *Razmnāmah*. I have discussed his final claim, namely that the *Razmnāmah* enunciates kingly advice. Additionally, he identifies religious and intellectual tensions that the *Razmnāmah* will resolve:

> When, with his perfect perception, [Akbar] found that the disputes between Muslims and the denials of the Hindus had become excessive and their rejection of each other appeared to be beyond all measure, [his] insightful mind decided to translate the revered books of each group into other tongues. The holy one of the age [Akbar] did this so that by the blessing of his words both sides would abandon faultfinding and rebellion in favor of becoming seekers of Truth [*haqq*] and, after having become aware of each other's virtues and faults, would make commendable efforts to correct themselves.[136]

Modern scholars have often emphasized communal conflicts between Hindus and Muslims when interpreting this passage.[137] Abū al-Faẓl indeed addresses interreligious discord ("their rejection of each other"), but he foregrounds "disputes between Muslims" (*nizāʿ-i farāʾīq-i millat-i muḥammadī*) and "denials of the Hindus" (*juḥūd-i hunūd*) and goes on to tackle issues within each group individually. As Rajeev Kinra has pointedly underscored, intracommunity relations were a significant part of a Mughal ruling strategy that is often described as *ṣulḥ-i kull*, which literally means "universal peace" but is perhaps more usefully rendered as "complete civility."[138] Moreover, as we will see, Abū al-Fażl also means to include intellectual and political controversies in these internal struggles. His solution to such disagreements is far more radical than scholars have recognized. Here the rest of the preface and larger courtly debates are essential to correctly understand Abū al-Fażl's politico-intellectual agendas.

Early in his preface, Abū al-Fażl outlines a specific dispute between Akbar and certain Muslim factions at court that the new *Razmnāmah* will decisively resolve. He begins broadly by explaining that people have long been ignorant and intolerant of the few who grasped real truth:

> For the entirety of recorded human history, the soul has been unenlightened and sight blind. . . . If sometimes good fortune grabbed some poor soul by the collar of existence and showed him hidden secrets . . . then good men in the world from their innocence and pitiful hearts and bad quarrelsome men from their bad inner nature and sedition sent [the poor soul] on the road of nonexistence and toward the house of oblivion and annihilation.[139]

Next, Abū al-Fażl describes how kings have typically left such matters in the hands of religious leaders who have proven themselves unworthy:

> Exalted kings—who are the pillars of the world and are usually expected to order the affairs of ordinary creatures—have typically not paid attention to the secrets of religious leaders in this matter [the rejection of the wise]. If by chance this reached their sublime ears, then [kings] have necessarily counted it among the affairs of religion [*dīn*] and entrusted it to religiously affiliated men who have taken over the office of issuing appropriate decrees, are connected with issues of Islamic law, and are leaders of the lords of traditional imitation [*taqlīd*]. Even though [religiously affiliated men] are ignorant and stupid leaders, [kings] have kept themselves from slander and speaking ill [of them].[140]

Abū al-Fażl declines to elaborate further at this point, but Akbar had been engaged in a power struggle with traditional Islamic leaders and certain

Sufi communities since the 1570s.[141] Akbar clashed with these groups on a range of issues, including tax laws, his numerous marriages (far beyond the Islamic upper limit of four), and the proper character of an Islamic empire in India. The members of this opposition tended to espouse a more conservative interpretation of Islam than Akbar. Perhaps more important, they desired to maintain direct influence in the expanding Mughal Empire. Akbar soon began to curtail the authority of such Islamic leaders by claiming an enhanced definition of the bounds of his own sovereignty and even persecuted certain individuals directly.[142] By the mid-1580s, the Mughal king had formulated a decisive answer to this imperial problem: Akbar removed powers previously exercised by the ulama, notably their prerogative to define the boundaries of Islamic knowledge, and invested them in himself as emperor.[143]

Alluding to this ongoing power struggle, Abū al-Faẓl declares that Akbar will no longer allow the supposedly learned of Islam undeserved authority. Instead, the king offers himself as a superior replacement.

> But today is the time for expressing the hidden name and the moment of overflowing, all-inclusive compassion. In accordance with divine inspiration and God's will, the chosen of mankind and the best of the children of Adam, the world of the soul and the soul of the world, meaning the king of the age, is guiding my loyal pen with a mere trace of his generosity. His insightful eye and discerning heart endorse the resources of lofty perception and the ascertainment of subtleties of knowledge [*taḥqīq-i tadqīqāt-i dānish*], and [thereby] he brings good fortune to the public and elite.[144]

Abū al-Faẓl's dense writing style could easily cause a noninitiated reader to miss much of his argument's force here. He proposes nothing less than that the king supplant the role of theologians by recalibrating the nature of knowledge.

A wider intellectual context helps explicate this dual claim of Akbar's new delineation of acceptable intellectual practices and his ability to exercise such power. Abū al-Faẓl uses the vocabulary of *taqlīd* (imitation) versus *taḥqīq* (inquiry) to talk about a fresh frontier of knowledge. For the ulama of the day, knowledge was *taqlīd*, which Abū al-Faẓl viewed as mind-numbing, rote repetition that limited one's intellectual purview to blindly following previous Islamic thinkers.[145] In contrast, under Akbar knowledge will now be *taḥqīq*, an active investigation that admits new sources of wisdom, including Sanskrit texts.[146] In a 1602 letter to Prince

Murad, Akbar mentions the *Mahābhārata* in particular as dissuading its readers from crass imitation:

> MURAD asks: If one or two volumes of books were sent that are recommended by [Akbar's] exalted mind and might promote the intellect and discourage blind imitation [*taqlīd*], they would enhance my education.
>
> AKBAR replies: In the marshland of *taqlīd* such a book is rarely found. But for [Murad] the translation of the *Mahābhārat*, which is a strange tale and has recently become available, has been sent.[147]

Later Abū al-Fażl also explicitly discusses how translating the *Mahābhārata* provides access to a previously unknown intellectual tradition.[148]

In his preface Abū al-Fażl pays homage to his patron with dozens of different formulations that focus largely on the emperor's erudition and perfect comprehension. He is the master of arts ranging from carpentry to philosophy who "ends the impenetrable night of false knowledge [*taqlīd*] and inaugurates the morning of discernment."[149] In this vein, later court texts often characterize Akbar as the "Perfect Man" (*insān-i kāmil*, an idea adapted from the twelfth- and thirteenth-century philosopher Ibn al-Arabī) who constantly searches for new sources of understanding that enhance his excellence.[150] In his preface, Abū al-Fażl upholds Indian learning as a key part of Akbar's revolution of knowledge. Speaking of the king, he says,

> He is a potent speaker who, having gained knowledge of different languages of people in the world, speaks with all types of men about their customs and the subtleties of various tongues. Particularly regarding Sanskrit [*zabān-i hind*], which is far from the road of those born of the Turks, having become a true master, he discourses on innovative meanings and esoteric topics.
>
> Ask him to decipher the secrets of subtle speakers
> since other than Solomon he alone knows the language of the birds.[151]

The claim that Akbar knew Sanskrit, "the language of India," is more flattery than historical fact. But Abū al-Fażl's larger point here stands: the king created access to Indian classical learning. In contrast, more hard-line Islamic thinkers at court often condemned reading the books of other religious traditions, including Brahmanical texts, because such works may mislead even a faithful Muslim.[152] Abū al-Faẕl declared that the *Razmnāmah* should settle "disputes between Muslims" in this larger context of contestations over the proper sources of Islamic knowledge and the appropriate leadership of imperial figures.

Abū al-Faẕl next accuses Muslim theologians of willfully deceiving their own followers and offers the *Mahābhārata* as the antidote to such ruses. Focusing on a specific contention about the age of the world, he posits, "Common people among the Muslims . . . believe that the beginning of humanity was some seven thousand years ago." As a result,

> The beneficent mind [of Akbar] decided that [the *Mahābhārat*], which contains the explanation of the antiquity of the universe and its beings, and is even totally occupied with the ancient past of the world and its inhabitants, should be translated into a readily understood language, so that this group favored by divine mercy should become somewhat informed and retreat from this distasteful belief [in the recent creation of the world].[153]

Here Abū al-Faẕl explicitly imbues a non-Islamic, Indian text with the authority to overturn juridically affirmed Islamic theology. This argument lends a striking amount of credence to a Brahmanical story, particularly in comparison with contemporary Indo-Islamic works. Writing in the early seventeenth century, ʿAbd al-Raḥmān Chishtī likewise accepted the validity of Indian views on cyclical time but also drew upon Sufi thought to reason that Sanskrit and Islamic ideas on the subject actually agreed.[154] In contrast, Abū al-Faẕl subverts Islamic authority by decrying Muslim views as false. Moreover, rather than relying on Islamic leaders, Akbar wishes to empower "common people among the Muslims" to judge such matters for themselves, based on a translation that Akbar has made available.

Abū al-Faẕl imposes some limits on the *Razmnāmah* as an authoritative text, however. Later in his preface, he discusses the variable credibility of the *Mahābhārata* and how he expects thoughtful readers to rebuff parts of what they read therein. A case in point is the text's thirteen conflicting accounts of creation:

> But a person of sound judgment does not rely on the falseness of those different ideas. There is a part that the wise will examine and throw out of circulation. There is part that the intellect will not be able to understand. And there is a portion of it that the wise will agree to accept or consent to after much study and a penetrating glance.[155]

Expanding this logic to the entire epic, Abū al-Faẕl proclaims, "This strange division is not specific to this chapter, but rather [all] chapters include many designs of this book of rarities except for the advice, guidance, and manners for inner and outer rulership narrated by wise [*ḥakīm*] Bhishma that are generally approved by the intellectuals and liked by the wise."[156] Later, he again emphasizes,

> Speech of this extent and breadth, with these strange things and wonders, is not present in the other various histories [*tavārīkh*] of the world. There is no trace of this amazing speech in the accounts [*ṭabaqāt*] of the world. . . . Although the lords of the circle of truth do not hesitate to refute the details of this story, nonetheless it is right that the mind of an intelligent person with discerning vision should reflect and place the essence of these reported things in the realm of possibility.[157]

The Mughals also use the narrative framework of the epic to signal their hesitations about its overall truthfulness. In their continual mentions of the Indian storytellers who transmit the tale, the translators typically use the verbs *āvardan*, *nivīshtan*, and *akhbār kardan* (to relay, to write, and to tell) to brand the work as alleged (rather than fully accepted) history.[158] Nonetheless, court histories attest that Akbar engaged in certain Sanskrit-inspired religious practices, like sun veneration, against the counsel of the ulama.[159] In such actions Akbar promoted his dual projects to expand the breadth of Islamicate learning and suppress the influence of jurists.

In addition to Islamic contestations, Abū al-Faẕl also targets problems within the Hindu community. He defines *hindūs* to mean primarily Brahmans and identifies the *Mahābhārata* as "containing most of the principles and beliefs of the Brahmans of India."[160] In his exposition of the imperial motives for the translation, he accuses Brahmanical leaders of leading the masses into false convictions and having "faith in their own religion beyond all measure."[161] Akbar's proposed corrective was to translate Indian texts such as the *Mahābhārata* with "clear expressions" into a language intelligible beyond elite circles. Abū al-Faẕl hoped that, once Brahmans are enlightened about the content of their tradition, "simple believers will become so ashamed of their beliefs that they will become seekers of Truth [*haqq*]."[162] In this passage, Abū al-Faẕl plays on the multivalence of the word *haqq*, which means both truth and the Islamic God. He also explicitly enjoins Brahmans to be more open to Islamic learning and argues that Indian religious leaders "regard the group of those who are connected to the religion of Muḥammad [*dīn-i Aḥmadī*] as utterly foolish, and they refute this group ceaselessly, although they are unaware of its noble goals and special sciences."[163]

Abū al-Fażl gives little indication that he intends Hindus to embrace Islam wholesale rather than accept parts of its religious and intellectual insights, as he encouraged Muslims to do with respect to Sanskrit texts. However, other Mughal intellectuals take Abū al-Fażl's logic a step further and praise full-scale conversion.[164] As mentioned, in his colophon to the translation, Naqīb Khān, one of the *Razmnāmah* translators, lauds Shaykh Bhāvan, an Indian collaborator on the project, for having accepted Islam at the urging of Akbar. Badāʾūnī, Akbar's most high-volume translator, echoes the language of Abū al-Fażl's preface when he brags in another text to having personally drawn Hindus away from their religion: "On this matter [reincarnation] I have, on different occasions, debated at length with [Hindu] learned authorities and, with divine blessing, made them see their errors, such that some of them turned away from their own religion."[165] Shantanu Phukan has argued that conversion functioned in the Mughal imagination as a literary trope just as much as a historical process.[166] This idea usefully highlights the intellectual and aesthetic stakes involved in conversion narratives. But we cannot ignore that individuals such as Naqīb Khān and Badāʾūnī purported to be speaking of actual changes in religious affiliation. At a minimum, Mughal intellectuals viewed the conversion of Hindus as a legitimate (although not especially central) goal. Even Abū al-Fażl, who shies away from endorsing outright conversion, undeniably acclaims the *Razmnāmah*'s humbling influence on Brahmanical arrogance.

Modern scholars have frequently argued that the *Razmnāmah* was meant to encourage kingdom-wide harmony.[167] Indeed the *Razmnāmah* was likely intended as part of Akbar's project of "universal peace" (*ṣulḥ-i kull*). But Abū al-Fażl's preface clarifies that creating a Persian *Mahābhārata* promoted this imperial objective because the epic disproves particular Islamic and Brahmanical ideas. In this view, "universal peace" does not mean anything as bland as mutual toleration but rather indicates a high-stakes process of honest evaluation and self-correction. Elsewhere, such as in the *Tārīkh-i Alfī*, Mughal authors expressed a similar perspective that Akbar wished members of different traditions to learn about one another's teachings and then reform their own convictions.[168]

Abū al-Fażl's preface quickly became a constitutive part of the *Razmnāmah* that served as an important lens through which readers encountered the Persian translation. As the preface circulated with the text, Abū al-Faẓl also became personally associated with the *Razmnāmah*. A marginal note on an illustrated folio from a 1598–1599 *Razmnāmah* produced for the imperial court attests, "The linguists of both groups, the Muslims and the Hindus, wrote out the *Mahābhārat* together with Shaykh Abū al-Faẓl."[169] Abū al-Faẓl's involvement in the original translation process is unsubstantiated by Mughal histories and Naqīb Khān's colophon. But his name quickly became inseparable from the text. The preface also exerted substantial influence on other translations from Sanskrit in the Mughal context and beyond. For example, many later translators follow Abū al-Faẓl's example concerning what types of information to include in introductions to Indian works.[170] However, later prefaces do not echo Abū al-Faẓl's concern with internal court contestations in the 1580s regarding Akbar's absolute sovereignty. Even Abū al-Faẓl himself treated the *Mahābhārata* in the 1590s in his *Āʾīn-i Akbarī* as part of the history of Delhi and surrounding regions rather than applicable to immediate imperial disputes.[171] Akbar's court perhaps also realized the narrow import of Abū al-Faẓl's preface and so returned to the *Razmnāmah* to explore other possibilities for the epic two further times in the next twenty years.

AESTHETIC REVOLUTION THROUGH FAYẒĪ'S *MAHĀBHĀRAT*

In the late 1580s, Fayẓī reworked the first two books of the *Mahābhārata* in a mixture of prose and verse.[172] He takes his prose directly from the *Razmnāmah*, adjusting the language and vocabulary at times. He then sprinkles his own verses liberally throughout the text, inserting lines at least every few paragraphs. He also opens and closes each book with a series of poetic verses. At the end of his reworking of the *Ādi Parvan*, Fayẓī expresses his ambition to "complete all eighteen books of the epic"[173] and claims,

> In these eighteen I will depict the tumult of battle
> as eighteen thousand sights to behold.
> I will enliven the events of old
> to poetically narrate story by story.[174]

Despite his initial intentions, Fayẓī discontinued his retranslation after the second book.[175] In his incomplete *Mahābhārat*, Fayẓī nonetheless explores the potential of fusing his poetics with an Indian epic to generate a novel work of Persian literature.

Fayẓī proclaims his firm foothold in both Indian and Persian literary traditions as critical to the aesthetic impact of his *Mahābhārat*. In his larger oeuvre, Fayẓī often foregrounds his innovation, which participates in a broader trend in Indo-Persian poetry of this time toward "freshness of speech" (*tāza-gū'ī*).[176] In his *Mahābhārat*, he speaks of the original quality of his poetry as directly linked with retelling an Indian tale:

With a hundred charms I am bringing an ancient book
from Hindi into Persian, the language of the court [*darī*].
I stroll to see with friends
the idol temple of Hindustan.[177]

In the next line, however, Fayẓī carefully notes, "I remain based in the fire temples of Persia."[178] In a self-descriptive poem elsewhere, Fayẓī makes the similar dual claim, "I am a clever [*nuktah-parvar*] Indian parrot who in imagination / matches the sweet-singing [*naghmah-zan*] nightingale of Persia."[179] As a result of bringing together two literary worlds, Fayẓī asserts that his new *Mahābhārat* so stretches the limits of expression that the wise will proclaim to him, "You have brought Persian literature [*sukhan*] to a new end."[180]

While Fayẓī's poetry is his main addition to the *Razmnāmah*, he also draws attention to the importance of his prose. He writes, "I have wet the pen with the blood of the heart / so that my prose is not inferior to my poetry."[181] Fayẓī elegantly rewords the *Razmnāmah*'s language in many places. For example, the *Sabhā Parvan* (*Book of the Court*) begins with the oft-repeated phrase "then the narrators of the events of this tale have relayed"[182] Fayẓī transforms this standard line to indicate that his *Mahābhārat* is not merely an alleged account of the past but also a literary masterpiece, writing, "The caretakers of this garden of poetic speech and the interpreters of this ancient story have relayed . . ."[183] Over the course of Fayẓī's work, these subtle changes cultivate a perceptibly lyrical tone in contrast to the *Razmnāmah*'s treatment of the text as reported history.

Fayẓī's intertwining of poetry and prose further augments the literary quality of his *Mahābhārat*. Persian histories and story collections had frequently blended verse and prose, and Fayẓī's *Mahābhārat* stands somewhere between these two genres.[184] Fayẓī's poetry is generally closely connected with the epic narrative but also invokes Persianate cultural resonances. For example, Fayẓī commences his tale by introducing the narrator:

> They say that in days past there was an ascetic called Lomaharshan who had set his heart in search for a true purpose out of exalted desires and lofty ambitions. He had a son dear to him called Ugrashravas who had learned the arts of wisdom and virtue from the wise men of the age and had mastered the knowledge of the Ved and Puran. Because of this, he had received the title of *sūtapūrānik*.[185]

Fayẓī then offers a few verses:

> Glory to that mine of water and dust
> that produces so many glittering jewels.
> May it be a happy day at the court
> that has such a star to illuminate the night.
> How fortunate is that garden
> from which friends' affection blooms.
> You call him a noble son
> because he elevates his father's name.[186]

These lines emphasize the royal milieu of the *Mahābhārata*'s recitation, but they also allude to the *Razmnāmah*'s own production context at the Mughal court. Moreover, the poetry evokes Persian tropes, including an emphasis on gardens and friendship.

Fayẓī also features Akbar prominently in his *Mahābhārat* by praising the king in his opening and closing verses to each book. He credits Akbar with envisioning this new Persian *Mahābhārat*, proclaiming, "The poetry is mine and the ambition the shah's."[187] In his retelling of the epic story, Fayẓī also further plays upon the few oblique references to the Mughals in the *Razmnāmah*. For example, I mentioned earlier how the *Razmnāmah* reformulates the story of Karna's conception to evoke Akbar's claim to be the manifestation of a divine light passed down through his Mongol ancestors. Fayẓī expands upon the *Razmnāmah*'s reference to Akbar's royal light (*farr*) by adding a few lines in praise of the sun that extol it twice with the Persian honorific *haẓrat*.[188] In short, Fayẓī viewed part of his task in composing a new *Mahābhārat* to more closely link the epic with Akbar through transforming the epic into Persian literature. As he succinctly puts his intentions in one of the closing verses to his *Ādi Parvan*, "I am the eulogizer of the throne of the King of Kings."[189]

Despite Fayẕī's attempt, Indo-Persian thinkers ultimately decided that the *Mahābhārata* did not possess the same aesthetic potential to become Persian literature as did other Sanskrit texts. Nobody penned another versified Persian *Mahābhārat* after Fayẕī.[190] In contrast, poets produced around two dozen Persian versions of the *Rāmāyaṇa*, many of which were versified, well into the nineteenth century.[191] Additionally, while Fayẕī's *Mahābhārat* was popular among Indo-Persian readers, they often confused both its contents and authorship. Fayẕī's work was frequently reabsorbed into the *Razmnāmah* in later manuscript copies, offered in lieu of the original Persian *Ādi* and *Sabhā parvans*.[192] Many manuscripts do not attribute Fayẕī's translation properly, whereas others mistakenly ascribe the entire *Razmnāmah* to the poet. Perhaps most tellingly, later copies often omit many of Fayẕī's verses, and most manuscripts either heavily abridge or exclude altogether his opening and closing lines of poetry.[193] In short, as with Abū al-Faẕl's preface, the specific contours and immediate court context of Fayẕī's project were lost over time.

While Fayẕī abandoned his rewriting of the *Razmnāmah* after two books, he continued to glimpse great potential in adapting Sanskrit materials and returned to an Indian story in his *Nal-Daman* (1594). *Nal-Daman* is a *mas̱navī* based on the love story of Nala and Damayanti, which Fayẕī heard from an Indian informant and is also told in book 3 of the *Razmnāmah*.[194] Fayẕī followed in a grand Indian tradition in both Sanskrit and vernacular languages of treating the saga of Nala and Damayanti as creative poetic material.[195] Whether Fayẕī was aware of this larger context remains uncertain, but he emphasizes that his *mas̱navī* is an Indian work, albeit one that will revolutionize Persian poetry.

> I have become exceedingly tipsy
> because I have wine from the sugar of India.
> When I sprinkle drafts across time
> "Well done!" will pour out of the wine and cup.[196]

However, unlike his *Mahābhārat*, which is a relatively close rewriting of a direct translation, his *Nal-Daman* fully integrates an Indian story within Persianate poetic frameworks. Most notably, Fayẕī consciously imitates the Persian poet Niẓāmī throughout the romance.[197] Fayẕī's *Nal-Daman* proved to be incredibly popular, was illustrated by Akbar's atelier, and was imitated many times in both Persian and Urdu.[198] Thus, it seems that Sanskrit stories provided plenty of raw aesthetic material for Persian poets, but they frequently needed to be thoroughly recast in a Persianate literary form.

REWRITING HISTORY IN ṬĀHIR MUḤAMMAD SABZAVĀRĪ'S ABRIDGED *MAHĀBHĀRAT*

Regardless of Fayẓī's muddled success in transforming the epic into literature, Persianate intellectuals continued to be intrigued by the *Mahābhārata*'s historical potential and returned to the story again in the early seventeenth century. Ṭāhir Muḥammad Sabzavārī retells the *Mahābhārata* as part of his universal history *Rawẓat al-Ṭāhirīn* (*Garden of the Pure*), which he began during Akbar's reign and completed in the early years of Jahangir's rule.[199] Ṭāhir Muḥammad was an Iranian immigrant who entered royal service in 1579–1580 and thereafter performed a number of tasks on behalf of his imperial employer.[200] In the *Rawẓat al-Ṭāhirīn*, he covers a broad range of events in five books, beginning with ancient Persia as described in texts such as the *Shāhnāmah* and ending with Indian-Portuguese relations and a treatment of Southeast Asia.[201] He describes his work as a "book of wonders" (*shagraf-nāmah*) and indeed employs *ʿajāʾib* tropes particularly in his description of more far-flung places.[202] In the fourth book of his history, Ṭāhir Muḥammad provides a chronological report of India's royal history based on Sanskrit materials. He divides book 4 into two successive sections that detail the avatars of Vishnu (seemingly following the *Bhāgavata Purāṇa*[203]) and the *Mahābhārata* saga, including the *Harivaṃśa*. He describes the two sections similarly as "a record of the events of the rulers of Hindustan who preceded the appearance of Islam and are called Brahmans."[204]

In his recapitulation of the *Mahābhārata*, Ṭāhir Muḥammad introduces the epic as an imperial text meant for Akbar's edification. Here he reiterates Abū al-Faẓl's conception of the epic as beneficial for kings:

> It has not remained hidden from the luminous, generous hearts of wise lords that the minds of men, particularly great kings, yearn to listen to histories. The most honorable one has made this knowledge beloved to their hearts so that the people of the age will take advice from listening to it and not forget noble times.[205]

Ṭāhir Muḥammad next names the *Razmnāmah* as the source for his abridgement. While he does not mention Abū al-Faẓl's preface, he draws heavily from it in his description of the epic's eighteen books, often repeating Abū al-Faẓl's words exactly.[206] However, Ṭāhir Muḥammad does not appear to follow Abū al-Faẓl or the *Razmnāmah* in highlighting the *Śānti Parvan* as a particular source of political advice. He gives the twelfth book no special treatment and shortens the text drastically. Whereas the *Śānti Parvan* constitutes roughly one-quarter of the *Razmnāmah*, it consists of only a few pages, around 4 percent, of Ṭāhir Muḥammad's *Mahābhārat*. Instead, Ṭāhir Muḥammad identifies the *Mahābhārata*'s political promise as more tightly linked with its status as a purported historical record.

In his *Mahābhārat*, Ṭāhir Muḥammad pares down the epic to its core story with an emphasis on enumerating the reigns of kings. He opens by tracing kingship back to the *dvāpar jug*, the third of four eras, and says that King Bharata ruled in Hastinapura, which is now called Delhi.[207] Beginning in this manner highlights what became the center of Indo-Islamic power on the subcontinent and provides a direct tie between the Mughals and ancient Indian kings. In his conclusion to the *Mahābhārata* proper, he briefly traces Yudhishthira's successors and notes the length of their reigns.[208] He then subdivides the *Mahābhārata*'s appendix, the *Harivaṃśa*, according to royal dynasties and individual rulers.[209] After the *Harivaṃśa*, Ṭāhir Muḥammad continues his history in his fifth and final book with the Islamic rulers of India that climax with Akbar. Thus Ṭāhir Muḥammad presents his *Mahābhārat* as a testimony of kingly rule in ancient India upon which Indo-Islamic rulers, above all Akbar, could build their political claims.

While discussing the reported history of the early subcontinent, Ṭāhir Muḥammad maintains distance from the stories he repeats in two ways and thereby voices the larger concerns of some Muslims who participated in Akbar's cross-cultural projects. First, he often invokes caveats about the credibility of such tales, characterizing them as Brahmanical "beliefs" or "learning,"[210] Ṭāhir Muḥammad also offers a short defense of using dubious Brahmanical history. He says that Brahmans have written these histories apart from Muslims and then asserts "the narration of heresy is not itself heresy" (*naql-i kufr kufr nīst*).[211] Here he echoes Badāʾūnī, who writes the same defense, word for word, regarding his translation of the *Rāmāyaṇa*.[212] Ṭāhir Muḥammad is comfortable simply stating that he is not assenting to the heresy he reports, but Badāʾūnī goes on to write out the Islamic statement of faith and begs Allah to forgive him for translating a cursed book.[213] Later translators of the Indian epics even include entire sections that justify bringing a non-Muslim story into Persian.[214] Thus, translating Sanskrit texts was fraught with anxieties for many members of the Indo-Islamic cultural sphere, not least because of the perceived challenges to their intellectual and religious traditions that Abū al-Fa̤zl encourages. However, these concerns were not overwhelming enough to prevent Ṭāhir Muḥammad from drawing on Sanskrit knowledge in order to construct a long arc of Indian history with Akbar at its pinnacle.

Contemporary and later Indo-Persian intellectuals further cultivated this connection between ancient Indian kings and the reigning Mughal sovereign by composing kingly lineages (*rājāvalīs*) in Persian that place Mughal rule at the end of a long chain of Hindu and Muslim sovereigns (see chapter 6). Whether any *rājāvalī* writers were inspired by the *Rawẕat al-Ṭāhirīn* remains to be explored, but Ṭāhir Muḥammad's work was notably popular.[215] Persian *rājāvalī* lineages often begin with none other than the kings of the *Mahābhārata*.[216] Other historians followed Ṭāhir Muḥammad in repeating stories from the *Mahābhārata* and additional Sanskrit sources within chronicles of pre-Islamic India.[217] The *Rawẕat al-Ṭāhirīn*'s fourth chapter also came to have a life of its own in later years and circulated independently. In this form, Ṭāhir Muḥammad's *Mahābhārat* became associated with other translations from Sanskrit and lost much of its original political edge.[218] But Ṭāhir Muḥammad aimed to cast the *Mahābhārata* as a pre-Islamic, most crucially a pre-Akbar, history of Indian kings.

CONCLUSION: POLITICS AND AESTHETICS

The *Razmnāmah* played a significant role in Akbar's court, in its initial translation, preface, and two subsequent reworkings. The four major textual projects discussed in this chapter each explore different ways for the *Mahābhārata* to participate in Indo-Persian literature and Mughal kingship. But all agreed that Sanskrit texts had the power to reshape Mughal political and aesthetic realities. Akbar's court viewed the *Mahābhārata* as a potentially transformative text because they conceived the work, as Abū al-Fa̤zl puts it in his preface, as "the most authoritative, important, and comprehensive book [among the Brahmans of India]."[219] Many premodern Indian sovereigns had also sponsored Sanskrit *Mahābhārata*s in order to articulate imperial claims, particularly through appropriating the epic's geography, which often overlapped with the actual spaces over which such rulers sought control. In regional translations, Indian rulers adapted the story line and its spatial mapping to speak to their local needs.[220] Akbar's translators did not seize upon the same aspects of the epic that had occupied earlier Indian monarchs. Nonetheless, the Mughals too saw immense politico-cultural potential in the *Mahābhārata* and through the text expressed themselves as an Indian dynasty.

In the initial *Razmnāmah*, the Mughals struck a balance between literal translation and literary creativity that imbued the text with a dynamic ability to transform Mughal culture. Ronit Ricci discusses the seemingly paradoxical relationship between textual fidelity and authority in her book on Tamil, Malay, and Javanese translations of Islamic works. She points out that twelfth-century Latin renderings of Islamic texts were painstakingly faithful because they were designed to discredit Islam. In contrast, for later South and Southeast Asian translations of the same materials, "distancing from the source in the form of creativity and poetic freedom was part of a powerful array of tools used to accredit earlier sources and present them as legitimate."[221] The Mughal translators adopted a moderate approach between these two poles. They closely followed Sanskrit texts, as evidenced by the many lists of names in the *Razmnāmah*. At the same time, they rewrote the *Mahābhārata*'s political advice and added poetry in order to make the epic vibrant within their own tradition. Some translation practices, such as mixed religious frameworks, incorporated aspects of both these proclivities. Akbar and his court sought the cultural specificity of the *Mahābhārata* and also its flexibility to become a foundational work in the Indo-Persian world.

In the translation's preface and two retellings, the Mughals explored the potential of the Persian *Mahābhārata* to become both imperial history and a work of literature. In terms of its historical value, Abū al-Fa̤zl and Ṭāhir Muḥammad seized upon the *Mahābhārata* as a record of the past but expressed its relevance to Persianate thought in different ways. For Abū al-Fa̤zl, in the midst of its exaggerations and tall tales, the *Mahābhārata* contained truths that facilitated a fuller understanding of the world. Ṭāhir Muḥammad distanced himself from questions concerning the *Mahābhārata*'s accuracy and developed its rhetorical value to provide the Mughals with a long view of their royal predecessors on the subcontinent. Both authors relied on the ability of translated texts to embody multiple meanings, often far beyond those intended in their first articulation, while still preserving the foreignness of a nonnative text. This "promise of the foreign," as Vicente Rafael has termed it, endows translation with some of its most powerful potential as a recurrent transformative force.[222]

Last, the *Razmnāmah*'s preface and two retellings are, at their core, works of literature, and in many respects, the Mughals pursued these projects because they wanted to change the Indo-Persian literary world. Fayẕī claimed that the *Mahābhārata*, as an Indian text, had a unique capacity to inspire truly revolutionary Persian poetry. Even Abū al-Faẕl's preface, an overtly political work, employs a specialized style of literary prose. It would flatten these texts to subsume their aesthetic qualities within some stale form of legitimation theory that privileges political claims above all else. We might transport our language for political hegemony into the aesthetic realm and posit that Akbar also attempted to conquer Indian literature or wished to appropriate Sanskrit literary discourse. But these formulations too fall short of capturing the subtle ways that literature wields its aesthetic and rhetorical powers. The Mughals did not so much colonize as dynamically interact with different aspects of Sanskrit and Persian aesthetics in their engagements with the *Mahābhārata*. The goal, at least in large part, was to reformulate the vocabulary, styles, and stories of the Mughals' Indo-Persian culture.

Over the next two decades, Persianate readers enjoyed all three versions of the *Mahābhārata* produced under Akbar and Abū al-Faẕl's preface, but they preferred the original *Razmnāmah*. Several subimperial illustrated *Razmnāmah*s were produced during the late sixteenth and early seventeenth centuries.[223] Illustrated manuscripts began to decline after Jahangir's reign, but the translated text continued to be voraciously copied and recopied.[224] During Aurangzeb's reign in the late seventeenth century, Basant Rae, a Hindu *munshī* in the retinue of Shaystah Khan, created a table of contents for the *Razmnāmah*.[225] This addition demonstrates a major shift that took place during the seventeenth century: the readership of Persian translations of Sanskrit texts began to include large numbers of Hindus. Hindus continued to read the *Razmnāmah* well into the nineteenth century. This legacy of the *Razmnāmah* is itself remarkable. A Persian translation that was produced in an Islamicate imperial court became one of the primary sources by which later Hindus encountered an ancient Sanskrit epic. This later reception awaits a separate study. But, regarding the Mughals, this afterlife indicates that Akbar's court succeeded in making the *Mahābhārata* an important part of Indo-Persian literary culture, even if the immediate political nuances of Akbar's projects often ceased to be relevant to later readers.

[4] ABŪ AL-FAẒL REDEFINES ISLAMICATE KNOWLEDGE AND AKBAR'S SOVEREIGNTY

In addition to direct translations, the Mughals also produced Persian accounts of Sanskrit literature and knowledge systems. The most extensive Mughal exposition of Sanskrit learning was easily Abū al-Faẓl's *Āʾīn-i Akbarī* (*Akbar's Institutes*), the final portion of a major history of Akbar's period, the *Akbarnāmah*. The *Akbarnāmah* consists of three large volumes devoted, in order, to the exploits of Babur and Humayun, an account of Akbar's reign, and the *Āʾīn-i Akbarī*.[1] The *Āʾīn-i Akbarī* itself is subdivided into five books that outline different facets of Akbar's India, including detailed information concerning Indian culture, history, and Sanskrit knowledge. This topical approach complements the earlier two chronological volumes of Abū al-Faẓl's history and rounds out an exhaustive portrait of the Mughal imperium. Here I analyze the structure and substance of Abū al-Faẓl's description of Indian, largely Sanskrit-based traditions. I argue that the Mughals developed a detailed exegesis of Indian, particularly Sanskrit, learning in order to formulate their sovereignty over the subcontinent and benefit from its multiple forms of knowledge.

Unlike many of the texts discussed in this book, the *Āʾīn-i Akbarī* is frequently cited by scholars who work on Mughal India. Many have drawn upon the text's unparalleled wealth of information, particularly its statistical data on Akbar's administration.[2] Others, foremost S. A. A. Rizvi, have identified Abū al-Faẓl as the mastermind of Akbar's imperial ideology in the second half of his reign.[3] While these approaches have usefully outlined some basic idioms of Mughal sovereignty, they are generally too broad in scope to look closely at Abū al-Faẓl's treatment of Indian traditions. Only a smattering of articles has taken up the question of how and why one of the most important works produced under Mughal support incorporated substantial information concerning Sanskrit knowledge systems.[4] I build upon this work to further excavate Abū al-Faẓl's political and intellectual contributions to the Mughal state.

Western scholarship on the *Āʾīn-i Akbarī* has long been hampered by overreliance on problematic translations. Colonial scholars rendered the work into English twice in the 1800s, and the later translation was updated in the mid-twentieth century.[5] This amended English version has been reprinted numerous times and has proved instrumental in making the *Āʾīn-i Akbarī* available to an English-speaking audience. But the translation is also riddled with ambiguities, inconsistencies, and questionable readings. Most problematically in terms of Abū al-Faẓl's characterization of Sanskrit intellectual culture, earlier translators loosely employ the religious term "Hindu" where the Persian original specifies a geographic- or linguistic-based community.[6] As with so many Indo-Persian works, scholars today commonly use translations of the *Āʾīn-i Akbarī* without accessing the Persian text.[7] A dearth of serious philological work has allowed many misleading interpretations of the *Āʾīn-i Akbarī* to be perpetuated for decades, and I begin to redress that situation here.

Abū al-Faẓl promulgates several broad ideas in his history that are crucial to understanding his treatment of Sanskrit knowledge. First and foremost, he voices Akbar's aspirations toward universal kingship. By the time Abū al-Faẓl wrote his *Akbarnāmah* during the 1590s, Akbar's earlier clashes with Islamic leaders in the 1570s and 1580s had largely subsided, and the royal court was able to focus on articulating its preferred idioms of rule.[8] The *Akbarnāmah* went through several redactions before its final version and expressed Akbar's comprehensive sovereignty in several ways. Akbar was destined to govern all Indians, regardless of their religious or ethnic backgrounds, and was also to be the supreme authority in all arenas of life. As we shall see, Abū al-Faẓl depicts his patron's kingship as stretching across time, traditions, and practices. Scholars have often focused on Akbar's projected authority in particular contexts, such as in the spiritual realm or as an unquestionable head of state.[9] But Abū al-Faẓl's larger point was that Akbar's rule expanded in all directions, encompassing everyone and everything.

Abū al-Faẓl embedded Akbar's universal sovereignty into the organization of the *Āʾīn-i Akbarī*. He begins with the royal household and courtly practices in book 1 and then works outward, in a loose concentric fashion, until he considers the whole of Hindustan.[10] Book 2 addresses primarily the army and imperial groups. Book 3 details the administrative units of the

Mughal imperium and includes Indian myths in the history of several provinces and cities. Book 4, the *Aḥvāl-i Hindūstān* (*Account of India*), adds temporal and intellectual depth to Akbar's empire by covering Indian knowledge systems. Within book 4, a section titled *Dānish-i Hindūstān* (*Learning of India*) explicates Sanskrit learning, including the nine philosophical schools and aesthetic theory. Book 5, by far the shortest section of the *Āʾīn-i Akbarī*, collects the sayings of Akbar and thus returns the text, and indeed the whole of the *Akbarnāmah*, to its crisp focal point: the emperor himself.[11]

Within this vision of all things in India ultimately being subsumed under Akbar's kingship, Abū al-Faẓl emphasizes Sanskrit-based knowledge. Abū al-Faẓl does not generally distinguish between Sanskrit-based ideas and those drawn from Hindi or other vernacular traditions. He tends to speak more generally about Indian (*hindī* or *hindū*) traditions but then often presents explicitly Sanskrit-derived information. He interlaces Sanskrit stories throughout book 3 and devotes the majority of book 4 to Sanskrit learning.[12] In book 4, he also expounds a radical vision for how the Mughals ought to redefine the Indo-Persian intellectual sphere by importing a broad base of specifically Sanskrit knowledge. Abū al-Faẓl closes the fourth and final section of his *Account of India* by linking pre-Islamic and Islamic India to situate traditional Indian learning within Mughal domains. In this vision Sanskrit knowledge systems provided a necessary foundation for Mughal imperial ambitions.

Throughout his treatments of Indian learning in the *Āʾīn-i Akbarī*, Abū al-Faẓl combines intellectual and political objectives in fluid configurations. He presents traditional Sanskrit learning as part of what the Mughals gained in establishing an Indian Empire. He also wishes to invigorate Mughal culture by introducing Indian ideas and even Sanskrit vocabulary. In this vision, intellectual objectives are not made to serve political ends (or vice versa). On the contrary, Abū al-Faẓl creates a framework for Akbar's court to simultaneously cultivate an unprecedented type of Indo-Persian political authority and a dynamic, multisourced intellectual culture. For the Mughals, the *Āʾīn-i Akbarī*, particularly its treatment of Sanskrit knowledge systems, constituted a major attempt to define Akbar's India.

MULTIPLE GENRES OF THE *AKBARNĀMAH* AND ITS *ĀʾĪN-I AKBARĪ*

Abū al-Faẓl wrote his *Akbarnāmah* as the pinnacle of several court-sponsored histories produced during Akbar's reign, and the text outlines a significantly different grounding for Mughal authority than earlier chronicles. For example, around 1580 ʿArīf Qandahārī authored his *Tārīkh-i Akbarī* (*Akbar's History*), which portrays Akbar as a model Islamic ruler and elides royal links with non-Muslim Indians.[13] Also beginning in the 1580s Akbar appointed a team of authors to compose the *Tārīkh-i Alfī* (*History of the Millennium*) in order to celebrate the first thousand years of Islam, which concluded in 1592. The *Tārīkh-i Alfī* commences with the death of the Prophet Muhammad and hails Akbar as the "Renewer of the Second Millennium" within an Islamic-centered narrative.[14] In his *Ṭabaqāt-i Akbarī* (*Generations of Akbar*, ca. 1590s), Niẓām al-Dīn Aḥmad traces the history of Islamicate rule over different regions in India. In contrast to these more Islamic-focused efforts, Abū al-Faẓl portrays Akbar's empire as based in multiple traditions and highlights the wider Indian context of the Mughal Empire.

While the *Akbarnāmah* as a whole is typically considered a history (*tārīkh*), there are aspects of this classification that are frequently overlooked. Above all, history was an intensely political genre in Mughal India that held glorifying its object (in the case of the *Akbarnāmah*, Akbar) as equally important to maintaining an accurate record of events. Persianate historians had long considered the true goal of their craft to be illuminating the meaning (rather than the mundane reality) of the past.[15] Scholars have often remarked that Abū al-Faẓl elides certain aspects of Akbar's rule and portrays the emperor as nearly divine.[16] But these features of the text are not isolated aberrations that can be brushed aside in favor of mining the work for facts. On the contrary, Abū al-Faẓl's political agendas were foundational to how he depicted the Mughal kingdom.

Abū al-Faẓl explicitly defines his project in the *Āʾīn-i Akbarī* as venerating his patron by charting Mughal imperial customs and institutions. He opens the work by paying brief tribute to Allah before announcing his intention to worship in a different manner: "I, Abū al-Faẓl-i Mubārak, return thanks to God by elaborating the glory of kingship and stringing royal pearls on the charming thread of description."[17] Abū al-Faẓl next outlines two further related reasons why he is embarking on this endeavor. First, he desires to convince his contemporaries of "the deep learning, incredible majesty, and great works of [Akbar]."[18] Second, Abū al-Faẓl wishes to install Akbar as a model ruler, a beacon for future generations. He proclaims, "I record some thoughts on the institutions of the ruler of the world and leave for everyone far and near an orderly work of wisdom."[19] He dedicates the remainder of his introduction to lauding

Emperor Akbar, whose royal institutes, as explained in this volume of the text, command unanimous admiration.

While Abū al-Faẓl makes grandiose claims of his universal audience, his writing style indicates his true orientation toward a narrow band of Islamicate elites. Only a learned class of Persianate readers would have been able to grasp his dense, ornate prose. Moreover, Abū al-Faẓl relies heavily on religious language that presumes familiarity with the Islamic tradition.[20] This intended readership again negates that persistent assumption in modern scholarship that all cross-cultural activities were aimed at integrating groups of people into the Mughal Empire. In the case of the *Āʾīn-i Akbarī*, Abū al-Faẓl's sights were set on those who already supported Akbar's claims to rule. He aimed to convince this influential group (among other things) of the virtues of infusing Sanskrit knowledge into the Indo-Persian thought world.

The *Āʾīn-i Akbarī*'s status as part of a politically oriented history did not preclude it from participating in several other genres as well. Following the influential book *Textures of Time*, several scholars have recently argued that Indo-Persian texts frequently operated across many genres, both in their original conception and later interpretations.[21] *Textures of Time* proposes "sub-genre markings," textual features that mark shifts between literary categories in clearly discernible ways (at least to a "native" reader).[22] The *Āʾīn-i Akbarī* certainly reads at different points as an ethical treatise, administrative manual, advice book for kings, and scientific work, in addition to a courtly history. Nonetheless, it is doubtful that premodern Persian texts were designed with systematic transitions between clearly demarcated genres.[23] A more likely explanation is that they were written to participate in numerous categories simultaneously. Consider how Abū al-Faẓl characterizes the simultaneous textual locations of his work in the close of the *Āʾīn-i Akbarī*:

> Praise be to God that I have completed this royal treasure book, a register of information, catalog of the notebook of wisdom, collection of imperial customs, slate of instruction in the school of etiquette, exemplar of the routines of wise men, manual of courtly practices, and mandate of correct behavior in the hall of justice and compassion.[24]

Among the many intersecting genres of the *Āʾīn-i Akbarī*, Abū al-Faẓl's reliance on Persian *akhlāq* literature is particularly crucial to understanding the import of his text. The *akhlāq* tradition addresses both the theory and practice of political culture in Islamicate societies and underscores the importance of social harmony. Muzaffar Alam has shown how *akhlāq* texts exerted significant sway over Mughal political thought and has highlighted the especially influential role of Naṣīr al-Dīn Ṭūsī's thirteenth-century *Akhlāq-i Nāṣirī* (*Nasirean Ethics*).[25] Abū al-Faẓl follows Ṭūsī in many aspects of the *Āʾīn-i Akbarī*, above all by portraying the king as embodying perfection and thereby regulating the conduct of his household, imperial groups, and realm.[26]

Several Persian works serve as relevant antecedents for Abū al-Faẓl's invoking Sanskrit knowledge systems in particular. Amīr Khusraw's *Nuh Sipihr* (*Nine Heavens*, 1318) describes Indian cultural life and specifically discusses Sanskrit.[27] Poets writing in Awadhi, a Hindavi dialect, had incorporated aspects of Sanskrit aesthetics since the fourteenth century.[28] Babur's memoirs provide a model for Abū al-Faẓl's project to craft a detailed administrative record of Mughal India that includes local information.[29] The most noteworthy precedent for Abū al-Faẓl's concentration on Sanskrit knowledge, however, is al-Bīrūnī's *India*. In the early eleventh century, Abū al-Rayḥān Muḥammad ibn Aḥmad al-Bīrūnī composed an extensive Arabic treatise on the subcontinent's intellectual and philosophical learning. This text, titled *Kitāb al-Hind* (*Book of India*) and commonly known as al-Bīrūnī's *India*, was unparalleled in the Islamicate world in terms of its depth and use of Sanskrit sources.[30] While al-Bīrūnī's *India* was not popular among early modern readers, the work was known to Abū al-Faẓl, who frequently emulates al-Bīrūnī's arguments and methods.[31] Both compare Sanskrit knowledge to the Greek tradition, emphasize discord between communities as a reason for producing their respective works, and stress the importance of accessing Sanskrit textual sources.[32] Despite these similarities, however, the social implications of the two treatises remain distinct. Al-Bīrūnī wrote his *India* outside the confines of direct royal patronage, and scholars have typically read the work as primarily an intellectual endeavor.[33] In contrast, Abū al-Faẓl's *Account of India* is intricately connected with Akbar's imperial project.

INDIAN TIME AND HISTORY IN AKBAR'S EMPIRE

Abū al-Faẓl first introduces significant traditional Indian knowledge in book 3 of his *Āʾīn-i Akbarī*, which covers the administration of imperial provinces (*ṣūbahs*). Three facets of Abū al-Faẓl's treatment here indicate imperial motivations in integrating Sanskrit learning into a court-sponsored history. First, the opening of book 3 compares different understandings of astronomy and time, including Sanskrit-based calculations. Second, Abū al-Faẓl recounts aspects of Sanskrit learning and India's sacred geography (perhaps known from Sanskrit materials) throughout his treatment of administrative provinces. Last, he provides a rich account of the efforts of Zayn al-Abidin, a fifteenth-century Kashmiri ruler, in translating Sanskrit materials. In these treatments, Abū al-Faẓl outlines several approaches to India's intellectual heritage that he builds on in book 4 of the *Āʾīn-i Akbarī*. Above all, he invokes information based on Sanskrit sources as an integral aspect of Akbar's India.

Abū al-Faẓl begins book 3 with a discussion of astronomy and temporal calculations that forefronts Indian opinions on both subjects. The Mughal court had created an official position for an Indian astrologer a few decades earlier, and the royal household regularly relied upon Sanskrit-based horoscopes (see chapter 1). In line with these developments, Abū al-Faẓl portrays Sanskrit astronomy as a valid intellectual system. For example, he names nine Sanskrit *siddhānta* texts as the discipline's textual foundation.[34] He also notes approvingly that Indian wise men have accurately transmitted this science for thousands of years.[35] Chains of transmission (*isnād*) were a common method of establishing the reliability of knowledge in the Islamicate world.[36] Earlier Persian accounts of Sanskrit learning had also invoked chains of transmission, such as the sixteenth-century *Baḥr al-Ḥayāt* (*Ocean of Life*) that traced yogic ideas back to Hindu deities as the original expositors.[37] Abū al-Faẓl deploys a similar model here, even though he decides not (or perhaps is unable) to produce the names of individual transmitters.

In the following section, Abū al-Faẓl explains the Indian calendar (*tārīkh-i hind*), but his presentation contrasts sharply with contemporary treatments of Indian time. In most other Islamicate texts, including Abū al-Faẓl's preface to the *Razmnāmah*, authors report that Indians divided time into four repeating *yugas* and often gave the vast numbers of years in each age. In the *Āʾīn-i Akbarī*, Abū al-Faẓl observes that Indian time is recurring, but instead of dwelling on the four eras he focuses on key rulers in the current Kali Yuga, the degenerate age.[38] He says that Raja Yudhishthira's rule opened the present period and next records the kings whose reigns marked the start of the *vikrama* and *śaka saṃvat* calendars. He then predicts that the end of the current cycle of *yugas* will be ushered in by a succession of sovereigns. This stress on royal history accords well with Abū al-Faẓl's concentration on kingship throughout his *Akbarnāmah* and underscores that Akbar's rule builds upon that of pre-Islamic Indian kings.

Other seekers of Mughal patronage also perceived an imperial interest in Indian calendars. For example, in 1589, the well-known Mughal artist Keśavdās (Kesu Das) painted a self-portrait that he dates according to the *vikrama saṃvat* year in a Hindi (Devanagari) inscription that also invokes wishes for Akbar's long life (*pātiśāhi ciraṃ jīva*).[39] Giridhardās, who authored a Persian *Rāmāyaṇa* in the early seventeenth century in order to solicit Jahangir's support, dates his text in both the *hijri* and *vikrama saṃvat* systems.[40] In his bilingual astrological lexicon written under Shah Jahan, Malājit Vedāṅgarāya explains how to convert between the Indian *śaka saṃvat* and the Islamic *hijri* calendar.[41] Such efforts attest to an ongoing Mughal attraction toward Indian calendric systems, which is most fully fleshed out in the *Āʾīn-i Akbarī*.

Abū al-Faẓl devotes the bulk of book 3 to regions of the Mughal Empire and weaves Sanskrit-related information into his narrative. Topographical features frequently prompt Abū al-Faẓl's digressions into Indian stories. For example, in the account of Bengal, he remarks that the learned men of India say that the Ganges flows from the hair of *mahādīv* (Shiva).[42] Later he notes that Indian pandits have penned many books eulogizing the Ganges, which no doubt refers to the plethora of Sanskrit praise poems (*stotras*) dedicated to the river goddess.[43] He briefly recounts the *Mahābhārata* story when discussing the battlefield of Kurukshetra.[44] He observes that Benares is historically called Kashi and has long been a place of traditional education.[45]

Abū al-Faẓl also connects Indian tales, available in both Sanskrit and vernacular texts and in oral culture, with the expansive ambitions of the Mughal Empire. For example, under the section on Lahore, he relays the story of how Shiva's wife sacrificed herself to protest the disrespect shown her husband at Daksha's sacrifice and was subsequently dismembered and scattered across the subcontinent.[46] This story is told in many Sanskrit sources that disagree regarding the number of places where her body fell. Abū al-Faẓl reports that parts of her landed in four areas: Kashmir, the Deccan, Kamrup, and Nagarkot.[47] It is likely no coincidence that these areas mark some of the outmost regions and aspirations of Akbar's imperium. Here Abū al-Faẓl collapses India's sacred and imperial geographies to advance Akbar's claims to rule over a vast Indian kingdom.

Among the areas he describes, Abū al-Faẓl devotes special attention to the history of Kashmir and here identifies a precedent for Mughal ties with the Sanskrit cultural world. He lists Kashmir's kings from its ancient rulers through Yaʿqub Khan, from whom Akbar took the region in the 1580s, and notes that he obtained much of this information from a Persian translation of the Sanskrit *Rājataraṅgiṇī* (*River of Kings*).[48] Abū al-Faẓl offers an approbative account of Zayn al-Abidin (r. 1420–1470), describing him in markedly similar terms to how Akbar is praised in Sanskrit texts from the late sixteenth century. For example, Abū al-Faẓl acclaims the Kashmiri ruler's compassion in canceling the taxes on non-Muslims and forbidding cow slaughter.[49] He also celebrates that Zayn al-Abidin refused to eat meat and dissuaded men from hunting, sentiments that Akbar also expressed (at least in moderation).[50] Most important, Abū al-Faẓl applauds Zayn al-Abidin's extensive translation activities, which stretched across many languages, including Arabic, Persian, Kashmiri, and Sanskrit.[51] Such a substantial royal precedent sets the stage for Abū al-Faẓl's comprehensive treatment in book 4 of Sanskrit and other Indian traditions as foundational for Akbar's sovereignty and Indo-Persian knowledge.

FRAMING THE *ACCOUNT OF INDIA*

Abū al-Faẓl dedicates book 4 of the *Āʾīn-i Akbarī*, titled *Account of India*, to South Asia's past and its learned traditions. The book contains four major sections: a combined geography and cosmography of India, a description of Sanskrit knowledge (*Learning of India*), a list of Islamic figures who traveled to the subcontinent, and a record of Indo-Islamic saints. The first two sections constitute the bulk of the book and rely primarily upon Sanskrit learning, whereas the latter two shorter segments draw upon Islamicate traditions. The pairing of Sanskrit and Islamicate knowledge systems is an important aspect of Abū al-Faẓl's project. Before pursuing this theme, however, it is helpful to explicate the overarching frame of book 4. In the opening of the book, Abū al-Faẓl outlines two politico-intellectual contexts that illuminate his objectives in this part of his imperial history.

First, Abū al-Faẓl names several world histories as his intellectual antecedents in addressing Indian learning and identifies the inadequacies of these works as one reason for producing his own. He writes,

> I do not know whether affection for my birthplace, an investigation into truth [*haqq-pizhūhī*], or describing reality [*haqīqat-guzārī*] has strongly inclined me toward this [record of Indian learning], because Banākatī, Ḥāfiẓ-i Abrū, and other ancients have constructed false visions and written down fictitious tales.[52]

Banākatī, who worked largely under Mongol support, completed his vast world history in 1317, and Ḥāfiẓ-i Abrū wrote his *Majmaʿ al-Tavārīkh* (*Collected Histories*) for the Timurid court of Herat in the early fifteenth century.[53] Both Banākatī and Ḥāfiẓ-i Abrū depended heavily on Rashīd al-Dīn's *Jāmiʿ al-Tavārīkh* (*Collection of Histories*, ca. 1300) in their sections on India.[54] Many other Islamicate writers had described Indian religions in Arabic and Persian and also generally recycled earlier materials.[55] Such world histories circulated in early modern India and were frequently cited.[56] In rejecting the works of these established authors as unreliable, Abū al-Faẓl signals his intention to base his work on direct translations of Sanskrit materials.

Abū al-Faẓl relied extensively on Sanskrit texts and informants for the fourth book of his *Āʾīn-i Akbarī*. He professes ignorance of Sanskrit early in his work and so used interpreters to access original sources: "Because I was not familiar with terms in the Sanskrit language [*zabān-i hindī*] and a desirable translator could not be found, laborious work went into repeated translations. [But] by a good turn of fate and the strength of my own will, I obtained my goal."[57] It is difficult to identify specific Sanskrit sources for most sections of the *Āʾīn-i Akbarī*, largely because much of the information is contained in multiple texts.[58] Nonetheless, Abū al-Faẓl displays his deep awareness of the Sanskrit tradition in many ways, including by giving the titles of dozens of works, particularly for *purāṇa*s and law books.[59] He also evinces familiarity with the material side of Indian manuscript culture early in the *Learning of India*, observing, "They used to write on palm and *tuz* leaves with a steel pen, but now they write on paper. They begin writing on the left and do not bind or stitch the pages together."[60] Abū al-Faẓl's Indian informants remain shrouded in mystery. Both sides are silent about the names or any other details concerning these individuals. Scholars have suggested the Jain intellectual Bhānucandra as one probable choice, which is a reasonable proposition since he spent considerable time at Akbar's court and tutored Abū al-Faẓl in the Sanskrit philosophical compendium *Ṣaḍdarśanasamuccaya* (*Collection of the Six Schools*).[61] Given the breadth and depth of his *Account of India*, Abū al-Faẓl likely employed multiple assistants, perhaps some of them Brahmans. Notably, he calls attention to the erudition of his unnamed informants, often honoring them with the appellations *ḥakīm* (learned) and *dānishvar* (educated). This recognition of Indian learnedness stands in pointed contrast to the treatment of native informants in direct translations as mere communicators of traditions that are, at least in part, false.[62]

In addition to the unreliability of earlier Islamicate expositions of Sanskrit knowledge, Abū al-Faẓl articulates a second, thoroughly imperial reason behind his *Account of India.*

> When I emerged from the privacy of isolation and discovered some of the ignorance of mankind and the discord of beings, I set about promoting peace and establishing friendship. . . . Although I had already set my pen to composing an account of the imperial provinces [*ṣūbahs*] and elaborated some of the conditions of India, my heart's intention now reached the time of realization. Being discontented with prior knowledge, I began begging hearts and solicited fresh instruction from impartial, learned men.[63]

This language of fostering social harmony builds upon Akbar's ideology of "universal peace" (*ṣulḥ-i kull*) that encouraged critical open-mindedness to others' ideas. Scholars have frequently conflated *ṣulḥ-i kull* with modern concepts of toleration that prioritize respecting different positions without assenting to them.[64] In contrast, however, *ṣulḥ-i kull* enjoined individuals to seriously weigh ideas from different traditions and adopt perspectives that superseded those espoused by their own community.[65]

Ṣulḥ-i kull contributed to the political interests of the Mughal Empire through both its social and intellectual dimensions. Modern scholars have often emphasized the potential of *ṣulḥ-i kull* to reduce sectarian strife, and Abū al-Faẓl addresses this societal benefit in his *Account of India.*[66] For example, at the conclusion of his section about Jainism, he states,

> A Brahman prefers to encounter a mad elephant or a roaring lion rather than to meet with one of [the Jains]. But in his search for truth in the world, King [Akbar] has partially dispelled the darkness of the age with the light of universal peace [*ṣulḥ-i kull*]. The different groups of mankind have ceased their conflict and revel in the establishment of concord.[67]

In reference to the *Account of India* as a whole, one scholar has suggested that the desire to stimulate amicable relations explains the infrequency of negative comments regarding Hindu beliefs.[68] But *ṣulḥ-i kull* was far more to Abū al-Faẓl than a pragmatic device to avert communal conflict. He also saw "universal peace" as an intellectual project to improve oneself by continually pursuing new sources of knowledge and a political opportunity to exert authority over the known world.

In the *Account of India*, Abū al-Faẓl identifies numerous causes of discord that *ṣulḥ-i kull* might cure, including superficial treatises, intellectual laziness, and false teachers.[69] He proposes that the world needs an inquisitive king "like Anushiravan" and a minister "like Buzurjmihr," who are both celebrated in the Persian tradition, including elsewhere in the *Āʾīn-i Akbarī*, for having sought out Indian knowledge and texts.[70] Most notably, Buzurjmihr (Burzui) is credited with traveling to India during the sixth century in order to find the Sanskrit *Pañcatantra* and translate the work into Middle Persian.[71] Having found suitable precedents for his project among early Persian kings (rather than Islamicate historians), Abū al-Faẓl stands ready to embark on his imperial mission of devising a fresh elaboration of Sanskrit learning and thereby redrawing the lines of the Indo-Persian intellectual tradition.

SOCIAL AND GEOGRAPHICAL LANDSCAPES OF THE SUBCONTINENT

In the first section of the *Account of India*, Abū al-Faẓl describes the subcontinent and its place in the world according to many measures. He delineates the people of India, the topography of the region, creation myths, astronomical calculations, Indian views of different climes of the world, the caste system, and local languages, flora, and fauna. Most of the data is based squarely on the Sanskrit tradition and outlines various ways of locating and defining the subcontinent. This whirlwind tour of Indian thought also exemplifies some major features of book 4 of the *Āʾīn-i Akbarī* more generally, including the central role of native informants and Abū al-Faẓl's ambition to be exhaustive.

At the outset Abū al-Faẓl commends the learnedness and fidelity of Indians. He sweepingly proclaims, "The inhabitants of this land are seekers of God, kindhearted, friendly to strangers, congenial, and pleasant. They are fond of knowledge, inclined toward austerities, committed to justice, content, hardworking, skilled, loyal, honest, and trustworthy."[72] Abū al-Faẓl next acclaims Indian soldiers as steadfast in battle before turning to educated men and praising Indians as quick learners who often surpass their teachers.[73] This dual emphasis on Indian warriors and intellectuals nicely complements the nature of power in the Mughal Empire, which relied on both military success and imperial ideology.

Abū al-Faẓl next takes up the issue of whether non-Muslim Indians are monotheists. His goal here is not a careful adjudication of different theological precepts, which he offers later in the book. Rather, he seeks to assure his readers that his Indian informants profess belief in God, a necessary prerequisite for admitting their ideas into the Perso-Islamic world.[74] Abū al-Faẓl contends,

> All [the inhabitants of this land] believe in the unity of God. As for the honor they show to images made of stone, wood, and other things that idiots consider idol worship, it is not so. The writer of this felicitous book has sat conversing with many wise and righteous men, and it is clear that they fashion images of some who have approached the court of the Purified One as aids to prevent the mind from wandering and render worship of God indispensable. In all their practices and customs, they seek favor from the world-illuminating sun and count the holy essence of incomparable God as higher than action.[75]

In short, Indians recognize an omnipotent God, and the learned can even explain the true purpose of idol veneration, a practice common in several Indian religions but generally frowned upon in Islam. Abū al-Faẓl remains a bit fuzzy whether he means to endorse the monotheism of all non-Muslim Indians ("all [the inhabitants of this land]") or more narrowly of the elites ("wise and righteous men").[76] Certainly the latter is what mattered, because it enabled Abū al-Faẓl to consider Sanskrit learning as a valid intellectual tradition.

Abū al-Faẓl dedicates the remainder of his opening section to outlining traditional understandings of India as a definable entity in terms of cosmography, geography, and the natural world. He explains Indian notation systems, all the while including comparisons to Greek thought. He also describes the topography of the subcontinent and covers Indian calculations of latitude and longitude. Last he includes accounts of social caste and class, a list of the languages spoken in different parts of the subcontinent, and descriptions of local flora and fauna. Throughout this section, Abū al-Faẓl offers a bewildering array of details. He frequently produces long lists, tables, and multiple opinions on a given point. Even in his moments of comparative brevity, he carefully notes what he omits. For example, he records that there are eighteen separate creation stories, although he recounts only three of them.[77] He aims to be as exhaustive as possible, although, as he warns his readers in the opening of the *Account of India*, "Now that I have provided a summary about India, I will delve into the details. Even if it is only a little out of much, I will write about one out of a thousand."[78] His approach suggests that there is not one way of knowing India but rather many vectors for comprehending what is now largely the Mughal Empire.

THE NINE INDIAN PHILOSOPHICAL SCHOOLS IN MUGHAL INDIA

Abū al-Faẓl surveys an astonishing range of subjects in his *Learning of India*, the second section of book 4 in the *Āʾīn-i Akbarī*. He begins with an extensive description of nine philosophical positions, which include six Brahmanical schools, as well as the thinking of Jains, Buddhists, and atheists. He then offers shorter vignettes on dozens of branches of Sanskrit learning, including the *Vedas*, *vedāṅgas* (six auxiliary disciplines), and numerous *śāstras* (technical disciplines). In this last section, literature (*sāhitya*) and music (*saṅgīta*) receive prolonged consideration before Abū al-Faẓl turns his attention to more religious topics, including the *avatāras* of Vishnu and Hindu theological precepts. He closes by describing sartorial and social practices such as marriage and death rites and acceptable clothing. Following his earlier pattern, Abū al-Faẓl's *Learning of India* is remarkably detailed, and modern scholars have been duly impressed by the scarcity of errors therein.[79]

The treatment of philosophical schools in particular showcases how Abū al-Faẓl viewed Sanskrit both as an ancient Indian tradition and an active part of the Mughal Empire. He begins by positioning himself as a detached adjudicator between the many Indian philosophical views: "As a gift for seekers of knowledge, I set down a detailed catalog of the nine fundamental systems and present the principles of each without disputation [*bī ḥujjat*]."[80] Here Abū al-Faẓl declares his desire to impartially communicate Sanskrit learning to his readers. Indeed, Abū al-Faẓl often comes across as a careful and thorough scholar who saw real value in providing an accurate account of the information he received from his Indian informants. However, he does not consider this goal incompatible with crafting his work to reflect the Mughal experience in India. On the contrary, Abū al-Faẓl situates his discourse on Indian philosophy deep in an imperial context and its attendant Islamicate assumptions. For instance, in spite of his professed neutrality, he freely condemns the one tradition that is unacceptable from an Islamic perspective: atheism. Using alliterative wordplay, he disparages Cārvāka, the founder of the atheist (*nāstika*) perspective, as an ignorant (*nāshināsā*) Brahman.[81] He then outlines *nāstika* beliefs in a few sentences as compared with his far lengthier descriptions of most of the other schools of thought. He concludes, "[The atheists] have written extensive books in contempt of others that serve as memorials of their own idiocy."[82]

Abū al-Faẓl's analysis of the other Indian philosophical schools similarly mirrors the Mughal court's ongoing encounters with Sanskrit intellectuals. Most notably, Abū al-Faẓl treats Jainism at greater length than any of the eight other viewpoints.[83] This choice echoes the heavy Jain presence at the Mughal court and hence the easy availability of information about this particular path. Abū al-Faẓl's elaborate commentary on Jain doctrine may also reflect the biases of his Sanskrit informants, whether Bhānucandra or one of the many other Jains who frequented Akbar's court.

Nonetheless, the Mughals were aware that Jainism was a minority tradition in India, and Abū al-Faẓl frames it as such in his *Learning of India.* He opens his exegesis of Sanskrit philosophy by grouping the six Brahmanical schools of thought together in contrast to the final three (Jain, Buddhist, and atheist), which are not accepted by mainstream (Brahmanical) opinion.[84] Moreover, in his section on Jainism, Abū al-Faẓl includes types of information that he does not address within the six Brahmanical traditions. For example, he discusses the Jain concept of different tiers in this world and the underworld and also describes religious practices associated with monks and laypersons, respectively. Abū al-Faẓl presents Brahmanical perspectives on such matters within his cosmography of Hindustan that precedes the *Learning of India* and his following section of religious practices. In short, Abū al-Faẓl understands Brahmanical ideas as dominant, standard Indian beliefs and others as deviant. Abū al-Faẓl treats Buddhism similarly to Jainism and separately mentions aspects of its cosmography along with Buddhist philosophy, although with far greater brevity.

Abū al-Faẓl depicts all nine Indian philosophical systems as historically grounded traditions. He carefully identifies the founder of each philosophy, such as Gautama for *nyāya* and Kapila for *saṅkhyā.*[85] He further positions the chronological growth of the schools in relation to one another where appropriate. Hence he records that *vaiśeṣika* preceded *nyāya* even though he addresses the two in the opposite order.[86] He often mentions important later expositors, such as Kumārila Bhaṭṭa, an influential seventh-century Sanskrit philosopher of *mīmāṃsā.*[87] Last, Abū al-Faẓl brings the progression of these systems into Mughal times by observing developments that account for the state of affairs in his day. In this vein, he remarks on the disappearance of all but traces of Buddhism from India.[88] Occasionally, he also comments on his cultural position vis-à-vis Sanskrit knowledge systems, such as when he discloses that he has no personal knowledge of the Digambara branch of Jainism.[89]

In addition to the content of Sanskrit philosophy, Abū al-Faẕl also introduces his readers to extensive Sanskrit terminology. He generally tries to follow correct Sanskrit pronunciation, often distinguishing Sanskrit terms from their common vernacular shortenings.[90] Once he defines a Sanskrit word or phrase, he often uses it again without any gloss, evidently expecting his readers to have thoroughly assimilated the Sanskrit vocabulary. As a result, many passages contain so much Sanskrit as to be unintelligible except to those who have mastered every term defined previously in the *Account of India*.[91] For example, a typical passage from the section on *mīmāṃsā*, the third philosophical school discussed, invokes substantial Sanskrit vocabulary introduced during the earlier exegesis of *nyāya*.

> According to [Kumārila] Bhaṭṭa and [Murāri] Miśra, there are six *pramāṇas*, four of which were described under *nyāya*. They count seven senses, adding *tāmasendriya*, through which darkness is cognized. They do not acknowledge *kevalānvayin* or *kevalavyatirekin*, and they do not admit *guru* or *mithyājñāna*. They admit *saṃśaya* and *viparyaya* as correct forms of knowledge. *Nyāya* thinks that air is perceived through inference, but this group through touch. The fifth [*pramāṇa*] is *arthāpatti*, which is observing the effect and positing the cause. The sixth is *anupalabdhi*, which is ignorance of things. They say that knowledge of the nonexistence of things arises from the nonexistence of knowledge of those things. [Murāri] Miśra, like *nyāya*, takes [*anupalabdhi*] as part of *pratyakṣa*.[92]

Abū al-Faẕl continues with a similarly dazzling density of Sanskrit vocabulary throughout his description of the nine philosophical positions. This approach strongly suggests that Abū al-Faẕl wished to educate his readers not only in Sanskrit ideas but also in Sanskrit terms and discourses for exploring those ideas.

Abū al-Faẕl confirms his interest in the language, in addition to the philosophy, of Sanskrit thought by methodically spelling out each Sanskrit word upon its initial usage. Few other intellectuals in Akbar's court show much precision in their transliteration of Sanskrit terms. Even the direct translations done in Akbar's court employed no standard system for expressing Sanskrit words in Perso-Arabic script, and as a result transliterated terms are often near illegible in later manuscript copies. In contrast, Abū al-Faẓl uses a type of Persian longhand that specifies the letters in each Sanskrit term as a safeguard against careless copyists. For instance, when he introduces the term *mīmāṃsā*, he says it is spelled with "an *m*, a long *ī*, an *m*, a long *ā*, an *n*, an *s*, and a long *ā*."[93] A bit later in his *Learning of India*, Abū al-Faẓl exercises a similar descriptive method to explain the Sanskrit alphabet.[94] Translated scientific texts sometimes invoke such spelling systems for Indian herbs and drugs that were used to treat illnesses.[95] Like the authors of these practical works, Abū al-Faẓl viewed Indian philosophy as a useful resource for his readers that required attention to the language of Sanskrit discourses.

PREPARING PERSIANATE READERS FOR SANSKRIT LITERATURE

Abū al-Faẓl further elaborates on the reasons behind his interest in Sanskrit terminology in his section on literature (*sāhitya*). Here Abū al-Faẓl elaborates primarily on the types of heroines (*nāyikā-bheda*), the complex classification of stock women who appear in Sanskrit erotic poetry. The system of *nāyikās* had become quite popular in early modern Sanskrit and vernacular languages and contained dozens of types and subtypes of heroines.[96] Abū al-Faẓl describes this system as follows: "In this excellent knowledge they describe relations between men and women and address the tumult of passionate love."[97] As we will see, at the end of this section, he implores readers to supersede his own research and go back to original Indian sources in order to learn more about this aesthetic tradition. Here Abū al-Faẓl makes a strong argument for the potential of repeated cross-cultural encounters to redefine the nature of Indo-Persian knowledge. Moreover, throughout his discussion he focuses on the metastructure of types of *nāyikās* in order to facilitate future inquires into these literary classifications.

Unlike for most of the *Āʾīn-i Akbarī*, we can identify the Sanskrit sources for at least parts of Abū al-Faẓl's section on literature. Most notably Abū al-Faẓl quotes several verses from Bhānudatta's *Rasamañjarī* (*Bouquet of Rasa*), a well-read literary treatise composed in the fifteenth century.[98] Additionally, Abū al-Faẓl borrows at least one example from Viśvanātha's fourteenth-century *Sāhityadarpaṇa* (*Mirror of Literature*).[99] Despite relying on specific Sanskrit texts, Abū al-Faẓl makes no attempt to render any Sanskrit examples into either Persian verse or poetic prose. Instead of capturing the aesthetic beauty of the Sanskrit lines, he focuses on accurately reproducing the classificatory information contained in this system. Accordingly he lists the Sanskrit names for dozens of *nāyikās*, much as he does earlier for philosophical concepts. But more often than not Abū al-Faẓl forgoes any examples and instead offers only a brief description of each type of woman.

For instance, in Sanskrit the woman whose husband has gone abroad (*proṣitabhartṛkā*) is depicted as so lovesick that she literally withers away. Bhānudatta gives this lovely verse as one of his examples:

> The dress is one you've worn before,
> and the bracelet on your wrist
> and the jeweled belt you carry on your hips.
> So why does it all seem too big,
> dear friend, on this lovely spring day
> that buzzing bees make lovelier?[100]

Here the woman has become so thin from longing for her husband that her clothes and jewelry now hang on her frail frame. The poet counterposes the woman's heartbreaking frailty with spring, a time of blossoming fecundity. About this same *nāyikā*, Abū al-Faẓl gives a short description that is devoid of any poetic quality. He says,

> *Proṣitabhartṛkā*. The husband has gone on a trip, and from his distance she is weak or thinking about leaving. She is distressed with fear.[101]

Other Indo-Persian authors who wrote about *nāyikās* provide a stark contrast to Abū al-Faẓl's utilitarian approach. For example, in the eighteenth century Āzād Bilgrāmī composed an Arabic treatise on Indian *nāyikās* that he later translated into Persian under the title *Ghizlān-i Hind* (*Indian Beloveds*). Unlike Abū al-Faẓl, Bilgrāmī illustrates the different women with Persian verses. For example, speaking of the same woman whose husband has gone abroad, he quotes this line from Saʿdī:

> Camel driver, go slow for my soul rests in the caravan.
> The camels have a load on their backs and I on my heart.[102]

In this verse, Bilgrāmī evokes the imagery of the beloved's departing caravan to culturally translate the Sanskrit system of *nāyikās*. Returning to the sixteenth century, literati in Akbar's court often used such tactics in re-creating Indian materials in Persian, such as the quotations of poetry in the *Razmnāmah.* However, in his account of Indian learning, Abū al-Faẓl offers a straightforward list of *nāyikā*s with terse prose descriptions that appears most concerned with reporting the ordering structures of Sanskrit literature rather than exploring their poetic draw.

Even when he translates poetic examples, Abū al-Faẓl frequently elides the larger literary and social contexts in which the heroines were originally understood. In Sanskrit poetry, numerous conventions and known story lines enabled authors to invoke a rich scene with a single, elliptical verse. Frequently familial relations and marital expectations played crucial roles. For instance, Bhānudatta offers the following lines to illustrate the secretive (*guptā*) *nāyikā* who invents a banal excuse for the marks of her extramarital affair in order to assuage her in-laws.

> Mother-in-law can rant, and friends
> condemn, and sisters-in-law reprove.
> How am I possibly to sleep
> another night in that house?
> That cat of theirs is forever
> springing out of a corner niche
> to catch a mouse, and you see what all
> she's done to me with her sharp claws![103]

Abū al-Faẓl quotes this verse in the *Learning of India* to exemplify the same secretive *nāyikā*, but he alters certain parts of the plot.

> *Guptā* conceals her conduct, covers her offenses, and skillfully hides her future intentions. She offers credible excuses such that if she has been scratched by her lover's fingernail, she says, "I cannot stay in this bedroom. A cat is running after a mouse and has scratched me in the chase."[104]

Here Abū al-Faẓl does not elaborate the family situation in which the woman needs to answer for her scratches; the mother-in-law has disappeared from his version. Yet Abū al-Faẓl explicitly mentions that the woman's scratches are the result of illicit lovemaking, which is merely implied in Bhānudatta's verse and would have been understood by educated Sanskrit readers. Yet suggesting this detail instead of overtly stating it was part of what made Bhānudatta's verse poetically appealing, at least in the minds of many Sanskrit readers and theoreticians.

At the close of his literary discussion, Abū al-Faẓl intriguingly directs his audience to Indian traditions to learn more about this branch of learning. After listing dozens of types of heroes and heroines, he writes, "In this art, they explain all the different behaviors of the *nāyaka* and *nāyikā* and offer many delightful stories. Everyone whose heart yearns should read the books of this [art], and he will find his heart's desire."[105] This enigmatic comment seems to call for readers to return to Sanskrit materials in order to unearth further texts on this topic. Of course, given Abū al-Faẓl's own ignorance of Sanskrit and his trouble locating competent interpreters, one wonders whether he thought that this was a reasonable suggestion. Allison Busch has proposed that given the language capabilities of Indo-Persian intellectuals at this time, Abū al-Faẓl must be referring here to Hindi texts.[106] Braj Bhasha works on *nāyikās* were certainly available, such as Keśavdās's *Rasikpriyā* (*Handbook for Poetry Connoisseurs*, 1591).[107] This quite plausible reading again introduces Hindi, the often-elusive third party, as an integral part of Mughal encounters with Sanskrit traditions. However, given Abū al-Faẓl's own quotations of Sanskrit materials here, it seems likely that he also meant to direct Indo-Persian attention to Sanskrit texts.

Abū al-Faẓl's endorsement of accessing Sanskrit or Hindi texts (or both) has intriguing implications for the intellectual project of his *Āʾīn-i Akbarī*. As I noted earlier, Abū al-Faẓl describes his *Account of India* as a much-needed correction to the Perso-Islamic tradition of regurgitating outdated information about the subcontinent. But, in addition to providing a fresh treatise, he also intended his account of Sanskrit knowledge systems to serve as a catalyst for further Persianate engagements with the Sanskrit thought world. Thus, Abū al-Faẓl sought to revolutionize the Indo-Persian tradition by placing cross-cultural projects and a consistent return to Sanskrit texts and ideas at its very core. To some extent he offers his work as a template. Yet he simultaneously encourages his successors to access Indian learning in a far more direct manner than his capabilities allowed. This long-term plan helps to explain why Abū al-Faẓl introduces such heavy Sanskrit vocabulary and names dozens of Sanskrit texts. He promotes repeated Sanskrit and Persian encounters as a mode of producing valuable, even revolutionary contributions to Indo-Persian learning.

Despite his lofty aspirations, Abū al-Faẓl's goal to reformulate the Indo-Persian intellectual sphere met with mixed success at best. Several writers over the next few centuries brought Sanskrit and other forms of Indian learning into Persian. For example, an anonymous (Zoroastrian?) writer authored the *Dabistān-i Maẕāhib* (*Book of Religions*, ca. 1650), which includes a section on Indian beliefs and philosophical schools.[108] Circa 1675, Mīrzā Khān ibn Fakr al-Dīn Muḥammad penned the *Tuḥfat al-Hind* (*Gift of India*), which includes extensive sections on Indian music, Braj Bhasha, and *nāyikā-bheda*.[109] But whether any of these later writers were inspired by the *Learning of India* remains unclear. When Āzād Bilgrāmī wrote his *Ma'āṣir al-Kirām* in the eighteenth century, he felt obligated to explain even the most basic concepts of Sanskrit literary theory, which suggests he expected his readers to be unfamiliar with such ideas.[110] Regardless of his success or lack thereof, however, Abū al-Faẓl's intention was not only to outline Sanskrit ideas and modes of discourse in Persian. He also desired to make repeated cross-cultural interactions a central method of inquiry for Indo-Persian intellectuals.

LINKING SANSKRIT AND ISLAMICATE TRADITIONS

After his account of Sanskrit knowledge systems, Abū al-Faẓl offers two relatively short sections to complete book 4 of the *Ā'īn-i Akbarī* that connect his survey of Indian learning with the Indo-Islamic world. First, he names Islamic figures who journeyed to India beginning with Adam, continuing through the early Indo-Persian rulers, and culminating in Babur and Humayun, the first two Mughal kings. Second, he lists Islamic saints who were born in India or came to the subcontinent. These two sections provide complementary ways to incorporate India as part of the Islamicate tradition and thus to interpret Sanskrit learning as the cultural inheritance of the Mughal Empire.

Abū al-Faẓl first addresses travelers to India who embody a specific narrative of how the subcontinent had always been part of the Islamicate past, from the first man on forward. He explains the relationship between this section and his exposition of Sanskrit learning thus: "Surveying the condition of India has stimulated me to review some of those who journeyed to this vast land and promote this extraordinary book by remembering great people."[111] Abū al-Faẓl openly recognizes that this early history is based on Islamicate sources and that Sanskrit texts do not confirm such reports.[112] Perhaps precisely this perceived gap in the Sanskrit tradition is what prompted Abū al-Faẓl to add this later section clarifying the longevity of Islam's connection with India. In this view, Sanskrit is a pillar of Indian learning that is complemented and completed by Islamicate knowledge, just as Islamicate knowledge gains from the incorporation of Sanskrit learning.

Abū al-Faẓl lists roughly forty-five comers to India in all and recounts brief stories regarding these individuals. Some of the narratives highlight previous inquiries into Indian learning, such as the adventures of Buzurjmihr, but more commonly the tales are of war and conquest. Abū al-Faẓl's lineage of those who entered Hindustan culminates with Humayun, who reclaimed the Mughals' Indian kingdom. Abū al-Faẓl exclaims in closing, "Thousands of praises to God that through the justice and dignity of [Humayun], ruler of the world, Hindustan became a meeting place for good men from the seven climes who fulfill the diverse desires of their hearts!"[113] This passage centers world history on India and also proclaims the Mughals to be operating within the strictures of fate in gaining control over this immense, intellectually rich land. Tellingly, Abū al-Faẓl excludes Akbar from this list of travelers. This omission stands to reason since Akbar was born in India. But more important, it marks a transition from a constant stream of newly arrived conquerors to Mughal kings who are now within a definably Indian royal tradition.

In the final section of book 4, Abū al-Faẓl pursues another strategy to identifying India with the Islamicate tradition and details Indo-Islamic religious figures, including many Sufis. He begins with an account of different orders of saints and Sufis and then describes individuals dating back to the eleventh century. The list concludes with several mid-sixteenth-century figures and ultimately Khizr and Elias, two archetypal Sufis who are also said to have traveled to India.[114] Abū al-Faẓl's reasons for offering this concluding section are somewhat obscure, and he cites only the pleasing nature of the topic.[115] There are a few potential connections related to specific saints. For example, Khizr is known for his assistance to rulers, most notably Alexander the Great, who was one of the earlier conquerors of India in the Islamicate tradition.[116] More generally, perhaps Abū al-Faẓl envisioned completing his account of India with a truly hybrid Indo-Islamic tradition.

CONCLUSION: THE POLITICS OF KNOWLEDGE

In his *Āʾīn-i Akbarī*, Abū al-Faẓl pursues an intricate set of imperial objectives related to Sanskrit knowledge systems. The work as a whole, particularly the *Learning of India*, is a momentous scholarly achievement and a keynote text in India's intellectual history. In addition, the *Āʾīn-i Akbarī* aggressively promotes Mughal political aims and operates as a cohesive part of an imperial history. As Edward Said reminds us, "All cultures tend to make representations of foreign cultures the better to master or in some way control them."[117] Akbar's court aggressively tried to move Sanskrit knowledge from the realm of the foreign into that of the familiar, but teasing out their specific ambitions requires a more nuanced formulation than the language of domination. Abū al-Faẓl outlines a dynamic relationship between Sanskrit traditions and Mughal sovereignty that often runs contrary to modern expectations.

Abū al-Faẓl's vision is clarified by a brief comparison with parallel efforts initiated by the British, the Mughal's far better studied imperial successors. Many scholars have argued that British colonists avidly produced different types of systematic knowledge as a means of colonizing India, such as sponsoring grammars of vernacular languages and conducting the first census of the subcontinent.[118] Many of these projects were without precedent, and so the British created new types of information that were previously unavailable to either Indians or Europeans. They used these innovative efforts in order to redefine the subcontinent and thereby created an India that they could control and conquer. In contrast, Abū al-Faẓl does not generate novel types of knowledge in the *Āʾīn-i Akbarī* but rather describes established Sanskrit learning to a fresh audience. Later writers exercised more initiative, such as Āzād Bilgrāmī, who invents new types of *nāyikā*s and *nāyaka*s.[119] But Abū al-Faẓl carefully restricts himself to known Sanskrit categories, even drily translating Sanskrit example verses rather than finding poetically comparable lines. He also imports Sanskrit vocabulary and modes of discourse wholesale into Persian, and, as a result, his Persian borders on unintelligible at times. Here an approach was at work that was rather different from the British attempt to produce an India on their terms. On the contrary, Abū al-Faẓl intended for Sanskrit ideas to alter the nature of Indo-Persian knowledge.

Moreover, Abū al-Faẓl wished to make repeated cross-cultural intellectual engagements a necessary part of ruling over Hindustan. He insists that Indo-Persian readers need to understand his work and also investigate branches of Sanskrit knowledge of their own volition. Here he presents a vision beyond what he could personally achieve where Indo-Persian intellectuals are fluent in the topics, discourses, and languages of both the Sanskrit and Persianate traditions. He imagines his *Account of India* as superseding previously shoddy Islamicate work on India, but not because it would be the definitive treatment of Sanskrit learning in Persian. Instead, he promulgates a highly ambitious model for placing cross-cultural contacts at the core of Indo-Persian imperial culture. In addition to redrawing the contours of Mughal knowledge, Abū al-Faẕl may also have held ambitions regarding Persianate thought more generally. At the time he was writing, India was a major center of the Persophone world; there were several times more people literate in Persian in India than there were in Iran.[120] Abū al-Faẕl would not have been numerically aware of the demographics, but he and many of his contemporaries conceptualized Mughal India as a hub of Persianate culture that was in dialogue and competition with Safavid Persia. This context highlights the intended force of Abū al-Faẕl's argument that Persianate culture should incorporate Sanskrit knowledge systems and thus be recentered altogether on the subcontinent.

Abū al-Faẕl's complex project communicates several fundamental aspects of Mughal power, and two points are worth highlighting in closing here. First, Akbar's court understood imperial authority in part as an intellectual endeavor. Mughal power certainly required secure alliances, a functioning administration, and a degree of control over the Indian people. But Abū al-Faẕl demonstrates that, alongside such coercive forms of authority, the Mughal kings also sought a type of power that operated within the world of ideas. There was no endgame application of this learned exposition to on-the-ground political aims. Rather, the Mughals understood imperial ambitions to operate within the domain of knowledge systems, which Abū al-Faẕl expanded to include Sanskrit traditions.

Second, Abū al-Faẕl does not equate this mode of intellectual power with domination. He does not advance a vision of the Mughals steamrolling over India's knowledge systems, nor does he think that imperial ambitions dictated knowledge as a form of conquest. Rather, he proclaims Akbar's sovereignty to lie in his ability to import a hitherto unknown tradition into the realm of Indo-Persian knowledge. Accordingly, Abū al-Faẕl's basic goal revolved around integrating Sanskrit discourses within Mughal learning in order to drastically change the latter in accordance with Akbar's royal wisdom. Later thinkers did not follow Abū al-Faẕl in outlining quite so extreme a view. But, as we shall see, many Sanskrit and Persianate thinkers recognized the substantial impacts of Akbar's cross-cultural projects on their literary and intellectual worlds.

[5] WRITING ABOUT THE MUGHAL WORLD IN SANSKRIT

JAINS AND Brahmans exhibited a range of reactions to digesting Mughal engagements with Sanskrit intellectuals, texts, and knowledge systems within their respective religious traditions and overlapping textual universes. Only a small sliver of each group actually visited the imperial court. But a far more robust number of Jains and Brahmans wrote about links between members of their communities and the Mughals in Sanskrit. Over more than sixty years, Jains wrote numerous Sanskrit texts chronicling the lives of ascetic and, to a lesser degree, lay leaders who spent time at the royal court. Jains also produced inscriptions that invoke their Mughal connections, particularly at the contested pilgrimage site of Shatrunjaya in southern Gujarat. Brahmans eschewed authoring narrative accounts of their imperial contacts but nonetheless addressed cross-cultural ties in other written ways. For example, dozens of poets crafted praise verses for a Sanskrit intellectual who gained political concessions from the Mughal crown. Jains and Brahmans also shared at least one type of literary reaction: composing Mughal histories in Sanskrit. In these diverse texts Jains and Brahmans promoted their own community interests, often through co-opting the power associated with Mughal rule.

Jains composed the most substantial body of Sanskrit materials that offer in-depth accounts of associations with the Mughals. A group of six works created between 1589 and 1652 form the core of this cache (table 5.1). Four biographies detail the lives of the three successive leaders of the Tapa Gaccha from the late sixteenth to the mid-seventeenth centuries, all of whom frequented the Mughal court.[1] In addition, a work dedicated to Bhānucandra, a prominent Tapa Gaccha monk active during the reigns of Akbar and Jahangir, addresses Jain-Mughal relations

TABLE 5.1 Jain Sanskrit Works That Discuss the Mughals

Author	Year	Text
Padmasāgara	1589	*Jagadgurukāvya* (*Poem on the Teacher of the World*)
Jayasoma	1594	*Mantrikarmacandravaṃśāvalī-prabandha* (*Account of the Genealogy of Minister Karmacandra*)
Devavimala	ca. early 17th century	*Hīrasaubhāgya* (*Good Fortune of Hīravijaya*)
Siddhicandra	ca. 1620	*Bhānucandragaṇicarita* (*Acts of Bhānucandra*)
Hemavijaya (finished by Guṇavijaya)	1624–1632	*Vijayapraśastimahākāvya* (*Great Poem in Praise of Vijayasena*)
Vallabha Pāṭhaka	1652	*Vijayadevamāhātmya* (*Greatness of Vijayadeva*)

more broadly.[2] Last, a biography of Karmacandra, a politician and lay Jain, discusses Akbar's relations with lay and ascetic Kharataras.[3] These six works, written by members of both the Tapa and Kharatara Gacchas, were directed at local, often sectarian communities.[4] They place themselves within different Sanskrit genres, including poetry (*kāvya*) and narrative literature (*prabandha* and *carita*) but are united by devoting substantial attention to events involving the Mughals.[5] Curiously, Jains produced several of these accounts after the 1610s, when ascetic connections with the royal court had ceased, and post-1650 works also refer to Jain-Mughal ties in a more limited fashion.[6] Even in the absence of ongoing relations between their religious leaders and the Mughal crown, Jain communities found value in stories about cross-cultural interactions.

Jain intellectuals confronted two overarching concerns in chronicling links between their leaders and the Mughal elite. First, Jains inherited the strong Sanskrit custom of not describing Islam as a distinct religious or cultural tradition. Since the late first millennium when Sanskrit authors began mentioning Islamicate individuals in inscriptions, they tended to slot Muslims into established roles, treating them as Indian rulers, warriors, and so forth. This method of incorporation without admitting distinctive cultural markers continued into the second millennium, when Muslims started to feature in full-length Sanskrit texts.[7] Accordingly, Jains most frequently depict the Mughal elite as operating within Sanskrit, and sometimes specifically Jain, cultural norms. However, some Jain writers also experimented with more unconventional possibilities, and a few offer striking admissions of the Perso-Islamic world in Sanskrit.

Second, Jain writers necessarily negotiated the complex theological implications of endorsing relations between monks and kings. Many Jain thinkers and followers believed that the secular political realm presented formidable obstacles to the spiritual obligations of renunciants. As one fourteenth-century Kharatara monk who attended Firoz Shah's court bemoaned to a nonpolitical monk, "I have failed to observe the strict life of a monk, night and day traipsing after the Sultan! I have no independence any more. You follow the correct behavior of a monk. The true behavior appropriate to a monk is preserved in your monastery."[8] Jains often advanced compelling counterpoints to such arguments, including in the Mughal context. But Jain discomfort with links between spiritual and worldly realms never fully subsided. An air of controversy frequently swirled around Shvetambara ascetics who involved themselves, even if only briefly, in the business of Indo-Islamic governance.

In addition to the internal concerns of Jains writers, we must take account of their historical sensibilities when analyzing these works. Jain narratives tend to fall somewhere between accurate reporting and imaginative retelling. Sanskrit writers overall embrace a porous line between history and literature. As Kumkum Chatterjee has suggested, there is a "close, virtual inseparability of pre-modern historiography with kavya."[9] Far from lessening their historical value, however, the creative impulses behind Jain Sanskrit works provide insight into the cultural and intellectual value of creating such written records for specific communities.

Jains, particularly members of the Tapa Gaccha, sought to develop authority claims for their religious traditions by either likeness or contrast with Mughal power. Many writers adapted Mughal models of authority to Jain contexts and thereby investigated some of the more radical possibilities for reframing their own communities in light of political modes of being. At the same time, other thinkers rigidly distinguished their ascetic leaders from the Mughal sovereigns in order to underscore the enduring strength of Jain religious devotion, even in an Islamicate setting. Both methods fit into known Jain literary practices. In these ways, Tapa Gaccha authors defined their community identity against an imperial backdrop and also indicate some of the apprehensions raised by this context.

The Jain verbosity about their imperial experiences are framed by an inverse reticence to pen narrative records on the part of Brahmans involved in similar cross-cultural exchanges. Brahmans far outnumbered Jains as recipients of Mughal patronage but were reluctant to describe their imperial interactions in Sanskrit texts. Thus, we have dozens of Brahmanical works that bear the Persian names of their Mughal patrons but otherwise offer no trace of the culturally charged environment of their composition. Modern scholars have tried to detect unacknowledged Persianate influences in early modern Sanskrit poetry and literary criticism, but such connections remain wholly unrecognized within the tradition itself.[10] The Brahmanical silence is deafening in its declaration that while Sanskrit intellectuals could participate in the imperial Persianate sphere, they could not allow narratives of such interactions to permeate their literary world. Brahmans never elaborated their reasons for this decision in writing. Nonetheless, the act of forgetting is often as important as remembering in the construction of a group's identity.[11] Moreover, Jain narratives demonstrate that Brahmans made a meaningful rather than an inevitable cultural choice in remaining mute and prompt us to look for other written ways that Brahmans responded to their links with the Mughal court.

Most notably, Brahmans from across the subcontinent authored Sanskrit verses and prose that laud Kavīndrācārya Sarasvatī for convincing Shah Jahan to rescind pilgrimage taxes. These praises were collected to form the *Kavīndracandrodaya* (*Moonrise of Kavindra*) and allow a rare window of insight into Brahmanical reflections on imperial links. Like Jains, Brahmans overall guarded against admitting markers of Perso-Islamic culture into Sanskrit. Nonetheless, nearly seventy authors contributed verses to the *Kavīndracandrodaya*, and many of them directly refer to Kavīndra's courtly activities and other aspects of Mughal life. These contributions showcase how Brahmans tried to enshrine a selective record of their cross-cultural encounters.

Last, Jains and Brahmans alike detailed aspects of Mughal political history in Sanskrit in works that have been nearly entirely overlooked by scholars. These materials include lists of Indian kings, narratives of Mughal conquests and succession wars, and a surprisingly close Sanskrit translation of the first portion of the *Akbarnāmah*.[12] Many of the texts are of unclear provenance, and they date from the late sixteenth to the early eighteenth centuries. Few appear to have circulated widely, although authors kept returning to similar topics over a period of at least one hundred and fifty years. A brief survey of these sundry works forms an appropriate coda to the story of Sanskrit in the Mughal Empire because they demonstrate the persistent lure for Indian literati of thinking through the legacies of Mughal power.

DESCRIBING ISLAMIC BELIEFS IN SANSKRIT

Devavimala penned his *Hīrasaubhāgya* (*Good Fortune of Hīravijaya*) in the early seventeenth century and therein discusses the Mughals at considerable length. The work traces Hīravijaya Sūri's life from birth until death and includes an authorial commentary. In this biography, Devavimala recounts many events set at the Mughal court, including a conversation between Hīravijaya and Abū al-Faẓl that involves one of the few open descriptions of basic Islamic beliefs in Sanskrit. This exchange took place during the Tapa Gaccha leader's first sojourn at the imperial court in 1583–1585. While many Jain writers divulge details of this extended visit, including that Hīravijaya met with Abū al-Faẓl, Devavimala alone recounts their debate about the merits of Islam versus Jainism.[13] The historical accuracy of the reported dialogue is dubious. But this section is noteworthy because it constitutes a striking and unprecedented sketch of Islamic religious ideas in Sanskrit. Moreover, Devavimala uses the exchange to glorify Hīravijaya as able to counter the particular theological challenges of Mughal-backed Islam.

At the beginning of this episode Devavimala frames both Abū al-Faẓl and Hīravijaya as religious scholars. He describes Abū al-Faẓl as "seeing the far edge of the ocean of Islamic learning" (*turuṣkaśāstrāmbudhipāradṛśvā*), which the commentary further specifies means that he knows Islamic scriptures such as the Qurʾan and Qurʾanic exegesis.[14] After a brief interlude during which Akbar found himself distracted and asked Abū al-Faẓl to meet with their guest, Devavimala again characterizes the vizier as "learned in the secrets of all *śāstras*" and glosses *śāstras* as "Islamic scriptures beginning with the Qurʾan."[15] Hīravijaya exceeded the vizier's accreditations from the start, however. Abū al-Faẓl recognized the Tapa Gaccha leader as a wise discriminator (*vivektāram*) "regarding both Islamic and Jain creeds that promote violence and compassion, respectively, and are opposed to one another" and so approached the sage respectfully, "like a student."[16] Then, having gathered a crowd of people to act as an audience for the exchange, Abū al-Faẓl asked Hīravijaya's opinion of

Muslim theology. This framing leaves no uncertainty that ultimately this debate will vindicate Tapa Gaccha views. But first Devavimala breaks from customary Sanskrit practice and includes Abū al-Faẓl's exposition of Islam along with Hīravijaya's response.

Abū al-Faẓl's reported speech is worth quoting at length for its astounding admission of Islam into Sanskrit as a cogent theological system. According to Devavimala, Abū al-Faẓl said,

> O Sūri, this was laid out by the ancient prophets in our scriptures—all Muslims [*yavana*] who are deposited on earth as guests of the god of death will rise at the end of the earth and come before the court of the Supreme Lord called *khudā*, just as they come to the court of an earthly king. He will cast good and bad qualities onto his own pure mind as if onto a mirror and bring about rightful judgment there, having refuted the false construction of mine versus another's. Having reflected, he will bestow the appropriate result of [the *yavana*s'] virtues and vices, just as the fertile soil generates plentiful grain from different seeds. Some will be brought to heaven by him, just as boats are led to the edge of the ocean by a favorable wind. Then they will find joy, nearly overwhelmed by floods of suitable, amazing pleasures. Others will be sent to hell by him because of sin. Like birds being crushed by hawks and pots being fired by potters, they will suffer great agonies at the mercies of hell's guards. O Sūri, what is the validity of this Qur'anic speech [*kurānavākyaṃ*]: is it true, like the speech of great-souled people, or is it false like a flower in the sky?[17]

Devavimala's open exposition of Muslim beliefs contrasts acutely with the durable preference for eliding Islam in Sanskrit texts. In particular, early modern philosophers overwhelmingly refused to incorporate Islam into Sanskrit discourse as a serious tradition that could be compared with Buddhist, Jain, and Brahmanical views.[18] Against this custom of unyielding rejection, Devavimala gives Islam a substantial platform as a theological tradition in a Sanskrit text. He further refers to a body of Islamic texts and employs several Perso-Islamic terms that are transliterated into Sanskrit and defined in the commentary (e.g., *paigambar* [*paighāmbar*] for "prophet," *doyaki* [*dūzakh*] for "hell," and *bhisti* [*bihisht*] for "heaven"). Thus, Devavimala presents Islam as a recognizable religious tradition with a solid textual basis and its own vocabulary for explaining reality.

In his commentary, Devavimala softens the brazen innovation of this passage by linking Islamic beliefs with traditional Sanskrit thought. For example, he explains why Allah will refute "the false construction of mine versus another's" by citing a famous Sanskrit sentiment that the entire world is a single family: "Only narrow-minded people make the distinction between being one of us or one of them. For the right-minded, the whole world is a family."[19] Variants of this verse appear in many places, and Devavimala quotes a version found in the *Hitopadeśa*, a ubiquitous book of instructive fables.[20] Devavimala explicates the description of hell's vicious guards with a Prakrit verse from Dharmadāsa's *Vidagdhamukhamaṇḍana* (*Ornament of the Clever-Mouthed*), a popular work of riddles dating from the mid-eleventh century or earlier.[21] Through such references, he attempts to render bewilderingly unfamiliar Islamic ideas explicable within Sanskrit intellectual frameworks, which suggests some sort of connectivity of commensurability between Indian and Islamic thought. Nonetheless, Devavimala's innovation in describing Islamic ideas at all is arresting. Furthermore, Hīravijaya's retort suggests a gulf of understanding between Islamic and Jain worldviews.

According to Devavimala, Hīravijaya supplanted Abū al-Faẕl's Islamic convictions by methodically overturning the logic of a creator god, heaven, hell, and judgment day. In lieu of Allah, Hīravijaya argued that the Jain doctrine of action (*karma*) governs all things:

> "He—who is free of dirt like a shell, devoid of defects like the sun, made of flames like fire, and without a body like the god of love—is the Supreme Lord. In what form does he attend court like a living being that adopts many appearances in his wanderings through existence? There he sets a person on the path to heaven or hell for what reason? A previous action, once ripened, has the power to grant both joys and sorrows. Thus, let action [*karma*] alone be recognized as the creator of the world, since otherwise [God] has no purpose." When the lord of ascetics [Hīravijaya] fell silent after speaking, Shaykh [Abū al-Faẕl] replied, "That book [commentary: Qurʾan] is recognized as false just as inconsistency is recognized in the speech of a garrulous, vile person." The lord [Hīravijaya] spoke again: "If the creator first made this world and then later destroyed it as if he were fire, he would have unparalleled distress. There is no creator or destroyer of the world whose variety is brought into being by its own *karma*. Therefore, the existence of a creator, like the birth of a son to a barren woman, appears false to me."[22]

Throughout his reply, Hīravijaya used established Jain thinking to refute Abū al-Faẕl point by point. Jains had long denied any God or gods as creators and instead contended that individuals control their own fate within the world (*loka*). They frequently promoted this view against Brahmans who identified a particular god as the maker of reality.[23] Even when Abū al-Fażl interrupted to proclaim that this argument falsifies the Qurʾan, Hīravijaya did not adapt his views for an Islamic audience. Later writers, such as Hemavijaya, sometimes present Tapa Gaccha representatives as creatively answering Mughal religious queries in ways that allow for convenient convergences with Islamic sensibilities. But Devavimala outlines a view solidly grounded in Jain theology and even cites religious treatises, such as the *Kalpasūtra*, in his commentary.[24] In closing, Devavimala declares that through his words Hīravijaya placed the *dharma* of compassion (*dayā*) in the heart of Abū al-Fażl.[25]

Whether anything approximating this exchange actually happened remains uncertain, and Abū al-Fażl's alleged conversion to Jainism is certainly a rhetorical flourish rather than a historical claim. But this narrative nonetheless presents three major insights on Jain perceptions of meetings with the Mughals. First, in this anecdote, Devavimala portrays Jain and Islamic theology as comparable, although highly unequal. Devavimala departs drastically from his predecessors and contemporaries in allowing Islam to permeate the boundaries of Sanskrit literature at all, much less as an alternative to a Jain understanding the world. He even allows Islam a fairly full hearing, equivalent in length to Hīravijaya's winning rebuttal. Here Devavimala invokes theology as a primary mode of expressing cross-cultural encounters.

Second, Devavimala uses the theological clash between Hīravijaya and Abū al-Fażl to advance a forceful argument that the Tapa Gaccha is a vigorous, competitive tradition within the Mughal imperium, a de facto Islamic space. In this sense, the Jain victory appears all the more potent for being against Abū al-Fażl, a prominent political figure and a leading intellectual of his day. Devavimala also promotes the strength of Jainism in the Mughal context in other ways throughout his text. For example, immediately following this episode, Devavimala narrates how Hīravijaya taught an almost ludicrously receptive Akbar about Jain *dharma*. Devavimala offers more detail regarding Jain ideas and practices in this exchange and also compares this meeting to political connections forged by earlier Jain leaders.[26] Hīravijaya's interaction with Akbar is also narrated in other texts and would have been familiar to Jain readers as a laudable case where a pious monk led a king to proper religious practice.[27] But Hīravijaya's discussion with Abū al-Fażl particularly highlights how the Tapa Gaccha could directly face and dominate politically backed Islam.

Last, Devavimala's description of Muslim convictions constitutes a break with the Sanskrit trend of denying Islam the status of a religious or philosophical system. Other exceptions surfaced periodically, but they were generally late and rather limited. For example, one thinker briefly denounced Islam in an eighteenth-century Sanskrit treatise, but he switched to Rajasthani for this section of the work.[28] Andrew Nicholson has suggested that some early modern Hindu criticisms directed against Buddhists and Jains are vague enough to have been interpreted by astute readers as applicable to Muslims.[29] Nonetheless, Devavimala seems to stand alone in providing a detailed Sanskrit explanation of Islamic theology in a historical context. This episode showcases the creative, previously unthinkable possibilities enabled, at least for Jain writers, by conversing with those who embodied Indo-Islamic authority.

NARRATIVES OF RELIGIOUS DIFFERENCE AT AKBAR'S COURT

Tapa Gaccha intellectuals record multiple occasions when Akbar called upon Hīravijaya and Vijayasena to explain the nature of "God" within Jain theology. Above all, the Mughals were alarmed that Jains might be atheists. Akbar and Jahangir tolerated different religious sensibilities at the royal court but perceived atheism as beyond the pale of acceptability. Imperial texts condemn those who lack belief in any god, and the Mughal kings even periodically jailed people, such as Naqīb Khān's son, for the offense.[30] In order to maintain their status as welcome members of the emperor's inner circle, Jains necessarily professed their monotheist notions before the Mughal assembly on several occasions. Moreover, Jains developed detailed Sanskrit accounts of these discussions for circulation within their communities (the conversations themselves almost certainly took place in either a form of Old Hindi or Persian). These religious debates and their narrativizations reveal how early modern Jains navigated religious difference and often reformulated aspects of their traditions in order to operate within a Mughal-defined world.

One remarkable case was the accusation of atheism lobbied against the Tapa Gaccha in the early 1590s. Vijayasena, who would soon take over leadership of the group, responded to Mughal horror at the prospect that Jains might deny the existence of God, and this discussion is recorded in notably dissimilar versions by Hemavijaya and Siddhicandra. Both wrote in the 1620s–1630s and include Vijayasena's testimony to Jain monotheism in larger hagiographies directed toward Jain audiences.[31] But they offer differing attestations of the Mughal charge of atheism and Vijayasena's answer, including different identifications of the Jain deity. Moreover, Hemavijaya emphasizes the dispute's immediate political consequences, whereas Siddhicandra underscores its significance in traditional Indian intellectual debates. Taken together, these two writers demonstrate erudition and flexibility to be great strengths of the Jain tradition that allowed its followers to flourish in Mughal environs and perhaps even enabled them to write about their experiences.

According to Hemavijaya, the central issue at stake was whether Akbar was convinced that the Jains accepted a monotheistic God. Trouble began when, upon seeing the Tapa Gaccha rise in Akbar's esteem, a nameless Brahman articulated a rather detailed case against the sect that resonates with basic Islamicate theology. He exclaimed,

> Those idiot Jains do not believe that there is a pure one, without a physical form, changeless, sinless, emancipated from rebirth, free of emotional agitations, passionless, independent, the slayer of all sins, and the maker of all happiness, namely God [*parameśvara*]. The path of those fools who do not believe God is the source of the world is always in vain like a fixed point without coordinates. Therefore, O Sun of the Courts of Shahs, the sight of those people is not good for kings like you, any more than the sight of menstruating women.[32]

As intended, the Brahman's words infuriated Akbar, who put a more basic query to Vijayasena: " 'These great-souled cheats of all mankind with hoards of worldly practices certainly do not believe in God [*parameśvara*]'—O Guru, let your words banish this doubt from my mind just as a cloth removes oil from water."[33] In his reformulation of the Brahman's denunciation, Akbar omitted many specific concerns, most notably the issue of a creator god, and asked more generally about a Jain supreme deity. This reduced allegation allowed Vijayasena to champion Jains as theists without disingenuously assenting to a creator. Moreover, Akbar narrowed a much broader set of largely Brahmanical objections to a possible dissonance between Islamic and Jain worldviews. Thus, Hemavijaya places this exchange firmly within its current circumstances as a moment of political peril for Jain ascetics who sought Mughal favor.

With the stage set for possible heresy and therefore expulsion of Jain monks from court, Vijayasena defended his imperial alliance. Hemavijaya records the response in sixty-one verses as the Jain leader weaved eloquent descriptions of God with more pointed statements about Jain theistic belief. In the middle of his speech, Vijayasena gave his most direct answer to the king's challenge:

> The Shaivas worship him as "Shiva" and the Vedantins as "Brahma." The Buddhists, who are sharp in logic, worship him as "Buddha" and the Mimamsakas as "Karma." Those who ascribe to the Jain scriptures worship him as "Arhat," and the Naiyayikas as "Creator." May that Hari, the Lord of the Three Worlds, give you whatever you desire.[34]

Thus, the God of the Jains is Arhat, also known as Jina, or an enlightened human teacher, and is comparable to chief deities in other Indian philosophies. This formulation of comparing Arhat to the gods (*deva* or *devatā*) of other systems mirrors Jain philosophical compendiums.[35] However, these compendiums often define theist (*āstika*) as an ethical rather than a doctrinal category that might be more aptly described as "nonmaterialist."[36] In this sense, Hemavijaya makes a far stronger claim than his philosophical predecessors that the Jains qualify as monotheists according to Islamic standards. Moreover, Hemavijaya judged even this formidable idea inadequate on its own merits. He relays that Vijayasena punctuated his demonstration of theistic comparability with a wish for Vishnu to ensure Akbar's well-being. Vishnu would likely have been more familiar than other Indian gods among the Mughal elite.[37] With this plea Hemavijaya reminds his readers that Akbar alone will determine the Jains' fate.[38]

In Hemavijaya's telling, Vijayasena devoted the other sixty verses of his reply to elaborating the twofold deity of Arhat. Vijayasena spent the first half of his speech describing a formless, eternal God "whose essence is knowledge and whose nature is inconceivable."[39] His descriptions often refute the specific Brahmanical objections that Jains do not consent to a God who is pure, changeless, and so forth. Vijayasena summarized at the close of his speech, "We always say that in this aspect, God has no beginning, no birth, is free of a soul that links him to this world, is made of knowledge, and is without equal."[40] In this view, Arhat is suitably vague and unqualified to be palatable to Islamicate sensibilities, which generally emphasize the all-powerful nature of God.[41] In other circumstances, the Mughals also pressured Brahmans to admit to a higher power devoid of form and attributes.[42] Yet such syncretic possibilities did not preclude the second half of Vijayasena's analysis, which is more specifically situated within Jain thought.

Over thirty-one verses, Vijayasena elaborated the intricate Jain imagery surrounding Arhat as a ford maker (*tīrthāṅkara*) who descended to earth to spread the Jain teaching. Vijayasena focused on the much-celebrated first sermon that Arhat gave as an enlightened individual that took place in a divine assembly hall (*samavasaraṇa*).[43] His imagery follows traditional Jain ideals to the letter as gods, men, and animals peacefully gathered to hear the Jina's teachings.[44] It is quite plausible that Vijayasena articulated much of this description before the Mughal court. Abū al-Faẓl crafted an extensive section on Jainism in his *Āʾīn-i Akbarī* and therein repeats some of these details, such as Arhat's fragrant breath and white flesh and blood.[45] Abū al-Faẓl also notes the dual nature of the Jain God as the incarnate founder of Jainism and "the supreme lord without qualities."[46] Nonetheless, the details of Arhat on earth would hardly have helped Vijayasena's case that the Jain God is comparable to transcendent Allah. Here, Hemavijaya's retelling seems designed to assure a Jain audience that admitting some similarities with Islam did not infringe on their distinct theological precepts.

At the end of Vijayasena's elaborate defense, Hemavijaya returns to the political risks in this debate and narrates that the Tapa Gaccha regained its place of pride in Akbar's estimation. The emperor's doubts were fully allayed.[47] As for the Brahmans, "When the Brahmans were defeated by the Sūri, they became so emasculated it is amazing the townspeople did not lust after them as if they were women."[48] The Jains, on the other hand, witnessed their fame expanding immeasurably as Vijayasena reveled in having gained increased political clout for the Tapa Gaccha.[49] For Hemavijaya, Mughal political power defined both the accusation of atheism and the benefits of overcoming this suspicion. Jain leaders were able to assuage Islamic concerns without compromising their theology precisely because their tradition understands God as possessing multiple aspects.

Siddhicandra relates a rather different version of these events than Hemavijaya that is far more grounded in traditional Indian philosophical disputes. He changes the audience for the exchange, the course of Vijayasena's argument, and the identity of the Jain God. Siddhicandra opens with an objection voiced by Ramdas Kachhwaha, a Rajput in the service of the Mughals, who said to Akbar, "These [Jains] are outside the Veda [*vedabāhya*], do not worship God [*paramātma*], and never do obeisance before the king."[50] Ramdas frequently advanced Vaishnava interests at the Mughal court and so it seems plausible that he sought to displace the Jains from imperial favor.[51] But Ramdas surrounded the central charge of atheism with two additional affronts. The last offense (refusal to bow) pointedly underscores that Jains risked losing Mughal favor if they did not meet imperial expectations. But the mention of the Vedas is more enigmatic.[52] Siddhicandra likely intended "Veda" here to be deliberately ambivalent. In the context of the Mughal court, he probably meant "Veda" in a broad sense of acceptable scriptures so that "outside the Veda" meant something like "separate from people of the book."[53] Akbar included Hindus within this protected category and was concerned about whether Jains also qualified. However, Jain readers would have recognized the phrase *vedabāhya* from disputes with Brahmans, where it meant that Jains "reject the Vedas." In this sense, Siddhicandra signals his intention to review long-standing doctrinal disputes between Brahmans and Jains.

According to Siddhicandra, Akbar next put the Rajput's accusation to Vijayasena, who denied everything. Then Bhaṭṭācārya, a Brahmanical (likely Shaivite) leader, contended, "It may be assented by them verbally, but nothing of the kind is found in their scriptures [*śāstra*]."[54] At this point, Akbar asked his vizier, Abū al-Faẓl, to settle the dispute and retreated from the scene. Siddhicandra repeatedly presents Abū al-Faẓl as a paragon of Sanskrit learning in his *Bhānucandragaṇicarita* (*Acts of Bhānucandra*). When he first introduces the vizier in the text, Siddhicandra marvels,

> The wisdom [of Shaykh Abū al-Faẓl] extended to all the *śāstras*, including Jainism, Mimamsa, Buddhism, Sankhya, Vaisheshika, Carvaka, Jaiminiya, literature [*kāvya*], yoga, Vedanta, lexicography, music, drama, aesthetic tropes, mythology [*purāṇa*], metrical works, the science of omens, astrology, mathematics, physiognomy, political science, erotics, veterinary science, and guardianship. There is nothing written [*vāñmaya*] that he has neither seen nor heard.[55]

In the current debate, Abū al-Faẓl exercised his erudition in the entirety of Sanskrit learning to facilitate a consolidated tour of old Jain-Brahman debates. Bhaṭṭācārya and Vijayasena moved rapidly through a sequence of condensed arguments that had been worked out by their intellectual predecessors over many centuries. Abū al-Faẓl judged the contest, but the standard of victory was not convincing an imperial patron but rather consistency within Jainism's own philosophical system.

Siddhicandra's cryptic narrative of the dispute between Bhaṭṭācārya and Vijayasena is difficult to follow and assumes familiarity with frequently rehearsed arguments. But the core question revolved around whether there is a creator god, an issue that was dropped at the beginning of the exchange in Hemavijaya's version. Toward the end of their verbal spar, Vijayasena summarized the Tapa Gaccha position: "If one who was dependent on action [*karma*] created, then he would not be independent and [instead] would be just like us. And given that all sorts of things are born from action [*karma*], then what need do we have of Shiva?"[56] Thus, *karma* is God for the Jains in the sense of accounting for cause and effect in the world, and all individuals initiate actions and are thus creators.[57] Moreover, Vijayasena contended in closing that it is ridiculous to require belief in a creator god in order to be considered theists:

> Given this line of reasoning, because of not assenting to the state of being a creator in respect to man but in respect to natural matter that is insentient, how are the Sankhyas believers in God? And saying that "this world arose unprecedented, born from a sacrifice recorded in the Vedas," how are the Vaisheshikas believers in God? And believing that "this world is an illusion, without God as a creator," how are the Vedantins believers in God?[58]

Thus, if Brahmans would deny that *karma* qualifies the Jains as theists, then they must also invalidate numerous other Indian schools of thought. Siddhicandra celebrates that Vijayasena rendered his Brahman opponent speechless with this "powerful ocean of reasoning."[59] Such logic would not appear to be particularly convincing to the Mughals, who inherited an Islamic-based conception of Almighty Allah. But here we are far from an Indo-Islamic court and deeply engulfed in Sanskrit philosophy. In case his readers doubted Vijayasena's intellectual victory, Siddhicandra next narrates that Abū al-Faẓl attested to Akbar that the Jains "spoke in accordance with their own teachings" and celebrations broke out in the streets.[60]

Thus, Siddhicandra and Hemavijaya agree on the basic argument that the Tapa Gaccha espouses a theistic system but individually emphasize distinct nuances within Jain thought. Taken together, one is struck by the ability of these authors to articulate divergent but yet consonant ideas. Hemavijaya promotes two compatible views of God as a transcendent deity and an incarnate teacher. Arhat is to be revered in both aspects and occupies a central place in Jain thought akin to Allah's position in Islam. Siddhicandra evades finding a Jain God that is to be worshipped and rather identifies the cycle of cause and effect as providing the same explanatory power in accounting for reality as God does in other religious systems. All these explanations are consistent with Tapa Gaccha philosophy and demonstrate substantial flexibility in how Jains could effectively present their views in Mughal India.

Hemavijaya and Siddhicandra both relay two formulations of the accusation of atheism: one from the perspective of a Brahman or Rajput and the second in the voice of the Mughal king. The precise content of these charges differs between the two texts, which further highlights the challenges of interacting with multiple religious communities in a space ultimately controlled by Islamicate elites. The lesson for Jain readers seems to be that while political alliances may give rise to many religious challenges, the Jain system is well equipped to transform such threats into opportunities for even greater gain precisely because of its multiplicity of perspectives. Additionally, when taken together, Hemavijaya and Siddhicandra attest that the Jain tradition perceived immense value in writing about these experiences for a local audience. Through such continual retellings, this debate and other Mughal encounters with Jain ascetics became integrated parts of the Tapa Gaccha's community narrative that were beneficial to invoke even in the absence of ongoing imperial connections. Perhaps the sophisticated ability to articulate congruent perspectives is also part of what rendered Jains capable of writing extensively and diversely about their experiences at the Mughal court, while Brahmans frequently remained tongue-tied.

MODELING JAIN AUTHORITY ON MUGHAL POLITICAL CULTURE

In many respects, Jains perceived the Mughal court as a space defined predominantly by imperial power. The Tapa and Kharatara Gacchas both depicted their ascetic leaders within this political context, often drawing upon established tropes for meetings between monks and kings. But the Tapa Gaccha found particular value in narrating connections with the Mughals, perhaps because they had never before exercised significant political influence. Kharataras had forged close relations with Delhi Sultanate rulers in the fourteenth century and developed the implications of those affiliations in written accounts.[61] But the Tapa Gaccha overall remained relatively limited and in the shadows of history until the second half of the sixteenth century, when the group came into prominence under Hīravijaya's leadership.[62] As the Tapa Gaccha stepped onto a world historical stage delineated by Mughal power, they formulated two opposing versions of Jain authority as alternatively modeled on the powerful ruling elite and distinct from Mughal worldly interests.[63] Particularly the former approach highlights that the Tapa Gaccha identified cross-cultural relations as a constructive, even essential exercise for conceptualizing and asserting their community. This attempt comes out most clearly in Tapa Gaccha descriptions of Hīravijaya, a leader often cast as embodying a Jain imperial authority perfectly suited to the Mughal dispensation.

In 1589, Padmasāgara composed the earliest Sanskrit text on Jain relations with Akbar's court (*Jagadgurukāvya* [*Poem on the Teacher of the World*]) and therein consistently depicts Hīravijaya according to Mughal standards of authority. He situates his boldest claim in the assembly of the Mughal governor of Gujarat, who had been ordered to send Hīravijaya to Fatehpur Sikri. This brief episode begins with a classic public glorification (*prabhāvanā*), a trope in Jain literature whereby refusing secular temptations underscored the devotion of politically involved religious leaders.[64] In a truly astonishing passage, Padmasāgara then compares Hīravijaya to the Islamic God:

> There the khan, a king called a sahib, who carried out the orders of glorious Padshah Akbar, invited the best of gurus [Hīravijaya] to his own assembly hall and honored him. He set out a large plate of jewels and gold that the best of gurus, the leader of all Jain ascetics, did not even touch. [Hīravijaya], foremost among the dispassionate, best of ascetics, who had the form of glorious *khudā*, was seen there, the likes of whom had not been seen anywhere else on earth. Thus, [the khan] sent [Hīravijaya] from his palace to the ascetic ashram in the company of Mughal soldiers and accompanied by praises, instruments, and drums.[65]

One could scarcely imagine a more evident adoption of Mughal, Islamic-based authority than invoking the Persian name of God (*khudā*). In other words, Hīravijaya stood on the highest level of the Islamic hierarchy, one step above any normal man and comparable to God himself. Akbar is often described in Persian texts similarly as the "shadow of God."[66] After appearing as a near divine, Akbar-like figure, Hīravijaya then proceeded to his ashram, although more in the fashion of a Mughal king than a Jain monk with an elaborate retinue of soldiers and panegyrists. Thus, when Hīravijaya embarked on his journey to Akbar's court in the next verse, he had already been declared the equal or better of the Mughal emperor.

When Hīravijaya arrived at the royal court, Padmasāgara reiterates his commensurability with the Mughal emperor. For example, he frequently equates Hīravijaya and Akbar with paired epithets such as "king of the earth" and "king of monks."[67] At the conclusion of their first meeting, Padmasāgara attests that Hīravijaya co-opted the markers of Mughal royalty in his procession from court:

> Then the lord of the earth [Akbar], following on foot, bowed down at [Hīravijaya's] feet and stood again. From his own home, he sent all his soldiers to [Hīravijaya], ordered musical instruments to be played stridently by men sitting on top of elephants and had his own splendor [*svaśriyam*]—complete with chariots, horses, and elephants—go before [Hīravijaya] Sūri.[68]

This imagery mirrors Hīravijaya's exit from the assembly of the governor of Gujarat, except on a grander, imperial scale. Here Akbar sent his own royal accoutrements, those things that announced to the world that he was the Mughal sovereign, to accompany Hīravijaya. Subsequent verses depict a Tapa Gaccha king who paraded through throngs of reveling people that threw expensive clothes on the ground before him.[69] In these ways, Padmasāgara casts Hīravijaya as an authority figure in a definably Mughal sense who adopted and elicited royal behaviors.

Later Jain Sanskrit authors often followed Padmasāgara's lead in framing Hīravijaya and his successors as sovereigns of an ascetic order. Paul Dundas has catalogued a number of references to the Tapa Gaccha's kingdom (*sāṃrājya*), earthly prosperity (*lakṣmī*), and royally modeled succession customs.[70] Even when describing practices thoroughly grounded in the Jain tradition, such as Hīravijaya's terminal fast at the end of his life, Devavimala compares him to a "king who never abandons justice."[71] The late seventeenth-century writer Meghavijaya represented the Tapa Gaccha's religious heads after Hīravijaya as Mughal-like warriors accompanied on their conquests by armies of monks.[72] Such characterizations were directed toward a Jain readership that would have been familiar with some fluidity between the characteristics of spiritual and political leaders. Nonetheless, earlier Jain authors had often extolled monks by showing their influence over the reigning king, occasionally even claiming that particular rulers converted to Jainism.[73] Padmasāgara and later authors pursue this strategy to varying degrees, such as Abū al-Fazl's inclination toward Jainism in the *Hīrasaubhāgya*, discussed earlier in this chapter. But Tapa Gaccha thinkers also allowed power to transfer in the other direction, so that their leaders and community were glorified by becoming like the Mughal king and his imperium.

UPHOLDING ASCETICISM AGAINST IMPERIAL COMMAND

While the Tapa Gaccha sought to imitate the Mughals in certain respects, they were also sensitive to the risk that political ties could undermine religious obligations. Moreover, intellectuals feared that lay followers and critics might infer laxity, whether or not it actually came to pass. Many authors deploy stock tropes to counter such worries, such as that ascetic leaders refused monetary rewards from the Mughal kings or declined to sit on luxurious carpets at court to avoid hurting small insects hidden underneath.[74] One thinker, Siddhicandra, offers a particularly galvanizing story about how he fervently clung to his ascetic vows despite immense pressure from Jahangir and his wife, Nur Jahan. Siddhicandra has featured in my discussion already as an author, but a few biographical details are helpful here. Siddhicandra was a Tapa Gaccha monk who was raised in Akbar's court and, by his own admission, learned Persian.[75] Perhaps because of his notably strong ties with the Mughal world, Siddhicandra exhibited more anxiety than his peers about accepting imperial patronage. In narrating the disagreement over asceticism, Siddhicandra develops a robust Jain authority in contradistinction to the worldly Mughals. Nonetheless, he also voices some strong objections to monks being located at royal courts. Ultimately, this unsettling account proffers an ambivalent moral about whether the benefits of Jain ascetic ties with the Mughal elite outweighed the dangers.

The story commences with Emperor Jahangir observing that in both age and nature, Siddhicandra was ill suited for a renunciant way of life:

> You possess signs that you are fit to be an earthly king.
> O friend, you are resplendent with the radiating beauty of youth.
> Given that your age is suited for pursuing fiery young women,
> why do you abandon sensual pleasures and give yourself to austerities?[76]

Siddhicandra chided Jahangir for poking fun at his serious commitment and retorted that the transience of the world makes people of all ages well advised to adopt asceticism. In rather poor form, Jahangir, "his eyes rolling about from the influence of drink," asked the monk straight up how he could help himself from thinking about sex.[77] In response, Siddhicandra waxed eloquently about the benefits of being detached from earthly things. Jahangir then quieted down in amazement at this strong reasoning, perhaps mixed with an alcohol-induced stupor, until Nur Jahan (here called Nur Mahal) walked into the assembly hall.

At this point, Siddhicandra's story slips into the realm of fantasy considering that purdah restrictions in the harem would have prevented Nur Jahan from appearing at court. But the value of this narrative for Siddhicandra is far less its historical viability than its promise as a potent illustration of a Tapa Gaccha monk's upholding his religious values while pursuing political influence.[78] Nur Jahan tried to undermine the monk by proclaiming, "Wherever there is youth, speech that reflects soundness of mind is impossible."[79] In response, Siddhicandra cited the example of the young king of Balkh who became a renunciant. Although the *Bhānucandragaṇicarita* does not specify the name of the ruler, this appears to be the story of Ibrahim ibn Adham, a figure renowned in the Perso-Arabic tradition for repudiating all worldly possessions, including his crown.[80] Siddhicandra introduces this Islamicate reference with the lone Hindi verse in his text to say, "Sixteen thousand palaces, eighteen lakh horses, and the city of Bilakkh [Balkh] were given up for the sake of his Lord."[81] This brief foray into the Perso-Islamic cultural sphere, including a language intelligible among the imperial elite, indicates the great political liability of this debate that called for the invocation of an idea designed to hit close to home for Jahangir and Nur Jahan.

After invoking Perso-Islamic culture in order to provide a precedent for young renunciants, Siddhicandra promptly steered the conversation back into his own tradition and frames both himself and his imperial interlocutors as speaking in Jain terms. Nur Jahan argued that it would be best to renounce as an old man, after having one's fill of sensual pleasures.[82] Siddhicandra responded that the degradation of the current age, the Kali Yuga, has had exactly the opposite effect, and people wantonly pursue pleasures virtually until the grave.[83] Next Jahangir, transformed from a drunkard into a skillful philosopher without explanation, articulated a sequence of compelling objections to Jain monks' participating in imperial affairs. Some of his arguments carry rhetorical force, such as when he exclaimed, "Young man! Why do you want to bring sorrows such as plucking out hair by the root on your body, which is as delicate as the stem of a *shirisha* flower."[84]

Jahangir's most convincing argument drew directly upon Jain thought. He proposed that the Jain doctrine of relativism or multiple viewpoints (*syādvāda*) made Siddhicandra's obstinacy untenable and that the monk should adopt a more relativist understanding of the universe as trumpeted by his own tradition. In the reported words of Jahangir, here described as "grasping Jain doctrine,"[85]

> Only the minds of men adjudicate between virtue and vice. Without the mind, there is no shirking of duty. Even if something is a sin here, it is to be repelled with good intentions, just as leanness caused by fasting is to be curbed by eating wholesome food. There are rules and exceptions in the *dharma* of ascetics, and both are to be remembered by all. Therefore it is foolish for everybody to grasp a single viewpoint. The truth of multiple viewpoints [*syādvāda*] is to be understood in all things by those who speak of relativism [*syādvāda*]. For them, endorsing a single view would be called falsity. O wise one, having abandoned your obstinacy and consenting to my speech, enjoy pleasures as you wish. What wise man would err in his own advice?[86]

Siddhicandra replied that exceptions to religious practice are for the weak and avoiding temptation altogether is the best method of resistance. But his only counter to Jahangir's use of *syādvāda* is to glibly quip that the doctrine itself admits that it cannot be taken as absolutely true and so dogmatism is sometimes justified.[87] This rhetorical sleight of hand signals the feebleness of Siddhicandra's position here, particularly in contrast to Jahangir's rather deft deployment of Jain thinking.

Siddhicandra does not allow his readers to dwell on the arguments, however, and next narrates that Jahangir's anger flared as the king shouted,

> Do you dare to show me contempt! Do you not know my power?
> When angered, I am the God of Death [*kṛtānta*] before your eyes,
> but when happy I am a wishing tree of paradise.
> Now you will reap what you have sown with your poisonous obstinacy.[88]

Siddhicandra still stood firm, at which point Jahangir once more demanded that he take a wife along with other worldly pleasures, including a position in the imperial administration, elephants, and horses.[89] When the monk refused, Jahangir ordered an elephant brought to crush him to death. When Siddhicandra rejected Jahangir's command to marry one last time, the elephant and the crowd together roared, but the monk stood perfectly still and appeared undisturbed. Impressed, Jahangir's fury dissipated slightly. He directed that the elephant be pulled back and imposed exile on the recalcitrant Jain ascetic instead of execution.[90] In addition, the king issued a *farmān*: "Other renunciants that wander my kingdom are to dwell in the forest since [the forest] alone is an appropriate residence for ascetics who are free of desires."[91]

The moral of this story thus far is murky at best. Siddhicandra stayed true to his vows despite repeated coercive efforts from the throne and staggering consequences for himself and other renunciants. Certain aspects of the tale communicate the strength of Jain ascetic vows to a sectarian audience, such as when Siddhicandra proclaims to Jahangir, "I will not violate the *dharma* I have chosen, even a hair."[92] But whether Siddhicandra justified his presence at court is a far more open-ended question. Tapa Gaccha followers were acutely aware of both the benefits and challenges their spiritual leaders faced in forging connections with the Mughal elite, but the former are what justified the latter. Given that Siddhicandra's stubbornness resulted in the eviction of Jain monks from court, he hardly demonstrated the value of the entire exercise.

Siddhicandra offers one more story to conclude his *Bhānucandragaṇicarita* that at least partially redeems politically affiliated monks. In brief, one day Jahangir noticed that Bhānucandra, the lone Jain ascetic allowed to remain at court, looked forlorn. The ruler inquired, and Bhānucandra confessed that he missed his star pupil. Hearing this, the emperor repented of his earlier harshness and called for Siddhicandra's return to court in a jubilant procession. Jahangir also decreed that all Jain ascetics could again go where they please, and with this the text closes.[93] Given this finale, it seems that the hazards of imperial life are worth the trouble of monks who will be vindicated, perhaps after significant hardship. Siddhicandra even puts a positive gloss on the entire affair by noting that Jahangir's wrath and order of exile afforded him the opportunity to work off some bad *karma* and thus enabled his spiritual growth.[94] But even at this happy conclusion, the well-worded objections of Nur Jahan and Jahangir continue to percolate in readers' minds. In particular, the king's *farmān* articulates an influential, time-honored position within many Jain sects: namely, monks belong in the forest rather than at court.

Jain intellectuals such as Siddhicandra vividly perceived the threats they faced by entering into a sphere where Mughal authority reigned supreme. Moreover, in enshrining their anxieties in writing they ensured that such concerns would be known to future generations. Siddhicandra's decision to narrate such a treacherous encounter might be explained as having an educational value for Jain readers who might form imperial links, but this is unlikely given that Jahangir again exiled Jain monks in 1618.[95] While he also quickly rescinded this second ban, Jain-Mughal relations never recovered, and no Jain ascetics are known to have been present at the Mughal court for any length of time after 1620. More likely, Siddhicandra wrote about this interaction because he found it valuable to the Tapa Gaccha community more generally. Perhaps in the 1620s, after nearly thirty years of sustained imperial relations, the sect's identity was too intertwined with the Mughals to be imagined on its own, at least by a young monk brought up in the royal court. Additionally, as the most powerful and one of the more thoughtful interlocutors available to Gujarati Jains in early modern India, the Mughals provided a useful foil for Tapa Gaccha thinkers to work through arguments for and against their own theological precepts.

ADJUDICATING POWER IN STONE AT SHATRUNJAYA

In addition to texts, Jains also negotiated the local impacts of their Mughal connections through inscriptions at pilgrimage locations, above all Shatrunjaya. Epigraphy had been a lively political and religious activity on the subcontinent since the advent of Indian literature in the final centuries B.C.E. Kings frequently demarcated their empires, both real and visionary, through inscriptions.[96] In the early modern period, Jain communities used inscriptions to celebrate their political alliances for a multilayered audience. On the one hand, these inscriptions constituted a form of public writing, situated squarely within the Mughal Empire, that were imagined as visible to society at large. Above all, however, Jains envisioned epigraphy as speaking to the faithful, who would come as pilgrims to places like the temple-laden Shatrunjaya. Both the Tapa and Kharatara Gacchas sponsored inscriptions about their Mughal ties to educate and invigorate their followers and also to compete with each other and Brahmanical groups.

Shatrunjaya was a crucial part of the religious geography of the premodern Shvetambara tradition. Building on the hill dates back historically to the sixth century C.E. But Jain stories envisage the location as a far older holy locale that is associated with Rishabha, the first Jina, and is said to have been visited by all but one of the twenty-four Jinas.[97] The area underwent several bouts of construction over the centuries and today houses nearly one thousand shrines and temples and more than five hundred inscriptions.[98] During the Mughal period, Shvetambara Jains esteemed Shatrunjaya as one of the purest spots on earth, and some even tendered that the mountain would survive the apocalypse.[99] It was a place of active religious practice, and in 1593 Hīravijaya led a large pilgrimage there. Additionally, Shatrunjaya was a repeated point in sectarian contests, and the Tapa and Kharatara Gacchas both gained control of the area through Mughal edicts at different times. These two groups also each carved a series of inscriptions between 1595 and 1629 that sketch out how their imperial links played into larger social and religious interests.

The Tapa Gaccha produced the longest and most prominent epigraph involving the Mughals in the Adishvara temple in 1595. Hemavijaya, who also authored one of the major Sanskrit texts chronicling imperial events, composed this sixty-eight-verse inscription eulogizing Tapa Gaccha leaders.[100] Twenty-one verses are dedicated to Hīravijaya and Vijayasena, including their Mughal connections.[101] The text is engraved in the temple's front entrance and boldly broadcasts the enviable position of Tapa Gaccha leaders at Akbar's court. Additionally, a shorter Tapa Gaccha inscription was executed at the same time to adorn a footprint icon (*pādukā*) near the Adishvara temple. This more concise epigraph announces a similarly integral place for Mughal links in the collective imagination of Tapa Gaccha members.

The Adishvara inscription introduces the Mughals in the context of political concessions that Hīravijaya gained from Akbar. These achievements are listed over several verses and include banning animal slaughter for six months; cancelling estate, jizya, and *śukla* (pilgrimage?) taxes; releasing prisoners, birds, and animals; securing control of Shatrunjaya; and establishing a Jain library.[102] The *pādukā* inscription contains a more succinct but similar catalog of royal decrees.[103] Both lists foreground the institutionalization of nonviolence, a theme that crops up repeatedly in Jain texts and inscriptions, often by noting that Akbar "granted lack of fear to living beings."[104] Continual mentions of this type of concession and the repeated use of this specific expression indicate that the Tapa Gaccha had developed an accepted framework for trumpeting the benefits of imperial ties.

The Adishvara epigraph contains a few additional noteworthy features. For example, it stresses Hīravijaya's strong rapport with Akbar and his effect on the Mughal ruler's religious sensibilities. Hemavijaya attributes each measure that advanced Jain interests to Hīravijaya's speech (*vāc*) or instruction (*upadeśa*).[105] He also compares Akbar to Shrenika, a king said to have met Mahavira.[106] Perhaps most strikingly, the epigraph credits Akbar with an intellectual vision in founding a Jain library: "Overjoyed by [Hīravijaya's] speech and with his mind trembling with compassion, [Akbar] established a peerless library of many texts that was like the home of Sarasvati."[107] Here Akbar is presented as internalizing Jain theological precepts and then promoting its learned culture. Devavimala, Hīravijaya's major Sanskrit biographer, confirms that Akbar indeed established a Jain library by gifting the books of Padmasundara, a Jain ascetic who visited Agra in the 1560s, to Hīravijaya.[108] Nonetheless Śānticandra and other Jain authors generally omit the founding of a Jain library from lists of political concessions (perhaps because it was Akbar's idea, not Hīravijaya's). The 1595 *pādukā* inscription also celebrates Akbar's Jain inclinations, describing the ruler as "possessing qualities such as being free of desire."[109]

In the Adishvara inscription, Hemavijaya next turns to Vijayasena and applauds his skills debating Brahmans in Akbar's court. He proclaims,

> [Vijayasena] established openly in the assembly of Shah Akbar that unparalleled Arhat was to be understood as being God [*parameśvaratva*] using such lofty words that the Bhattas, lords of the Brahmans, whose babbling was sheer madness, became blinded by powerful proofs like thieves confronted by a great light.[110]

Here Hemavijaya refers to Jain defenses of being monotheists in Akbar's court and also indicates sectarian interests in specifying that Vijayasena was victorious over Brahmanical opponents. Hemavijaya next lists a few political concessions granted to Vijayasena that were similar to those earlier solicited by Hīravijaya.[111] The Adishvara inscription closes its section on the Mughals by celebrating that an illustrious person like Vijayasena lives in Gujarat.[112]

Kharatara Gaccha members also produced inscriptions at Shatrunjaya that mention the Mughals, although not until the 1610s. In the late sixteenth century they directed their epigraphic energy elsewhere, and a 1594 inscription at a Parshvanatha temple in Patan, Gujarat, offers insight into how Kharatara Gaccha affiliates initially publicized their group's imperial ties.[113] This inscription acclaims connections between Kharatara leaders and Akbar in ways designed to counter Tapa Gaccha courtly links. For instance, the Patan inscription heralds royal edicts that Jinacandra received from Akbar that banned animal slaughter and prohibited fishing in the Gulf of Cambay.[114] Both concessions mirror *farmāns* gained by Hīravijaya in the 1580s, particularly one that forbade fishing in a lake near Fatehpur Sikri. The Patan inscription also announces that a prior Kharatara leader, Jinahaṃsa, convinced Sikander Lodhi to release five hundred prisoners, which parallels the third concession that Hīravijaya gained on his initial royal sojourn.[115] Here Kharatara Gaccha members show their awareness of the Tapa Gaccha's successes with the Mughals and also exhibit a keen desire to emulate and supersede these imperial rivals.

At Shatrunjaya, the Kharatara Gaccha sponsored seven epigraphs mentioning the Mughals in 1619 and then one each in 1626 and 1630. All were carved after a Kharatara monk had enraged Jahangir by predicting an early end to his rule and also following the second and final expulsion of Tapa Gaccha ascetics from Jahangir's court. But none acknowledge these recent troubles. On the contrary, Kharatara Gaccha authors proudly claimed their royal ties, particularly the titles individual members received from the Mughal sovereigns. Even more prominently, the epigraphs stress the link between a strong Mughal state and a vigorous Jain tradition. All seven of the 1619 Kharatara inscriptions at Shatrunjaya begin identically by positioning themselves "in the kingdom of victorious Sultan Nuruddin Jahangir Savai."[116] The later inscriptions offer similar formulations with the one dated after Jahangir's death updating the phrase to "in the kingdom of victorious glorious Padshah Shah Jahan."[117] One inscription at the base of an image clarifies how Kharatara followers envisioned the expansive domain of the Mughal Empire by describing Akbar as "lord of the Indians and the Turks."[118]

The Kharatara Gaccha and other Indian communities had often projected a bond between political stability and religious vitality. But, as Phyllis Granoff has argued, "in the late medieval period Jains retreated from the pan-Indian rhetoric which linked proper worship with the security of the state as a whole and shifted their focus from that larger community to the smaller community of the Jain faithful."[119] In large part, Granoff contends, this change was induced by the advent of Indo-Islamic rule, which introduced a certain degree of insecurity to the subcontinent. Steven Vose has challenged the accuracy of this historical characterization, and inscriptions and texts from the fourteenth century celebrate Kharatara links with the Tughluq court.[120] With the dawn of the Mughal Empire, Jains from both the Tapa and Kharatara Gacchas found new ways that a healthy polity could bolster their communities. Particularly at Shatrunjaya, a location deep in Mughal-controlled Gujarat, it made good sense to publicly pronounce the intertwined strength of religion and the state.

COMMEMORATING KAVĪNDRĀCĀRYA'S NEGOTIATIONS WITH SHAH JAHAN

While Brahmans produced no Sanskrit narratives of their time at court comparable to Jain texts and inscriptions, they responded to ties with the Mughal world in other written ways. One of their most momentous reactions was the *Kavīndracandrodaya* (*Moonrise of Kavīndra*), a collection of Sanskrit praises that commend Kavīndrācārya Sarasvatī for convincing Shah Jahan to annul a pilgrimage tax on Benares and Prayag (Allahabad).[121] A literati named Kṛṣṇa compiled the work and describes the encomium as a cooperative effort:

> Composed by the glorious luminaries of Kashi that are good poets, the similar inhabitants of Prayag, and residents of all lands who delight in great learning, this collection of verses was written down by glorious Kṛṣṇa and is dedicated to glorious, venerable Kavīndra, who is a treasure house of knowledge [*vidyānidhāna*], known by the name "teacher" [*ācārya*], and yoked with the title *sarasvatī*.[122]

The *Kavīndracandrodaya* features contributions from sixty-nine named individuals as well as a number of anonymous sections. While most of the authors remain unidentified beyond their names, a few, such as Brahmendra and Pūrṇendra Sarasvatī, were leaders in the Benares-based Brahmanical community.[123] Altogether, the work contains over three hundred Sanskrit verses, several lengthy prose passages, and a handful of Prakrit and Marathi lines.[124] The *Kavīndracandrodaya* showcases an act of selective remembrance in the Sanskrit tradition regarding how Brahmans interacted with the imperial Mughal court. But this enshrined memory was hardly a uniform vision. The work's many authors demonstrate the limits and points of contestation among early modern Brahmans regarding how to formulate social and historical commentaries in Sanskrit on imperial relations.

Kṛṣṇa opens with several dozen verses that set the tone and reception context for the encomium. Mostly he lauds Kavīndra, often in the second person, and the *Kavīndracandrodaya* has rightly been dubbed the "first festschrift in Sanskrit."[125] But Kṛṣṇa also envisioned a broader reception for the work, writing, "Warding off the cover of utter darkness, eradicating the anguish of all wise men, let this composition called the *Moonrise of Kavīndra* traverse the world."[126] Kṛṣṇa's wide intended readership for the *Kavīndracandrodaya* diverges acutely from the Brahmanical silence on many of their cross-cultural activities, such as assisting with Mughal translations of Sanskrit texts. Even when Brahmans admitted certain imperial involvements, such as serving as royal astrologers, they generally mentioned such actions briefly rather than treating them as bases for entire texts. But Brahman literati judged that Kavīndra had engaged with the Mughals in a manner that it was proper to commemorate at length in Sanskrit. Thus, while the *Kavīndracandrodaya* was certainly composed for Kavīndra, the larger impetus behind this work was for the Brahmanical Sanskrit community to memorialize relations with the Mughal elite.

While the Sanskrit contributors all applaud Kavīndra for negotiating tax relief from Shah Jahan, relatively few overtly discuss the Mughal court. Given that Sanskrit literati frequently erased social contexts, it is difficult to infer anxiety from this omission. Instead, cultural preference seems to have inclined most contributors toward conventional eulogizing tropes. Many poets marvel at Kavīndra's extensive learning, often listing the Sanskrit subjects in which he was proficient. Numerous authors liken Kavīndra to Hindu gods and their incarnations, such as Vishnu's avatars, who are known for saving the world. Many authors laud Kavīndra's generosity, his compassion (*kṛpā, dayā*), and his empathy (*kāruṇya/karuṇa*) with the hardships faced in the world.[127] The trio of Bali, Dadhici, and Karna arises in a few verses, all of whom are celebrated for their selfless munificence.[128] One literati lifts his entire prose section directly from Bāṇa's seventh-century *Kādambarī*.[129]

While most authors of the *Kavīndracandrodaya* remain safely within Sanskrit points of reference, a few divulge telling details about how Brahman elites perceived Mughal culture and Kavīndra's time at the royal court. For instance, a few poets celebrate that Kavīndra received the Sanskrit title of *vidyānidhāna* (Treasure House of Knowledge) from Shah Jahan.[130] Pūrṇānanda Brahmacārin presents several verses that cite this designation, which he attributes to Kavīndra's ability to instruct Shah Jahan in Sanskrit learning. For instance, he wrote,

Kavīndra, lord of the three worlds, teaches the Lord of Delhi every day
according to knowledge of the Vedas, sacred texts, and *śāstras*.
Even though famous for releasing major pilgrimage sites from royal tax
and honored with [the title] *vidyānidhāna*, [Kavīndra] does not fall prey
to pride.[131]

Numerous other contributors also praise Kavīndra's role as a purveyor of Indian knowledge, often placing him in line with great Sanskrit literary figures who were popularly renowned for teaching kings, such as Vālmīki, Vyāsa, and Kālidāsa.[132] A few verses also offer more creative formulations of how Kavīndra's wisdom enabled him to gain Mughal favor, such as Nīlakaṇṭha's contribution, which plays on a double entendre (*śleṣa*):

O Kavīndra! Freed by you from the grasp of imperial taxes through [teaching the king] commentaries [*bhāṣya*], poetry [*subhāṣita*], etc., glorious Kashi is glorified by the feet of sages and enlightens people in good and bad speech, just as the *Kāśikā* commentary, freed by your own hand, O World-ruler, with [your] writing about the [*Mahā*]*bhāṣya*, illuminates correct usage and provides wisdom concerning speech and mis-speech.[133]

Some Brahmans extolled the virtues that set Kavīndra apart from the worldly Mughal court, even when these are not fully historically accurate. For example, one writer celebrates that Kavīndra rejected Shah Jahan's offer of wealth and instead demanded relief for religious pilgrims.

For the hordes of elephants and horses, gold, and lines of jewels
that were being offered, Kavīndra had no thirst.
He was committed to the deliverance of all pilgrimage places.
Surely a mass of rain clouds takes no pleasure in rain?[134]

Jain sources likewise praise their leaders for refusing Mughal financial compensation,[135] but in the case of Kavīndra this boast is wholly misleading. Persian sources attest that Kavīndra accepted payments from the Mughals for his services as a vernacular singer, and European visitors perceived this arrangement as also due to Kavīndra's erudition.[136] While Sanskrit literati generally gloss over (or even flatly deny) this aspect of Kavīndra's courtly activities, they were aware of both his singing and remuneration. In the *Kavīndracandrodaya*, one writer explicitly notes Kavīndra's dual roles of singer and scholar for the Mughals: "The illustrious Svāmi

Kavīndra learned knowledge and studied songs for everybody's sake, in order to rescue cows and Brahmans from fear."[137] Moreover, in terms of money, the few Marathi verses included in the *Kavīndracandrodaya* contain a plea for Kavīndra to loan the poor author two hundred rupees, presumably out of his more lucrative Mughal stipend.[138]

A poet named Hīrārāma Kavi lists the different social and ethnic groups present at Shah Jahan's court in one of the most unique and striking verses in the entire encomium. He draws upon both old and new categories in order to express the heterogeneous composition of the Mughal elite:

> In the assembly of glorious King Shah Jahan, those born in Kashmir, Iraq, Karaskara,[139] Darada,[140] Khurasan, and Habshan [Abyssinia], Bengalis, Arabs, Firangis [Westerners], Turks, Shakas [Scythians], Badakhshanis, Multanis, those from Balkh, Qandaharis, even the lords of Kabul who rule the earth, Magas [Iranians], and Ottomans—they all praise you, Kavīndra![141]

This list mixes traditional Sanskrit groups with more contemporary communities. The Karaskaras, Daradas, and Shakas all appear frequently in classical Indian texts, and the latter two are even said to have fought in the *Mahābhārata* war.[142] Many other groups were more recently introduced into the Sanskrit imaginaire, including the imported Persian term *firangī* (*phiraṅga* in Sanskrit), meaning Europeans.[143] Hīrārāma also displays a nuanced appreciation of places in Central Asia that were politically salient identity markers in Mughal culture. In this verse, Hīrārāma indicates some of the disputed lines of the Sanskrit literary tradition, and the verse stands alone in the *Kavīndracandrodaya* for its attempt to make sense of the complex social landscape of the imperial court.

In these diverse ways, the Brahmanical community at large celebrated Kavīndra's success with Shah Jahan. One verse in the *Kavīndracandrodaya* even says that Kavīndra worshipped both Shiva and Vishnu, which perhaps signals that his popularity cut across sectarian lines.[144] The Brahman contributors to the *Moonrise of Kavīndra* agreed on the need to memorialize a particular vision of Kavīndra's relations with Shah Jahan, although they hardly present a uniform final picture. Moreover, in addition to the dozens of Sanskrit literati who wrote for the *Kavīndracandrodaya*, many vernacular poets contributed to a parallel (although significantly shorter) Hindi encomium titled the *Kavīndracandrikā* (*Moonlight of Kavīndra*).[145] The relationship between these two texts awaits further study, but it is worth noting that a few individuals authored verses for both volumes.[146] For example, Hīrārāma Kavi penned a vernacular verse for the *Kavīndracandrikā* that includes an assortment of place-names rather similar to his Sanskrit verse quoted above.[147] Many other poets also wrote exclusively for the *Kavīndracandrikā*, which demonstrates the multiple options available to Brahmans who wished to venerate relations with the Mughal crown in particular ways and perhaps within certain linguistic traditions.

MUGHAL POLITICAL HISTORY IN SANSKRIT

Jains and Brahmans both wrote Sanskrit histories in response to cultural, political, and social changes associated with the Mughal Empire. These texts generally emerged from far beyond the imperial court and reveal the manifold options available to Sanskrit intellectuals for writing about major imperial events. A few authors from the late sixteenth century dramatically reconstituted the recent Mughal past and the imperial present. Other writers engaged more directly with the tradition of Indo-Persian chronicles, including drafting a literal Sanskrit translation of the first portion of the *Akbarnāmah*. Several later writers integrated the Mughals into lists of Indian monarchs that frame the Mughal dispensation as the culmination of a long tradition of subcontinental kingship. These disparate works often address the impacts of Mughal rule more generally rather than limiting themselves to burgeoning cross-cultural relations. Moreover, there are few clear connections between them, and they represent a diffuse rather than a continuous set of literary projects. Nonetheless, these works demonstrate that the Mughals were a recurrent topic for Sanskrit writers who were thinking seriously and diversely about the implications of massive political shifts for their literary and intellectual traditions.

Several Sanskrit authors exploited the poet's liberty to reinvent the past by altering the course of Mughal historical events. One of the most striking cases of such imaginative reworking occurs in Padmasāgara's *Jagadgurukāvya* (*Poem on the Teacher of the World*), which contains the first known Sanskrit account of the Mughal rise to power. Padmasāgara wrote this narrative work in 1589 primarily to eulogize the life of Hīravijaya, the Tapa Gaccha leader at the time, but he devotes nearly one-third of the poem to a creative recounting of the military exploits of Humayun and Akbar.[148] Padmasāgara crafts an astoundingly innovative story line for the early days of the Mughal Empire that changes the dynasty's origins, founder, and early development. Through this substantial rewriting, he furthermore depicts the coerced establishment of Mughal rule as engendering the flourishing of Indian cultural and religious traditions.

Padmasāgara opens by describing the Mughals as an Indian dynasty, even before they established their empire. In reality, the Mughals claimed ancestry from Genghis Khan, a thirteenth-century Mongol emperor, and Timur, a late fourteenth-century Turkish ruler. But, for Padmasāgara, the Mughals originated within the geographical and cultural boundaries of India.

> In the glorious land of India [*bhārata*], where more than twenty-five lands exist that have been graced by incarnations of the best of men such as the great, illustrious Jina and Vishnu, the wonderful heartland contains shining palaces, idols, great libraries and is inhabited by worthy people. Here, near the good land of Khurasan, lies a great city called Kabul that is filled with good men and known as the dwelling place of heroes. In Kabul, a hundred thousand Mughals, their power unbroken and a terror to demonic Hindus [*hindvāsuratrāsakaṃ*], feast with great pleasure upon hundreds of delicacies at will.[149]

Thus, the Mughals hailed from Kabul, which is itself in the heartland (*madhyadeśa*) of India and houses temples, incarnations, and idols. Sanskrit authors from Akbar's time typically described Kabul and Khurasan as outside *bhārata* and part of a culturally distinct land, often characterized by exotic fruits and horses.[150] Persianate historians of the period likewise conceived of Kabul and surrounding areas as a homeland that the Mughals left in order to conquer *hindūstān*, which was by definition a foreign place.[151] Padmasāgara erases this history of migration by portraying the Mughals as geographically and culturally Indian from the beginning.

Padmasāgara next narrates how the Mughals expanded their control over the subcontinent, but he significantly condenses the military timeline. First, he expunges Babur from the record altogether and presents Humayun as the first Mughal king.[152] Padmasāgara relays three stories involving Humayun: his acquisition of Delhi from Sher Shah Suri, his capture of Gujarat and Malwa from Bahadur Shah, and his untimely death. According to Persian sources, the first event never happened and the latter two unfolded in 1535–1536 and 1556, respectively, with Humayun's fifteen-year exile from Hindustan separating the two. But Padmasāgara portrays these three events as following in quick succession by dating the conquest of Delhi to when Akbar was eight years old and Humayun's death to when Akbar was twelve.[153] In this way, Padmasāgara erases entirely the embarrassing episode of the Sur interregnum when Humayun lost control of his Indian kingdom and proclaims that only four years (as opposed to the actual thirty) separated the Mughals' first conquest of Delhi from Akbar's enthronement.[154]

Throughout his streamlining of Humayun's victory over India, Padmasāgara emphasizes the causal link between forceful Mughal expansion and broad cultural flourishing. For example, at the close of the Humayun-Sur clash, he praises Humayun for ensuring freedom and wealth:

> When the Sur king had been defeated, [Humayun] made the Sur warriors his own servants, who, free from punishment and happy, inhabited that land. Then he established a kingdom without fear where elephants, horses, oxen, camels, and men traveled on the road between Kabul and Delhi and millions of houses on tall mountains were adorned with heaps of pearls, gems, and gold.[155]

As Padmasāgara observes, the security of the Kabul-Delhi road benefited economic interests and individual travelers. Both were active concerns for the Gujarati Jain community, which had long been involved in trade and supported travel for both monks and lay pilgrims.[156] More generally, Padmasāgara asserts that Humayun brought prosperity to Gujarat and Malwa upon their inclusion in the empire.

> Having established prosperity in the great lands of Gujarat, Malwa, and so forth, the Mughal ruler, abounding with a hundred virtuous qualities, came to Delhi. He possessed the best kingdom, one united, free of enemies, and happy. For when good fortune itself is watching, who does not obtain everything he desires?[157]

In these ways Padmasāgara proclaims a direct relationship between a strong Mughal Empire, whose domination of India was quick and uncontested, and the subsequent thriving of Indian communities.

Other Sanskrit writers pursued a similarly loose approach to recounting the recent imperial past, but they often held rather different views of the Mughals. For instance, Rudrakavi, a Deccani court poet, wrote his *Rāṣṭrauḍhavaṃśamahākāvya* (*Great Poem on the Rastraudha Dynasty*) in 1596, only seven years after Padmasāgara's revision to Mughal history. In the work, Rudrakavi describes how Bahadur Shah of Gujarat defeated Humayun in 1535–1536, when in reality the battle went the other way.[158] Rudrakavi was likely unfamiliar with Padmasāgara's text, but these two works attest that reworking past events was a broader practice in early modern Sanskrit literature. Contemporary Mughal sensibilities also allowed for great leeway in reformulating reality. For example, Akbar often had episodes omitted from his imperial histories, and Jahangir commissioned paintings of unreal events, such as his beheading of Malik Ambar.[159] For Sanskrit intellectuals, imperial events were equally malleable and could be adapted to suit local agendas.

Taking a different approach to representing Mughal events, one Indian writer translated the Persian chronicle *Akbarnāmah* into Sanskrit. The Sanskrit version is known as the *Sarvadeśavṛttāntasaṅgraha* (*Collection of Events Across the Land*) and survives in a few incomplete manuscripts. A colophon page that likely postdates the rest of the manuscript and is appended to the British Library copy ascribes the translation to Maheśa Ṭhakkura, the ruler of Mithila in the early sixteenth century.[160] The text's modern editor upheld this authorial claim because the British Library manuscript shows linguistic influences from Maithili.[161] However, this attribution is almost certainly false, not least because the *Akbarnāmah* was written in the 1590s. Accordingly, Maheśa Ṭhakkura would have needed to live to an improbably old age in order to author the Sanskrit translation (despite writing nothing else after 1540).[162] A more likely scenario is that a writer composed the Sanskrit rendering in the seventeenth or eighteenth century, and it was later attributed to Maheśa Ṭhakkura because of popular traditions that associated his dynasty with the Mughals.[163] Even absent clear authorship or date, however, the *Sarvadeśavṛttāntasaṅgraha* attests that some Sanskrit literati possessed significant awareness of the Indo-Persian historical tradition and explored how it might be brought into Sanskrit.

Nobody has yet analyzed the *Sarvadeśavṛttāntasaṅgraha*, and it is outside my purposes to conduct a thorough examination here. But even a cursory look at the text confirms that it is indeed a rather close translation of both the prose and poetry of the *Akbarnāmah*, even when the cultural resonances are lost. For example, the Persian chronicle opens with praises of God, such as,

> What is this utterance that appeared
> and unveiled the eighteen thousand?
> There is no feast more intoxicating, nor any stronger rival.[164]

In Persian, these verses are laden with religious meaning. The utterance (*sukhan*) refers to the Arabic letters that God spoke at the dawn of creation, and the eighteen thousand symbolizes the totality of God's creation. Sanskrit lacks the cultural framework to capture these specific ideas, but the translation nonetheless renders the lines quite literally:

> What is this speech that unveils all universes?
> Since when the world was visible,
> there was no one more intoxicated.
> Even though strong, there was no equal.[165]

The translator seems to muddle some of the grammar but otherwise renders the verse rather exactingly. What Sanskrit readers would have made of such obscure imagery remains uncertain.

Aside from the opening lines, the *Sarvadeśavṛttāntasaṅgraha* is written in prose. The work follows the Persian history quite faithfully. The Sanskrit version even adopts some Persianate conventions, such as using honorary titles for deceased members of the Mughal family (transliterated into Sanskrit). The text breaks off shortly after an episode in Akbar's childhood where he overpowered an older cousin in a wrestling match.[166] It is unclear whether the remainder of the translation was lost or was simply never finished. We know nothing about the reception history of the *Sarvadeśavṛttāntasaṅgraha*, and the work is anomalous, so far as I know, as a direct Sanskrit translation of a Persian chronicle. However, other, later Sanskrit intellectuals also wrote Mughal histories. Most notably, in the eighteenth century, Lakṣmīdhara penned two Sanskrit accounts of post-Aurangzeb imperial events that have yet to be examined in any detail.[167]

Sanskrit literati also integrated the Mughals into more all-embracing visions of Indian history. For example, the anonymous and undated *Bhaviṣyapurāṇa* describes the line of Mughal kings through Shah Alam II (d. 1806) and includes a ninety-seven-verse section titled "Description of Padshah Akbar" (*akabarabādaśāhavarṇana*).[168] Among other things, this work discloses that several Hindu sages were reincarnated as figures in the royal Mughal court, such as Devāpi, who was reborn as Birbal, a trusted Brahman adviser to Akbar.[169] Additionally, a kingly lineage (*rājāvalī*) titled the *Rājavaṃsavarṇana* (*Description of Royal Dynasties*, ca. early eighteenth century?) chronicles Indian kings from the Pandavas through the Mughals. Such works followed upon a trend of pre-Mughal Sanskrit inscriptions that listed subcontinental rulers through the Delhi

Sultanate.[170] Notably, the *Rājavaṃsavarṇana* posits Timur as the immediate predecessor to Babur, which signals a loose treatment of historical facts similar to the approaches followed by Padmasāgara and Rudrakavi.[171] It is difficult to pinpoint the precise cultural and political values of narrating Mughal history in works whose dates and contexts remain obscure. Nonetheless, the existence of numerous texts in this vein leaves little doubt that the Mughals loomed large in the imaginations of Sanskrit intellectuals well into the eighteenth century.

Beyond their immediate contexts, Sanskrit texts about Mughal events demonstrate that Indian literati employed various historical approaches in order to think through political shifts that were changing the world around them. The decision to write histories at all may well have been informed by the explosion of Persian and Hindi historical works at roughly the same time.[172] While the Sanskrit texts never formed a cohesive genre or tradition, they share several key characteristics. Most notably, most of the works freely blend fact and fiction, even when they touched upon recent or well-known occurrences. The goal was likely not to alter commonplace knowledge about the past but rather to privilege imagination over reality within the Sanskrit literary realm. What readers made of such works generally remains elusive. But Sanskrit authors returned to the Mughals repeatedly for centuries, which indicates that writing creatively about this dynasty was fertile ground for pursuing political, religious, literary, and local interests.

CONCLUSION: SANSKRIT INTELLECTUAL CULTURES

Jain and Brahman literati discussed Mughal cross-cultural activities and imperial rule in Sanskrit in ways that intersected with literary, religious, and historical concerns within their communities. Jain writers narrated their experiences at the royal court in order to formulate distinct relationships between their religious traditions and the Mughal Empire. Several authors recounted theological conflicts in order to blazon the fortitude of Jain thought in a Mughal-defined world, even in the face of imperially endorsed Islam. Tapa Gaccha writers were also keen to compare spiritual and imperial authorities in Mughal India. Although individual thinkers differed on whether to project their spiritual leaders as powerful by virtue of their difference or similarity to the Mughal emperor. Both Tapa and Kharatara Gaccha Jains publicized their Mughal connections (largely to each other) through inscriptions at major pilgrimage locations. While Brahmans avoided composing detailed Sanskrit accounts about their imperial relations akin to Jain works, they cultivated other forms of cultural remembrance. The verses and prose of the *Kavīndracandrodaya* offer a textured picture of how different members of a Brahmanical community wished to formulate a Sanskrit record of cross-cultural ties. Additionally, both Jain and Brahmanical authors penned Sanskrit works about Mughal history and attest that this was a dynamic topic for several centuries. Taken together, these works highlight vital features of early modern Sanskrit intellectual culture, including a heterogeneous historical consciousness, the importance of representation, and the close relationship between religion and politics.

First, Sanskrit writers were keenly interested in thinking and writing about the Mughal past and present. Over the past few decades, many scholars have devoted renewed energy to investigating trends within early modern Sanskrit philosophical and literary traditions (e.g., the Sanskrit Knowledge-Systems Project). The general consensus is that Sanskrit intellectuals frequently continued to engage with questions that had occupied Indian thinkers for generations, albeit often with new approaches.[173] Alongside conventional concerns, however, a considerable number of Jains and Brahmans mobilized Sanskrit to comment on the new cultural and political conditions within the Mughal dispensation. These thinkers tried to adjust their inherited practices to current historical circumstances, and particularly Jain writers developed fascinating textual records. Jains need to be integrated into the history of Sanskrit literary culture more generally if we are to accurately characterize this rich and varied tradition. We also ought to retire the inaccurate view of Sanskrit intellectuals as disengaged from real-world events. The texts discussed here illustrate some of the ways that Indian literati responded to and participated in Indo-Islamic rule.

Both Jains and Brahmans faced a thorny set of questions regarding how to write in an Indian classical tongue about relations with the Mughals. It is worth emphasizing that many literati opted out of these concerns altogether and adopted vernaculars for such topics instead of Sanskrit. Jains authored a series of Gujarati works that explore connections with the Mughal elite and have yet to be researched in any detail.[174] Brahmans often turned to Braj Bhasha to comment on Mughal authority.[175] Vernacular cultures presented their own mores with which writers needed to reckon, but they also mark, in part, the limits of what early modern Jains and Brahmans chose to embrace in Sanskrit. Nonetheless, the Sanskrit tradition was not yet obsolete or calcified in early modern India. Many writers felt animated by its unique set of literary and historical tools for probing the impact of Mughal rule on their social, religious, and literary communities.

In their varied works, many Sanskrit writers viewed representation as a key concern, sometimes irrespective of empirical truth, because of the power of texts to shape both memory and future realities. In this regard, Sanskrit intellectuals and the Mughals thought more alike than anybody cognized at the time. Akbar and his successors carefully cultivated their sovereignty through texts, images, architecture, and other imperial practices in order to bring into being a certain type of Indo-Persian polity. As a result, they successfully built a stable political system that was grounded not only in military subjugation but also in well-articulated modes of Persianate (and, as I have argued here, Sanskrit) culture and authority. Jain and Brahmanical writers lacked the political means of the Mughal kings, but they intuited the creative energy of representation all the same. They used memory, forgetting, and Sanskrit reworkings of the past in order to reimagine themselves in an increasingly Indo-Persian world.

Last, Sanskrit responses to ties with the Mughal court indicate a complicated, fertile relationship between religion and power in early modern India, particularly for Jains. Scholars working on colonial and postcolonial India frequently lament the perceived shift on the subcontinent from traditional modes of pluralistic faith toward narrow religious ideology.[176] Speaking of changes in Indian modernity, for instance, Sudipta Kaviraj has drawn a distinction between thick and thin religion where "thick religion" is a layered belief system that is generally tolerant of other views, is practiced locally, and is typically separate from politics. In contrast, "thin religion" is an intolerant brand of broad identity focused on a political end.[177] This sort of distinction may highlight trends in Indian modernity, but it does not accurately capture how Jains experienced religion in Mughal India as a deeply political phenomenon that recognized limits of tolerance while also propagating specific ideas. Crucially, the mutual saturation of politics and theology did not flatten religion for Jain thinkers. Rather, it enabled Jains to pursue groundbreaking paths, such as writing about the taboo topic of Islamic beliefs in Sanskrit, reframing debates about Jain theological precepts, and disobeying Mughal orders.

[6] INCORPORATING SANSKRIT INTO THE PERSIANATE WORLD

THE EXPLOSION of imperial links with the Sanskrit sphere, especially in the 1580s–1590s, elicited a wave of responses in early modern Indo-Persian culture. Literati took an interest in Akbar's initiatives, particularly his translations, almost immediately, and the reactions continued throughout the seventeenth century. Some ardently condemned the cultural and political ambitions embedded in the Akbari translations; others enthusiastically produced their own copies of translated texts. After Jahangir rose to power, Akbar's endeavors frequently lost their original intended valence and took on unanticipated meanings as intellectuals fashioned new fusions of Sanskrit and Persian literary and imperial idioms. During the reigns of Shah Jahan and Aurangzeb ʿAlamgir, Sanskrit knowledge became increasingly commonplace in the Indo-Persian tradition and was often invoked absent any direct connection with the set of cross-cultural initiatives situated in the late sixteenth-century Mughal court. While the content of the responses differed greatly, many early modern Persianate intelligentsia felt compelled to engage with the Mughal introduction of Sanskrit narratives and learning into the Indo-Persian thought world.

Indian-based Persianate writers developed a gamut of methods for integrating (or confronting and rejecting) Sanskrit-based information. Two interconnected processes were at work in such projects. First, encounters with Sanskrit ideas spurred cultural ingenuity and change. Modern scholars generally recognize that Persian-medium poets on the subcontinent often wrote in ways that distinguished them from their Iranian and Central Asian–based peers. Many have criticized the anachronistic and pejorative phrase "the Indian style" (*sabk-i hindī*) that supposedly describes a more bombastic version of Persian. In its place, recent scholars suggest, we might more fruitfully examine the self-proclaimed desire to "speak fresh" (*tāza-gū'ī*) from the late sixteenth century onward and the accompanying interest in writing about novel topics.[1] Examining the integration of Sanskrit ideas and stories offers a promising avenue for investigating the unique features of Persian literature in India.

Second, Sanskrit and Persian encounters help to map out political debates that linked Indo-Persian centers across the early modern subcontinent. Writers working in Deccani courts, princely households, and subimperial environs responded to Mughal activities. This learned community was attuned to the aesthetic and political possibilities—often most pertinent in their own local contexts—that could be realized through grappling with Sanskrit-based ideas. Crucial here is to recognize, as Roy Fischel has eloquently pointed out regarding the Deccan Sultanates, that not all early modern Indian polities saw themselves as imperial in a Mughal sense.[2] Many individuals disapproved of specific Mughal cross-cultural endeavors, particularly those pursued under Akbar. Many more conceived of other modes of sovereignty and alternative relationships between languages, literatures, and power. Early modern Persophone Indians saw diverse ways that Sanskrit stories and learning could reshape the Indo-Persian sphere, especially in terms of political possibilities.

The full Indo-Persian reception history of Mughal engagements with Sanskrit is a lifetime's work and more, rather than the subject of a single chapter. Nonetheless, select texts produced in Deccani courts and other courtly contexts speak eloquently to the larger questions I address throughout this book concerning the interplay of literature and politics as well as the relationship between imperial centers and regional powers. Moreover, even the bare bones of this wider reception indicates the far reaches of Mughal cross-cultural activities. I outline here some of the major features of how Persianate thinkers both within and beyond the Mughal court viewed Mughal multicultural activities as generating new, potentially threatening literary and political modes of being.

RECEPTIONS OF AKBAR'S *RĀMĀYAN*

The Akbari translation of the Sanskrit *Rāmāyaṇa*, completed in the 1580s, was the first full Persian rendering of this epic and was designed as a royal work. Akbar idealized Rama, an avatar of Vishnu's and the hero of the epic, as a model Indian monarch.[3] Imperially illustrated manuscripts of the translation overtly parallel the two men and suggest what other Sanskrit texts state explicitly: Akbar was another incarnation of Vishnu.[4] Examining the original Akbari translation holds much promise for understanding how Akbar's sovereignty built upon Sanskrit precedents. However, the Akbari *Rāmāyan* has never been published, and the master imperial copy has been inaccessible to scholars for decades.[5] Additionally, several mysteries surround Akbar's *Rāmāyan*, including conflicting claims about its authorship and the constitution of the text, which appears to have been somewhat fluid.[6] Especially without access to the master copy, these challenges render work on the original translation difficult.

Given the close ties between Mughal royal identity and the *Rāmāyan*, reacting to this work was a way of commenting upon Akbar's exercise of power. Perhaps unsurprisingly then, of all the Mughal cross-cultural endeavors, the translation of the Sanskrit *Rāmāyaṇa* into Persian engendered the most extensive and long-lasting set of responses. Akbar's *Rāmāyan* provoked numerous comments, illuminated manuscripts, and retellings. Many thinkers balked at the political claims that Akbar sought to advance in this epic. Others eagerly sought to replicate the Mughal interest in this Sanskrit tale, such as by sponsoring further illuminated manuscripts. Both types of reactors correctly understood the Mughals' not-so-subtle message that the *Rāmāyaṇa* had been remade into a work about Mughal sovereignty.

Some authors cleaved the story of the *Rāmāyaṇa* from Mughal politics and expanded the tale's potential in alternative directions, often seizing upon the Persianate literary possibilities of its mingling of war and romance. There is no denying that Rama's tale spoke to many Indo-Persian poets. By the end of the nineteenth century, literati had created more than two dozen distinct Persian *Rāmāyans*, many of them versified, of which there are collectively thousands of extant manuscripts.[7] Nonetheless, it took decades for writers to conceive of Persian *Rāmāyans* as belonging outside the Mughal court. In this sense, the Mughal claim over Rama's story stood strong, even in the minds of those who imagined other cultural and literary purposes for the tale.

THAT BLACK BOOK: BADĀʾŪNĪ'S OBJECTION TO MUGHAL TRANSLATION

Badāʾūnī was Akbar's most prolific translator and participated in the rendering of several Sanskrit texts into Persian under royal orders.

Nonetheless, Badāʾūnī found translating Sanskrit materials distasteful and disparages such work several times in his unofficial history of the period. He reserves his harshest comments for the *Rāmāyaṇa* and condemns the text as "that black book," a phrase that highlights the potentially threatening nature of the epic. Badāʾūnī also recounts how he defied Akbar's direct command to write a preface for this translation. Badāʾūnī's objections are hardly straightforward, however, and need to be understood in the context of theological and imperial battles being waged at the late sixteenth-century Mughal court. Particularly when considered in tandem with Abū al-Faẕl's preface to the Persian *Mahābhārata*, Badāʾūnī's protests demonstrate the intertwined religious and political challenges that he perceived in creating a Mughal *Rāmāyan*.

Badāʾūnī vividly narrates his refusal to compose a preface to Akbar's *Rāmāyan*. He begins by calmly describing the practicalities of bringing the Sanskrit story into Persian. He relates the time frame of the translation and its length, noting that it was much admired at court. But Badāʾūnī was alarmed by Akbar's directive to write an introduction and takes the opportunity in recollecting this event to express his angst in having translated the epic at all.

> [Akbar] ordered me to also write a preface [to the *Rāmāyan*] in the style of the authors. Because I found little benefit and also had to write the *khutbah* without praise of the Prophet [*bī naʿt*], I desisted. I seek refuge in God from that black book, which is as rotten as the book of my life. The narration of heresy is not itself heresy, and I utter the declaration of faith against heresy. Why should I fear—God forbid!—that this text, which was written against my will and by the force of imperial command, carries a curse? *O God! I verily take refuge in You from associating anything with You, and I know, and I beg your forgiveness for that which I know not, and I repent of it, and say: There is no God but God and Muhammad is his Messenger.* My repentance is not a fearful repentance and is accepted in the court of the merciful and generous God![8]

Here Badāʾūnī proffers two related reasons for refusing to pen a preface for the Akbari *Rāmāyan*. First, providing an introduction would not have served his interests ("I found little benefit"). Second, the preface would have had to be written without praise of Muhammad, which would go against his religious convictions when he had already skirted heresy by translating the *Rāmāyaṇa* at all. Badāʾūnī's objections both stem from politico-religious tensions in Akbar's court.

First, Badāʾūnī's pragmatic assessment that he would not profit from composing a preface refers to his position within conflicts regarding the interpretation of Islam among the Mughal ruling class. Badāʾūnī had a reputation in imperial circles for adhering to hard-line Islamic views that Akbar denigrated.[9] Badāʾūnī himself records that Akbar once called him a "bigot" (*mutaʿaṣṣib*) in contrast to an "adherent of Sufism" (*ṣūfī-mashrabī*).[10] More pointedly, Akbar suspected that Badāʾūnī's views might corrupt his translations from Sanskrit and on one occasion openly accused him of covertly interpolating Islamic theology into the *Mahābhārata* (see chapter 3). Despite such frictions, however, Badāʾūnī was Akbar's most productive translator and was assigned to render part or all of at least five separate Sanskrit texts into Persian, four of which he completed.[11] There were perhaps workaday reasons why Akbar assigned the task of bringing texts across cultural and linguistic boundaries to someone he distrusted, such as the dearth of other writers. Even so, the emperor's repeated selection of Badāʾūnī as a translator seems strange. For other translations, Akbar invoked the services of members of his trusted inner circle, such as his vizier and poet laureate. Badāʾūnī certainly stood outside this elite group but was nonetheless at the center of translation activity at court.

In his preface to the *Razmnāmah*, Abū al-Fażl provides an important clue to explaining this apparent asymmetry when he states that one major goal of that translation (and presumably others) was to prompt conservative Muslims to reconsider their beliefs.[12] This objective was partially a theological intervention, but it also had a strong political edge. Akbar sought to wrestle power away from Islamic jurists, who had traditionally held significant sway in Islamicate polities, and invest it in himself by establishing a new, enlightened intellectual era that heralded the contributions of Sanskrit knowledge. In the case of Badāʾūnī, Akbar apparently sought for translations to open peoples' minds beginning with the translator. When Badāʾūnī claims he resisted writing a preface for the *Rāmāyan* because he would not benefit from the exercise, he likely indicates his disapproval of this agenda.

Badāʾūnī's second objection, that he would need to compose an introduction "in the style of the authors" (*rasm-i muṣannifīn*), no doubt referred to Abū al-Fażl's preface to the Persian *Mahābhārata*. Abū al-Fażl wrote this preface in 1587 as a masterpiece of literary prose that quickly became an integral component of the *Razmnāmah*. This introduction also provided a guide for conceptualizing Persian translations of Sanskrit works as a Mughal cross-cultural activity more broadly and was often cited in other translated texts.

Badāʾūnī explicitly attests that he rejected this model because Abū al-Faẓl omitted the conventional praise of Muhammad.[13] Elsewhere in his *Muntakhab al-Tavārīkh* Badāʾūnī also deprecates Abū al-Faẓl's preface for other reasons. These remarks further elucidate the motivations behind Badāʾūnī's disinclination to write a similar introduction for the Persian *Rāmāyan.*

Badāʾūnī volunteers two comments about the *Mahābhārata* preface that indicate deep discomfort with Abū al-Faẓl's religious and political visions. First, while discussing his own participation in the *Razmnāmah* project, Badāʾūnī says that in the span of three or four months, he "translated two out of the eighteen fabricated, worthless books [of the *Mahābhārat*], which baffle the eighteen thousand worlds."[14] In his mention of "the eighteen thousand worlds" Badāʾūnī plays off the opening verses of Abū al-Faẓl's preface, which praises God with the lines,

> O You, for whom the eighteen thousand worlds are drunk with yearning,
> heads on the path of searching and souls in the palms of their hands.
> So many writing tablets have been blackened and so many pens broken.
> Yet they have not drawn so much as a line comparable to your creation.[15]

These verses became emblematic of the Persian *Mahābhārata*, and later copies of the translation often quote them, even when they exclude the rest of Abū al-Faẓl's preface.[16] For Badāʾūnī, the hyperbole of such praise supplied a way to lampoon the outlandish *Mahābhārata* as confusing rather than enlightening God's creation.

A few lines later in his *Muntakhab al-Tavārīkh*, Badāʾūnī objects that Abū al-Faẓl's preface contradicts an earlier commentary by the same author on the Qurʾan, presumably because of the different theological leanings of the two texts. Badāʾūnī then calls out to God in Arabic: "We flee to God for refuge from infidelities and unprofitable words!"[17] This outburst is designed to mark Badāʾūnī's allegiance to a monolithic Islamic tradition as opposed to Abū al-Faẓl's attempt to diversify the base of Indo-Islamic knowledge. In his discussion about the *Rāmāyaṇa*, Badāʾūnī invokes the *kalima* to similar effect, drawing on the long-standing use of this particular phrase serving as a site of Muslim memory and identity.[18] The text of Akbar's *Rāmāyan* also evinces a similarly guarded attitude and invokes the phrase "God knows best" (*allāh aʿlam*) at the end of certain chapters to signal a desire to shield against rather than celebrate the content of this epic.[19]

In another work, titled *Najāt al-Rashīd* (*Salvation of the Rightly Guided*), Badāʾūnī clarifies that he rebukes non-Islamic books because they could alter the convictions of Muslims. He describes how a weak believer, when exposed to false theological ideas, may mistakenly wonder if such notions are actually God's guidance for how to live one's life.[20] Additionally, non-Muslim works lack the inimitable nature of the Qurʾan and so may contain interpolations that even the learned cannot sort out.[21] Abū al-Faẓl agrees with Badāʾūnī about both possibilities, but he gladly embraces the potential of Indian texts, such as the *Mahābhārata*, to disprove unwarranted Islamic beliefs, as I discuss in chapter 3. Here we can see the opposing positions of different thinkers within Akbar's court on the appropriate role of non-Muslim knowledge within Islamic thought.

In addition to its theological threat, Badāʾūnī was also concerned with the political implications of Sanskrit knowledge. In a broad sense, Badāʾūnī was intensely uncomfortable with royal authority that extended into religious domains. Ali Anooshahr has documented how Badāʾūnī repeatedly reproaches both Akbar and other kings who attempted to propagate religious practices of their own invention.[22] Likewise, Badāʾūnī fervently opposed divine kingship and even rewrote the stories of pre-Mughal kings to elide such suggestions.[23] Elsewhere in his history, Badāʾūnī indicates his particular concern with Sanskrit-based ideas about sacred sovereignty and condemns Brahmans who praise Akbar as like Rama.[24]

Thus, disagreements over both power and theology lay behind Badāʾūnī's unwillingness to write a preface to Akbar's *Rāmāyan*. By creating a Persian *Rāmāyan*, Badāʾūnī had already granted Akbar access to potentially explosive knowledge. But he draws the line at composing an introduction that would have spelled out the king's claims regarding the epic's imperial value. Such a work would have made Badāʾūnī not merely complicit but also an active participant in promoting Akbar's vision of royal authority as transcending multiple religious traditions. While Badāʾūnī does not elaborate further in his history, presumably refusing the king's demand was no light matter and signals the high stakes of this conflict. Perhaps precisely the combination of imperial and theological dangers is what prompted Badāʾūnī to openly disobey Akbar. Badāʾūnī appears to have abided by his decision, and Akbar's *Rāmāyan* as we have it today lacks a preface.

ROYAL READERS OF AKBAR'S *RĀMĀYAN*

Upon its completion, Akbar's *Rāmāyan* became quite popular in elite circles, and two copies survive from the late sixteenth century that belonged to the royal family. The master imperial copy produced for Akbar's court was completed in 1588 and held in the imperial library. This manuscript was passed down through the line of Mughal sovereigns, and flyleaf inscriptions confirm that it was viewed frequently. One note dating from Shah Jahan's reign even records that the manuscript required repairs, which indicates it had been handled extensively.[25] Additionally, another illuminated royal *Rāmāyan* was produced in 1594. It remains unclear who ordered this second manuscript, but seals and inscriptions show that it was owned by Hamida Banu Begum, Akbar's Persian mother.[26] Hamida Banu Begum was an avid collector of books, and one portrait even shows her holding a stamp used to mark manuscripts that entered her collection.[27] Her library primarily consisted of classical Persian texts, and so it is not immediately obvious why she was interested in an Indian epic. By comparing the reading and valuation practices of these two imperial manuscripts in the early seventeenth century, a few key points emerge regarding the initial royal interest in Akbar's *Rāmāyan*.

Jahangir inherited the master imperial copy of Akbar's *Rāmāyan* in 1605 and personally inscribed the manuscript with a brief comment a month after he ascended the throne. The note indicates Jahangir's appreciation of the epic as a good story that could inform Mughal kingship. The inscription reads,

> On the fifth of Azar during the first regnal year, this book entered the library of this supplicant at the divine court. Written by Nur al-Din Jahangir Shah, son of Akbar Padshah Ghazi in the year 1014 [November 1605]. This book, the *Rāmāyan*, is one of the celebrated books of the ancients of India. My father ordered it translated into Persian. It contains strange and incredible stories [*ʿajīb ū gharīb*] that are truly incomprehensible to the intellect [*ʿaql*].[28]

First and foremost, Jahangir calls attention here to Akbar's agency in transporting the *Rāmāyaṇa* into Persian. He declines to name any of the Mughal translators who worked on the text, a common feature of such notes, and instead focuses on the imperial instigator. Jahangir's emphasis on Akbar likely also served as an endorsement of his father's cultural politics. Jahangir initiated few Persian renderings of Sanskrit texts as an emperor, although he had sponsored several as a prince.[29] Here—early in his reign—he stresses his approval of translated Sanskrit works, a defining feature of the Akbari dispensation.

Jahangir's mention of "strange and incredible stories" draws attention to the *Rāmāyan*'s narrative within the common Indo-Persian framework of fantastical elements (*ʿajāʾib*). Mughal authors were enthralled by this mode of describing the Indian Other, even as Sanskrit ideas and intellectuals were increasingly becoming a staple of imperial cultural life. The *Rāmāyaṇa* is a strange story indeed from a Persianate perspective and includes oddities such as talking animals and superhuman feats. As Azfar Moin has pointed out, extraordinary events that occurred within a sovereign's realm were considered pertinent for royal reflection because they might have implications for the health of the polity.[30] Even more so than other Mughal emperors, Jahangir is well known for having a taste for the exotic, which is indicated at several places in his memoirs and confirmed by foreign visitors.[31]

Both royal copies of the Akbari *Rāmāyan* were assigned a monetary worth in accordance with valuation practices that were developed during Akbar's rule and codified under his successors. The valuation was typically based on several factors, including the type of work, the fame of the calligrapher, and the illustrations.[32] Only a handful of the master copy's 176 illustrations have been published, but art historians have repeatedly emphasized their aesthetic merits.[33] Additionally, the majority of Mughal master painters whom Abū al-Faẓl mentions in his *Āʾīn-i Akbarī* participated in this project.[34] In contrast, the copy owned by Hamida Banu Begum contained only around 55 paintings in its original form, and these illustrations are generally considered inferior to those of the master copy. Yet the Hamida Banu Begum *Rāmāyan* was valued at 5,550 rupees, whereas the master imperial copy was given a worth of only 1,516 rupees.[35] The motives behind this accounting are uncertain, but perhaps the bizarrely high value of the later copy was connected with the restricted access to this translation. After Hamida Banu Begum died in 1604, her *Rāmāyan* went to Jahangir, who also owned the master imperial *Rāmāyan* after Akbar's death in 1605. This means that more than twenty years after the translation was completed, two of the three known manuscripts were in the Mughal imperial library. At least initially, the Mughal *Rāmāyan* was truly a royal work.

RAḤĪM GETS THE STORY WRONG

ʿAbd al-Raḥīm Khān-i Khānān owned the third known copy of the Akbari *Rāmāyan*, which he directed his atelier to copy and illuminate around the turn of the seventeenth century. The text and illustrations are based on the master imperial copy, although both show some variations.[36] Moreover, Raḥīm's *Rāmāyan* contains a curious note written in Raḥīm's own hand on an opening flyleaf. This inscription constitutes one of the most extensive extant reflections on how the imperial elite understood Akbar's translation projects and is worth quoting in full. Raḥīm writes,

> This book, which is known as the *Rāmāyan*, is among the esteemed books of India. It is an account of Ramchand, who was one of the great kings of India [*pādshāhān-i buzurg-i hind*]. His external and spiritual graces were exemplary, being manifestations of divine attributes. According to Valmiki, who was among the greatest darvishes of India, it is said that he [Ramchand] is the son [*pisar*] of Shiva [*mahādīv*]. [These] discourses are an account of [Ramchand's] graceful attributes, pleasing virtues, great victories, and conduct, which show his magnificence. At the order of the officials of His Majesty Akbar, Naqīb Khān of Qazwīn, who was among the high-ranking lords and became exalted in the companionship and service of the king of kings, was honored and made eminent by the love of the king. He translated [this book] into Persian from the Sanskrit language [*zabān-i sanskrit*], in which Indian learning [*ʿulūm-i hind*] was recorded at the time. There was a Brahman by the name of Deva Miśra who would interpret the meaning of the *shloka*s and Naqīb Khān would translate [that] into Persian. The king, who possessed Jamshid-like magnificence, desired that on this occasion paintings be executed in this book. Upon completion of that [work], this slave reared by the kindnesses of the emperor, ʿAbd al-Raḥīm, son of Bayram Khān (may he rest in peace), requested that as I had the privilege of seeing this book, I be allowed to have a copy made. By royal favor, permission was granted. This work was prepared and illustrated by the scribes and painters of this well-wisher of the king. Thus, it may be viewed by people. This work was completed in the year A.H. 1007 [A.D. 1598–1599]. The beginning of the work and illumination of this work were made in the year 996 Hijra [A.D. 1587–1588]. The total number of paintings is 135 and the number of leaves is 349. It was completed under the term of the supervision of the loyal and gracious Mullā Shakībī Imāmī and reached completion by the mercy of God.[37]

This comment contains substantial information regarding the subimperial reception of the Persian *Rāmāyan*. Most notable are Raḥīm's misstatement of Rama's parentage and need for special permission to copy the imperial text.

In this note, Raḥīm incorrectly identifies Rama as Shiva's son, which is a noteworthy error because of both its context and source. As Seyller points out, Akbar's *Rāmāyan*, which is itself based on Vālmīki's Sanskrit text, repeatedly emphasizes that Rama is an incarnation of Vishnu.[38] Moreover, this divine identity was widely known among Akbar's inner circle and comes up in a variety of sources. Abū al-Faẓl details the incarnations of Vishnu in his *Āʾīn-i Akbarī* and therein records Rama's earthly and divine origins.[39] A synopsis of the *Rāmāyaṇa* story is contained in the *Razmnāmah* (although Raḥīm did not sponsor his copy of this epic until the 1610s). Brahmans also repeatedly told Akbar that he was an incarnation of Vishnu, like Rama, and others at court, such as Badāʾūnī, overheard these conversations (see chapter 1). Rama's worship of Shiva was an integrated part of *Rāmāyaṇa* lore, but worshipper and son are quite different things.[40] It seems that Raḥīm was unclear about even the general outline of Rama's relationships with different gods, and this slip raises doubts concerning what precisely Indo-Persian readers understood of translated Sanskrit texts. Despite the confusion he displays here, Raḥīm was a reputed polymath of Indian languages and a patron (and author) of Hindi poetry. It is difficult to reconcile these sustained interests in Indian traditions with his pronouncement that Shiva is Rama's father. We are thus left with the puzzling question, why did someone reputed to be a cross-cultural intellectual appear to know so little about a popular Indian narrative?

Raḥīm's blunder suggests that the content of translations from Sanskrit did not constitute their only value in the Indo-Persian sphere. But if not as a relevant tale, then what was the importance of Akbar's *Rāmāyan* for Raḥīm, a Mughal general and presumed connoisseur of Indian culture? Raḥīm situates the translation in a political context by mentioning Akbar and the central Mughal court several times in his note. Perhaps Raḥīm sought to reflect some of the imperial court's prestige onto himself by reproducing a royal manuscript. In this scenario, the exact text may not have been as relevant to Raḥīm as the fact that the Persian *Rāmāyan* had been created for the royal household.

Raḥīm discloses that he applied to Akbar to "be allowed to have a copy [of the *Rāmāyan*] made." This reference reminds us that Akbar, like his successors, tightly controlled who was able to see royal texts, which in turn shaped the impacts of translations from Sanskrit. The Mughal court initially did not intend for many translated works to be widely read and thought of these cross-cultural projects as operating within clearly demarcated courtly spaces. As I discuss in chapter 3, scholars have often been misled on this point and have interpreted Mughal texts, particularly Abū al-Faẕl's preface to the *Razmnāmah*, as outlining an expansive role for translations in Indian society. Akbar certainly desired Mughal encounters with Sanskrit to be revolutionary in his project to build an empire and, at times, in Indo-Persian culture more broadly. But Raḥīm's requirement for authorization to copy the *Rāmāyan* underscores precisely how restricted access to Persian translations of Sanskrit texts actually elevated the value of these works and sparked interest within the second tier of Mughal courts. Indeed, after Raḥīm's death in 1627 his *Rāmāyan* was owned by a series of nobles who worked under Shah Jahan and Aurangzeb.[41] This top-down system also hints at one type of power that the Mughals cultivated under Akbar. They did not seek popular legitimation through their interest in Indian tales but rather grounded their sovereignty in an elite culture of limited access.

Additionally, the level of illustration in Raḥīm's *Rāmāyan* may have created the prerequisite of royal permission. The two royal copies of the *Rāmāyan* were both lavishly illuminated, which was often a distinguishing mark of imperial manuscripts. In this sense, perhaps Raḥīm required permission to reproduce a royal text on a royal level.[42] Raḥīm's motivations for financing such a sumptuous copy remain murky. He certainly challenged Mughal authority at times and often had a rocky relationship with Jahangir.[43] Nonetheless, at least in his *Rāmāyan*, he seems to remain wholly within imperial Mughal modes of expressing power and so aligns himself with the empire and its ways of relating to Indian culture.

RETELLING THE *RĀMĀYAṆA* EPIC FOR JAHANGIR'S COURT

Despite the initial vision of a circumscribed imperial epic, Akbar's *Rāmāyan* helped reshape Indo-Persian literary culture far beyond his court and marked the beginning of repeated retellings of the *Rāmāyaṇa* story in Persian that continued to be generated well into the nineteenth century. These new *Rāmāyan*s were often based on Sanskrit or vernacular versions of the epic or simply oral knowledge of the tale rather than the Akbari translation. While the broad spectrum of Persian *Rāmāyan*s remains beyond my scope here, it is useful to briefly survey the two earliest retellings: Saʿd Allāh Masīḥ Pānīpatī's *Dāstān-i Rām ū Sītā* (*Tale of Ram and Sita*), also known as *Rāmāyan-i Masīḥī*, and Giridhardās's *Rāmāyan*. The works were both written for a Mughal courtly audience (although outside direct imperial patronage), but the authors developed their respective narratives in dissimilar ways. Masīḥ Pānīpatī crafted his *Rāmāyan* as a love story, whereas Giridhardās cast his poem as a heroic tale. Together they showcase the vivacity of Sanskrit-derived materials for Indo-Persian literati and begin to outline some of the rich possibilities for retelling the *Rāmāyaṇa* in Persian.

Masīḥ Pānīpatī constructed his *Rāmāyan*, titled *Tale of Ram and Sita*, as a versified Indo-Persian romance dedicated to Jahangir. In the opening section, he emphasizes that his poem expresses a truth grounded in love:

> I must speak eloquently of Hindustan
> because the dust of this land is infused with love [*ʿishq*].
> From that I spoke the tradition [*ḥadīs̱*] of Ram and Sita.
> It is not a legend [*afsānah*] but history [*tārīkh*] here.[44]

Later he again states that "this love [*ʿishqī*] of which I speak is not a legend [*afsānah*]. / Every pearl I pierce shines like the sun."[45] Masīḥ Pānīpatī's insistence that the *Rāmāyaṇa* possesses historical legitimacy echoes the understanding of Sanskrit texts translated under direct Mughal support. But whereas Akbar's translators labeled texts such as the *Mahābhārata* a record of India's royal past, Masīḥ Pānīpatī accentuates the emotional honesty of the *Rāmāyaṇa*'s love story. Masīḥ further recast this Indian tale within the Persianate framework of a romance. As one scholar has put it, "Masih canonizes the Rama story among the other Islamicate legends as a tragedy of love. Rama and Sita come to embody the similar trope of a lover and beloved who must surmount numerous obstacles."[46] Romances had long been tightly linked with courts and kingship in the Persianate tradition.[47] In telling the Indian tale within this romantic-political framework, Masīḥ may also have intended to provide ethical or even spiritual instruction to his projected imperial audience.[48]

In contrast, Giridhardās reimagined the epic as Rama's story exclusively and set out to write an account of an Indian hero. He authored his *Rāmāyan* in 1623–1624, dedicated the poem to Jahangir, and described his work as the "book of Ram" (*nāmah-i rām*).[49] Giridhardās follows Vālmīki's version quite closely and so includes the story of Sita within the text.[50] But when Giridhardās sketches an initial table of contents, he outlines Rama's good nature, his exile, and the war against Ravana with no mention of Sita. Even when it seems he must name Sita in order to explain the reason for battle with Lanka, he prefers vague references to how "disaster suddenly befell" and "countless soldiers prepared for war."[51] Giridhardās ends his prologue by focusing on Rama's glorious rule in Ayodhya (Oudh) after he returned triumphant over Ravana.

> After the promised time of fourteen years,
> the crown and good fortune together returned to Oudh.
> The world was full of equity and justice.
> He delighted the world with righteousness.[52]

In the closing line of his summary, Giridhardās reiterates that he is going to narrate "[Ram's] adventures."[53]

Giridhardās's excising of Sita mirrors the opening of Akbar's *Rāmāyan*, which also includes a brief summary of the epic and likewise characterizes the tale as Rama's story. The synopsis in Akbar's *Rāmāyan* reads,

> It has not remained hidden from the hearts of the lords of truth that this is a book famous among the Indians [*ahl-i hind*] and called *Rāmāyan* in Sanskrit [*zabān-i hindī*]. It is an account of the adventures of Ramchand from the time of his birth until his death. He was an Indian king and sovereign lord of an empire. The majesty and splendor of the city of Ayodhya, which is now known as Oudh, is famous. Among Ramchand's stories is that he built a bridge over the salt ocean and vanquished Lanka, a well-known city among islands, with total strength and composure. He killed Ravan, a strong demon with ten heads, whose line had held sovereignty over that land for thousands of years, and he destroyed that lineage. Valmiki, a Brahman who was very learned and an ascetic, versified this story [*afsānah*] from beginning to end in Sanskrit [*zabān-i hindī*] and became famous in this land.[54]

We do not know whether Giridhardās was familiar with Akbar's *Rāmāyan*. But it seems that there was a common interpretation of this epic as a hero's tale in Mughal India, especially in works directed toward the Mughal king.

Even this cursory glance at the retellings of Masīḥ Pānīpatī and Giridhardās illustrates how select Sanskrit stories proved to be successful as creative materials in Indo-Persian literature. Many other Sanskrit-based narratives were also popular during this period, and some had been part of Indo-Islamic culture far before the advent of Mughal rule. Most notably, animal fables from the *Pañcatantra* (*Five Tales*) and the *Hitopadeśa* (*Good Advice*) had been translated and reformulated in Arabic and Persian since the sixth century.[55] Interestingly, however, even poets working outside the royal court viewed Persian *Rāmāyans* in particular as demanding an imperial reception. Both Masīḥ Pānīpatī and Giridhardās dedicated their poems to Jahangir (whether he received them is unclear).[56] Elite Mughal culture exerted such a profound influence on Indo-Persian literature that poets continued to imagine Persian incarnations of Rama's story as belonging within the royal court.

FIRISHTAH: A DECCANI PERSPECTIVE ON THE *MAHĀBHĀRATA*

Writers beyond the Mughal Empire also engaged with imperial translations, such as Muḥammad Qāsim Firishtah, who worked under Ibrahim ʿAdil Shah II (r. 1580–1627), ruler of Bijapur in the Deccan. Firishtah wrote his *Gulshan-i Ibrāhīmī* (*Ibrahim's Rose Garden*), more commonly known as *Tārīkh-i Firishtah* (*Firishtah's History*), in the early seventeenth century and includes an account of pre-Islamic India that draws on Mughal texts.[57] Firishtah's overarching project was to trace the rise of Indo-Islamic power. He promotes his chronicle as "containing the events of Islamic kings [*vāqiʿāt-i pādshāhān-i islām*] and anecdotes about great *shaykhs* who are [respectively] known as the external and internal rulers over the provinces of Hindustan."[58] As part of this endeavor, Firishtah opens his history with an extended introduction on "the beliefs of the Indians [*muʿtaqadāt-i ahl-i hind*], an account of Hindu kings [*rāyān*], and a detailed description of the appearance of Islam in that land."[59]

Scholars have typically paid little attention to the prefatory section of the *Tārīkh-i Firishtah*, partly because modern sensibilities condemn it as historically inaccurate. In addition, the major English translation of the text silently and severely truncates Firishtah's treatment of the pre-Islamic subcontinent.[60] In this long-neglected section, Firishtah presents two competing histories of early India, one of which is drawn from Sanskrit materials that the Mughals had introduced into Persian. Firishtah offers a useful viewpoint on Mughal cross-cultural activities in two respects. First, he directly relies on texts that emerged out of Mughal interactions with Sanskrit literature, above all the *Mahābhārata*, and thereby provides insight into how these works were circulated and perceived beyond imperial circles. Second, he worked under royal non-Mughal patronage, which imbues his text with a set of political concerns at once parallel to and contrasting with those of Mughal-sponsored intellectuals.

In the opening of his history, Firishtah recounts the *Mahābhārata*'s basic story. He names Akbar's *Mahābhārata* as one of his major sources and attaches a significant but qualified importance to this translation. He highlights the centrality of this Sanskrit epic to Indians (*ahl-i hind*), writing, "There is no more comprehensive and authoritative work than that [*Mahābhārat*] among this group today."[61] Having lauded the epic as a foundational work, Firishtah attests that it was translated under Mughal sponsorship, and subsequently, "The author of these lines has undertaken the work of making an abridgment and offers it here."[62] Firishtah then commences his overview of the *Mahābhārata*, starting with a description of Indian cyclical time divided into four ages (*yugas*). He relates the basic plot of the epic, including the main characters' lineages, how the Pandavas lost their kingdom, and the Great War. Firishtah next discusses Krishna's story because, as he explains, Krishna is a particularly famous character among Indians. He concludes with Vyāsa writing the *Mahābhārata* at the request of Arjuna's grandson.[63]

Despite his claims to rely on Akbar's *Mahābhārata* throughout this summary, Firishtah's language betrays that he actually drew on Abū al-Faẕl's preface to the Persian text rather than the Akbari translation itself. Firishtah reproduces Abū al-Faẕl's wording exactly at times, including his quoted verses of Persian poetry.[64] He also unwittingly points to his true source by mistakenly attributing the entire Persian *Mahābhārata* to Abū al-Faẕl when in fact only the preface can be rightfully ascribed to him. In a sense, Firishtah's dependence on Abū al-Faẕl's introduction parallels how Raḥīm conceptualized Akbar's *Rāmāyan* as a text to be acquired and invoked rather than seriously read. But, unlike Raḥīm's mischaracterization of one aspect of the *Rāmāyan*, Firishtah accurately relayed the story of the *Mahābhārata*. At the end of his summary, he even claims some original research in evaluating its Sanskrit title:

> [Vyasa] called this book the *Mahābhārat*. I have heard that the reason for this title is that *mahā* means great and *bhārat* means war. Because this book records great battles, he called it the *Mahābhārat*. But this is wrong because *bhārat* does not mean war in the vocabulary of the Indians [*lughat-i ahl-i hind*]. Clearly because this book contains tales of the illustrious offspring of Raja Bharat, it was given his name, and in usage the *-a* was lengthened. God knows best![65]

While Firishtah uses the epic's Persian preface, he does not subscribe to Abū al-Faẕl's political interpretation of the *Mahābhārata*. In particular, he discards Abū al-Faẕl's postulation that the text contains intellectual truths that supersede Islamic notions. Wherever Firishtah finds any conflict between the Sanskrit record and Islamicate (including Persian) sources, he declares the former incorrect. As I discuss in chapter 3, Abū al-Faẕl gives the example of how some Muslims erroneously believe that the earth is only seven thousand years old, which the *Mahābhārata* controverts by sketching out a much longer temporal arc. In contrast, Firishtah holds that "from the age of Adam until the time of writing these lines, not more than seven thousand years have passed. What the Indians [*hindū'ān*] say about hundreds of thousands of years is an exaggeration and a pure lie."[66] The *Mahābhārata*'s speciousness does not prevent Firishtah from using the epic to reconstruct ancient Indian history according to the Indians. But, perhaps because of the text's perceived fallibility, he falls short of integrating the epic story into his overarching historical narrative.

After Firishtah finishes his retelling of the *Mahābhārata*, he launches into a new version of India's pre-Islamic past that he detaches from the Sanskrit epic's depiction. He transitions to this second narrative with the straightforward claim, "The reality [*taḥqīq*] is that India was populated by the descendants of Adam, just like the rest of the habitable world."[67] He then elaborates the story of the great flood and the subsequent dispersal of Noah's children around the globe, including to India. Firishtah thus brackets the epic within the realm of reported history and then offers a second, more reliable tradition based on a Muslim prophet. Earlier Persianate authors frequently offered multiple historical narratives but typically confined themselves to Islamicate traditions.[68] Given this precedent and Firishtah's own disposition toward Islamic history, it is striking that he chose to include the *Mahābhārata* at all. Here Firishtah signals the long-reaching effects of Mughal encounters with Sanskrit texts on Indo-Persian literary and historical sensibilities. The epic may not have been "comprehensive and authoritative" for Firishtah as it was for early modern Brahmans, but the text quickly became an essential part of the Indo-Persian tradition. As such it demanded inclusion in a history of ancient India, even if it was ultimately overwritten by another past.

In his second vision of pre-Islamic India, Firishtah situates the subcontinent as integrated into the Perso-Islamic tradition well before the dawn of Indo-Islamic dynasties. Firishtah describes Indians as the direct descendants of the early Abrahamic prophets, which was a time-honored Islamic strategy for incorporating new groups of people.[69] For example, ninth- and tenth-century Persian and Arabic writers cast Persians as the progeny of early Muslim figures in order to assimilate Iran into the Islamic world.[70] This method of integrating previous outsiders into an Abrahamic narrative was a broader phenomenon also shared by Christians. For example, eighteenth-century colonial scholars articulated a parallel idea that Indians were descendants of early Christian figures.[71] For his part, Firishtah records that all Indians are descended from Hind, the son of Ham and the grandson of Noah. In this deft move Firishtah also provides an etymology for the Perso-Arabic name for India (*hind*). He further postulates that Hind had four sons, who gave rise genealogically and linguistically to the different regions of India. Accordingly, Bang populated Bengal, Dakhin established himself in the Deccan, and so forth.[72]

Firishtah also sets forth religious correspondences between India and Persia, such as their movement toward (and ultimately away from) idol worship. He writes,

> It is said that Hind, just as he had seen and heard from his father Ham, the son Noah, obeyed and worshipped the incomparable Creator. His children, generation after generation, followed his example. Until, during the time of Maharaj, someone came from Iran who introduced sun worship. That became popular, and many became star worshippers and also fire worshippers. But when the practice of idol worship [*rasm-i butparastī*] appeared, most became followers. This is because a Brahman [from Jharkhand] told Suraj that whoever made a representation of his own predecessor in gold, silver, or stone and worshipped it would find the road to salvation. As a result all kinds of people crafted large images of those who had come before and worshipped them.[73]

Here Firishtah paints Indians as originally monotheists. Prior Indo-Islamic writers, such as Shaykh Rukn al-Dīn (d. 1575/1576), the son of ʿAbd al-Quddūs Gangōhī (d. 1537), had made a similar claim that early Indians professed divine unity (*tawḥīd*) but later became corrupt.[74] This vision that multiple world areas were privy to pure knowledge in ancient times was well attested in Islamic thought. The eighth to tenth century Abbasid translation movement drew upon this idea in order to lend credence to newly introduced Greek materials.[75] In the *Tārīkh-i Firishtah*, linking India's religious evolution with that of ancient Persia also suggested that Islam would one day restore India (like Persia) to its idol-free roots.

Last, Firishtah attempts to demonstrate how India's past was intricately bound up with that of the larger Islamicate world through the actions of several key individuals. In some cases, Firishtah relays what we consider to be accurate history today, such as Alexander the Great's entry into India.[76] In other instances, Firishtah's stories are more dubious, such as when he records that the legendary Persian hero Rustam visited the subcontinent and placed a new king on the throne.[77] Firishtah's account of pre-Islamic India predictably ends with the rise of Muslim dynasties on the subcontinent, the primary topic of his work.

Thus, for Firishtah, India's history revolved around Islam. Indians were descended from Noah, originally monotheists, and were ultimately bound to be ruled by Muslims. Even in the intervening centuries when idol worship and non-Muslim sovereigns prevailed, India was always connected to the Islamic world. Whereas Akbar's court often conceived of the Mughals as heirs to the Sanskrit tradition, Firishtah depicts India as subsumed within Islamic history. The *Mahābhārata* does not fit easily into this perspective, but nonetheless Firishtah opens his text by recapping this epic. He treats the *Mahābhārata* as a work that must be addressed as part of the Indo-Islamic tradition, even if it is ultimately rejected in favor of a different story.

COUNTING KINGS IN SEVENTEENTH-CENTURY INDIA

Later Indo-Persian authors increasingly perceived Sanskrit-derived information about India's past as legitimate history. One notable trend in this direction is the appearance of independent royal lineages (*rājāvalīs*) in Persian that connect ancient and contemporary Indian rulers. These texts feature lists of kings, typically based in Delhi, that begin with pre-Islamic figures and continue through the lines of Indo-Islamic sovereigns to conclude with the reigning Mughal emperor. Such texts spoke to a deep imperial interest in royal predecessors. The Mughals often celebrated their genealogical ancestors in texts and paintings.[78] Akbar and Jahangir even had gems engraved with their names alongside those of their Timurid forerunners.[79] However, as Corinne Lefèvre has pointed out, the Mughals' Genghis-Timurid past was not well suited for an Indian audience that would have responded better to other types of authority claims.[80] To this observation I would add that the Mughals' Central Asian heritage also left gaps in the self-narrative of the ruling elites, who saw themselves, in no small part, as Indian sovereigns. Persian *rājāvalīs* offer one example of how intellectuals built upon earlier cross-cultural endeavors under Akbar and Jahangir to construct an integrated history of Indo-Islamic kingship.

One exemplary and understudied work is the *Tārīkh-i Rājhā-yi Dilhī* (*History of the Kings of Delhi*), which was penned during Shah Jahan's rule (1628–1658). The authorship of the *Tārīkh-i Rājhā-yi Dilhī* is uncertain, but the Persianate tradition connects the work with Shah Jahan's court. The text survives today in a single known copy that is ascribed to Chandar Bhān Brahman.[81] Chandar Bhān Brahman was Shah Jahan's imperial chief secretary (*mīr munshī*), and he produced a number of important literary works.[82] Chandar Bhān is emblematic of one major way that Brahmans were integrated into the Mughal court, namely as members of the imperial service, and here emerges as somebody who also had an interest in Sanskrit-derived ideas. To my knowledge, there is no mention of this royal lineage in any of Chandar Bhān's other works, and the writing style is too cryptic to offer supporting evidence for his authorship.[83] However, the text is datable to the mid-seventeenth century because it concludes with Shah Jahan's reign and thus offers insight into the later imperial reception of Sanskrit-based history.

The *Tārīkh-i Rājhā-yi Dilhī* promotes a succinct vision of the Mughal Empire as the culmination of a succession of pre-Islamic and Islamic Indian dynasties. Approximately half of the work is devoted to kings predating the dawn of Islamic rule, from Yudhishthira until Prithviraj Chauhan. The records on the earliest kings are brief, typically detailing only the length of each one's tenure on the throne, often down to the precise number of days. The author also occasionally marks dynastic changes and other crucial events, particularly the further forward the work moves in time.[84] The text highlights the transfer of power from pre-Islamic to Islamic rulers while still maintaining the continuity that all are Delhi-based kings. The author describes how Shihab al-Din Ghori and Prithviraj Chauhan battled for the throne, which ended with the establishment of padshahs who rule India.[85] The text then goes through various Indo-Islamic polities. For the Mughal sovereigns, the work even gives an overview of the intrigues for the throne that often accompanied succession struggles, including the brief reigns of Shahriyar and Davar Bakhsh Bulaqi before Shah Jahan rose to power with the help of Asaf Khan.[86]

The *Tārīkh-i Rājhā-yi Dilhī* demonstrates two significant developments beyond previous works that incorporated Indian knowledge into Persian for imperial purposes. First, the text uses a concise format to link ancient India to the Mughal present. Abū al-Faẓl, Ṭāhir Muḥammad Sabzavārī, and Firishtah all pursued similar goals of presenting Islamic rulers as inheritors of India's pre-Islamic past. But their projects each run thousands of pages and were intended for elite audiences. In contrast, the *History of the Kings of Delhi* is a short, readable work that numbers a mere twenty folios in large handwriting. One predecessor of the *Tārīkh-i Rājhā-yi Dilhī*'s may be a list and short narrative account of Delhi's sovereigns that Abū al-Faẕl includes in his *Āʾīn-i Akbarī*.[87] But whereas recounting Delhi's rulers was part of a colossal project for Abū al-Faẕl, here it stands alone. Given this format, the author imagined a quite different audience from the learned, necessarily patient readers envisioned by earlier literati. This later author, whether Chandar Bhān or somebody else, offers a comprehensive and concise view of India's royal past that reached its pinnacle with the Mughals.

Second, the *Tārīkh-i Rājhā-yi Dilhī* treats Sanskrit sources as accurate, reliable texts that are comparable to Arabic and Persian works. In a brief introduction, the author claims that he relied on both "Indian books" (*kutub-i hindī*) and Islamicate histories, such as the *Majmūʿ* of Niẓām al-Dīn Aḥmad Khān.[88] Earlier thinkers, such as Firishtah, tended to treat Sanskrit sources separately from the rest of history, which was by definition Islamic. In contrast, this slightly later writer united Sanskrit (and possibly also Hindi) and Islamicate works in order to build a synthesized vision of India's past. The line of kings beginning with Yudhishthira no longer constituted a separable chapter in Indian history but rather partook of the same Indian sovereignty now enjoyed by Indo-Islamic dynasties.

After the *Tārīkh-i Rājhā-yi Dilhī*, literati such as Banvālī Dās, a *munshī* in Dara Shikuh's retinue, composed further independent *rājāvalī*s in Persian.[89] Eighteenth-century authors included similar lineages of kings from Yudhishthira to the reigning Mughal sovereign within larger historical works.[90] Some Rajputs pursued an inverted project of incorporating Persianate sources into their royal histories by invoking *Shāhnāmah* characters among their ancestors, for example.[91] This later history lies beyond what I can analyze here, but the ongoing production of royal chronicles that operated across traditions attests to the enduring relevance and appeal of Sanskrit knowledge in the Indo-Persian world.

DARA SHIKUH'S PRINCELY PROJECT

In the 1640s and 1650s, the Mughal prince Dara Shikuh sponsored a series of Sanskrit and Persian encounters that was sharply distinguished from earlier Mughal projects. Dara Shikuh was Shah Jahan's eldest son and the heir apparent to the Mughal crown before he was outmaneuvered and executed in 1659 by his elder brother, Aurangzeb ʿAlamgir (r. 1658–1707). Prior to his demise, however, Dara Shikuh was based at the royal court and enjoyed a wealth of free time and resources to use at his leisure.[92] During the 1640s–1650s, he forged links with Indian religious and intellectual communities and supported numerous translations. For instance, Dara Shikuh was involved in offering a land grant to a man named in Persian sources as Gosain Vithalrai, a religious leader in Gokul in 1643.[93] In the early 1650s, he sought out Bābā Lāl, a Punjabi spiritual leader, for philosophical conversations.[94] Dara Shikuh also supported numerous Sanskrit intellectuals, some with strong Advaita Vedanta leanings, within his princely household. Many of these thinkers assisted with translations.[95] One of these pandits also penned a Sanskrit letter on Dara Shikuh's behalf to a Brahmanical leader in Benares.[96] Dara's affinity with Indian religious figures was frequently memorialized in Persianate texts and paintings.[97]

While Dara Shikuh's projects bear broad similarities to Akbar's earlier endeavors in that both are cross-cultural, Dara Shikuh's interests demanded a separate approach to Sanskrit texts and knowledge systems. Accordingly, his endeavors are most fruitfully considered in contrast to earlier imperial efforts. In his translations, Dara Shikuh focused overwhelmingly on Sanskrit religious and philosophical texts. For example, working under Dara's support, Banvālī Dās produced a Persian adaptation of the *Prabodhacandrodaya* (*Moonrise of Enlightenment*), an allegorical play based on Vedanta philosophy written in the eleventh century. The Persian translation identifies the work as a "text of Sufism" and underscores its relevance to spiritual pursuits.[98] Translations of several other Sanskrit mystical works are also associated with Dara Shikuh's patronage, including two Advaita Vedanta works, the *Aṣṭāvakragītā* (*Song of Ashtavakra*) and the *Ātmavilāsa* (*Play of the Soul*).[99] Dara Shikuh is personally attributed with a Persian *Bhagavadgītā*.[100] He commissioned another version of the *Yogavāsiṣṭha*.[101] Perhaps the most well-known translation associated with Dara is a Persian rendering of fifty *upaniṣads* titled *Sirr-i Akbar* (*Greatest Mystery*).[102]

Within many of his translations, Dara Shikuh promoted an agenda of reconciling Hindu and Muslim ideas, often specifically Vedantic and Sufi notions. For example, the preface to the *Sirr-i Akbar* describes the Sanskrit *upaniṣads* as "not only in agreement with the noble *Qur'ān*, but a commentary upon it."[103] Here Dara Shikuh presents Sanskrit texts as complementary to and in fact subsumed within the Islamic tradition. Dara Shikuh also underwrote independent works along similar lines. Most notably, he sponsored a treatise on the convergence of Vedantic and Sufi metaphysics titled *Majmaᶜ al-Baḥrayn* (*Confluence of Two Oceans*). This work was also translated into Sanskrit shortly after its composition under the title *Samudrasaṅgama* (*Confluence of Oceans*).[104]

Dara Shikuh's interests in philosophical and particularly religious convergences were hardly an aberration and had a long, rich history in Indo-Persian (including Mughal) royal contexts, as Supriya Gandhi has aptly shown.[105] Nonetheless, emphasizing Hindu-Muslim similarities marked a shift from the overarching arc of earlier Mughal cross-cultural activities, which tended to be more concerned with political power, historical questions, and literary innovations. One distinction worth highlighting is that Akbar's court generally celebrated the uniqueness of Sanskrit knowledge systems, whereas Dara's projects sought to show Sanskrit's commensurability with Perso-Islamic traditions. Mughal thinkers formulated many different relationships between Indian and Perso-Islamic worldviews, but few before Dara Shikuh had so drastically reduced the distinctiveness of the Sanskrit tradition. In this sense, scholars have been mistaken in surmising that Dara Shikuh completed Akbar's vision of the "unity of beings" (*waḥdat al-wujūd*).[106] On the contrary, Dara Shikuh avoids mentioning Akbar in his writings, and his cross-cultural projects do not evoke earlier royal Mughal models.[107]

Despite his engagements with the Sanskrit world being largely separate from earlier Mughal projects, one similarity is that Dara Shikuh was also no doubt motivated to engage with Sanskrit texts and ideas by political ambitions. As Munis Faruqui has recently argued, Dara attempted to build a network of diverse alliances and a healthy princely household as a stepping-stone to becoming the next Mughal sovereign.[108] Supriya Gandhi has pointed out that he was highly concerned with balancing rulership and his specially appointed spiritual role.[109] Dara may well have viewed his actions as supporting a bid for the throne, and yet he defined his interests (including in Sanskrit) far more narrowly than had his predecessors in a series of missteps that ultimately contributed to his demise. For instance, Dara Shikuh's excessive involvement with the Miyan Mir lineage of Qadiri Sufis alienated other Sufi orders that otherwise could have provided crucial imperial support.[110] In a similar fashion, his narrow emphasis on Advaita Vedanta, as opposed to a range of Brahmanical (not to mention Jain) viewpoints, constituted a significant contraction of Mughal interests in the Sanskrit world.

CONCLUSION: REMAKING THE INDO-PERSIAN WORLD

Mughal connections with the Sanskrit world, particularly their translations of Sanskrit texts, were culturally powerful into the mid-seventeenth century and beyond. Many authors agreed with the Mughals about the potency of integrating Islamicate and Sanskrit ideas, although not everybody approved of this project. The diverse opinions on imperial interactions with Sanskrit are well illustrated by reactions to Akbar's *Rāmāyan*. Badāʾūnī, who translated the text, condemns the epic on religious and political grounds. The translation was consumed in limited elite circles, although how and even to what extent it was read remain unclear given Raḥīm's enigmatic flyleaf note. Regardless, the Akbari *Rāmāyan* was understood as a text about the evolving institution of Mughal kingship. For some, this was reason to reject it altogether, whereas for others its royal relevance elevated its status.

Those writing after Akbar's reign found further meanings for the *Rāmāyan* within the Indo-Persian world. Jahangir thought of the epic as a fantastical tale, Masīḥ glimpsed the potential for a romance, and Giridhardās crafted the narrative into a martial story. The new Persian *Rāmāyans* advanced the larger Mughal mission of using Sanskrit stories to redefine Indo-Persian culture, but in rather different ways than Abū al-Faẓl had imagined within Akbar's court. In his *Learning of India*, Abū al-Faẓl strove to introduce Sanskrit ideas to Indo-Persian intellectuals and prepare them to further engage with the Sanskrit tradition. In contrast, Giridhardās and other authors of Persian *Rāmāyan*s transculturated the epic story by liberally drawing on existent Persianate genres and literary tropes. There was no single mode of cross-cultural exchange in Mughal India, and even under Akbar Fayẓī had followed a similarly adaptive method of retelling the Nala and Damayanti saga. But the vision of returning to source Sanskrit texts seemed to fade as time went on, even as Indo-Persian poets continued to see enticing political and literary resources in stories such as the *Rāmāyaṇa*.

As we move outside the space-time frame of the Mughal courts of Akbar and Jahangir, Firishtah and the author of the *Tārīkh-i Rājhā-yi Dilhī* offer perspectives as individuals who had inherited (rather than helped to create) the presence of Sanskrit materials in Persianate knowledge. In his history, Firishtah remains ambivalent about the place of Sanskrit visions of the past in an Islamicate tradition. He acknowledges the *Mahābhārata* as the starting point for ancient Indian history but ultimately brands the text unreliable and disconnects it from the rest of his narrative. The *Tārīkh-i Rājhā-yi Dilhī* envisions equality and fluidity between the Sanskrit and Persian traditions and outlines how the former leads into the latter through the dynastic lines of Delhi-based kings. In so doing, the work reveals an important shift in the status of Sanskrit knowledge in Indo-Persian political thought.

In addition to the political receptions I have outlined, Mughal cross-cultural activities also became integrated within the Indo-Persian literary and cultural spheres far beyond the confines of courts. For example, ʿAbd al-Raḥmān Chishtī (d. 1683) penned a work titled the *Mirʾāt al-Makhlūqāt* (*Mirror of Creation*) that incorporates aspects of the *Mahābhārata* story. Muzaffar Alam has recently drawn attention to ʿAbd al-Raḥmān's argument that Sanskrit Puranic materials furnish evidence for Muslim prophets.[111] Many additional Indo-Persian texts emerged in the seventeenth and eighteenth centuries, including retranslations of popular works such as the *Rāmāyaṇa* and the *Bhagavadgītā*. Most such crossover works remain unanalyzed, but there were many impacts and afterlives of the Mughal interest in Sanskrit. These later projects continued the process that was kicked into action under the Mughals of significantly changing the nature of Persian literary culture on the subcontinent. We might even say that repeated engagements with Sanskrit-based ideas are a major part of what constitute the *Indo* part of the Indo-Persian tradition.

CONCLUSION

POWER, LITERATURE, AND EARLY MODERNITY

SCHOLARS HAVE long ignored the very existence, not to mention the political ramifications, of connections between the imperial Mughal court and Sanskrit intellectuals, texts, and knowledge systems. Many Mughal historians have relied exclusively and uncritically on Persian histories, usually produced under royal support, which frequently offer a purposefully inaccurate vision of Mughal culture as limited to Perso-Arabic traditions. Additionally, the false notion remains prevalent that Sanskrit literary developments unfolded without reference to political events and social changes. Both views ignore large caches of materials, including Persian retellings of Indian stories and Sanskrit works that explicitly discuss the Mughals. Above all, however, the presumption that the Mughals were a Persianate dynasty in a restrictive sense has precluded any major imperial role for Sanskrit texts and ideas before such a possibility was even considered. In short, we have lacked the imagination to recover the complex, multilingual culture of encounters that flourished under Akbar, Jahangir, and Shah Jahan.

In this book, I have reconstructed the social links between the Mughal elite and Jain and Brahman Sanskrit intellectuals and the series of literary engagements that they separately and jointly produced. In these networks, the royal court occupied a key position as a perceived cultural center. Many thinkers, both Persianate and Sanskrit, viewed the imperial court as a principal hub for negotiating the boundaries of their respective traditions. The Mughals bolstered this image by bestowing lavish patronage on people working in Persian, Sanskrit, Hindi, and other languages. Diverse royal sponsorship brought members of multiple traditions into close proximity and encouraged ongoing exchanges. Even writers who operated outside imperial support regarded the Mughals as recipients of innovative texts and so dedicated cross-cultural works to the ruling elite. Many texts produced both under and for the Mughals circulated far beyond the central court, and writers throughout the subcontinent grappled with the implications of these manifold cross-cultural projects.

Connections with the Sanskrit cultural world played a crucial role in the evolution of Mughal power and also significantly altered dynamics within Indian literary and religious communities. In order to grasp the political and cultural implications of Mughal-Sanskrit connections we must be open to aspects of power that do not rely on large audiences.[1] For the Mughals, Sanskrit texts and ideas offered a way to be rulers of India. This was not an exclusionary opportunity, and the Mughals also cultivated ruling identities within the Persianate realm, the Islamicate world, and so forth. But the Mughals saw unique possibilities in the Sanskrit tradition to know India in historical, mythic, and empirical senses, as indeed had many kings before them. For Jain and Brahman elites, encounters with the central court enabled them to participate in Mughal rule, to define themselves in politically salient ways, and to bring new ideas into the Sanskrit literary tradition. The interplay between politics and culture flowed both directions, and larger shifts, particularly within the Sanskrit literary ecumene, ultimately led to the decline of Mughal engagements with this tradition. These diverse encounters over the course of roughly one hundred years continued to exert vibrant effects for centuries in numerous literary and cultural contexts on the subcontinent. Awareness of this history ought to significantly change how we understand the Mughal Empire, early modern Jain and Brahman communities, and Sanskrit and Indo-Persian literary dynamics. Moreover, my analysis offers several broader applications to studies of sovereign identity, literary cultures, and India's early modernity.

MUGHAL MULTICULTURALISM

The Mughals have been a major topic of scholarly research for decades and are also invoked in popular culture and political settings in contemporary India and Pakistan. In all contexts, much disagreement persists concerning how to properly characterize Mughal multiculturalism. Certainly the royal Mughal court had many facets, and part of my goal is to highlight a hitherto overlooked aspect of how the Mughals forged links with a particular literary and intellectual tradition. However, the stakes in this project are higher than excavating one discounted aspect of a notably diverse court. The imperial interest in Sanskrit usefully highlights some of the defining features of the social and intellectual environment that the Mughals fostered in the core of their kingdom. Accordingly, my arguments suggest a few substantial realignments to how we understand the cultural fabric of the royal court and Mughal imperialism.

First, the Mughals identified cross-cultural meetings as foundational to their imperial practices and so crafted their royal court as a space defined by multiple cultural frontiers. Frontiers are most frequently identified as the geographical edges of a given polity. In this land-based usage, frontiers are unknown quantities that remain uncharted from the viewpoint of the imperial center and demand to be investigated from an alternative perspective based within the frontier itself. As Manan Ahmed has recently put the case for dedicating significant attention to regions on the margins of empires, "Situating ourselves in the frontier reveals new topographies, varied perspectives, networks and routes that are invisible to the imperial eye."[2] Cultural frontiers follow a similar logic as geographical ones. They are horizons that allow insight into important ideas and trends that are often obscured from a more center-based perspective.

Akbar and his successors established their empire across the very geographical space in which Sanskrit had thrived for centuries as the premier Indian language of literature and learning. In so doing, they suddenly found a tradition that was largely unknown to them at the very heart of their political formation. Moreover, instead of rejecting Sanskrit as an inconsequential language for imperial purposes, the Mughal kings expended considerable energy toward incorporating Sanskrit intellectuals, stories, and knowledge systems into their court culture. By extending patronage to Jains and Brahmans, sponsoring renderings of Sanskrit works, and producing Persian accounts of Indian knowledge systems, the Mughals established Sanskrit as an important cultural and intellectual tradition within their imperial dispensation. In many cases, they even made such encounters a pivotal part of their political ambitions.

In addition to Sanskrit, the Mughals identified several other traditions as vital in their court. Hindi poets enjoyed liberal royal support, and the majority of Mughal patronage was devoted to Persian, the Mughals' administrative medium of choice. Sanskrit thinkers forged a variety of relationships to these other traditions. Hindi was often the mutual tongue of Sanskrit and Persian intellectuals and therefore mediated imperial access to Sanskrit works. Sanskrit and Hindi traditions also shared certain cultural spaces in the Mughal context. Critically, when the Mughals brought Sanskrit, Hindi, and Persian traditions into various configurations within the imperial court, the result was not a single syncretic culture. Francesca Orsini has recently argued, "Both the single-language and 'composite culture' narratives exclude large swathes of literary production."[3] Assuming a single cultural milieu, whether we characterize it as monolingual or diverse, obscures the Mughal interest in Sanskrit. Instead, characterizing Mughal cross-cultural interests as ongoing encounters along a cultural frontier usefully highlights the processes whereby members of largely discrete traditions came into contact with one another and worked out dynamic relationships between their cultural and political worlds.

The Mughals never focused solely on absorbing the Sanskrit tradition into the Indo-Persian world but rather repeatedly forged numerous types of connections. Certain projects such as Abū al-Fażl's *Āʾīn-i Akbarī* sought to robustly introduce Sanskrit ideas and discourses into Persian. But Akbar, Jahangir, and Shah Jahan also supported Sanskrit literary production as a largely independent activity in which they could participate as patrons. Responding to indications from the ruling elite, regional figures dedicated Sanskrit works to the Mughals. These praise poems asserted a political role for Sanskrit in the Mughal imperium and also integrated the Mughals into Sanskrit aesthetic paradigms. Royally sponsored and dedicated translations of the Indian epics expanded manifold visions for how to productively fuse aspects of Sanskrit and Islamicate traditions. Both during and after the height of Mughal links with Sanskrit, Persian and Sanskrit existed as distinct entities that nonetheless each showed significant evidence of having crossed paths in a Mughal imperial context. For the Mughals, repeated exchanges were crucial to integrating Sanskrit in their rich cultural tapestry.

Curiously, the Mughals did not identify their inability to comprehend Sanskrit as a major hurdle to engaging with this tradition. In some cases, the Mughals relied on translations (into Persian and Hindi) in order to understand Sanskrit texts. But in other instances Sanskrit works project an imperial reception without specifying any means of being linguistically understood. In chapter 2, I suggest three ideas for a transverse Mughal understanding of Sanskrit texts: the works may have been verbally translated into Hindi, the Mughals may have understood some spoken Sanskrit, and some works may have been received as gifts (including, perhaps, appreciation of alliteration and other sound-based features).

There are exceptions to the lack of Mughal concern with linguistic competence. Most notably Abū al-Faẕl strove to teach Sanskrit technical discourse to Persianate readers, although even he stopped short of explaining Sanskrit grammar. Overall, however, neither the Mughals nor their Sanskrit interlocutors recognized Sanskrit-Persian bilingualism as a necessary prerequisite for cross-cultural interactions. The persistent gap between language abilities and imperial interests will no doubt prove difficult for many modern scholars to accept.[4] But we must strive to understand a cultural world that allowed for generative, and perhaps today unimaginable, dynamics between textual traditions absent full linguistic comprehension.

While there is a strong temptation to celebrate Mughal cross-cultural activities, we wade here into murky waters. Modern thinkers have often mischaracterized the Mughals as exhibiting a protoversion of modern religious toleration or even secular tendencies. To take a prominent example, the well-known economist Amartya Sen lauds Akbar's policies of "religious neutrality of the state" and his "tolerant multiculturalism," championing these approaches as forerunners for postindependence Indian secularism.[5] Mughal historians have likewise extolled Akbar's evenhanded treatment of religions and endorsed his rational thought as "an indelible contribution to our [Indian] national history."[6] There may be great political value in interpreting the Mughal past to foster a precedent for contemporary tolerance, but the truth of the matter is more complicated than this prosecular, prodemocracy narrative.[7]

The Mughal brand of multiculturalism was not an open stage where all traditions were equally esteemed, nor was it a utopia of religious toleration. Mughal engagements with Sanskrit were fueled by political, literary, and intellectual interests that often led imperial elites to harshly judge specific ideas, texts, and practices. Accordingly, the Mughals sought access to a previously unknown chapter of history in Persian translations of the Sanskrit epics, but they had no qualms about condemning the inaccuracies in such materials. They identified incredible potential in importing Sanskrit knowledge systems into Persian, although this invitation did not extend to unthinkable traditions such as atheism. In many cases, the Mughals sought to harness Sanskrit discourses to speak to ongoing imperial projects. For example, they sponsored full Sanskrit grammars of Persian in the decades immediately after the establishment of Persian as the primary language of administration. The Mughals were interested in Sanskrit precisely because it could change the contours of their literary and political culture (within acceptable limits). It was not neutrality, appreciation, or a desire for academic debates that attracted Akbar and his successors to Indian traditions. Rather, a yearning for fresh, transformative ideas impelled the Mughals to continually encounter the Sanskrit cultural world.

Mughal engagements with Sanskrit intellectuals and texts were a significant aspect of their imperial order from the mid-sixteenth through the mid-seventeenth centuries that ought to be more central in modern analyses of the Mughal Empire. More broadly, my work demonstrates the need to consider literary traditions beyond the Persianate realm if we are to accurately recover the dynamics of Mughal culture and power. No longer can we cite Mughal cross-cultural activities as sideshow curiosities that are eclipsed by the hegemonic story line of a Persianate empire. Multiculturalism was foundational to the imperial dispensation and ought to be carefully analyzed and treated prominently in future accounts of the Mughal state.

AURANGZEB'S TROUBLED LEGACY

The central Mughal court did not maintain direct, ongoing links with Sanskrit intellectuals after the mid-seventeenth century. Imperial interest in Sanskrit appears to have waned to some degree during Shah Jahan's reign, and Aurangzeb's ascension marked the break of the few lingering ties between the royal court and the Sanskrit world. Mughal connections with Sanskrit thinkers came to a close, at least in the forms first articulated under Akbar, due to a combination of literary and political trends, as I discuss in the following. But the timing of this end can also be easily slotted into a deceptive image of Aurangzeb as instituting a new era of religious orthodoxy and oppression that remains widespread in both scholarly and popular discourses. As a corrective to this wearisome narrative, it is helpful to dwell briefly on the demise of Sanskrit as a major tradition at the Mughal court and the alternative cross-cultural activities that replaced this earlier model.

When Shah Jahan fell ill in 1657, a war of succession broke out among his four adult sons. After two years, when the dust of conflict had cleared, Aurangzeb emerged as the victor and ruled the Mughal Empire for nearly fifty years until his death in 1707. Scholars have long recognized that Aurangzeb ʿAlamgir's reign marked a major shift in Mughal political fortunes. On the one hand, Aurangzeb expanded Mughal control further than any of his predecessors, pushing deep into the Deccan and even parts of southern India.[8] But after Aurangzeb's death the Mughal Empire quickly fragmented, and the early eighteenth century witnessed the rise of regional powers on the subcontinent.[9] Many modern assessments of Aurangzeb's reign have been marred by unhelpful value judgments that frame Aurangzeb as a religious conservative at best and a bigoted fanatic at worst.[10] These analyses are generally based on some truth in that, so far as we can tell, Aurangzeb personally subscribed to a more conservative interpretation of Islam than his ancestors. For example, he prayed with greater regularity and abstained from wine. However, until recently, few scholars have investigated how Aurangzeb's religious inclinations informed Mughal policy.[11] Even today it is alarmingly common to see entirely unsubstantiated comments about Aurangzeb's purported religious intolerance and his alleged penchant for destroying temples, manuscripts, and anything else of cultural value.[12]

Scholars have recently begun to question the long-held assumption that Aurangzeb's personal devotion rigidly restricted Mughal culture and disrupted its previously heterogeneous facets. For example, Katherine Schofield has proposed that while Aurangzeb was not inclined to music, he did not ban it as scholars previously thought, and musical traditions actually flourished during his reign.[13] Azfar Moin has pointed out that many imperial and subimperial activities under Aurangzeb did not reflect the king's individual preferences. Aurangzeb's sons and Mughal nobles continued much as they had before in terms of revelry, patronizing poets and music, drinking wine, and celebrating various religions' holidays.[14] This disconnect between the emperor (or, in some instances, his royal court) and broader imperial culture potentially signals a significant change in the calibration of power under Aurangzeb. Here the Akbari model of emanating authority and, to a great degree, culture from the throne seems to fall by the wayside in favor of a more diffuse model of cultivating imperial claims.[15] Further work is required to parse the relationship between the royal center and the Mughal kingdom in the latter half of the seventeenth century. However, in light of at least some detachment between Aurangzeb's interests and Mughal culture, the notion that Aurangzeb single-handedly killed off imperial interest in Sanskrit because he was an illiberal, cultural dolt lacks explanatory power. We need to consider broader cultural and political developments in order to understand the end of Sanskrit as a major component of Mughal court life.

Two major trends in the seventeenth century led to the cessation of the active, continuous ties that the central Mughal court had enjoyed with the Sanskrit cultural world since Akbar's rule. First, Sanskrit was increasingly being supplanted by Hindi, both in India at large and specifically within the Mughal imperial context. Shah Jahan's court gave no sign of being particularly aware of this shift (or at least needing to comment upon it). Indeed, the Mughals had often found it unnecessary to distinguish between Sanskrit and Hindi when describing the original language of certain texts, for example.[16] From the perspective of the Mughal elite, there may have been few epistemological differences between the two.[17]

Second, Aurangzeb's ascension resulted in a direct schism in royal support of Sanskrit intellectuals. Most likely, Dara Shikuh's princely engagements with Sanskrit during the 1640s–1650s rendered this particular mode of cross-cultural encounters unappealing to Aurangzeb, his younger brother and rival for the throne. When Aurangzeb prevailed over Dara Shikuh and became the sixth Mughal emperor, he understandably sought to distinguish the language of his authority claims from those of the previous heir apparent. Thus, Aurangzeb dissolved the remaining Mughal ties with the Sanskrit world, most notably discontinuing the imperial stipend to Kavīndrācārya Sarasvatī, not because he was flatly opposed to all cross-cultural activities but rather to distance himself from his elder brother's chosen idioms of kingship. In other words, Aurangzeb's decision to terminate Mughal links with the Sanskrit cultural milieu was not an expression of overarching orthodoxy but rather a sensible political act driven by a recently resolved, formidable rivalry.

Despite Aurangzeb's lack of attention to Sanskrit, interest in this classical Indian tradition did not instantly disappear among Mughal elites. Aurangzeb's reign is still lightly studied in comparison to those of earlier Mughal rulers. Nonetheless, there are several known examples of more limited and sporadic connections between the Mughals and the Sanskrit world in the latter half of the seventeenth century. Beyond the royal court, for instance, Shaystah Khan, a maternal uncle of Aurangzeb's, sponsored several engagements with Sanskrit stories and texts. He ordered Basant Rae, a Hindu *munshī* in his employ, to produce a detailed table of contents for the *Razmnāmah* in the 1680s.[18] During the same decade, Shaystah Khan also supported a Sanskrit intellectual known as Caturbhuja, who compiled an anthology titled *Rasakalpadruma* (*Wishing Tree of Aesthetic Emotion*) in order to please his Mughal patron.[19] Several verses in this work praise Shaystah Khan.[20] The *Rasakalpadruma* also includes verses attributed to

Shaystah Khan, which introduces a fresh way for Mughal elites to participate in Sanskrit literature as authors.[21] Especially given that a significant disconnect arose between Aurangzeb's royal court and other venues of Mughal imperial culture in the late seventeenth century, it is imperative to consider such nonroyal exchanges when trying to accurately reconstruct the cultural possibilities of this period.

Moreover, even within Aurangzeb's court, there were occasional contacts with Indian intellectuals who participated in Sanskrit and vernacular traditions. At least two Jain monks are said to have met with Aurangzeb, Lāl Vijaya and Bhīmavijaya. Both encounters are recorded in vernacular works.[22] We lack evidence that Aurangzeb directly supported Sanskrit literary production, although some authors still hoped to gain imperial support. Kavīndrācārya, for instance, lobbied Aurangzeb for some time (unsuccessfully) to reinstate his stipend.[23] Writing from Delhi in 1663, the astrologer Īśvaradāsa included an entire chapter on Aurangzeb's lineage in his Sanskrit work *Muhūrtaratna* (*Jewel of Time*).[24] Īśvaradāsa's father, Keśava Śarma, had previously served as Jahangir's *jotik rai* (royal astrologer), and Īśvaradāsa perhaps sought to rekindle the association between his family and the Mughals by praising Aurangzeb.[25] Certainly the link between Brahmans and astronomy more generally remained alive in Aurangzeb's court. For example, a Dutch traveler who was a temporary part of Aurangzeb's large retinue employed four Brahmans to keep track of time, and a painting of this cross-cultural activity survives today.[26] In many respects, Mughal culture under Aurangzeb did not break as sharply from its previous formulations as modern scholarship would have us believe.

Despite lingering associations, there is little doubt that the high point of Mughal relations with Sanskrit intellectuals had come and gone before the dawn of Aurangzeb's reign. However, identifying an end date for such cross-cultural activities is not an easy task. Even to the extent that Aurangzeb did institute certain fissures, such as halting royal payments to Kavīndrācārya, later sporadic connections disprove any notion that this break was clear-cut and irrevocable. Above all, it seems that scholars have only recently begun to ask the right sorts of questions about Aurangzeb's reign. Aurangzeb formulated the relationship of himself as emperor to his larger kingdom (and that of his royal court to lower courts) rather differently than his predecessors. Accordingly, we may be best served by employing alternative methods to investigate his rule. In terms of relations with Sanskrit in particular, future researchers may find looking at subimperial courts more fruitful than an emphasis on the central royal milieu. Additionally, given literary trends in seventeenth-century India, vernacular sources may prove particularly useful to reconstructing cultural exchanges during Aurangzeb's tenure on the throne.

LITERARY DYNAMICS IN INDIA'S EARLY MODERNITY

Links between Sanskrit traditions and the imperial court were also an important part of complex cultural changes under way in sixteenth- and seventeenth-century India. Over the past few decades, scholars have devoted significant attention to intellectual and literary production during India's so-called early modern period, roughly 1500 to 1800.[27] The centuries just prior to colonialism constituted the final moments of India's literary traditions before substantial Western contact and major shifts, in different ways, for Sanskrit, Persian, and vernacular cultures in South Asia. Many scholars have underscored the key roles that cross-cultural networks played in developing vernacular traditions in northern India. For example, the emerging genre of literary analysis in Braj Bhasha relied heavily on Sanskrit aesthetic categories, and Hindavi romances established a style that was at once cosmopolitan and composite.[28] Scholars are also increasingly analyzing the early modern Indo-Persian tradition (a project in which this book participates).[29] However, the effects of cross-cultural literary encounters on the Sanskrit tradition during this transitional period remain comparatively unexplored.

The "early modern period" is a categorization that has become current among historians of India during the past few decades and has prompted serious debate. The term first became common in European historiography in the 1970s and has proven popular in South Asian studies as a replacement for "medieval" or "premodern" that focuses attention on the conventionally neglected centuries just before the consolidation of colonial rule.[30] Scholars have concentrated on different facets of India's early modern past and have accordingly characterized this period in different ways. Looking at social and political trends, John Richards identified several shared features of societies across much of Europe and Asia between 1500 and 1800 that signaled the beginnings of modernity.[31] Focusing on intellectual developments, Sheldon Pollock has cautioned that parallels between early modern India and the West extend only so far and that there were also major differences.[32] An extended comparison beyond India lies outside the scope of my project here. But Mughal engagements with Sanskrit highlight some hallmark features of literary cultures, particularly Sanskrit, during this period that have typically been overlooked.

Within the early modern Sanskrit tradition, contact with the Mughal court prompted novel sorts of intellectual, aesthetic, and historical possibilities. This newness was generally unmarked as such, and authors tended to stress continuity rather than rupture with prior practices. In this regard, Sanskrit authors who formed imperial ties were notably different from their contemporary philosophical counterparts, who often proudly heralded themselves as "new" (*navya, navīna*) intellectuals but in fact followed closely on the heels of their received tradition. Speaking of those writers, Sheldon Pollock has argued,

> What these scholars produced was a newness of style without a newness of substance. The former is not meaningless and needs careful assessment and appreciation. But, remarkably, the new and widespread sense of discontinuity never stimulated its own self-analysis. No idiom was developed in which to articulate a new relationship to the past, let alone a critique; no new forms of knowledge—no new theory of religious identity, for example, let alone of the political—were produced in which the changed conditions of political and religious life could be conceptualized.[33]

My work here suggests that substantive novelty arose elsewhere in the early modern Sanskrit tradition. In particular, the multicultural interactions that occurred at the imperial Mughal court often elicited innovative responses from both Jain and Brahmanical Sanskrit intellectuals.

Jains and Brahmans reacted differently to their imperial ties, as we have seen. The agency exercised by each group (and by particular individuals) highlights the array of choices available within the Sanskrit cultural realm in the sixteenth and seventeenth centuries. Brahmans developed new types of textual production in certain subjects, chiefly astrology, astronomy, and grammar. Some of these texts prompted intellectual controversies within the wider Brahmanical community, although silence predominated as the main Brahmanical response to proliferating imperial ties. Gujarati Jains authored narrative accounts of their encounters with the Mughals that offer a largely untapped resource for reconstructing both Mughal history and the diverse historiographic possibilities of early modern Sanskrit texts. Both Brahmans and Jains identified poetry and aesthetics as particularly fertile areas for engaging with the Mughals, even though the actual novelty embedded in individual works can be difficult to tease out.

The increased Sanskrit interest in history is a particularly noteworthy trend during this period that appears to be closely linked with Indo-Islamic culture and courts. Jains and Brahmans had written about real-world events in Sanskrit before Mughal rule, utilizing a variety of genres that strike different balances between historical accuracy and poetic creativity.[34] But particularly the Jain Sanskrit works that discuss the Mughals indicate calibrations of historical sensibilities that had not previously been fully realized in the Sanskrit tradition. Brahmans also participated in this trend through certain (admittedly far less numerous) poetic texts as well as what can best be described as deliberate historical forgetting. The full intellectual history of Sanskrit memories of Indo-Islamic dynasties remains to be written, but it is certain that texts about the Mughals will be a major part of the story. Moreover, this surge of historical interest may well be part of what marks this period of Indian intellectual production as different from earlier time frames. What remains to be further excavated is precisely how Sanskrit thinkers addressed specific Indo-Islamic dynasties and key historical actors before and after the height of Mughal control.

In addition to the dawn of fresh literary and intellectual possibilities, a second major shift happened within the early modern Sanskrit tradition: its decline. The date(s), nature, and dynamics of Sanskrit's demise remain highly controversial. There is little consensus about when (not to mention why) Sanskrit literati ceased to produce exciting new texts, stopped copying old ones, and ultimately lost interest in most Sanskrit intellectual discourses altogether.[35] But few would contest that Sanskrit is no longer an energetic, living intellectual or literary tradition in modern South Asia. Most of its core knowledge systems are considered obsolete, and the few that have survived, such as traditional medicine (*āyurveda*), have been significantly changed by the forces of colonialism and modernity.[36] I have found no compelling evidence that events at the Mughal court precipitated the broader cultural move away from Sanskrit. If anything, the influence flowed in the other direction, and it was the decline of Sanskrit that slowly nudged the Mughals toward Hindi at Sanskrit's expense during the seventeenth century. Nonetheless, Sanskrit's downward spiral is significant for thinking about the legacy of Mughal connections with Jain and Brahman intellectuals because it introduces the potential of an immutable break within India's early modernity, even before the advent of its eventual, colonial-induced modernity.[37]

Modern scholars have often sensed a problem with the suggestion of discontinuities in India's path to modernity. For example, Dipesh Chakrabarty has recently argued that if there was an Indian early modernity in intellectual terms, then it ought to inform twenty-first-century South Asian thought:

> If it is true that thinkers in India in the "early modern" period engaged in self-reflexive debates about institutions that eventually constituted our modernization, then historians ought to be able to bring to life such ancestors from precolonial India whose reflections on their own times are worthy of our contemporary passions and disagreements.[38]

Such a view captures some of the teleological problems (at least from a Western perspective) embedded in the concept of South Asian "early modernity." However, other thinkers have suggested that, despite the terms themselves, we ought not to assume that early modernity led to modernity. As Arif Dirlik, a Sinologist, has recently put it, "In order to avoid teleology, the two periods taken as the 'modern' and the 'early modern' are better viewed as contradictory rather than as evolutionary phases in the history of modernity."[39] But, if much of this intellectual past does not inform the present, then why call it modern except as a value judgment that fits our contemporary agenda to level the playing field of history between East and West?[40] If we are to seriously consider such issues, we need a better picture of the actual substance of early modern Indian thought, including Sanskrit intellectual discourse in its final moments.

Mughal engagements with Sanskrit culture offer a few major contributions to discussions concerning the content of Sanskrit thought shortly before the beginning of colonial rule. First, imperial links prompted certain new literary and intellectual developments in the Sanskrit tradition. Scholars would be well served to consider these trends and texts when formulating broad theories about the early modern Sanskrit cosmopolis, especially in discussions about novelty therein. To date, many scholars have sought newness in the same genres of Sanskrit works that had earlier proven so fertile (e.g., philosophy, sciences). But it appears that often early modern Sanskrit intellectuals turned to newer types of works to express their creative energies. Historical and poetic discourses were highly contested during this period and often featured key contributions from minority communities within the Sanskrit world. Particularly Jain writings ought to be taken more seriously (for starters, discussed at all) in accounts of India's intellectual past. Regardless of whether we choose to label Jain Sanskrit works as "early modern" or use different terminology, the fact remains that there are many such texts that must be analyzed in order to accurately recover the contours of Sanskrit literary culture shortly before the advent of the colonial encounter.

INDO-PERSIAN CULTURE

Cross-cultural activities at the Mughal court were also a powerful defining force within Indo-Persian literary culture. In chapter 6, I trace some of the most immediate Persianate responses to the imperial interest in Sanskrit, such as retellings of the *Rāmāyaṇa* in Persian and attempts to integrate the Mughals into lineages of Indian kings. Here I wish to pose the question of how Mughal engagements with Sanskrit fit into the wider Persianate tradition, especially as it was manifested on the subcontinent. Some scholars have emphasized the "extraordinarily unified culture" of the early modern Persianate world, largely as a legacy of Timurid rule, which linked Mughal India with other cultural and imperial centers in Asia.[41] Indeed the Mughals often viewed themselves as operating in a larger Persianate (and sometimes specifically Timurid) context, particularly in terms of their Persian-medium intellectual and literary output. Scholars such as Mana Kia have highlighted the continued mobility and migration that integrated the Persophone community throughout the eighteenth and even early nineteenth centuries.[42] My arguments here do not negate the links between Mughal India and other Persianate regions and empires, but my work pointedly underscores identifiably Indian aspects of Persianate intellectual and literary culture on the subcontinent.

The imperial projects of Akbar, Jahangir, and Shah Jahan introduced significant Indian ideas, vocabulary, and stories into the Persianate thought world. The infusion of Indic ideas cannot be traced exclusively to Mughal activities. Deccani courts, Sufis, nonimperial poets, and others also made major contributions to this broader cultural process. Yet Indo-Persian literary culture as it stood in the mid-seventeenth century is inconceivable without Mughal-sponsored and Mughal-inspired texts. The Mughals consciously played a key role in encouraging the growth of Indo-Persian culture and often sought to recenter the Persophone world on the subcontinent. Moreover, many of their cross-cultural projects had active afterlives within the Indo-Persian tradition that continued to stimulate literary production for well over a century after the fall of the Mughal Empire in all but name in the early to mid-eighteenth century.

Even with the rapid degeneration of Mughal authority and patronage after Aurangzeb's death in 1707, Persian does not appear to have flagged as a political or literary tongue on the subcontinent. On the contrary, Persian remained the language of government across much of India throughout the eighteenth century.[43] The British also adopted Persian as their administrative language for decades and switched to English only in the 1830s. Even when Persian began to fall out of favor during the course of the nineteenth century, many Indo-Persian poetic practices were carried on into Urdu.[44] In Persian and also in Urdu, Mughal-supported translations were a significant shaping force. For example, Sanskrit-inspired tales that were first introduced into Persian under Mughal sponsorship, such as the *Rāmāyaṇa* and the love saga of Nala and Damayanti, inspired numerous retellings in Persian and Urdu well into the nineteenth century. The Akbari translation of the Sanskrit *Mahābhārata* remained popular into the colonial period and became a major way that Hindus accessed their own tradition. Early Orientalist scholars also read Mughal translations, and thus such works molded initial European attempts to understand what they would dub "Hinduism."[45]

In short, the Indo-Persian literary world from the late sixteenth century onward was largely defined by the dynamic presence of Sanskrit-related works that had been composed at the central Mughal court and their later reverberations. This reality highlights several defining features of the broader Persianate realm in India. First, Indo-Persian was a complex tradition that functioned in both South Asia and the wider Persianate world. Particularly given the trend toward speaking loosely of broad traditions and cosmopolitan cultures in current scholarship on South Asia, we ought to be vigilant in looking for more local influences as well. More fundamentally, there was an identifiably Indo-Persian culture in early modern India that is worth demarcating as such. This literary tradition is partly defined by the presence of Sanskrit-derived stories, knowledge, and even vocabulary, largely introduced by the central Mughal courts of Akbar through Shah Jahan.

WORLD FRONTIERS: NEW METHODS FOR IMPERIAL HISTORY

In addition to their importance within India, the Mughals are also a useful case study for thinking about imperial histories more broadly. After experiencing a period of decline, empire has been a growing topic over the past few decades across academic disciplines as far ranging as history, political science, religion, anthropology, and literary studies.[46] This emphasis has become so profound in recent years that it has even prompted one scholar to exclaim in relation to empire and its partner, colonialism, "'Imperialism', as a word, has gone imperial; 'colonialism' has colonized our languages."[47] The renewed prominence of imperial formations in modern scholarship no doubt reflects contemporary political concerns, but it also holds much promise for advancing our understanding of the past. Jane Burbank and Frederick Cooper remind us that "for most of human history empires and their interactions shaped the context in which people gauged their political possibilities, pursued their ambitions, and envisioned their societies."[48] Questions of political ideology and authority remain prevalent for many scholars today, although we often lack even a rudimentary understanding of how power worked in earlier societies. My work here offers several methodological strategies and conceptual tools to those seeking to explore power and empire, particularly in the precolonial world.

First, Mughal links with Sanskrit culture emphasize the need to identify new archives and develop fresh historical methods for recovering the past. In the case of the Mughals, the imperial interest in Sanskrit was long obscured by the perceived lack of historically reliable information. The story of Madhusūdana exemplifies this ongoing problem. Oral legend posits that Madhusūdana Sarasvatī, an influential sixteenth-century Sanskrit scholar of Advaita Vedanta philosophy, met with Akbar in order to discuss the correct Mughal response to some ascetics (*sanyāsins*) who had taken up arms against Muslim foes.[49] This story is intriguing because Persian sources concur that Akbar met with militant Hindu ascetics (although they were fighting among themselves) but do not mention Madhusūdana by name.[50] Nonetheless, a Madhusūdana appears in the list of learned men in the *Āʾīn-i Akbarī*, whom scholars have debated may or may not be the famous Advaita Vedantin.[51] Thus, living memory recalls a relationship between the Sanskrit thinker Madhusūdana Sarasvatī and Akbar's court that is suggested but far from proven in available Persian documents.[52] Neither the Brahmanical Sanskrit tradition nor Mughal Persian histories provide much help in sorting out such tantalizing possibilities.

In the case of Madhusūdana, his remembered ties with the Mughal elite may never be fully confirmed or invalidated. However, the ambiguity of this particular episode does not prohibit the possibility of retrieving many aspects of Mughal cross-cultural activities, and scholars have made two major errors in this regard. First, many have taken individual cases where uncertainty remains as evidence that the entire network of Mughal relations with Jain and Brahman intellectuals is unrecoverable. On the contrary, Sanskrit texts provide a wealth of information that may not sort out the Madhusūdana-Akbar connection but offer insight into a myriad of other cross-cultural encounters, most of which remain unknown to Mughal historians (who generally do not learn Sanskrit). Second, many Indologists have declared Sanskrit materials unreliable for accessing historical fact instead of trying to parse their particular historical sensibilities.[53] On the contrary, much of the Mughal past can be reconstructed only from Sanskrit texts. Modern historical methods provide many tools that help us responsibly use these materials. But, equally important, Sanskrit materials allow us to supplement our modern attachment to finding out what actually happened with critical attention to the histories of perception, representation, and literary memory.

In the course of this book, I have repeatedly criticized the narrow preoccupation with on-the-ground facts that has led academics to ignore key literary and cultural aspects of their source materials. One of the major prizes of investigating the complex dynamics of early modern Indian texts is the opportunity to deepen our understanding of historical sensibilities. This project opens up new ways of understanding the past. Speaking of early modern Hindi works Allison Busch has elected to "stress the diversity of historical texts in Mughal India and the need for a broader definition of what can be accounted as history."[54] Taking a slightly different but complementary approach, Sheldon Pollock has suggested that "instead of assessing whether Indian texts are history or myth, we might ask whether the texts themselves invite us to transcend this very dichotomy."[55] If we look beyond our own circumscribed definition of "history," we find an array of options for how to construct narratives about the past in Sanskrit and other Indian tongues (including Persian). Many of these viewpoints and commemorations fall outside the contemporary notion of history in its narrowest sense but nonetheless add great depth to our understanding of precolonial societies. So often what people believed tells us far more than a dry litany of facts about who they were and what they valued.

Additionally, Mughal encounters with Sanskrit demonstrate that we must be highly attuned to the implications of using any given set of sources. In this book, I have drawn upon written works and entire traditions earlier deemed irrelevant to the study of the Mughal Empire, such as Sanskrit works assumed to be disconnected from real-time political affairs and Mughal translations of the Sanskrit epics that were previously taken to be strictly religious or literary endeavors. In the study of other empires, it may also be illuminating to explore texts that were produced outside the standard languages, courts, and genres typically judged pertinent. Moreover, I have shown that many canonical sources, especially Persian court chronicles, have been gravely misrepresented as a result of being read outside their imperial context and demonstrated the value of more critical, sensitive interpretations. Few historians would contest that texts ought to be read in context, but the case study of Sanskrit at the Mughal court powerfully underscores the need to be creative and vigilant in our philological methods and to broaden our understanding of which texts and contexts are relevant.

Last, Mughal engagements with Sanskrit were often deeply aesthetic in nature and, as a result, had profound implications for the formulation of Mughal imperial ambitions. The Mughals fused politics and aesthetics in creative ways that cannot be reduced to a simple legitimation formula. As Daud Ali has put it, "[legitimating royal authority] has tended to assume that political power is constituted outside the realm of ideation, to which it then desperately repairs in order to gain post facto 'legitimacy.'"[56] Against the assumption that power is divorced from the literary realm, cross-cultural events at the central Mughal court prompt us to reflect on the nature of power itself as an aesthetic practice. Most clearly, numerous Mughal attempts to rework the *Mahābhārata* and the *Rāmāyaṇa* in Persian explored the dual political and aesthetic possibilities of uniting Persianate literature and the Indian epics. Sometimes the goal was to find political resources in Sanskrit texts, whereas other translations aimed to introduce the revolutionary potential of Sanskrit stories into the Indo-Persian literary world. In all cases, a consistent feature is that the Mughals deemed the aesthetic and political possibilities of Sanskrit literature to be imperially pertinent.

In studies of empire more broadly, we ought to consider how literary, intellectual, and other cultural pursuits were foundational to the construction of power. As I have argued throughout this book, such projects were often directed toward a select group of elites and, at times, exclusively the emperor. This facet of power—by the ruling class, for the ruling class—permeated the premodern and early modern worlds. Scholars who work on the West have periodically highlighted this royal prerogative, such as Paul Binski, who points out that massive architectural projects such as Westminster Abbey were often directed "not to some notional 'public', but rather to the community which produced it in the first place."[57] The case study of the Mughal Empire underlines the vivacity and the ultimately far-reaching impacts of royal self-fashioning. The Mughals also passed along their interest in self-definition through cross-cultural encounters to their Indian interlocutors, and both Jains and Brahmans utilized their imperial meetings to cultivate and contest new community identities that made sense within the Mughal dispensation.

In short, the study of empire involves all kinds of topics beyond military conquest, administration, and economic policies. Chief among the concerns of those who want to parse imperial formations ought to be literature, aesthetics, and cross-cultural exchanges. I have argued in multiple forms throughout this book that the Mughals produced and reproduced their imperial power in conversation with Sanskrit literati and Sanskrit learned traditions. The actual operation of politics within individual transcultural endeavors varied greatly, and much remains to be explored. But I have established the relevance of such an exercise for thinking about the nature of the Mughal Empire, Sanskrit and Persian traditions in early modern India, and connections between literature and imperialism. Perhaps because we live in an increasingly multicultural world with rising (and falling) empires, parsing the possibilities of prior exchanges between traditions is a mounting priority for many scholars. The Mughals offer a wealth of detailed resources for exploring how narratives of power unfold across cultures.

APPENDIX 1: BILINGUAL EXAMPLE SENTENCES IN KṚṢṆADĀSA'S *PĀRASĪPRAKĀŚA* (*LIGHT ON PERSIAN*)

In his Persian grammar of Sanskrit, Kṛṣṇadāsa gives a series of bilingual example sentences in order to demonstrate the different cases, many of which feature Akbar and the Mughal court. I give the relevant examples here in transliterated Persian and Sanskrit and English translation. I base the transliteration on the 1965 printed edition, but there are slight variations in the manuscripts, particularly regarding the use of the halant and interchanging certain letters (e.g., *ba* and *va*).

Nominative:
Persian: *hajarat śāhe akabara dera be mānad*
Sanskrit: *śrī-akabaraśāhaś ciraṃ jīvatu ityarthaḥ*
Long live glorious Shah Akbar!

Vocative:
Persian: *ye hajarat śāhe jallāladīn dastagīra śava marā dara dīna va duniā*
Sanskrit: *he śrīśāha jallāladīn mama hastāvalambaprado bhava amutreha cetyarthaḥ*
O glorious Shah Jalaluddin, come to my aid in this world and the next!

Accusative:
Persian: *śāhān śāhī śasta rā mesāyad*
Sanskrit: *mahīmahendro 'ṅgalitrāṇaṃ ghaṭayatītyarthaḥ*
The king of kings prepares to hunt.

Persian: *ālamapanāha hajarata āphtābarā mebīnad*
Sanskrit: *jagadekaśaraṇyaḥ śrīsūryyaṃ paśyati ityarthaḥ*
The protector of the world sees the glorious sun.

Persian: *śāhajallāladīna aj yadālati khud kaliyuga rā satyayuga kardd*
Sanskrit: *śāhajallāladīno 'tīvadhārmmikaḥ śrīmadakabaro nijasunayapratāpāt kaliyugaṃ satyayugam akarod ityarthaḥ*
Glorious Akbar [Sanskrit: who is very ethical] made the Kali Age into the Era of Truth by his own justice.

Persian: *hukume ātaś śāhe akavara duśmane jaṅgala rā khākistar mekunad*
Sanskrit: *śāha-akavaraśāsanāgniḥ śatruvanaṃ bhasmasāt karotītyarthaḥ*
Shah Akbar's fierce rule reduces a forest of enemies to ash.

Persian: *ba darabāra rā meravad*
Sanskrit: *rājadvāraṃ prativrajatītyarthaḥ*
He goes to court.

Dative:
Persian: *hajarata akabara śāha bā bujurgāṃ khitāba medihad*
Sanskrit: *śrī-akabaraśāho mahadbhyaḥ padavīṃ dadāti*
Great Akbar Shah gives titles to important people.

Persian: *bā rabbānī mandī mekunad*
Sanskrit: *parameśvarāya namaskaroti ityarthaḥ*
He praises God.

Persian: *barāy kāre akabarśāha sare khud rā nigāh medāram*
Sanskrit: *akabaraśāhakāryyāya śira ātmanaḥ sandhārayāmītyarthaḥ*
I devote myself to the work of Akbar.

Ablative:
Persian: *īṃ phīla aj ke as / aj akabaraśāha ityādi*
Sanskrit: *ayaṃ hastī kasyāsti iti praśne akabaraśāhasyetyarthaḥ*
This elephant belongs to whom? To Akbar!

Genitive:
Persian: *hukum śāharā*
Sanskrit: *ājñā rājña ityarthaḥ*
The king's order.

APPENDIX 2: FOUR SANSKRIT VERSES TRANSLITERATED IN THE *RAZMNĀMAH* (*BOOK OF WAR*)

THE AKBARI translation of the Sanskrit *Mahābhārata* contains four verses that are transliterated (rather than translated) into Persian. I have reconstructed the quoted Sanskrit verses here, which correspond closely with the Devanagari recension variants cited in the critical edition of the *Mahābhārata*.

RECONSTRUCTED SANSKRIT VERSES[1]

asitaṃ[2] *cārtimantaṃ ca sunīthaṃ cāpi yaḥ smaret*
divā vā yadi vā rātrau nāsya sarpabhayaṃ bhavet

yo jaratkāruṇā jāto jaratkārau mahāyaśāḥ
āstīkaḥ sarpasatre ca pannagān yo 'bhyarakṣata
taṃ smarantaṃ mahābhāgā na māṃ hiṃsitum arhatha

sarpāya sarvabhadraṃ te dūraṃ gaccha mahāviṣa
janamejayasya yajñānte āstīkavacanaṃ smara

āstīkasya vacaṃ śrutvā yaḥ sarpo na nivartate
śatadhā bhidyate mūrdhni śiṃśavṛkṣaphalaṃ yathā
janamejayasya yajñānte āstīkavacanaṃ smara

ENGLISH TRANSLATION

Whoever remembers Asita, Artimant, and Sunitha,
whether day or night, will have no fear of snakes.

When I remember that illustrious Astika,
who was born to Jaratkaru by Jaratkaru and protected the snakes at the snake sacrifice,
let you, eminent ones, be unable to harm me.

All blessings upon you snake! Go away great poisonous one!
Remember the words of Astika at the completion of Janamejaya's sacrifice.

Whichever snake does not flee when he hears the words of Astika,
his head will split into a hundred pieces like the fruit of the shimsha tree.
Remember the words of Astika at the completion of Janamejaya's sacrifice.

NOTES

INTRODUCTION

1. Rodney Barker offers a brief overview of recent scholarship in *Legitimating Identities*, 12–15.
2. Ibid.
3. Rajeev Kinra discusses the biases of Mughal historians toward political and military history in "Secretary-Poets in Mughal India," 10–14. Muzaffar Alam and Sanjay Subrahmanyam offer a more in-depth treatment of post-1950 Mughal studies in *Writing the Mughal World*, 11–32.
4. For declarations of the unimportance of Sanskrit and other Indian languages at the Mughal court, see, e.g., Alam, *Languages of Political Islam*, 148; Asher and Talbot, *India Before Europe*, 247. Thackston declares, "The history of literature in the Mughal empire is basically the history of Persian" ("Literature," 84).
5. E.g., Asher and Talbot, *India Before Europe*, 5. Muzaffar Alam has criticized this dichotomy of peaceful or antagonistic as politically motivated on both accounts ("Competition and Co-existence," 37).
6. Eaton, *India's Islamic Traditions*, 9–11; Thapar, "Tyranny of Labels."
7. For a recent criticism of assuming "religion" as a universal, distinct sphere of human life, see Nongbri, *Before Religion*. While I think that Nongbri overstates the lack of religion in premodernity, I find useful his more basic point, also made by many others, that religion as we typically understand the concept today has a modern, Protestant history.
8. *Venture of Islam*, 1:57–60. See Eaton's comments regarding some of the problems with the Islamicate-Indic dichotomy (*India's Islamic Traditions*, 13–14).
9. Asher and Talbot endorse a largely composite culture view in *India Before Europe*.
10. Recently Sanjay Subrahmanyam has raised the concern of assuming perplexity instead of searching for understanding in his *Courtly Encounters*.
11. "Retelling the Muslim Conquest of North India," 31 (italics in original). Many other scholars, such as Tony Stewart, have attacked syncretism on similar grounds ("In Search of Equivalence," 261–62).
12. "Shifting Semantics," 156–57.

13. Sheldon Pollock has outlined the idea of the Sanskrit cosmopolis (*Language of the Gods*, particularly 10–19). Several scholars have used this as the model for the "Persian cosmopolis." E.g., Kinra, "Fresh Words," 129, Hakala, "Diction and Dictionaries," 267, and, most convincingly, Eaton and Wagoner, *Power, Memory, Architecture*, 18–27. Others have also spoken of a "Muslim cosmopolis," "Indo-Persian cosmopolis," and "Arabic cosmopolis" (Alavi uses the prior two phrases in "Creation of a Muslim Cosmopolitanism," and Ricci offers a compelling argument for the last one in *Islam Translated*, 13–20).
14. For the early history of Persian in Middle Eastern courts, see Meisami, *Medieval Persian Court Poetry*.
15. Madhav Deshpande elaborates on different uses of the term *śiṣṭa* in *Sanskrit and Prakrit*, particularly chapters 4–6.
16. I adapt the idea of fuzzy communities from Kaviraj, *Imaginary Institution of India*, 13–14 and 193–94. Sanskrit literati were also "fuzzy" in Kaviraj's sense of the word because they were unenumerated.
17. In some cases, Jains and Brahmans who were not connected with the Sanskrit world forged connections with the Mughals. Most notably, Jain merchants had links with the Mughal elite. I largely leave aside such ties here.
18. On Chandar Bhān Brahman, see Kinra, *Writing Self, Writing Empire*.
19. Todar Mal sponsored the productio n of a Sanskrit compendium titled *Ṭoḍarānanda* (*Todar's Bliss*).
20. Siddhicandra, a Jain Tapa Gaccha monk, claimed to know Persian. Kṛṣṇadāsa and Kavi Karṇapūra, the authors of the two Sanskrit grammars of Persian that were produced under the patronage of Akbar and Jahangir, respectively, knew both languages. I talk about these three individuals in further detail in chapters 1 and 2.
21. Patel and Leonard, *Indo-Muslim Cultures*, 3. Muzaffar Alam discusses Persian under the Mughals in "Persian in Precolonial Hindustan," 159–74.
22. E.g., Babur's great-grandson, Jahangir, boasted fluency in Turkish in his memoirs (*Jahangirnama*, 77 in Thackston's translation). An English ambassador, William Hawkins, confirmed Jahangir's ability to converse in Turkish (*Hawkins' Voyages*, 400–401).
23. Abū al-Faẓl lists all these languages except for European tongues in the *Āʾīn-i Akbarī*, 1:115 (all citations are to the Calcutta edition unless otherwise noted). For a list of some of the European works held in Akbar's library, see Pinheiro as quoted in Maclagan, "Jesuit Missions to the Emperor Akbar," 68–69.
24. E.g., Keśavdās's image of four men, including a self-portrait that features the artist holding a scroll with Devanagari writing (ms. Staatsbibliothek zu Berlin, Preußischer Kulturbesitz, no. 117, fol. 25a). The image has been printed several times, most recently in Guy and Britschgi, *Wonder of the Age*, 69.
25. *Poetry of Kings*, 130–65.
26. Both Azfar Moin and Francesca Orsini have recently underscored the need to take account of oral cultures in early modern India (Moin, "Peering through the Cracks," 507–8; Orsini, "How to Do Multilingual Literary History?" 242–43).
27. Busch discusses the evidence for Akbar's facility in Hindi (*Poetry of Kings*, 135). Jahangir and Shah Jahan both had Rajput mothers and presumably spoke a dialect of Hindi from an early age.
28. Among other places, this story of Burzui appears in the *Shāhnāmah* (7:361–73) and in the preface to the Arabic *Kalila wa Dimna* (Marroum, "*Kalila wa Dimna*," 524–27).

29. Ḥusayn Vāʿiẓ Kashifī (d. 1504–1505) wrote his *Anvār-i Suhaylī* (*Lights of Canopus*) at the request of Amīr Shaykh Aḥmad al-Suhaylī, who advised Husayn Bayqara (Roxburgh discusses the dedication in *Prefacing the Image*, 85–86). Even al-Bīrūnī, an eleventh-century polymath who wrote extensively on Sanskrit knowledge systems (see chapter 4), laments the corruptions that translators had poured into the *Pañcatantra* and wishes he had time to render a fresh translation (*Alberuni's India*, 1:159).
30. See manuscripts mentioned in Khandalavala and Desai, "Indian Illustrated Manuscripts," 129, 131.
31. The *Panchākhyānah* (*Five Stories*) of Muṣṭafá Khāliqdād ʿAbbāsī and the *ʿIyār-i Dānish* (*Touchstone of the Intellect*) of Abū al-Faẓl, based on the *Anvār-i Suhaylī*.
32. On the treatment of Indian topics in the *Jāmiʿ al-Tavārīkh*, see Jahn, *Rashīd al-Dīn's History of India*.
33. Allsen, *Culture and Conquest*, 83–102.
34. Respectively, Blair, *Compendium of Chronicles*, 31, and Findly, *From the Courts of India*, 22–25.
35. Gabbay, *Islamic Tolerance*, 35.
36. Granoff translates and discusses the stories of Jinaprabhasūri at the Tughluq court ("Jinaprabhasūri and Jinadattasūri").
37. On the *Bṛhatsaṃhitā* translation, see Jalali and Ansari, "Persian Translation of Varāhamihira's Bṛhatsaṃhitā." Sreeramula Rajeswara Sarma lists six Persian translations of Sanskrit texts produced under Firuz Shah's orders, only two of which have survived ("Translation of Scientific Texts," 70).
38. There were early cross-cultural endeavors about which the Mughals were ignorant. E.g., in the early eleventh century Mahmud of Ghazni minted bilingual coins that proclaimed the Islamic statement of faith in Arabic on one side and in a loose Sanskrit translation in Nagari characters on the other (Sircar, *Studies in Indian Coins*, 19). This experiment was not repeated on the subcontinent, however, and the Mughals likely knew nothing about it. Interestingly, similar Arabic-Latin coins were made on the Iberian Peninsula for a short period in the seventh to eighth centuries, which suggests that this particular cross-cultural approach was linked to the early introduction of Islam (Gallego, "Languages of Medieval Iberia," 110–11). Mahmud of Ghazni was also the recipient of a praise poem written in either a literary register of Hindi or Sanskrit (*Lughat-i Hindavī*) (Flood, *Objects of Translation*, 81).
39. Sunil Sharma, "Genre of Historical Narratives," 115.
40. The bilingual inscription is translated and discussed by Yazdani and Chhabra in *Epigraphia Indo-Moslemica* 1935–1936, 48–49. Also see the correction note by Yazdani in ibid., 1939–1940, 47.
41. Kapadia, "Last Cakravartin?" Also see chapter 4 of Kapadia's 2010 dissertation ("Text, Power, and Kingship in Medieval Gujarat").
42. Shukla, "Persian Translations of Sanskrit Works," 188.
43. Slaje discusses the *Rājataraṅgiṇīs* in *Medieval Kashmir and the Science of History*, 6–23. On Śrīvara, also see Slaje, "Śrīvara's So-Called '*Jaina-Rājataraṅgiṇī*.'"
44. The *Kathākautuka* was printed in 1901 in the Kāvyamālā series.
45. *Āʾīn-i Akbarī*, 1:584.
46. Chaudhuri, *Muslim Patronage to Sanskritic Learning*, 101–9 and 111, respectively.

47. E.g., a Persian translation of the Sanskrit *Kokaśāstra*, a sexual treatise, was dedicated to ʿAbdullah Qutbshah (r. 1626–1672) (see description of ms. British Library, Persian Additional [Add.] 17,489 in Rieu, *Catalogue of the Persian Manuscripts*, 2:680).
48. E.g., Kugle, *Sufis and Saints' Bodies*, 239–52. Rizvi details a wider variety of responses on the part of Sufis to Hindu ideas and practices (*History of Sufism*, 2:390–432). A Sanskrit text on tantra and yoga, the *Amṛtakuṇḍa* (*Pool of Nectar*), was widely known across the Islamicate world in Persian, Arabic, and Turkish versions (Ernst, "Islamization of Yoga," 203–6).
49. Aditya Behl's posthumously published book discusses these Sufi romances in depth (*Love's Subtle Magic*).
50. On the peripatetic court under Babur and Humayun, see Ruby Lal, *Domesticity and Power*, 69–102. John Richards discusses how Akbar used the movement of the royal court to concentrate authority in the person of the emperor ("Formulation of Imperial Authority," 136–39).
51. Richards details the major military and administrative shifts during Akbar's early years (*Mughal Empire*, 14–28).
52. Rizvi, *Religious and Intellectual History*, 104–40; Rezavi, "Religious Disputations and Imperial Ideology." Brand and Lowry collect mentions of the *ʿibādatkhānah* in different historical works of Akbar's period (*Fatehpur-Sikri*, 108–22). Also note the famous miniature painting of a diverse crowd in the *ʿibādatkhānah* held in the Chester Beatty Library (In 03.263).
53. Alam and Subrahmanyam, "Frank Disputations," 463.
54. Discussions in the *ʿibādatkhānah* were suspended in 1581, and the fate of the institution thereafter remains unclear (Rezavi, "Religious Disputations and Imperial Ideology," 202). Jahangir mentions being sent by Akbar to the *ʿibādatkhānah* as a sort of infirmary to recover from his alcohol addiction in the early seventeenth century (discussed ibid., 202–3).
55. Akbar gave some Sanskrit books to Hīravijaya in the early 1580s, as I discuss in chapters 1 and 5.
56. Such assumptions run throughout the generally insightful work of scholars such as Muzaffar Alam, Rajeev Kinra, and S. A. A. Rizvi.
57. Several scholars have emphasized the importance of the emperor not as a private individual but rather as a social figure. E.g., Blake, "Patrimonial-Bureaucratic Empire"; Faruqui, *Princes of the Mughal Empire*; Moin, *Millennial Sovereign*. Rajeev Kinra eloquently points out the need for more work on other members of the Mughal courts, who frequently worked across the reigns of two or more kings ("Handling Diversity").
58. E.g., see Niʾmat Allāh's comment about Jahangir bringing back Islam (quoted in Faruqui, *Princes of the Mughal Empire*, 269).
59. As I discuss in chapter 3, Prince Salim sponsored a translation of the *Yogavāsiṣṭha* (*Vasishtha's Treatise on Yoga*) in the late sixteenth century.
60. E.g., Jahangir's seal is found on a manuscript of Vāmana's *Kāvyālaṃkārasūtravṛtti* that later entered Kavīndrācārya's library (Athavale, introduction to the *Kavīndrakalpadruma*, xxii).
61. Busch, "Hidden in Plain View," 294–300; Brown, "Did Aurangzeb Ban Music?" 103–8.
62. For recent scholarship on Dara Shikuh's projects involving Sanskrit texts, see D'Onofrio, "Persian Commentary to the Upaniṣads"; Gandhi, "Mughal Engagements with Vedānta"; Ganeri, "Transmission of the Upaniṣads."

63. While scholars have begun to correct the bias against Aurangzeb in more recent years, we remain woefully uninformed about many aspects of literature and culture during his reign. For criticisms of standard Mughal historiography for this period, see Kinra, "Infantilizing Bābā Dārā," 166–67; Brown, "Did Aurangzeb Ban Music?" 112–16.
64. Ms. British Library, Persian Add. 5641, fols. 7b–14b; ms. British Library, India Office [IO] Islamic 2517.
65. Babur's Turkish memoirs are the major exception, which were rendered into Persian under Akbar's orders and read primarily in translation thereafter.
66. Richard Eaton makes this point for the Delhi Sultanate period ("Temple Desecration and Indo-Muslim States," 268–69).
67. Faruqui, *Princes of the Mughal Empire*, 182.
68. *Millennial Sovereign.*
69. *Princes of the Mughal Empire.*
70. *Poetry of Kings*, 130–65; "Hidden in Plain View."
71. For this perspective, see Irfan Habib as quoted in Kumar, "Qutb and Modern Memory," 153.
72. Among the scholars who have made some attempt to investigate Sanskrit-Mughal connections, Jatindra Bimal Chaudhuri deserves special mention for publishing, in the 1940s–1950s, a pioneering series of thin books on Mughal patronage of Sanskrit authors and editing some important Sanskrit encomia to Mughal figures. More recently, David Pingree, S. R. Sarma, and Christopher Minkowski have made important contributions to incorporating Sanskrit texts into our understanding of the Mughal past.
73. My critique here borrows heavily from Sheldon Pollock's discussion in *Language of the Gods*, 511–24.
74. *Princes of the Mughal Empire*, especially chapter 4.
75. On India, see Pollock, *Language of the Gods*. On the political role of aesthetics in early modern Japan, see Ikegami, *Bonds of Civility*.
76. The phrase is from Rodney Barker (*Legitimating Identities*, 5).
77. http://www.columbia.edu/itc/mealac/pollock/sks/.
78. Sheldon Pollock identifies the mid-seventeenth century Mughal court and early nineteenth-century colonial Bengal as the final two historical moments of Sanskrit's life as a vibrant literary tradition that produced innovative thought ("Death of Sanskrit," 404–14). Yigal Bronner and David Shulman contest Pollock's denial of newness in early modern Sanskrit and moreover point out that his argument ignores the sheer volume of Sanskrit textual production ("Sanskrit in the Vernacular Millennium," 28–29).
79. E.g., Bronner and Shulman, "Sanskrit in the Vernacular Millennium."
80. I adapt the phrase from Tavakoli-Targhi, who uses it to talk primarily about works that do not fit neatly into nationalist histories (*Refashioning Iran*, 8–15).
81. Rao, Shulman, and Subrahmanyam, *Textures of Time*. For a sharp criticism of the book, see Pollock, "Pretextures of Time."
82. On the importance of historical memory and literary retellings in South Asia, see, e.g., Sreenivasan, *Many Lives of a Rajput Queen*, and Prachi Deshpande, *Creative Pasts*. Gujarati and Hindi works raise similar methodological concerns in many genres (e.g., *rāsa*).

83. Pollock, "Death of Sanskrit," 417; Pollock, "New Intellectuals," 5–6. Yigal Bronner, Jonardon Ganeri, Jan Houben, Lawrence McCrea, Christopher Minkowski, Gary Tubb, Dominik Wujastyk, and others have also written about the "new intellectuals."
84. Yigal Bronner and Gary Tubb highlight the need to distinguish among "orders of innovation" in early modern Sanskrit thought ("New School of Sanskrit Poetics," 619–20).
85. Pollock, *Language of the Gods*, 430–31.
86. Most recently, Moin, *Millennial Sovereign*. Also see, e.g., works by Stephen Blake, Stephen Dale, and Francis Robinson.
87. On Mughal ties with Central Asia, see, e.g., Balabanlilar, *Imperial Identity*; Faruqui, "Forgotten Prince"; Foltz, *Mughal India and Central Asia*. On Mughal genealogical techniques, see, e.g., Lefèvre, "Mughal Genealogical Strategies." On the Mughals and Europe, see, e.g., Subrahmanyam, *Mughals and Franks*, and "Taking Stock of the Franks."
88. Pollock, "Comparison Without Hegemony," 188–89.

1. BRAHMAN AND JAIN SANSKRIT INTELLECTUALS AT THE MUGHAL COURT

1. As I discuss in the introduction, the category of "Sanskrit intellectuals" excludes Brahmans and other "Hindus" who became *munshī*s or otherwise entered the Persian-medium imperial service. While these individuals also benefited from increasing Mughal comfort with Indian traditions, this assimilation is a distinct phenomenon that merits a separate treatment (see Kinra, "Secretary-Poets in Mughal India," 121–34).
2. So far as we know, Digambara ascetics did not visit the Mughal court. But they were aware of the Mughals and occasionally mention them in inscriptions and texts (e.g., respectively, Jain, "Piety, Laity and Royalty," 77, and Rājamalla's *Jambūsvāmicarita*; Banārasīdās's *Ardhakathānaka*).
3. There was a serious philosophical issue with history in Sanskrit, particularly within certain Indian schools of thought (Pollock, "Problem of History"). Nonetheless, this intellectual objection often did not map onto actual intellectual practices.
4. A good example of embellishment is when Siddhicandra describes Nur Jahan's walking into the Mughal court completely unveiled, which would contradict everything we know about harem norms at the time (*Bhānucandragaṇicarita* 4.259–68). Nonetheless, the larger story of Siddhicandra's argument with Jahangir is attested in multiple sources from competing traditions (see chapter 5).
5. *Akbarnāmah* of Abū al-Faẕl, 2:254 (all references are to the Calcutta Persian edition unless otherwise noted. Wheeler M. Thackston has undertaken a new translation of the *Akbarnāmah*, but as of the time of writing only the first volume was available, which goes through roughly chapter 28 of volume 1 in Beveridge's translation). It is unclear whether *hindī* means Hindi or Sanskrit here. As I discuss in the following, Sanskrit intellectuals were simultaneously identified with vernacular culture from nearly the beginning of their interactions with the Mughals. Badāʾūnī also notes that Mahāpātra (*mahāpātar* in Persian) joined this embassy (quoted in Wade, *Imaging Sound*, 108).

6. *Geetaprakash* of Krishnadas Badajena Mohapatra, ed. Sri Nilamadhab Panigrahi (Bhubaneswar: Orissa Sangeet Natak Academy, 1983).
7. *Siṃhavājapeyīvaṃśāvalī* v. 31, quoted in Mahapatra, "Some Forgotten Smṛti-Writers of Orissa," 7. Narasiṃha also later authored several Sanskrit texts, most notably the *Nityācārapradīpa* (*Light on Obligatory Good Conduct*). Orissan literati more broadly were also aware of Mughal power and incorporated mentions of the Mughal Empire into their works. E.g., a scribe copying the *Kādambarīkathāsāra* (*Summary of the Kadambari Tale*) in 1584 under the orders of Vīrabhadra locates himself "in the kingdom ruled by the Glorious Ghazi, Padshah Jalaluddin Muhammad Akbar" (British Library, IO, Sanskrit [Sans.] 3948, cited in *Catalogue of the Sanskrit Manuscripts in the Library of the India Office*, vol. 2, part 2, p. 1530).
8. *akabaranṛparucyartham* (*Nartananirṇaya*, 3:4.2.675). On the patronage relationship between Akbar and Puṇḍarīkaviṭṭhala, see the introduction to the *Nartananirṇaya*, 1:15–21. Scholars have often dated Puṇḍarīkaviṭṭhala's entry into the Mughal court to the 1550s–1560s, but Gode discusses why this postulation is incorrect and a slightly later date is more reasonable ("Works of Puṇḍarīkaviṭṭhala").
9. Scholars cite both 1586 and 1589 as the years of Tansen's death (e.g., Wade, *Imaging Sound*, 108 and 115).
10. For an overview, see Delvoye, "Indo-Persian Literature on Art-Music."
11. Brown, "Evidence of Indo-Persian Musical Synthesis?" 89 and 91.
12. Gode discusses Puṇḍarīkaviṭṭhala's Kachhwaha support ("Works of Puṇḍarīkaviṭṭhala," 121–23). Bharmal Kachhwaha (Man Singh's grandfather) became acquainted with Akbar's court in the 1550s, and relations accelerated from 1562 onward, after the marriage of Akbar to Bharmal's daughter (Afzal Husain, *Nobility Under Akbar and Jahangir*, 88–89).
13. Chaudhuri, *Muslim Patronage to Sanskritic Learning*, 33–35; Raghavacharya, "Akbarīya-Kālidāsa Alias Govindabhaṭṭa," 565–67. Akbarīya Kālidāsa's verses praising Akbar are found in several different collections, and often the same verse is cited in multiple texts (e.g., compare *Rasikajīvana* 2.29 to the verse cited from three different works in Chaudhuri, *Muslim Patronage to Sanskritic Learning*, 95). Chaudhuri lists Akbarīya Kālidāsa's known verses in *Muslim Patronage to Sanskritic Learning*, 37–38. Gode notes that Akbarīya Kālidāsa also penned a few verses praising Todar Mal, Akbar's finance minister ("Quotations from the Śṛṅgāra-Sañjīvinī," 213).
14. Persian-medium intellectuals also often transitioned from subimperial to imperial patrons in Mughal India (Lefèvre, "Court of ʿAbd-ur-Raḥīm Ḵẖān-i Ḵẖānān," 88–94).
15. Mahāpātra was affiliated with the courts of Sher Shah and Islam Shah (*Muntakhab al-Tavārīkh*, 2:76 in Calcutta edition and 2:53 in Tehran edition; citations are to the Calcutta edition unless otherwise noted). Puṇḍarīkaviṭṭhala earlier served a Muslim patron in the Deccan known as Burhan Khan (Gode, "Works of Puṇḍarīkaviṭṭhala," 124–25).
16. Harṣakīrti's *Dhātutaraṅgiṇī* quoted in the introduction to the *Akbarasāhiśṛṅgāradarpaṇa*, xxii.
17. Quoted in the introduction to the *Akbarasāhiśṛṅgāradarpaṇa*, xx.
18. Bhandarkar, *Search for Sanskrit Mss.*, 42–44; Patkar, *History of Sanskrit Lexicography*, 133–34.

19. While the historical accuracy of Harṣakīrti's list is doubtful, scholars have long taken these lines as fact rather than fiction (e.g., Dasharatha Sharma, "Three Earliest Jain Influencers of Mughal Religious Policy," 146; Vrat, *Glimpses of Jaina Sanskrit Mahākāvyas*, 74).
20. This meeting is recorded in numerous texts (e.g., Padmasāgara's *Jagadgurukāvya* vv. 122–89; Devavimala's *Hīrasaubhāgya*, chapters 13–14; and Siddhicandra's *Bhānucandragaṇicarita* 1.78–128). Note that there are some attestations that in 1568 Sādhukīrti of the Kharatara Gaccha debated Buddhisāgara of the Tapa Gaccha before Akbar's court on the topic of a Jain religious ceremony. Both Sanskrit and vernacular sources recount this episode, but I find reason to question this supposed encounter given its early date (1568) and its similarity to later Jain discussions before the Mughals. The meeting is mentioned in Sādhusundara's commentary on the *Dhāturatnākara* without mentioning Buddhisāgara's name (quoted in Desai, "Introduction," 14n17, and Peterson, *Fifth Report*, 159, v. 16) and in the *Śrisādhukīrtijayapatākāgītam* printed in *Aitihasik Jain Kavya Samgraha*, 137–38. For secondary sources, see Rizvi, *Religious and Intellectual History*, 137; more recently, Jain, "Jain Community and the Mughal Royalty," 34.
21. *Hīrasaubhāgya* 14.93–128. This is a relatively early attestation that Sanskrit texts were housed in the Mughal library.
22. The Nagapuriya Tapa Gaccha originated earlier but was considered an affinal lineage of the Tapa Gaccha in early modernity (Dundas, *History, Scripture and Controversy*, 224n88).
23. E.g., *Jagadgurukāvya* and *Bhānucandragaṇicarita*.
24. Several secondary sources describe Mughal relations with Jain religious leaders from Hīravijaya onward (most thoroughly Desai, "Introduction," 1–75). Also see, e.g., Gopal, "Jain Community and Akbar"; Jain, "Jain Community and the Mughal Royalty"; Krishnamurthi, "Jains at the Court of Akbar," 137–43; Pushpa Prasad, "Akbar and the Jains," 97–108.
25. Jain-authored Sanskrit texts repeatedly emphasize the good standing of Jains at the Mughal court. More convincingly perhaps, Western travelers and Persianate authors confirm that Akbar favored Jains (see, respectively, Father Pinheiro's comments quoted in Maclagan, "Jesuit Missions to the Emperor Akbar," 70, and Badāʾūnī's complaints about the preferential treatment of Jain ascetics and Brahmans in *Muntakhab al-Tavārīkh*, 2:256–57).
26. The positive description of the Jains is found in a *farmān* issued by Akbar (quoted in Malcolm's translation in Desai, "Introduction," 77). The negative depiction of Brahmans is from Abū al-Faẓl's "Muqaddamah" (19).
27. O'Hanlon details the growth of a Brahmanical culture in Benares during this period that was partially built upon Mughal infrastructure ("Speaking from Siva's Temple," 254). Despite early modern Benares being included within the Mughal polity, however, Minkowski emphasizes that Sanskrit scholars there were "free from the control of Delhi" ("Advaita Vedānta in Early Modern History," 220).
28. *Jagadgurukāvya* vv. 40 and 122–39; *Hīrasaubhāgya*, chapters 10–12. The *Jagadgurukāvya* reports that Akbar heard about Hīravijaya from a Jain ascetic, whereas the *Hīrasaubhāgya* says that the king learned of Hīravijaya from his courtiers.
29. *Hīrasaubhāgya* 13.121–22.
30. The *farmān* is dated June 1584 (see the English translation in Malcolm, *Memoir of Central India*, 2:163–65n).

31. Translated ibid., 2:164n.
32. *Jagadgurukāvya* vv. 182–84. However, a Gujarati text records that Akbar did not grant this request (*Hīravijayasūrirāsa*, quoted in Vidyavijayji, *Monk and a Monarch*, 37–38).
33. *Jagadgurukāvya* vv. 182 and 185, and *Hīrasaubhāgya* 14.195. In the commentary on the *Hīrasaubhāgya*, Devavimala credits Śānticandra with convincing Akbar to ban fishing in the pond.
34. *svayaṃ sāhinā khānitatvān mahattayā prasiddhaṃ ḍāmara ityākhyā* (*Hīrasaubhāgya*, comm. on 14.195).
35. *Jagadgurukāvya* v. 185.
36. Vidyavijayji lists some of the people who may have accompanied Hīravijaya (*Monk and a Monarch*, 31–34). Also see Desai, "Introduction."
37. See *farmāns* collected and translated in Commissariat, "Imperial Mughal Farmans in Gujarat," 26–56; Desai, "Introduction," 77–91; Nahar and Ghosh, *Epitome of Jainism*, appendix B; and Vidyavijayji, *Monk and a Monarch*, 97–122. Findly lists Jahangir's *farmāns* relating to Jains in "Jahāngīr's Vow of Non-Violence," 253. Some relevant Tapa Gaccha inscriptions are given in *Epigraphia Indica*, 2:34–86 (Buhler, "The Jaina Inscriptions from Śatrumjaya").
38. For the Tapa Gaccha, see the Adishvara inscription in *Epigraphia Indica*, 2, no. 12; also note the multiple references in Siddhicandra's *Bhānucandragaṇicarita*. For the Kharatara Gaccha, see, e.g., Jayasoma's *Mantrikarmacandravaṃśāvalīprabandha* v. 397.
39. On this letter, see Sastri, *Ancient Vijñaptipatras*, 19–42. Pramod Chandra discusses the illustrations in "Ustād Sālivāhana," 25–34.
40. Jain, "Jain Community and the Mughal Royalty," 47. As Jain notes, these idols were taken from Sirohi but returned to Bikaner, which suggests a regional interest was also at work in this exchange.
41. Ibid., 46–51.
42. Many of these *farmāns* are reproduced and translated into English, Hindi, and Gujarati by Jhaveri (*Imperial Farmans*). Also see Mukherjee and Habib, "Akbar and the Temples of Mathura." Kumkum Chatterjee notes the involvement of individuals such as Ramdas Kachhwaha, Todar Mal, and Bharmal ("Cultural Flows," 155).
43. "Justifying Defeat," 359. Raja Man Singh was a notable supporter of temple construction, including the Govinda Deva temple.
44. *Travels in the Mogul Empire*, 326–27. It is possible that Bernier confuses Brahmans and Jains here.
45. In 1568, a Mughal order certified the management rights (*adhikāra*) of one Jīva Gosvāmī over two temples in Mathura (Mukherjee and Habib, "Akbar and the Temples of Mathura," 235–36). Shah Jahan later made a parallel decree that a devotee of Jīva Gosvāmī should have control (*adhikāra*) of Vrindavan temples (Mukherjee and Habib, "Mughal Administration and the Temples of Vrindavan," 290).
46. Ansari collects the relevant *farmāns* in *Administrative Documents of Mughal India*, docs. 1–20. Also see the discussion in Anooshahr, "Fatalism and Agency in Indo-Persian Histories," 220–22.
47. A possible but unconfirmed exception is Nṛsiṃhāśrama (separate from the great Advaita philosopher), whom V. Raghavan describes as having convinced Akbar to halt cow slaughter and pilgrimage taxes ("Kavīndrācārya Sarasvatī," 159). A collection of praises for Nṛsiṃhāśrama, compiled by his pupil Saccidānandāśrama, is described in Shastri, *Descriptive Catalogue of Sanskrit Manuscripts*, 4:81–85.

48. Kavīndrācārya writes in his *Kavīndrakalpadruma* that he convinced the king (*mahendra*) to relinquish taxes on Kashi and Prayag (*kāśīprayāgau*, v. 4); he again mentions the event and the two pilgrimage sites in his *Kavīndrakalpalatā* (p. 2, v. 14, *kāsīkī aru prāgakī*). Raghavan suggests that taxes may have been canceled at other pilgrimage sites also ("Kavīndrācārya Sarasvatī," 162).
49. The *Kavīndracandrodaya* (*Moonrise of Kavindra* [Sanskrit]) and the *Kavīndracandrikā* (*Moonlight of Kavindra* [Hindi]). On Kavīndra's interactions with the Mughals as a Sanskrit intellectual, see Pollock, "Death of Sanskrit," 407–8, and as a Hindi intellectual, see Busch, "Hidden in Plain View," 289–92.
50. *Muntakhab al-Tavārīkh*, 2:213.
51. E.g., the *Razmnāmah* colophon and ʿAbd al-Raḥīm Khān-i Khānān's flyleaf note.
52. Muṣṭafá Khāliqdād ʿAbbāsī's translation of the *Pañcākhyāna* (*Five Tales*) probably comes from the Jain-influenced *tantrākhyāyika* family of *Pañcatantras* (English introduction to the *Panchākhyānah*, 10–11).
53. *Millennial Sovereign*, 11.
54. For a more detailed discussion of the office of *jyotiṣarāja* and the individuals who filled it, see Sreeramula Rajeswara Sarma, "Jyotiṣarāja at the Mughal Court"; Pingree, *From Astral Omens to Astrology*, 84–85 and 92–93; Minkowski, "Learned Brahmins and the Mughal Court."
55. *Jahāṅgīravinodaratnākara* v. 10, quoted in Pingree, *Census of the Exact Sciences in Sanskrit* [*CESS*], series A 5:211.
56. Sreeramula Rajeswara Sarma, "Bilingual Astrolabe."
57. Pingree, "*Sarvasiddhāntarāja*," 269.
58. Sarma, "Jyotiṣarāja at the Mughal Court," 365–66.
59. *Jahāṅgīravinodaratnākara* v. 11, quoted in Pingree, *CESS*, series A 5:211.
60. Pingree outlines some of this history in *From Astral Omens to Astrology*, 79–90. Jains had previously engaged in astrological and astronomical exchanges involving the Persianate tradition within Islamicate milieus (e.g., see Sreeramula Rajeswara Sarma's discussion of Jains and astrolabe manuals in Firuz Shah Tughluq's court in "Sulṭān, Sūri and the Astrolabe," 140–44).
61. The chapter is part of a larger work titled *Siddhāntasaṃhitāsārasamuccaya* (*Compendium of Essential Points Concerning the Siddhāntas and Saṃhitās*). On this text, see Minkowski, "On Sūryadāsa," 329–30.
62. Quoted in Minkowski, "On Sūryadāsa," 330 (translation is my own).
63. Sarma, "Jyotiṣarāja at the Mughal Court," 369–70. Also see the excerpts of Vedāṅgarāya's *Pārasīprakāśa* printed in Bendrey, *Tārīkh-i Ilāhī*, appendixes A and B.
64. "*Sarvasiddhāntarāja*," 270.
65. *Muntakhab al-Tavārīkh*, 2:326 (2:227 in Tehran edition).
66. *Pārasīprakāśa* of Kṛṣṇadāsa, p. 1, vv. 2–4. Verse 2 has *pratīyate* instead of *pragīyate* in the Weber edition ("Über den Pârasîprakâça des Kṛishṇadâsa," 24) and ms. Jodhpur Man Singh Pustak Prakash 626(c) (fol. 1a).
67. The *Allopaniṣad* is undated. My estimate is based on the timing of Akbar's experimentation with various politico-religious ideas that were eventually largely abandoned (e.g., *ʿibādatkhānah* in 1575–1576, *maḥẓar* in 1579, and rewriting of the *kalima* 1579–1580).
68. The Sanskrit text of the *Allopaniṣad* is printed in *Light of Truth*, 721, and in the nineteenth-century *Śabdakalpadruma*, 1:121.

69. Richards, *Mughal Empire*, 72.
70. Moin, *Millennial Sovereign*, 144.
71. *allo rasūlamahāmad[ar]akabarasya allo allām* (*Allopaniṣad* vv. 3 and 10 in *Light of Truth*, 721).
72. On the importance of the *kalima*, see Ricci, "Citing as a Site," 333–40.
73. *Muntakhab al-Tavārīkh*, 2:273.
74. E.g., see Abū al-Faẓl's preface to the *Razmnāmah* ("Muqaddamah"), which lacks praise of Muhammad. Also note Badāʾūni's comments about declining to write a preface for the Akbari translation of the *Rāmāyaṇa*.
75. Moin details these measures as recorded by Badāʾūnī (*Millennial Sovereign*, 153–54). As Haider points out, 990 A.H. was the turning of the Islamic millennium according to some calculations in Akbar's court ("Monarch and the Millennium," 77).
76. Akbar's *tawhīd-i ilāhī* likely never expanded beyond twelve people. For a discussion of the basic tenets of this program, see Moin, *Millennial Sovereign*, 142–45.
77. For independent *Allopaniṣad* manuscripts, see Raghavan et al., *New Catalogus Catalogorum*, 1:410. Otto Schrader discusses a few copies that made it as far south as Madras (*Descriptive Catalogue of the Sanskrit Manuscripts in the Adyar Library*, 1:136–37).
78. Ernst discusses nineteenth-century debates over the *Allopaniṣad* in "Muslim Studies of Hinduism?" 191–92. Particularly, see Babu Rajendralala Mitra's condemnation of the text using Western philological methods in "Alla Upanishad," 170–76.
79. *Bhānucandragaṇicarita* 2.67–71.
80. Ibid. 2.106–7.
81. *Muntakhab al-Tavārīkh*, 2:260–61 and 2:322. Montserrat, a late sixteenth-century Jesuit visitor to the Mughal court, confirms that Akbar saluted the sun at dawn (*Commentary of Father Monserrate*, 184).
82. *Akbar and the Jesuits* of Du Jarric, 68.
83. *Qānūn-i Humāyūnī*, quoted in Faruqui, *Princes of the Mughal Empire*, 63, and Orthmann, "Court Culture and Cosmology," 206–7.
84. On Illumination philosophy in Mughal India, see Ernst, "Limits of Universalism in Islamic Thought," 5–8. A. Azfar Moin points out that Suhrawardi (d. 1191) composed Arabic prayers to the sun and that a similar set of prayers by Abū Maʿshar (d. 886) were included in the *Tārīkh-i Alfī* (*Millennial Sovereign*, 209). On Akbar's relations with the Nuqtavis, see Moin, "Peering through the Cracks," 520. On Akbar's connections with Zoroastrians and Ishraqi philosophy, see Maneck, *Death of Ahriman*, 49–70. Note that much of our information concerning Zoroastrians at Akbar's court comes from a nineteenth-century text (*Mahyar Name*). However, Zoroastrians were also part of the Mughal historical consciousness, as evidenced by their appearance as sun worshippers in the *Ḥamzanāmah*, the single most lavish manuscript ever produced in Akbar's court (Moin, "Peering through the Cracks," 513). Badāʾūnī also links Zoroastrians with Akbar's veneration of the sun during Nauruz, the Persian New Year (Blake, "*Nau Ruz* in Mughal India," 125–26).
85. Respectively, ms. 157 at the Museum of Islamic Art, Doha (printed and discussed in Guy and Britschgi, *Wonder of the Age*, 49), and Grobbel, *Der Dichter Faiḍī*, 53–55.
86. Alam, "Debate Within," 149.
87. *Mantrikarmacandravaṃśāvalīprabandha* vv. 390–95

88. *Hīrasaubhāgya* 13.136.
89. Ania Loomba summarizes much of this repeated misunderstanding in "Of Gifts, Ambassadors, and Copy-cats," 54–56.
90. *Āʾīn-i Akbarī*, 1:233–35 (note variant reading that renders Hīravijaya's name more clearly in n. 9 on 1:233).
91. *Vijayapraśastimahākāvya* 12.68–70 and commentary. According to Siddhicandra, Nandivijaya's performance aroused the jealousy of Hindus at court (*Bhānucandragaṇicarita* 4.17–19).
92. On Akbar's desisting from consuming meat, see *Āʾīn-i Akbarī*, 1:59. Findly discusses Jahangir's temporary cessation of hunting and eating meat in "Jahāngīr's Vow of Non-Violence" (on the influence of Jains in this decision, see pp. 252–56).
93. *Mantrikarmacandravaṃśāvalīprabandha* vv. 359–64.
94. Most notably, Badāʾūnī seems to mention nothing about Akbar's honoring Jain images in his *Muntakhab al-Tavārīkh*. The *Maʾāṣir al-Umarā* notes that Akbar adopted some Hindu practices but also falls short of Jayasoma's account (e.g., see the description under the entry on Abū al-Faẓl in 2:619–20).
95. In addition to Jayasoma, Siddhicandra wrote about this ceremony in Sanskrit (*Bhānucandragaṇicarita* 2.140–68), and a Gujarati work called *Hīravijayasūrirāsa* also records the episode (Vidyavijayji, *Monk and a Monarch*, 42). Siddhicandra's version contains some obvious hyperboles, but nonetheless he had little incentive to include this event in which Kharatara members took the lead except that it was actually true.
96. E.g., Hemavijaya's *Vijayapraśastimahākāvya* 12.145.
97. One Sanskrit work presents Akbar as remembering, "I used to deeply love Padmasundara, moon of the learned, like a friend. He did not tolerate the pride of Paṇḍitarāja, just as winter does not tolerate a line of lotuses" (*Hīrasaubhāgya* 14.91).
98. Samayasundara was a learned monk in the upper levels of the Kharatara Gaccha's hierarchy and often a spokesperson for the sect (Balbir, "Samayasundara's *Sāmācārīśataka*," 255). He traveled extensively and wrote important works in Gujarati (Yaschandra, "From Hemacandra to *Hind Svarāj*," 571–74).
99. For discussions of the *Artharatnāvalī*, see Apte, "Artharatnavali of Samaya Sundaragani," and Vrat, *Studies in Jaina Sanskrit Literature*, 180–81.
100. In this reading, the sentence goes *rājā no dadate saukhyaṃ*, and *rājā* = *śrīsūrya*. Samayasundara explains this meaning as *śrīsūryadevatābhaktajanānāṃ vacanam* (*Artharatnāvalī*, 1).
101. Ibid., 65.
102. Ibid., 65–66.
103. Samayasundara breaks down the sentence as *rā-a-aja-a-a no dadate saukhyaṃ* (*rā* = *śrī*, *a* = the letter *a*, *aja* = *brahma* = *ka*, *a* = *vāyuḥ* = *va*, *a* = *agni* = *ra*); *Artharatnāvalī*, 65–66.
104. *Bhānucandragaṇicarita* 4.168–73; also see discussion in Findly, "Jahāngīr's Vow of Non-Violence," 253–54.
105. Quoted in translation in Desai, "Introduction," 83–84.
106. *Jahāngīrnāmah*, 249; all further citations are to the Persian edition unless otherwise noted. Desai questions whether Jinasiṃha ever made such a prediction, but Jahangir clearly thought that he had ("Introduction," 18).

107. Azad, *Religion and Politics in India*, 119–21.
108. *Bhānucandragaṇicarita* 4.237–337.
109. On the side of the Tapa Gaccha, Siddhicandra records that he and Bhānucandra were responsible for Jahangir's rescinding the banishment order (*Bhānucandragaṇicarita* 4.338–58). But the Kharatara tradition widely claims that Jinacandra appeased Jahangir (Kalipada Mitra, "Jain Influence at Mughul Court," 1070; Azad, *Religion and Politics in India*, 119).
110. The *farmān* attests that Vivekhaharṣa, Vijayadeva, and Nandivijaya (all Tapa Gaccha affiliates) ensured the free travel of all Jains in 1616 (printed and translated in Commissariat, "Imperial Mughal Farmans in Gujarat," plate 1 and pp. 26–27, respectively).
111. *Embassy of Sir Thomas Roe*, 1:123–24.
112. *Jahāngīrnāmah*, 249.
113. Ibid., 250; my translation is indebted to Thackston's rendering in *Jahangirnama*, 251. Banārasīdās also discusses the effects of this second banishment order in his *Ardhakathānaka* (Jain, "Piety, Laity and Royalty," 74–75).
114. *Majālis-i Jahāngīrī*, 272.
115. Azad, *Religion and Politics in India*, 119–20.
116. *Majālis-i Jahāngīrī*, 111.
117. Dundas, *Jains*, 147.
118. Bhīmavijaya secured imperial relief for multiple monasteries in 1679, and Saubhāgyavijaya records that Lal Vijaya obtained a monastery from Aurangzeb (Azad, *Religion and Politics in India*, 236).
119. See discussion in Jnan Chandra, "ʿAlamgir's Tolerance in the Light of Contemporary Jain Literature."
120. E.g., see Shah Jahan's *farmāns* concerning Śāntidās (Commissariat, "Imperial Mughal Farmans in Gujarat"). Also see Jain, "Piety, Laity and Royalty," 77–84; Mehta, *Indian Merchants*, 102–5.
121. Mehta, *Indian Merchants*, 91–109; Jain, "Piety, Laity and Royalty," 77–89.
122. For the meetings of Jahangir and Jadrup: *Jahāngīrnāmah*, 202–3, 284, 286, 316, 317 (two meetings), and 318 (this last one may or may not be a separate encounter). In Thackston's translation: *Jahangirnama*, 209, 283, 285, 313 (three meetings), and 314. Muʿtamad Khān's *Iqbālnāmah* also records at least one meeting between Jahangir and Jadrup (Alvi, "Religion and State," 114). Modern scholars have often been baffled by Jahangir's remark on Vedanta and Sufism (*Jahāngīrnāmah*, 203), although this specific equivalence was not uncommon in early modern South Asia. E.g., Persian notes on copies of two Sanskrit *Bhagavadgītās* identify the text as part of "the discipline of Vedanta, i.e., Sufism" (*fann-i bidānt yaʿnī taṣavvuf* [mss. British Library, IO, Sans. 2244 and Sans. 2387]). A text titled *Sharīq al-Maʿrīfat* (*Illuminator of Gnosis*) that is sometimes attributed to Fayẓī posits a series of links between Sufi thought and Indian philosophy (including Vedanta). On this work, see Ernst, "Fayzi's Illuminationist Interpretation of Vedanta." Dara Shikuh often equated Vedanta and Sufi ideas (Gandhi, "Mughal Engagements with Vedānta").
123. *Jahāngīrnāmah*, 203. Jadrup is mentioned in the *Āʾīn-i Akbarī* as one of the learned men of the age in the second of five groups, "masters of the heart" (1:233). Jadrup

may be the same as Chitrarupa discussed in the *Dabistān-i Mazāhib*, but this identification remains tentative (M. Athar Ali, "Pursuing an Elusive Seeker," 368n18; Moosvi, "Mughal Encounter with Vedanta," 16).

124. *Jahāngīrnāmah*, 318.
125. *Ā'īn-i Akbarī*, 2:59–60.
126. Kinra, "Handling Diversity," 268; Alvi, "Religion and State," 114.
127. The image of Jadrup with Akbar is in the Fogg Museum, Harvard University, 1937.20 (dated 1625–1630). The image of Jadrup with Jahangir is in the Musée national des arts asiatiques–Guimet, Paris, acc. 7171.
128. The image is in the Victoria and Albert Museum, London (IS.94-1965). See the discussion in Gadon, "Note on the Frontispiece."
129. *Majālis-i Jahāngīrī*, 95–98. I am grateful to Corinne Lefèvre for the reference.
130. *Padyaveṇī* v. 153.
131. Ibid. v. 159. Parvez was a serious contender for the Mughal throne before drinking himself to death in 1626 (Faruqui, *Princes of the Mughal Empire*, 36).
132. Harideva Miśra's brother, Raghudeva Miśra, is often credited with a *virudāvalī* in praise of Shah Jahan. However, the work never mentions Shah Jahan, and even the foreword to the printed edition doubts this connection (1–2).
133. The *Kavīndracandrodaya* specifically mentions *subhāṣita* (v. 92). On the *Yogavāsiṣṭha*, Dara Shikuh commissioned a Persian translation of the work (Ernst, "Muslim Studies of Hinduism?" 184). Additionally, Kavīndra was known to be learned in the *Yogavāsiṣṭha* (*Kavīndracandrodaya* v. 12) and produced a Hindi summary of the text (Busch, "Hidden in Plain View," 289). The *Kavīndracandrodaya* also mentions that Kavīndra read *bhāṣya* with the Mughals (v. 92), which V. Raghavan took as Śaṅkara's *Bhāṣya* ("Kavīndrācārya Sarasvatī," 161). However, I think that *bhāṣya* here more likely refers to philosophical commentaries generally. The verse is a *śleṣa*, and in its second meaning, *bhāṣya* likely refers to Patañjali's *Mahābhāṣya* (I am grateful to Victor D'Avella for the suggestion).
134. The *Kavīndracandrodaya* and the *Kavīndracandrikā* both commemorate this event, but Persian histories do not mention it. Allison Busch has pointed out that this omission is unsurprising given the tight control that Shah Jahan exerted over his public image ("Hidden in Plain View," 291).
135. On this work, see Rahurkar, "Bhāṣā-yogavāsiṣṭhasāra."
136. Busch, "Hidden in Plain View," 289.
137. Busch, *Poetry of Kings*, 148–51. On the connection between *dhrupad* and Hindi, see Wade, *Imaging Sound*, 80–81.
138. *ʿAmal-i Ṣāliḥ*, 3:122.
139. E.g., *Kavīndracandrodaya* v. 126.
140. *Travels in the Mogul Empire*, 341.
141. Pollock explores Sanskrit's intellectual decline in seventeenth-century northern India in his "Death of Sanskrit," 404–12. Bronner and Shulman point to the volume of textual production during this period as one reason to question Pollock's narrative ("Sanskrit in the Vernacular Millennium," 28).
142. Pollock discusses the rise of southern and northern Indian vernaculars and their complex relationships with Sanskrit in *Language of the Gods*, particularly chapters 9–10.
143. Gode, "Manuscript Library of Kavindracharya Sarasvati"; more recently, Pollock, "Death of Sanskrit," 407–8. Bernier does not give Kavīndra's name, but this

identification is well established (see P. K. Gode's table in "Bernier and Kavīndrācārya Sarasvatī," 370–73). For Bernier's physical description of Kavīndrācārya, see *Travels in the Mogul Empire*, 341.

144. Gode, "Manuscript Library of Kavindracharya Sarasvati," 54–55.
145. Ernst mentions some intellectuals who frequented Dara Shikuh's court in "Muslim Studies of Hinduism?" 184. Dara Shikuh also employed literati to compose works in Sanskrit (Gode, "Identification of Gosvāmi Nṛsiṁhāśrama") and to assist with Persian translations (D'Onofrio, "Persian Commentary to the Upaniṣads").
146. Asher and Talbot, *India Before Europe*, 205–7; Richards, *Mughal Empire*, 286–88.
147. *Bhāminīvilāsa*, 106, v. 44.
148. Jagannātha has one verse praising Jahangir and four that refer to the "king of Delhi" in his *Rasagaṅgādhara* (quoted in L. R. Vaidya's introduction to the *Bhāminīvilāsa*, 8n).
149. *Rasagaṅgādhara*, 2:812.
150. Pollock, "Death of Sanskrit," 408–12. Even if we recognize Persianate influences in Jagannātha's poetry, these are notable largely because they are unacknowledged.
151. E.g., see the articles by Yigal Bronner and Gary Tubb examining Jagannātha Paṇḍitarāja's scholarship, particularly in relationship to Appayya Dīkṣita, an important sixteenth-century thinker: "New School of Sanskrit Poetics" and "Blaming the Messenger."
152. *Bādshāhnāmah* of ʿAbd al-Ḥamīd Lāhawrī, 1b:56, 1b:102, and 2:5 (2:5 mentions that Jagannātha sings in "the language of Karnataka," *zabān-i karnātak*). Also see references in Qanungo, "Some Side-Lights on the Character and Court-Life of Shah Jahan," 49–50.
153. *Bādshāhnāmah* of ʿAbd al-Ḥamīd Lāhawrī, 2:5; the mention of forty-five hundred rupees is found on 1b:56. Hindustani musicians were generally well remunerated by the Mughals (Schofield, "Reviving the Golden Age Again," 498, based on Seyller's work in "Inspection and Valuation"). Also, the imperial elite may have particularly prized Jagannātha as a singer because he came from the south (see Schofield's discussion of how Mughal connoisseurs believed southern Indian musical traditions to be authoritative in "Reviving the Golden Age Again," 499–501).
154. M. Athar Ali, *Apparatus of Empire*, no. S884.
155. Nalini Delvoye mentions Jagannātha's *dhrupads* collected in the *Anūpasaṅgītaratnākara* ("Les chants *dhrupad*," 169). Sheldon Pollock mentions the *bhajan* collection titled *Kīrtanapraṇālīpadasaṃgraha* in "Languages of Science in Early Modern India," 42n31.
156. Athavale, "Life of Paṇḍitarāja Jagannātha."
157. Cited and translated in Pollock, "Sanskrit Literary Culture," 97–98. As Pollock notes, we have no compelling reason to doubt the authenticity of these verses (98n125).
158. Athavale, "Life of Paṇḍitarāja Jagannātha," 418. The Braj text, titled *Sampradāyakalpadruma*, refers to Lavaṅgī as a daughter of the shah (*sāhasutā*), which I am disinclined to take narrowly but certainly signals some connection with the Mughal world.
159. Introduction to the *Kavīndrakalpadruma*, xvi.
160. Bronkhorst, "Bhaṭṭoji Dīkṣita on Sphoṭa," 15.
161. Bronner and Tubb recount this legend in "Blaming the Messenger," 87–88.

162. Ibid., 88.
163. E.g., Lolimbarāja, a doctor who lived in Maharashtra and was active in the late sixteenth century, married a Muslim woman, who adopted the name Ratnakalā. He wrote repeatedly about her loveliness and erudition, and his *Camatkāracintāmaṇi* features Ratnakalā posing a series of medical questions (Dominik Wujastyk, "Contrasting Examples of Ayurvedic Creativity," 139–40). Also note the love affair of Dayādeva and the Muslim woman Cimanī that took place in the mid-seventeenth century and is memorialized in the *Cimanīcarita* (Gode, "Historical Background of the Cimani-carita").
164. E.g., Khaṇḍadeva's *Mīmāṃsākaustubha* quoted in Pollock, "Languages of Science," 34–35.
165. Vaṃśīdhara Miśra, a Sanskrit poet, also appears to have spent some time at Shah Jahan's court (Chaudhuri, *Muslim Patronage to Sanskritic Learning*, 77).
166. Moin, *Millennial Sovereign*, 212–13; Richards, *Mughal Empire*, 121–23.
167. Busch, *Poetry of Kings*, 147–48.
168. Ibid., 156–58.
169. Brown, "Did Aurangzeb Ban Music?" 82–116.
170. Patkar, "Moghul Patronage to Sanskrit Learning," 174–75; Patkar, "Muhūrtaratna," 83. Azad cites some favorable vernacular verses in *Religion and Politics in India*, 234.
171. E.g., Caturbhuja served Shaystah Khan, Aurangzeb's maternal uncle (Chaudhuri, *Muslim Patronage to Sanskritic Learning*, 78–80).
172. E.g., a sixteenth-century biography of the tenth-century monk Balibhadra describes how he was appointed by royal intervention and was later cast out by his community (Granoff, "Politics of Religious Biography"). During the early seventeenth century, Jain merchants were also able to push through official title changes on occasion, such as the merchant Śāntidās, who successfully got his favorite monk promoted to *ācārya* (Mehta, *Indian Merchants*, 100–101).
173. *Hīrasaubhāgya* 14.93.
174. *Bhānucandragaṇicarita* 2.172. The title *sārvabhauma* had been used since the reign of the Tughluqs for the Islamicate sovereign that ruled from Delhi. Writing in the fourteenth century, Jinaprabhasūri and Vidyātilaka both use a Prakrit variation (*savvabhomo*) for the Tughluq sultan (*Vividhatīrthakalpa*, 46 and 96; I thank Steven Vose for the references). Writing in the seventeenth century, Veṇīdatta glosses *dillīpati* as *sārvabhauma* (*Pañcatattvaprakāśa*, ms. Biblioteca Nazionale, Rome, Orientali 172, fol. 1b, v. 18). In the mid-seventeenth century, multiple contributors to the *Kavīndracandrodaya* use *sārvabhauma* to refer specifically to the Mughal king (twice in prose on p. 29 and once on p. 31).
175. *Bhānucandragaṇicarita* 2.173a. Abū al-Faẓl also explains this hierarchy in his *Āʾīn-i Akbarī* (2:108).
176. *Bhānucandragaṇicarita* 2.173b–75.
177. Ibid. 2.176.
178. Ibid. 2.177–78.
179. Throughout this paragraph, I paraphrase *Bhānucandragaṇicarita* 2.179–86.
180. Ibid. 4.48–49. This episode continues through 4.67.
181. Ibid. 4.60 and 4.63, respectively.
182. *Mantrikarmacandravaṃśāvalīprabandha* vv. 431–32. For the announcement of the new title, see v. 442.

183. Ibid. v. 440.
184. Ibid. v. 441.
185. *Ā'īn-i Akbarī*, 1:156–57.
186. *tasalīmeti yavanabhāṣayā dakṣiṇapāṇiśiraḥsaṃyogapūrvikā vinayapratipattiḥ* (*Mantrikarmacandravaṃśāvalīprabandha*, p. 70).
187. Ibid. vv. 457–64. At the same time as these two titlings, several titles were also given to other members of the Kharatara Gaccha but not by Akbar it seems (v. 465).
188. Respectively, *Mantrikarmacandravaṃśāvalīprabandha* v. 442, and *Yugapradhānasūri*, cited in Azad, *Religion and Politics in India*, 121. Both titles are also mentioned in a series of 1619 inscriptions at Shatrunjaya (*Epigraphia Indica*, vol. 2, nos. 17, 18, 19, 20, 23, and 24).
189. E.g., *Epigraphia Indica*, 2:37.
190. Andhare, "Imperial Mughal Tolerance of Jainism," 225.
191. *Millennial Sovereign*, 214.
192. These honorary titles were known by a variety of Sanskrit terms, most commonly *biruda* but also *nāma* and *ākhyā*.
193. *Hīrasaubhāgya* 14.203–5. The *Hīrasundaramahākāvya*, an earlier version of the *Hīrasaubhāgya*, gives Munisundara's title as *vādigokulasaṇḍhaka* (glossed as *saṇḍa*), meaning "bull of orators" (14.201).
194. "Authority and Innovation," 51–57.
195. Prasad, "Akbar and the Jains," 100. The enduring cultural power of Mughal-bestowed titles is also demonstrated by later works, such as Kāntanātha Bhaṭṭa's *Bhaṭṭavaṃśakāvya* (published 1903), in which he claims his ancestor Nārāyaṇa Bhaṭṭa was titled *jagadguru* by Akbar (Minkowski, "Learned Brahmins and the Mughal Court," 109n19).
196. Raghunātha's *Muhūrtamālā* as quoted in *CESS*, series A 5:376; also see Sarma, "Jyotiṣarāja at the Mughal Court," 367. Raghunātha also refers to himself as the son of Jyotirvitsarasa in colophons to multiple works (*CESS*, series A 5:376). It is unclear whether or not Nṛsiṃha held any official position at court at this time (Pingree, *From Astral Omens to Astrology*, 92). Raghunātha says that Nṛsiṃha's title was granted during the siege of Asirgarh fort, which occurred in 1600–1601.
197. Siddhicandra does not mention the date, but Abū al-Faẓl departed for the Deccan in January 1599. He was recalled by Akbar a few years later in order to help address Prince Salim's rebellion.
198. *Bhānucandragaṇicarita* 1.77. As printed, *dalathambhana* appears to be a Prakrit form. I have been unable to consult the original manuscript.
199. On Nandivijaya's title, see *Bhānucandragaṇicarita* 4.18 and *Vijayapraśastimahākāvya* 12.135. On Siddhicandra's title, see his *Bhānucandragaṇicarita* 4.85.
200. Respectively, *ṭīkā* of *Kādambarī*, 483, v. 5, and *ṭīkā* of *Vasantarājaśākuna*, 1, v. 9. Note that in both cases the verse is misprinted because of confusion over the Persian title; for correct printings, see excerpts in the *Bhānucandragaṇicarita*, appendix 1, pp. 58 and 53, respectively. In his *Kāvyaprakāśakhaṇḍana*, the title is mentioned in the colophons of all ten chapters except chapter 9 (75).
201. This seal is described in the introduction of Siddhicandra's *Kāvyaprakāśakhaṇḍana* as "a seal in the Nasta'liq variety of Arabic script. Its colour is black. It reads: 'Bhanchand murid-e-Khush Fahn 1008'" (6). The seal appears on two manuscripts of texts by Siddhicandra (*Kāvyaprakāśakhaṇḍana* and *Laghusiddhāntakaumudī*) that

were last known to be held in the Jaina Bhandar of Pannyasa Saubhagya Vimalji in Ahmedabad.

202. *Hīrasaubhāgya* 14.294.
203. *Vijayadevamāhātmya*, chapter 17.
204. Ibid. 17.32; also see 17.42, where the title is given as *pātisāhijahāṅgīramahātapā* (Padshah Jahangir's Great Ascetic). Meghavijaya lists the title simply as *mahātapā* (Great Ascetic) in his *Devānandamahākāvya* (2.127).
205. Siddhicandra mentions the two titles in his *Anekārthopasargavṛtti* and *Jinaśatakaṭīkā* (Desai, "Introduction," 65). Marshall also reports that Jahangir fashioned *guṇavinaya kavirāja* (King of Poets). (*Mughals in India*, vol. 1, no. 553).
206. *Āsaphavilāsa*, 96. In manuscripts Jagannātha's title is sometimes given in a slightly vernacularized form as *paṇḍitarāya* (e.g., the title is given in both forms in ms. Pune BORI 732.iii of 1886–92, fol. 23b).
207. Several verses mention both Kavīndra's title and its origin with Shah Jahan (e.g., *Kavīndracandrodaya* vv. 39, 116, 118). Page 31 (no. 13 of the prose) gives the more elaborate version of the title. Note, however, that a verse from the *Kavīndrakalpalatā* attests that this title was conferred by the Brahmanical community (quoted by Athavale, introduction to the *Kavīndrakalpadruma*, xxvi, n. 14).
208. E.g., *Kavīndracandrodaya* vv. 7–8 mention Kavīndra's three titles (*kavīndra*, *vidyānidhāna*, and *ācārya*) but omit Shah Jahan's role in the middle appellation.
209. "Hidden in Plain View."
210. Persian histories and Hindi songs record Jagannātha's titles. See note 152 for Persian references. Athavale mentions the Hindi references in "Life of Paṇḍitarāja Jagannātha," 420.
211. On Ramdas Kachhwaha's Mughal-bestowed title, see Desai, "Introduction," 39n54. Birbal was fashioned *kavirāy* by Akbar (Busch, "Hidden in Plain View," 276). Akbar honored Man Singh as *rāja* after the death of his father, Bhagwant Das.
212. In the seventeenth century, Hussain Khan gave the title *kaṇṭhābharaṇa* (Garland or Necklace) to an author who composed a poem in mixed Sanskrit and Prakrit (Chakravarti, "Muslim Patronage to Sanskrit Learning," 181–82). Man Singh is reported to have bestowed the title of *kavicandra* (Moon of Poets) on Viśvanātha and later sent him to Akbar's court, although the sources for this information are unclear (Mohanty, *Colonialism and South Asia*, 155).
213. Ironically, given his recurrent opposition to such relations, Badāʾūnī's illicit Persian account of the period provides some of the most detailed information on the activities of Jains and Brahmans at court.

2. SANSKRIT TEXTUAL PRODUCTION FOR THE MUGHALS

1. The seven works are Śānticandra's *Kṛpārasakośa* (for Akbar), Rudrakavi's four works (*Dānaśāhacarita* for Danyal, *Khānakhānācarita* for ʿAbd al-Raḥīm Khān-i Khānān, *Jahāṅgīracarita* for Jahangir, and *Kīrtisamullāsa* for Khurram), Harideva Miśra's *Jahāṅgīravirudāvalī* (for Jahangir), and Jagannātha Paṇḍitarāja's *Āsaphavilāsa* (for Asaf Khan).
2. Slaje, "Śrīvara's So-Called '*Jaina-Rājataraṅgiṇī*.' "
3. Shah, "Śabda-vilāsa or Pārasīnāmamālā."
4. Patel, *Text to Tradition*, 122–23.

5. On Bhānudatta's works and patronage, see Pollock, introduction to the *Bouquet of Rasa and River of Rasa.*
6. Chattopadhyaya, *Representing the Other?* 41–44.
7. Van der Kuijp explores a potential early exception to the general tendency not to discuss religious markers of Muslims in Sanskrit ("Earliest Indian Reference to Muslims," 169–202).
8. Chattopadhyaya, *Representing the Other?* 28–60. Kapadia discusses a fifteenth-century example of describing an Indo-Persian figure as a *cakravartin* ("Last Cakravartin?").
9. *Muntakhab al-Tavārīkh*, 2:326.
10. "How to Do Multilingual Literary History?" 242–43.
11. *Islam Translated*, 3.
12. Wink discusses the multiple sources that attest to Akbar's illiteracy (*Akbar*, 11–14).
13. "Two Histories of Literary Culture in Bengal," 511–13.
14. E.g., multiple eyewitnesses attest that Akbar was proficient in a literary register of Hindi. Abū al-Fażl says that Akbar was skilled in "composing Hindi poetry" (*guftan-i naẓm-i hindī*) (*Akbarnāmah*, 1:270–71). Shaykh Mustafa Gujarati, a visitor in the mid-1570s, records that Akbar delighted in vernacular *dohras* (MacLean, "Real Men and False Men," 203).
15. Harideva's *Jahāṅgīravirudāvalī*, e.g., uses heavy alliteration at times.
16. The *Akbarasāhiśṛṅgāradarpaṇa* was published in the Anup Sanskrit Library series in 1943, and a facsimile of an Allahabad manuscript was printed in 2006 under the title *Śṛṅgāradarpaṇa*. All citations refer to the Anup edition unless otherwise noted. Vrat discusses this treatise (*Studies in Jaina Sanskrit Literature*, 98–102).
17. E.g., the commentary on Bāṇa's *Kādambarī* authored by Bhānucandra and Siddhicandra. Also see Jagannātha Paṇḍitarāja's numerous works.
18. Āzād Bilgrāmī penned Arabic and Persian verses exemplifying *nāyikā-bheda* (Sunil Sharma "Translating Gender"; Ernst, "Āzād Bilgrāmī's Depiction of *Nāyikas*"). Allison Busch suggests that the Mughals may have been reading about such typologies in Hindi texts beginning in the late sixteenth century (*Poetry of Kings*, 140).
19. Kunhan Raja, prefatory note to *Akbarasāhiśṛṅgāradarpaṇa*, xv.
20. *Akbarasāhiśṛṅgāradarpaṇa* 1.1.
21. Before Padmasundara, a handful of Sanskrit inscriptions and coins referred to the Islamic God with Sanskrit terms. E.g., a thirteenth-century Sanskrit inscription consecrates a mosque for the worship of *viśvanātha* (lord of the world), who is both *śūnyarūpa* (devoid of form) and *viśvarūpa* (of many forms) (*Epigraphia Indica*, 34:141–50). However, the name Rahman had been limited in Sanskrit largely to texts that directly engaged with Islam or Persian. E.g., Salakṣa defines Rahman (*rahamān*) in his Sanskrit-Persian lexicon titled *Śabdavilāsa* (1365) (ms. Patan Hemacandra Jnana Mandir 995, fol. 1a, v. 11). A fifteenth-century treatise on building mosques penned in Gujarat is titled *Śrīrehamānaprāsādalakṣaṇam* (Chattopadhyaya, *Representing the Other?* 75n29).
22. *Akbarasāhiśṛṅgāradarpaṇa* 1.2.
23. Ibid. 1.3
24. Ibid. 1.4–7.
25. Ibid. 1.5 (compare with his list of nine *rasas* in 1.11).
26. *Śṛṅgāratilaka* v. 1.

27. *River of Rasa* 1.1. Also see Keśavdās's *Rasikpriyā* 1.2.
28. The *Akbarnāmah*, *Ṭabaqāt-i Akbarī*, and *Tārīkh-i Akbarī* all record that Akbar had a mystical experience during a hunt in 1578 (*Akbarnāmah*, 3:241–42; *Ṭabaqāt -i Akbarī*, 2:337–38). Rizvi discusses all three mentions of this episode (*Religious and Intellectual History*, 126–27).
29. Akbar causes others to experience only the amazing (*adbhuta*) *rasa*, whereas Shiva prompts the following: disgusting (*bībhatsa*), fearful (*bhayānaka*), amazing (*adbhuta*), and comic (*hāsya*).
30. *Akbarasāhiśṛṅgāradarpaṇa*, pp. 11, 21, 33, and 46 (also see Allahabad facsimile in *Śṛṅgāradarpaṇa*, 17, 32, 48, and 65, and ms. Jodhpur Rajasthan Oriental Research Institute 19607, fols. 8a, 14a, 21a, and 28a).
31. *Akbarasāhiśṛṅgāradarpaṇa* 2.74.
32. E.g., ibid. 4.27, 4.44, 4.83, 4.84, and 4.85.
33. Ibid. 4.83.
34. Ibid. 4.84.
35. E.g., compare ibid. 4.83, and *Śṛṅgāratilaka* 3.65; *Akbarasāhiśṛṅgāradarpaṇa* 4.84 and *Śṛṅgāratilaka* 3.67.
36. *Akbarasāhiśṛṅgāradarpaṇa* 4.100. Cf. *Śṛṅgāratilaka* 3.85.
37. *Kṛpārasakośa* vv. 13–17.
38. Ibid. vv. 8–12.
39. Ibid. vv. 18–20 on Babur and vv. 21–25 on Humayun.
40. *Colī* refers to the queen's wanderings in the desert (*chūl* in Persian) after Humayun was ousted from his throne (Vincent Smith, "Confusion Between Hamida Bano Begam," 556). Coli Begum is named as such in other Sanskrit sources (e.g., *Epigraphia Indica*, 2:55, v. 34). Antoni Montserrat, a Jesuit visitor to Akbar's court at around the same time as Śānticandra, also referred to Akbar's mother by this name (*Commentary*, appendix, ix).
41. *Kṛpārasakośa* vv. 25–26, respectively.
42. Ibid. v. 37.
43. Bauer, "Dohada," 163.
44. *Kṛpārasakośa* v. 38. On Coli Begum's compassion, also see vv. 39–40.
45. Ibid. v. 44a. *B* and *v* are often used interchangeably in early modern Sanskrit.
46. Ibid. v. 18.
47. *Jambūsvāmicarita* 1.9.
48. *Kṛpārasakośa* v. 67.
49. E.g., see *Jagadgurukāvya*, *Jambūsvāmicarita* (chapter 1), and *Bhānucandragaṇicarita* (chapter 1).
50. *Kṛpārasakośa* v. 77.
51. Ibid. vv. 78–89.
52. Ibid. v. 81.
53. Ibid. v. 84.
54. On the political import of the conquering of the four directions, see Pollock, *Language of the Gods*, 240–49.
55. *Kṛpārasakośa* v. 89.
56. Frances Taft discusses the political implications of Mughal marriages to Rajput women ("Honor and Alliance"). I am uncertain what to make of Śānticandra's reference to Akbar's marrying even a lacking (disfigured?) Rajput woman (*striyam aṅgahīnāṃ*, *Kṛpārasakośa* v. 92).

57. *Kṛpārasakośa* v. 94.
58. *Āʾīn-i Akbarī*, 1:158–61.
59. John Cort argues for a continuum of Jain perspectives on kingship that range from a non-Jain king who patronized the community to a king such as Kumārapāla, who converted ("Who Is a King?" 85–106).
60. Devavimala's *Hīrasaubhāgya* also draws a parallel between Akbar and Kumārapāla (Dundas, *History, Scripture and Controversy*, 60; Granoff, "Authority and Innovation," 55).
61. *Kṛpārasakośa* v. 113. Akbar is also compared to Kumārapāla in v. 98.
62. Ibid. v. 111.
63. Ebba Koch has discussed Mughal attempts to model themselves on Solomon; e.g., "Mughal Emperor as Solomon."
64. *Kṛpārasakośa* v. 100.
65. On *hindū* as an ethnic or geographic description in early modern India, see Talbot, "Inscribing the Other," 700–701.
66. *Vividhatīrthakalpa*, quoted in Vose, "Making of a Medieval Jain Monk," 404.
67. *hindū viprādir āstiko lokaḥ* (*Saṃskṛtapārasīkapadaprakāśa* v. 222).
68. *Kṛpārasakośa* vv. 106, 102, and 103, respectively.
69. *Śrīmadakabarabādaśāhapratibodhakṛte* (*Kṛpārasakośa*, p. 1) and *pātasāhiśrī-akabara-mahārājādhirājapratibodhakṛte* (21, hyphens in printed Sanskrit text). Harideva makes a similar claim that his work "enlightens glorious heroic Padshah Jahangir" (*pātisāhavaravīraśrījahāṅgīraprabōdhanāya*; *Jahāṅgīravirudāvalī*, p. 3).
70. *Kṛpārasakośa* vv. 126–27. These verses (and verse 128) are missing in ms. Ahmedabad LD Institute of Indology 11878.
71. E.g., *Kavīndracandrodaya* v. 116
72. *Kalpasūtrāntravākya* of Ratnacandragaṇi, ms. Ahmedabad LD Institute of Indology 11654, fol. 82.
73. *Hīrasaubhāgya* 14.271.
74. According to Sheth, "In A.D. 1576–7, [Śāntichandra] defeated Vadibhushana, a Digambara monk, in the Court of Nārāyana of Idar. He won another victory over Digambara Gunachandra at Jodhpur." (*Jainism in Gujarat*, 273).
75. *Kṛpārasakośa* v. 128.
76. This verse is omitted in ms. Ahmedabad LD Institute of Indology 11878.
77. *Kṛpārasakośa* vv. 1–7.
78. Guha, *Environment and Ethnicity*, 64–65.
79. During Akbar's time, Baglan was attached to the *ṣūbah* of Gujarat but treated as a separate territory (Habib, *Atlas of the Mughal Empire*, no. 7A).
80. *Rāṣṭrauḍhavaṃśamahākāvya* (printed in Gaekwad's Oriental Series, 1917).
81. In the title, *dānaśāha* is a *śleṣa* with the double meaning of Shah Danyal, the name of the recipient, and the shah of generosity. On the date, see *Dānaśāhacarita* 4.11 (note that Chaudhuri misprints the *śaka* date here as 1515; the correct reading is 1525, as printed in Har Dutt Sharma, "Poet Rudra and His Works," 242–43). Also see the date written in the margins of ms. British Library, Buhler 70, fol. 18a.
82. For a brief account of Raḥīm's public career, see Seyller, *Workshop and Patron*, 45–48.
83. The last mention we have of Pratap Shah as the ruler of Baglan is 1620 (Naravane, *Short History of Baglan*, 38). Har Dutt Sharma has suggested ca. 1616 as a date for the *Kīrtisamullāsa* because of Khurram's military activities in the Deccan at this time ("Poet Rudra and His Works," 243–44). This idea is possibly supported by Rudrakavi's

use of the title "shah" for Khurram, which was granted to him by Jahangir just before he departed for the Deccan in 1616 (e.g., *Kīrtisamullāsa* v. 13). But Buhler suggests that certain verses referring to Jahangir indicate that the *Kīrtisamullāsa* was penned not long after Akbar's death in 1605 (*Catalogue of the Sanskrit Manuscripts in the Library of the India Office*, vol. 2, part 2, p. 1186).

84. Karambelkar, "Nabābakhānakhānācaritam," 245.

85. The *Khānakhānācarita* was edited by J. B. Chaudhuri in *Works of Rudra Kavi*, and all citations refer to this edition. Note that the first two verses printed by Chaudhuri likely belong only to the *Dānaśāhacarita*, and an alternative opening verse is given in some manuscript copies (Karambelkar, "Nabābakhānakhānācaritam," 242–43; also see ms. British Library, Buhler 70, fol. 5a).

86. "Navab" is not a royal title in the Mughal context. But I doubt that Rudrakavi would have appreciated this fine distinction, and he likely does not mean to call attention here to Raḥīm's nonkingly status.

87. *Khānakhānācarita* 1.6. In his *Āʾīn-i Akbarī*, Abū al-Faẕl lists the regents of the ten directions (four cardinal directions, four intercardinal directions, up, and down), and so it is plausible that Raḥīm was familiar with these gods (2:53).

88. *Khānakhānācarita* 1.4.

89. E.g., ibid., p. 9.

90. We might consider this a form of "praise by blame" (*nindāstuti*) or "feigned praise" (*vyājastuti*). On these literary devices, see Bronner, "Change in Disguise."

91. *Khānakhānācarita*, pp. 6–8.

92. Ibid., p. 7. This particular *śleṣa* had a long history of Sanskrit. E.g., see the praise of King Shudraka in the opening of Bāṇa's *Kādambarī*, which includes a similar formulation of mixing colors versus castes (*Princess Kādambarī*, 18–19; *citrakarmasu varṇasaṃkarā*).

93. On Raḥīm's patronage in general, see Seyller, *Workshop and Patron*, 48–58; Schimmel, "Khān-i Khānān Abdur Rahīm as a Patron"; Lefèvre, "Court of ʿAbd-ur-Raḥīm K͟hān-i K͟hānān." While Raḥīm always gave far more support to Persian poets, he also sponsored Hindi authors (Naik, *Literary Circle*, 463–97; also see Lefèvre's more sober account in "Court of ʿAbd-ur-Raḥīm K͟hān-i K͟hānān," 78–86). On Raḥīm's Hindi production, see Busch, "Hidden in Plain View," 282–84, and "Riti and Register," 108–14.

94. Rahim's purported Sanskrit verses are collected in the *Rahīmgranthāvalī*, 171–74. The mixed astrological text is titled *Kheṭakautuka*. The work has been published several times, and a translation is available in Chaudhuri, *Contributions of Muslims*, 126–48. Another partial translation was published by S. D. Udhrain under the title *Star-Lore*.

95. *Maʾās̱ir al-Umarā*, 1:709.

96. E.g., late in Jahangir's reign, Raḥīm supported Prince Khurram's rebellion against his father.

97. *Khānakhānācarita* 1.7.

98. Ibid. 4.1.

99. Ibid. 4.2–3.

100. Pratap Shah's role in the Ahmednagar campaign is described in the *Rāṣṭrauḍhavaṃśamahākāvya*, chapter 20. William Finch mentions a seven-year siege of Baglan by Akbar that ultimately failed (*Early Travels in India*, 136–37).

101. *Khānakhānācarita* 4.4–5; read verse 4.5 with the variants given in Karambelkar, "Nabābakhānakhānācaritam," 245. Verse 6 as printed by Chaudhuri should be omitted (note break in ms. British Library, Buhler 70, fol. 13a, and also the omission of this verse in other manuscript copies).
102. The story of Vishnu's dwarf incarnation was translated by the Mughals in the *Harivaṃśa* (see illustration in Hendley, *Memorials of the Jeypore Exhibition*, plate CXLVII). Nonetheless, it is problematic to easily presume that Raḥīm read the Mughal renderings of the Sanskrit epics (see my discussion of his *Rāmāyan* in chapter 6).
103. Īraj was titled Shāhnavāz Khān by Jahangir after the composition of the *Khānakhānācarita*.
104. *Maʾāṣir al-Umarā*, 2:645–48 and 2:14–17, respectively.
105. In the mid-1610s, both of Raḥīm's sons participated in a major defeat of Malik Ambar's forces in the Deccan and the subsequent burning of his capital in Khirki (i.e., Aurangabad). But, based on the date of the *Khānakhānācarita*, Rudrakavi must be referring to the earlier 1602 engagement here.
106. I am grateful to Phyllis Granoff for her assistance in interpreting this verse. Pradyumna would have been familiar to the Mughals from the *Mahābhārata* translation, although he was not always portrayed in a positive light (e.g., *Razmnāmah*, 4:252–53).
107. *Jahāngīrnāmah*, 225–26. A Dutch chronicle from the first quarter of the seventeenth century confirms that Pratap Shah and the Mughals were on good terms (quoted in *Rudrakavi's Great Poem*, 129).
108. Busch, "Poetry in Motion," 202, citing the *Jahāngīrnāmah*.
109. *Jahāṅgīracarita*, ms. Baroda Oriental Institute, Acc. No. 5761.
110. I base my assessment of the *Jahāṅgīracarita*'s original length on the folio numbers of the Baroda manuscript, which begin with 52.
111. *Jahāṅgīracarita* 3.18 is from the *Rāṣṭrauḍhavaṃśamahākāvya* (6.8), and 3.19 is from the *Khānakhānācarita* (1.10). In chapter 4, at least eleven of seventeen verses are recycled from Rudrakavi's other three praise poems for Mughal figures, and all the prose is reused from the *Khānakhānācarita* (vv. 4.1–9, 4.12, 4.16, and prose fols. 55b–59b and fols. 61a–63b). In chapter 5, at least four of ten surviving verses (5.1 and 5.3–5) are repeated from the *Khānakhānācarita* and the *Kīrtisamullāsa*, but the final prose passage appears to be new (fols. 69b–74b). It remains unclear whether Rudrakavi composed his poem for Jahangir or Khurram first. Several verses overlap between these two and are included in my calculations here. In all, seven of the eighteen verses and both prose sections in his *Kīrtisamullāsa* are recycled.
112. *Jahāṅgīracarita*, fols. 53b–54a, v. 4.3. With the appropriate name changes in the first line, this verse is also found in *Dānaśāhacarita* 3.4 and *Khānakhānācarita* 2.15.
113. *Rāṣṭrauḍhavaṃśamahākāvya* 11.36.
114. E.g., compare Jagannātha's *Prāṇābharaṇa* and *Jagadābharaṇa* (see analysis in introduction to the *Pandita Raja Kavya Samgraha*, viii–x). An example from Indo-Persian literature is Zuhūrī (d. 1616), who reused verses in works composed for the ʿAdilshahis and the Nizamshahis (Sunil Sharma, "Nizamshahi Persianate Garden," 169). Another instance is Muṭribī Samarqandī's *Tazkira-i shuʿarā* (written for the Ashtarkhani ruler Wali Muhammad), which he revised and later presented to

Jahangir under the new title of *Nuskha-i zibā-yi Jahāngīrī* (I am grateful to Corinne Lefèvre for this example).

115. Munis Faruqui even suggests that circumstantial evidence strongly points to Prince Salim's having a role in instigating Danyal's death (*Princes of the Mughal Empire*, 240–41).
116. On Khusraw's rebellion and Jahangir's response, see ibid., 221–31.
117. *Jahāṅgīracarita* vv. 4.10–11, 4.13–15, and 4.17.
118. Ibid., fols. 68a–b, 5.7.
119. Ibid., fols. 72a and 72b, respectively.
120. E.g., Prithu's story is told in the *Śānti Parvan* (*Book of Peace*) of the Persian *Mahābhārata* produced under Akbar (*Razmnāmah*, 3:34–37).
121. Jahangir's mother was Indian, and so he presumably learned Hindi as a child. He further sponsored numerous Hindi poets and was the audience for Braj Bhasha works such as Keśavdās's *Jahāngīrjascandrikā* (Busch, *Poetry of Kings*, 141).
122. For Harideva, the meanings of some of his appellations seem to be secondary to their sound. The three given above mean "the embodiment of taxes," "best of heroes," and "whose arrows are fierce" (*Jahāṅgīravirudāvalī*, 21).
123. There are at least two other Sanskrit praise poems that are sometimes connected with Jahangir, but both are problematic. First, there is an incomplete and unpublished work preserved in the Bodleian Library and written in Sharada script that Stein lists as *Jahāṅgīrakāvya* (ms. Bodleian Stein Or. G. 3). But, to date, the work has not been identified with Jahangir beyond the title. Additionally, a work attributed to Kavīndrācārya titled *Jagadvijayacchandas* is sometimes identified as a praise poem to Jahangir (Raja, introduction to the *Jagadvijayacchandas*, xxix–xxxvi). Kunhan Raja's reasoning regarding the addressee is certainly plausible but by no means convincing, especially since Jahangir is not explicitly mentioned in the extant manuscripts. Even if Kunhan Raja is correct, then quite unlike the encomia I discuss here Kavīndra is ambivalent concerning the addressee of his poem (one manuscript claims it is directed toward Shiva). I am not the first to doubt Kunhan Raja's reasoning in this regard (Chakravarti, "Review of *Jagadvijayacchandas* ed. Raja," 321).
124. *Āsaphavilāsa*, 96 (*rāyamukundenādīṣṭena . . . paṇḍitajagannāthenāsaphavilāsākhyeyam ākhyāyikā niramīyata*). The *Bādshāhnāmah* records an occasion when Jagannātha was ordered not to accompany Shah Jahan to Kashmir and instead to stay behind and work on his songs (1b:56). Whether this was the occasion of visiting Mukunda Raya remains unclear.
125. *Bhāminīvilāsa*, 106, v. 44.
126. On the central role played by Asaf Khan in Shah Jahan's ascension, see Flores and Subrahmanyam, "Shadow Sultan," 88–92.
127. *Āsaphavilāsa* v. 2. Shah Jahan is named in the preceding prose passage, which leads into the verses with "and also."
128. Zutshi, *Languages of Belonging*, 28–34.
129. *Āsaphavilāsa*, 95.
130. Ibid. Jagannātha refers to Asaf Khan here as "Āsapha Jāhī," an alternative title that also provides a nice alliterative effect with *-avagāhī* (bathes).
131. Abū al-Faẕl covers Sanskrit aesthetic theory at some length in his *Learning of India*, part of the *Āʾīn-i Akbarī* (*Āʾīn-i Akbarī*, 2:130–34). In addition, several musical works

that draw on Sanskrit aesthetics were available in both Hindi and Persian by the mid-seventeenth century (e.g., *Kitab-i Nauras* by Ibrahim ʿAdil Shah II). On the Indo-Persian interest in Hindustani music more broadly, see Schofield, "Reviving the Golden Age Again," 495–503.

132. *Āsaphavilāsa*, 96.
133. Koch mentions that this garden had nine terraces, as noted by Lahawrī (*Complete Taj Mahal*, 74).
134. It is not clear to me how far back this legend dates, but it is retold in many modern sources.
135. E.g., see Chandar Bhān's description of Kashmir (translated in Kinra, "Secretary-Poets in Mughal India," 466–68).
136. Zutshi, "Past as Tradition," 204–5; also see her discussion of the *Tārīkh-i Kashmīr* (206–10).
137. *navābāsaphakhānamanaḥprasādena . . . paṇḍitajagannāthena* (*Āsaphavilāsa*, 96).
138. Introduction to the *Pandita Raja Kavya Samgraha*, viii. I find the suggestion that the *Āsaphavilāsa* is incomplete unwarranted given the existence of a full colophon.
139. Kosambi, "Introduction," xlvii.
140. Pollock, *Language of the Gods*, 162–84.
141. Sreeramula Rajeswara Sarma addresses Sanskrit grammars and lexicons of Persian in his many articles (particularly "Sanskrit Manuals for Learning Persian" and "From Yāvanī to Saṃskṛtam"). Also see Truschke, "Defining the Other."
142. Kṛṣṇadāsa mentions his courtly sponsorship in his opening verse (*Pārasīprakāśa* of Kṛṣṇadāsa, 1, v. 1) and also in multiple colophons (E.g., *Pārasīprakāśa* of Kṛṣṇadāsa, 39, 42, 45, 51, 91, and 97). All citations refer to the Varanasi edition published in 1965. Weber also published the lexicon portion of text along with his own analysis in 1887 under the title "Über den Pârasîprakâçades Kṛishṇadâsa." Some scholars have suggested that the lexicon and grammar sections were originally two separate, identically named works (Scharfe, *Grammatical Literature*, 196–97). However, as I discuss elsewhere, this argument has limited supporting evidence, and manuscripts attest that readers early on considered the treatise as a unified whole ("Defining the Other," 645–46).
143. *Pārasīprakāśa* of Kṛṣṇadāsa, 1–2, vv. 5–6.
144. *nātra saṃjñāsaṅgrahaḥ kvacid apekṣayā saṃskṛtasaṃjñayaiva kāryasiddher vakṣyamāṇatvāt* (*Pārasīprakāśa* of Kṛṣṇadāsa, 25).
145. On genitive substitution, see Kahrs, *Indian Semantic Analysis*, chapter 5.
146. *bhuvaḥ śuda bhūtārthe* (*Pārasīprakāśa* of Kṛṣṇadāsa, 54).
147. Walter Slaje makes the case for Kṛṣṇadāsa's reliance on the Sārasvata system of grammar rather than Paninian or Kātantra methods, as has often been previously assumed ("Der Pārasīprakāśa").
148. Alam, *Languages of Political Islam*, 129.
149. Reading was generally important for Mughal service, although elsewhere in India people were considered to be fluent in Persian even in the absence of being able to read the script. E.g., the Hindu interpreters at Goa in the first half of the seventeenth century translated texts from Persian but hired Muslims to read out the Perso-Arabic script to them (Flores, "How Cosmopolitan Were the Hindu Interpreters of Early Modern Goa?").

150. The Jain monk Siddhicandra claimed to have learned Persian at the royal court and subsequently read Persian texts to the king and princes (*Bhānucandragaṇicarita* 4.90 and 4.104). So far as we know Siddhicandra never wrote in Persian, however.
151. In addition to Kavi Karṇapūra, Siddhicandra remained at court early in Jahangir's rule.
152. The earliest known Sanskrit-Persian lexicon is Salakṣa's *Śabdavilāsa* (dated 1365). On this work, see Shah, "Śabda-vilāsa or Pārasīnāmamālā."
153. Kṛṣṇadāsa's *Pārasīprakāśa* survives in dozens of manuscript copies scattered across the subcontinent, which indicates it was widely read. For a preliminary (although not exhaustive) list, see *New Catalogus Catalogorum*, 12:38.
154. During Akbar's reign the Mughals decided to promote Persian as the official administrative tongue (Alam, *Languages of Political Islam*, 122–40).
155. *Pārasīprakāśa* of Kṛṣṇadāsa, 42 and 43, respectively. See appendix 1.
156. Ibid., 43. See appendix 1.
157. E.g., Abū al-Faẓl's preface to the *Razmnāmah* ("Muqaddamah," 21–22), *Tārīkh-i Firishtah* (1:6–7), and *Rawẓat al-Ṭāhirīn* of Ṭāhir Muḥammad Sabzavārī (ms. Bodleian Elliot 314, fols. 387b–88a and fols. 421b–22a).
158. *Pārasīprakāśa* of Kṛṣṇadāsa, 44. See appendix 1.
159. A native Persian speaker known as Sībawayh (Sībūya) (fl. late eighth century) authored the foundational text of Arabic grammar, called by one commentator "the *Qur'ân* of grammar" (Versteegh, *Arabic Linguistic Tradition*, 39). Also see the discussion of continued Iranian participation in Arabic grammar and lexicography traditions in Danner, "Arabic Literature in Iran," 578–80.
160. Jeremiás draws on lexicography to suggest some emendations to the standard narrative that Persians did not produce grammars of their own language until the mid-nineteenth century ("Native Grammatical Literature of Persian").
161. On Kavi Karṇapūra's background and entry into the Mughal court, see Truschke, "Defining the Other," 652–53.
162. *Saṃskṛtapārasīkapadaprakāśa* v. 2.
163. Karṇapūra may have conceptualized the two sections of his text as distinct (although connected) works and penned separate praise and introductory verses for each part (ibid. vv. 1–2 and vv. 326–328). For an analysis of this work, see D. D. Sarma, "Saṃskṛtapārasīkapadaprakāśa."
164. Sreeramula Rajeswara Sarma has also noted the lucidity of Karṇapūra's exegesis as compared with that of Kṛṣṇadāsa ("From Yāvanī to Saṃskṛtam," 85).
165. In contrast to dozens of manuscripts of Kṛṣṇadāsa's *Pārasīprakāśa*, to date I have identified four copies of Karṇapūra's *Saṃskṛtapārasīkapadaprakāśa*: mss. Calcutta Asiatic Society of Bengal [ASB] 24327, Pune Bhandarkar Oriental Research Institute 1502 of 1891–1895, Varanasi Sarasvati Bhavan Library 43704, and the Nepali manuscript on which the printed edition is based (introduction to the *Saṃskṛtapārasīkapadaprakāśa*, 1).
166. *Saṃskṛtapārasīkapadaprakāśa* v. 3; ms. Calcutta ASB 24327, fol. 1b, v. 3, has some variant readings but the same meaning.
167. Ibid. v. 6b.
168. Ibid. v. 7; read *yavana-* as in ms. Calcutta ASB 24327, fol. 1b, and printed in Sarma, "Saṃskṛtapārasīkapadaprakāśa," 190. In the context of Jahangir's court, this comment could refer to the lack of Persian grammars available.
169. Gordon, *Robes of Honour*.
170. *Languages of Political Islam*, 135.

3. MANY PERSIAN *MAHĀBHĀRATAS* FOR AKBAR

1. Abū al-Fażl penned a preface for the *Razmnāmah* in 1587 that is printed in the Tehran edition of the translation. There are two retellings of the *Razmnāmah*: Fayżī's mixed prose and poetry reworking of the first two books of the epic, which Akbar directly sponsored, and Ṭāhir Muḥammad Sabzavārī's abridgement of the *Mahābhārata* in his *Rawżat al-Ṭāhirīn*.
2. Akbar wrote a letter to his son Murad in which the king notes sending a copy of the *Razmnāmah* for the prince's edification. The letter is preserved in an earlier draft of the *Akbarnāmah* (ms. British Library, Persian Add. 27,247, fols. 403a–403b, and translated by I. A. Khan in Moosvi, *Episodes in the Life of Akbar*, 94).
3. The best analyses of the *Razmnāmah* are based on Abū al-Fażl's preface (e.g., Ernst, "Muslim Studies of Hinduism?" 180–82; Rizvi, *Religious and Intellectual History*, 209 and 212–14). Much has also been written on illustrations of the *Razmnāmah* (e.g., Das, *Paintings of the Razmnama*; Das, "Daswant"; Seyller, "Model and Copy"; and, more recently, Rice, "Persian Mahabharata"). I have previously written on the *Razmnāmah* in "Mughal *Book of War*."
4. E.g., see Lefevere's discussion of conceptual and textual grids ("Composing the Other") and Appiah's idea of "thick translation" ("Thick Translation").
5. Shukla provides the most complete and largely accurate list of Mughal-sponsored translations of Sanskrit texts ("Persian Translations of Sanskrit Works"). Also see Ernst, "Muslim Studies of Hinduism?"
6. Badāʾūnī, Fayżī, and Ibrāhīm Sirhindī consecutively failed to translate the *Atharva Veda* (*Muntakhab al-Tavārīkh*, 2:212–13).
7. Badāʾūnī claims to have produced a translation of the *Siṃhāsana-dvātriṃśikā* (renamed *Nāmah-i Khirad Afzā* [*Wisdom-Enhancing Book*]), although this version went missing from the imperial library during Badāʾūnī's lifetime (*Muntakhab al-Tavārīkh*, 2:377). Chaturbhuj Das authored a separate adaptation of the *Siṃhāsana-dvātriṃśikā*, titled *Shāhnāmah* (*Book of Kings*) (Sachau and Ethe, *Catalogue of the Persian, Turkish, Hindustani, and Pushtu Manuscripts in the Bodleian Library*, vol. 1, no. 1324).
8. Fayżī's *Līlāvatī* was printed in 1827, and Marshall lists many manuscripts (*Mughals in India*, no. 468). On this work, see Winter and Mirza, "Persian Version of Līlāvatī."
9. Akbar sponsored at least two Persian versions of the *Pañcatantra*: one titled *ʿIyār-i Dānish* (*Touchstone of the Intellect*) that reworked an earlier Persian rendition (Haider, "Translating Texts," 117) and another called *Panchākhyānah* that was based on a Jain recension of the Sanskrit work (English introduction to the *Panchākhyānah*, 10–11). There are conflicting reports about whether there were one or two Persian *Rājataraṅgiṇī* translations under Akbar (M. Athar Ali, "Translations of Sanskrit Works at Akbar's Court," 43–44). Abū al-Fażl mentions only one Persian *Rājataraṅgiṇī*, and, while he treats it as a single text, it appears to have been Kalhaṇa's work paired with the continuations by Jonarāja and Śrīvara (*Āʾīn-i Akbarī*, 1:578).
10. E.g., on the Akbari *Mahābhārata* and *Rāmāyaṇa* illustrations, see the articles and monographs of Asok Das and John Seyller.
11. Niẓām al-Dīn Pānīpatī made a translation of Abhinanda's *Laghuyogavāsiṣṭha* for Prince Salim in the late sixteenth century (Mujtabai, "Persian Translations of Hindu Religious Literature," 20–21). Rajeev Kinra mentions that Mir Findiriskī introduced the work into Safavid circles ("Handling Diversity," 270).

12. The two Persian *Rāmāyaṇas* for Jahangir are by Giridhardās and Saʿd Allāh Masīḥ Pānīpatī. An author known as Bhāramal (or Bhārāmal) composed his Persian *Siṃhāsana-dvātriṃśikā* (ca. 1610) during Jahangir's reign (Marshall, *Mughals in India*, no. 308). Ṣūfī Sharīf Qutbjahānī dedicated his Persian *Yogavāsiṣṭa* to Jahangir (Mujtabai, "Persian Translations of Hindu Religious Literature," 21).
13. Ibn Harkarn wrote his *Siṃhāsana-dvātriṃśikā*, seemingly based on earlier Persian versions, at Shah Jahan's request (ms. British Library, Persian Add. 6597).
14. Busch, *Poetry of Kings*, 147. Additionally, Jan Kavi presented his *Buddhisāgar*, a version of the *Pañcatantra*, to Shah Jahan (Busch, "Poetry in Motion," 197).
15. Respectively, Badāʾūnī, *Muntakhab al-Tavārīkh*, 2:320–21, and 2:399–400.
16. The master imperial copy, known as the Jaipur *Razmnāmah*, was highly valued by the Mughals at 4,024 rupees (Seyller, "Inspection and Valuation," 307). Additionally, the illustrious Lucknow *Harivaṃśa* (A.N. 57,106) was also likely produced for imperial consumption.
17. Inspection notes on the imperial *Razmnāmah* attest to frequent viewings and recitations at the imperial court (Seyller, "Inspection and Valuation," 307).
18. See Cort's critique in "Making It Vernacular in Agra."
19. Flood offers a compelling use of the notion of translation (*Objects of Translation*).
20. Muzaffar Alam's recent work on the *Mirʾāt al-Makhlūqāt* (*Mirror of Creation*) is a notable exception (Alam, "Mughal Sufi Story of Creation"). Also see Shankar Nair's scholarship (e.g., "Sufism as Medium and Method of Translation").
21. E.g., take the history of Spain that is related successively in two separate versions by ʿAbd al-Sattār in his *S̱amarat al-Falāsifah* (*Fruit of the Philosophers*). While he narrates the Arabic sources quite loosely, he cites dates, exact names, and other markers of careful translation for the portion based on Western sources (Lefèvre, "Europe–Mughal India–Muslim Asia," 134–35).
22. Sunil Sharma suggests that many Mughal readers saw parallels between Persian translations of the Sanskrit epics and the *Shāhnāmah* and sometimes used similar iconography in illustrating these texts ("Production of Mughal *Shāhnāmas*," 91–94).
23. Pollock, *Language of the Gods*, 223–24.
24. E.g., Edward Said tries to distinguish between Foucault's idea that "knowledge in the end serves power" and his own observation that reading leads to human enlightenment in his chapter "Return to Philology" (*Humanism and Democratic Criticism*, 66).
25. Abū al-Faẕl lists three of these translators as having translated the *Mahābhārata* and names Mullā Shīrī separately as having translated the *Harivaṃśa* (*Āʾīn-i Akbarī*, 1:115–16). Badāʾūnī mentions all four without specifying which portions individuals translated (*Muntakhab al-Tavārīkh*, 2:320–21). Elsewhere in his *Muntakhab al-Tavārīkh*, Badāʾūnī reiterates the key roles of Naqīb Khān and Sultan Thānīsarī as beginning and completing the translation, respectively (3:80, Tehran edition).
26. Naqīb Khān contributed to the *Tārīkh-i Alfī* and is described by Jerome Xavier, a visitor to Akbar's court, as one "whose office is to read [the king] histories" (quoted in Alam and Subrahmanyam, "Frank Disputations," 482). He was the son of Akbar's tutor and grandson of the celebrated historian Mīr Yahyā (Rizvi, *Religious and Intellectual History*, 86). Badāʾūnī describes Mullā Shīrī as an Indian poet (*shāʿir-i hindī*; *Muntakhab al-Tavārīkh*, 2:55), and he is known to have composed

verses in Persian (Naik, *Literary Circle*, 400; *Muntakhab al-Tavārīkh*, 3:171–73 in Tehran edition). Mullā Shīrī died in 1586 along with Birbal in Kashmir (*Muntakhab al-Tavārīkh*, 3:173 in Tehran edition). Sultan Thānīsarī was the financial officer in charge of Thānīsar (in modern-day Haryana) and the father-in-law of Aḥmad Sirhindī (Rizvi, *History of Sufism*, 2:406). After participating in the *Mahābhārata* translation, he fell out of favor with Akbar, and ʿAbd al-Raḥīm Khān-i Khānān helped to temporarily smooth over some of the difficulties (Badāʾūnī, *Muntakhab al-Tavārīkh*, 3:80–81 in Tehran edition; Schimmel, "Khān-i Khānān Abdur Rahīm as a Patron," 207). Akbar eventually ordered Sultan Thānīsarī executed in 1598 (Rizvi, *History of Sufism*, 2:406–7).

27. Ms. British Library, Persian Add. 5642, fol. 481b; ms. British Library, Persian Or. 12076, fol. 138b; and ms. British Library, IO Islamic 1702, fol. 411a. The colophon is translated (with the names of the Sanskrit informants largely obscured) in Ali, "Translations of Sanskrit Works at Akbar's Court," 41. This colophon is also available in later manuscripts, although often lacking *bih hindī* ("in Hindi"; e.g., Delhi National Museum Persian 63.47). Ms. Bibliothèque nationale de France [BNF], Supplément Persan 1038, gives the colophon with some additional emendations.
28. Hodivala, *Studies in Indo-Muslim History*, 564–65. E.g., see *Muntakhab al-Tavārīkh*, 2:321.
29. Shaykh Bhāvan, a convert to Islam, had previously disappointed the Mughals with his shaky interpretation of the *Atharva Veda* (*Muntakhab al-Tavārīkh*, 2:212–13). Deva Miśra also assisted with the initial Mughal rendering of the *Rāmāyaṇa* (see Raḥīm's flyleaf note on Freer *Rāmāyan*, fol. 1a, also printed and translated in Seyller, *Workshop and Patron*, 73–74). Caturbhuja may have previously translated the *Siṃhāsanadvātriṃśikā* into Persian
30. The Hindi line is found in the fourteenth book of the epic (*Razmnāmah*, 4:389).
31. *Dāstān-i Nal va Daman*, 35.
32. E.g., note the story of Barbarik that I discuss later in this chapter, which is unknown in the Sanskrit textual tradition but common in oral folk retellings of the epic stretching from Tamil Nadu to Himachal Pradesh (Hiltebeitel, *Rethinking India's Oral and Classical Epics*, 414–38). Unsurprisingly, the *Razmnāmah* version is closest to renditions of the story prevalent in central and northern India (e.g., compare *Razmnāmah*, 3:3–5, and the Marwari version recorded in Hiltebeitel, *Rethinking India's Oral and Classical Epics*, 432). Nonetheless, the *Razmnāmah* preserves some memory that this story was popular in the south by identifying Barbarik's homeland as near Lanka (3:3).
33. Scholars have long distinguished two broad approaches to translation: making the text appear as part of the target culture versus emphasizing a work's foreignness.
34. For a discussion of *Mahābhārata* recensions and versions, see Sukthankar, "Prolegomena," 1:vii–cvii; also Edgerton, "Introduction," 2:xxxi–l. All *Mahābhārata* citations are to the critical edition.
35. The regional versions of the *Mahābhārata* are typically not distinguished by any features tied to their location (see Pollock's discussion in *Language of the Gods*, 229–33).
36. The *Razmnāmah* may also hold important implications for the constitution of the critical edition of the Sanskrit *Mahābhārata*. Sukthankar mentions that he did not consult the Persian text, which was unedited at the time ("Prolegomena," 1:xxviii).

37. Milo Beach has argued that we should view the *Harivaṃśa* as a distinct project from the *Razmnāmah* because Abū al-Faẓl mentions it separately as translated by Mullā Shīrī (*Imperial Image*, 60). However, Abū al-Faẓl recognizes the *Harivaṃśa* as an integral part of the epic in his preface to the translation ("Muqaddamah," 40). The Jaipur *Razmnāmah* contains the *Harivaṃśa* as its fourth volume, although with new pagination.
38. Hendley, *Memorials of the Jeypore Exhibition*, 4:3.
39. Indologists have long asserted that Mughal-era translations stray so far from their Indian sources that the Sanskrit is best forgotten altogether. This erroneous idea dates back to William Jones, who proclaimed, ". . . my experience justifies me in pronouncing that the Mughals have no idea of accurate translation, and give that name to a mixture of gloss and text with a flimsy paraphrase of both" (quoted in Habibullah, "Medieval Indo-Persian Literature Relating to Hindu Science," 167). Francis Gladwyn made a similar pronouncement that the *Razmnāmah* "was nothing more than an extract, very indifferently executed" (quoted in Sreeramula Rajeswara Sarma, "Translation of Scientific Texts," 72). Scholars through the twentieth century agreed with Jones and Gladwyn, postulating that, "It may be worth while to sound a note of warning regarding the exactness of these Persian translations [from Sanskrit]: it is futile to expect a close approximation to the original text" (Habibullah, "Medieval Indo-Persian Literature Relating to Hindu Science," 167).
40. Ms. Srinagar Oriental Research Library [ORL] Persian 188, fols. 11b, 12b–13a, 14a, 16b–18a, 19a, 23a, 24a–25b, 27a, and 30b.
41. I have checked key components of all eighteen books of the *Razmnāmah* against the critical edition of the Sanskrit *Mahābhārata* as well as Abū al-Faẓl's preface, in which he summarizes the table of contents given in the opening of the *Mahābhārata* (*parvasaṅgraha*). Since books of the *Mahābhārata* often circulated separately, checking each book individually is crucial. I have not determined the *Harivaṃśa* recension. Book 14 is the exception in not following the northern recension, as I discuss later. For Abū al-Faẓl's summary, compare "Muqaddamah," 37–40, and *Mahābhārata* 1.2.
42. This analysis presents significant challenges since the Mughals did not adopt any standardized transliteration system and the names often vary between *Razmnāmah* manuscripts. Moreover, the master copy of the translation produced for Akbar's court, while extant, has been inaccessible to scholars for decades. Last, the Sanskrit manuscripts of the northern recension are themselves rarely as old as the Mughal translation, and therefore a certain amount of temporal dislocation taints any comparison. In my analysis, I have compared the Sanskrit critical edition to both the printed *Razmnāmah* and select late sixteenth- and early seventeenth-century manuscript copies. Despite the obstacles I have detailed here, the evidence is overwhelming.
43. In addition to a variety of shorter checks, I have analyzed three lists of names in detail that I selected for their length, variants, and distribution: the snake names in book 1 (*Mahābhārata* 1.52.5–17; *Razmnāmah*, 1:52–53), the names of Shiva that appear in book 12 of much of the Devanagari corpus (*Mahābhārata*, vol. 16, app. 1, no. 28, lines 160–346; *Razmnāmah*, 3:394–408), and a list in book 13 (*Mahābhārata* 13.151.2–50; *Razmnāmah*, 4:211–13). Chief among the early manuscripts I consulted are British Library, Persian Add. 5641/5642 (dated 1598–1599), Aligarh Muslim University, University Collection No. Persian/Ikhbar 2 (1604–1605), and Birla

Razmnāmah (1605). In addition British Library, Or. 12076, which contains books 14–18, is dated 1598–1599 (on this manuscript, see Meredith-Owens and Pinder-Wilson, "Persian Translation of the *Mahābhārata*"), and the Lucknow State Museum *Harivaṃśa* A.N. 57,106 likely dates to the 1590s (Skelton, "Mughal Paintings from Harivaṃśa Manuscript," 52).

44. Art historians have known for well over a century that the fourteenth book of the *Razmnāmah* follows the *Jaiminīyāśvamedha* (Hendley, *Memorials of the Jeypore Exhibition*, 4:29). But they have generally not commented on the implications of this source beyond the illustrations.
45. J. Derrett dates the *Jaiminīyāśvamedha* to between 1100 and 1200 on the basis of its textual references ("Greece and India," 22–27). On the work's popularity and vernacular versions, see Koskikallio and Vielle, "Epic and Puranic Texts," 70–75. In his introduction to the critical edition's *Aśvamedha Parvan*, Karmarkar summarizes the *Jaiminīyāśvamedha*'s contents in comparison with the canonical version (18:xxiv–xliv). Gita Press has published the Sanskrit text, and an English translation came out in 2008 (*Jaiminiya Ashvamedha Parvan*).
46. Koskikallio and Vielle mention the *Jaiminīyāśvamedha*'s emphasis on Krishna in "Epic and Puranic Texts," 67; also see the discussion in Shekhar Kumar Sen, "Introduction," 40–44. Most likely the Mughals were not drawn to the *Jaiminīyāśvamedha* due to its theological bias. On the contrary, they avoided theology in the *Razmnāmah*, as I discuss subsequently.
47. The references for these stories are as follows: the kingdom of women (*Razmnāmah*, 4:292–94), tree-born men who live a single day (295), Arjuna's head problems (354–56 and 365–66), Arjuna's conflict with his son (350–56), and adventures from the *Rāmāyaṇa* (309–50). On the *Jaiminīyāśvamedha*'s description of the kingdom of women (*strīrājya*), see W. L. Smith, "Strīrājya," 472–75.
48. The single most famous work is the *ʿAjāʾib al-makhlūqāt wa-gharāʾib al-mawjūdāt* (*Marvels of Creation and Rarities of Existence*) of Zakariyyāʾ al-Qazwīnī (d. 1283).
49. Berlekamp, *Wonder, Image, and Cosmos*, 23–24; Hunsberger, "Marvels." Von Hees has criticized the Western tendency to portray *ʿajāʾib* as imaginary or fictitious when the Islamicate tradition often emphasizes precisely their reality ("Astonishing," 104–5).
50. "Wiles of Creation," 24.
51. *Love's Subtle Magic*, 119–40. On the Islamicate interest in Indian *ʿajāʾib* generally, see Behl, "Magic Doe," 197–99; Berlekamp, *Wonder, Image, and Cosmos*, 170–71; Flood, *Objects of Translation*, 19.
52. *Millennial Sovereign*, particularly 60–62 and 202–3.
53. Badāʾūnī presents the *Atharva Veda* as a rather strange work (*Muntakhab al-Tavārīkh*, 2:212–13). Also note the description of the *Atharva Veda* in the seventeenth-century *Dabistān-i Maẕāhib* (1:139).
54. [*mahābhārat*] *qiṣṣahhā-yi gharīb dārad* (*Akbarnāmah*, ms. British Library, Persian Add. 27,247, fol. 403b; also see Moosvi, *Episodes in the Life of Akbar*, 94).
55. *Muntakhab al-Tavārīkh*, 3:173 in Tehran edition; also cited in Naik, *Literary Circle*, 401.
56. "Muqaddamah," 24 and 24–25, respectively.
57. Ibid., 34. Previous scholars have suggested, incorrectly I think, that the *Razmnāmah* represented Akbar's "waning concern for fantastic or mythological narratives"

(Beach, *Mughal and Rajput Painting*, 48). For the Mughals, there was little conflict between the fantastic and the historical.

58. *Razmnāmah*, 4:291.
59. Some later Indo-Persian literati knew the separate source of the Mughal *Aśvamedha Parvan*. E.g., a colophon to a 1729 manuscript notes that this version was associated with Jaimini (ms. Aligarh Muslim University, Sir Suleman Collection 35/22, as reproduced in Zaidi, *Hinduism in Aligarh Manuscripts*, 22). At some point a Persianate writer also went back to the Sanskrit tradition and rendered the canonical *Aśvamedha Parvan* into Persian, which survives in at least two manuscript copies today (ms. Aligarh Muslim University, Sir Suleman Collection 27/14, and ms. Royal Asiatic Society of London, Persian No. 15, fols. 1b–37a).
60. Despite not being the longest, book 14 is the most heavily illustrated *parvan* of the Jaipur *Razmnāmah* (Seyller, "Model and Copy," 46). For comparisons of illustrations of book 14 among the earliest illuminated manuscripts, see Das, "Notes on Four Illustrations," 74–78; Seyller, "Model and Copy," 46–50.
61. Compare *Mahābhārata* 12.56.35 and *Razmnāmah*, 3:26.
62. Compare *Razmnāmah*, 3:86, and *Mahābhārata* 12.102.4–5.
63. This story is found in *Razmnāmah*, 1:53–54. I have reconstructed the Sanskrit verses and translated them in appendix 2.
64. "Citing as a Site," 348.
65. ʿAbd al-Raḥmān Chishtī reproduces a garbled Sanskrit *śloka* as evidence of his use of Sanskrit sources in his seventeenth-century *Mirʾāt al -Makhlūqāt* (*Mirror of Creation*) (Alam, "Mughal Sufi Story of Creation," 159n26). Sumīr Chand transliterates the first line of Sanskrit poetry (*ādikāvya*) in his early eighteenth-century *Rāmāyan* (Ms. Rampur Raza Persian 5008, p. 12).
66. E.g., ms. Bodleian Ouseley 326 (dated 1730). Ms. Bodleian Wilson 422b contains a blank line in place of the verse (fol. 42a), which suggests that the scribe's unfulfilled intention was to write the verse in red ink.
67. Ms. Patna Khuda Bakhsh Persian 2714, fol. 29b; ms. Srinagar ORL Persian 1294, fol. 31b; ms. Bodleian Ouseley 239, fol. 55b. The single Hindi quotation so far identified in the *Razmnāmah* involves a similar concern with poison. But the Hindi phrase (*us ko na bikhā dejō*) is immediately translated into Persian ("Don't poison him!") and does not seem to have held the same impenetrable linguistic power as the quoted Sanskrit verses (*Razmnāmah*, 4:389).
68. Respectively, *Razmnāmah*, 1:269–72, 4:211–13, and 1:122–25.
69. *Alberuni's India*, 1:299–303.
70. *Baburnama*, 335–50.
71. E.g., ms. Birla *Razmnāmah*, vol. 2, fols. 481a–82a. Persian treatises on Indian music also sometimes included diacritic marks (Delvoye, "Indo-Persian Accounts on Music Patronage," 258).
72. For examples of overlining, see ms. Patna Khuda Bakhsh Persian 2718–2719 (dated 1770) and ms. British Library, IO Islamic 1641–1643 and 1512 (dated in the early 1770s). For a numbered list (plus overlining), see ms. Bodleian William 422b, fol. 74b (dated 1806).
73. Also note the separate phenomenon where some later manuscripts, generally written by Hindu scribes, replace mentions of *khudāvand* with *bhagavān* (e.g., *Tarjumah-i Razmnāmah*, ms. Hyderabad Oriental Manuscript Library Tarikh 266).

74. *Razmnāmah*, 1:2. Earlier Islamicate writers had also identified the Hindu God as Allah and honored him with appropriate Arabic phrases (e.g., Friedmann, "Medieval Muslim Views of Indian Religions," 216).
75. *Razmnāmah*, 2:475.
76. Ibid., 4:334.
77. *Mahābhārata* 3.54.16–20.
78. *Razmnāmah*, 1:300.
79. *ay gushāyandah-i kārhā-yi bastah va ay rāhnumā-yi gumshudigān* (*Razmnāmah*, 1:300).
80. *Al-fatāḥ* and *al-hādi*, respectively. I am grateful to Hossein Kamaly for this insight.
81. Behl surveys the frameworks of the major Hindavi romances in *Love's Subtle Magic*, 34–46.
82. In their edition, Naini and Shukla supplement the *Razmnāmah*'s meager *Bhagavadgītā* with the fuller version attributed to Dara Shikuh (introduction to the *Razmnāmah*, 2:3; Dara Shikuh's version can be found in *Razmnāmah*, 2:11–110). The *Razmnāmah*'s *Bhagavadgītā* is available in Vassie, "Persian Interpretations of the *Bhagavadgītā*," 265–68, corresponding to *Mahābhārata* 6.23–40. Also see *Mahābhārat-i Fārsī: Bhīkham Parb*, 7–10.
83. *Mahābhārata* 9.29–53.
84. Some modern scholars have asserted that Naqīb Khān omitted the *Bhagavadgītā* out of respect for Akbar's poet laureate, Fayẓī, who had previously translated the work (introduction to the *Razmnāmah*, 3:32). However, we lack evidence that Fayẓī ever translated the *Bhagavadgītā*, much less before the completion of the *Razmnāmah* (e.g., see Dayal's comments on the alleged translation by Fayẓī, despite his unsubstantiated conclusion, in *Gita in Persian*, xi–xii). In any case, the Mughals typically had no qualms about retranslating texts.
85. Quoted in Ernst, "Fayzi's Illuminationist Interpretation of Vedanta," 358.
86. There are multiple early modern Persian translations of the *Bhagavadgītā*, several of which are attributed to either Fayẓī or Abū al-Faẓl. More manuscript work is needed to sort out the dates and correct authors of these texts (Ahuja, "Persian Prose Translation of the Gita").
87. Vassie, "Persian Interpretations of the *Bhagavadgītā*," 265; *Mahābhārata* 6.23.20–25.
88. ʿAbd al-Raḥman Chishtī's later Persian version of the *Bhagavadgītā* also tempers Krishna's divinity, in his case by presenting Krishna as reflecting God's divinity (Vassie, "ʿAbd al-Raḥman Chishtī and the Bhagavadgita," 372–73).
89. Vassie, "Persian Interpretations of the *Bhagavadgītā*," 268.
90. E.g., Krishna is equated with *khudā* in *Razmnāmah*, 1:240.
91. *Tarjumah-i Barāhī*, ms. British Library, IO Islamic 1262, fols. 2a–5a. The translator was ʿAbd al-Azīz Shams Bahā-yi Nūrī, also known as ʿAbd al-Azīz Shams Thānīsarī (Jalali and Ansari, "Persian Translation of Varāhamihira's Bṛhatsaṃhitā," 162–63).
92. *Razmnāmah*, 3:36–37.
93. The translators almost certainly quote from Indo-Persian and lesser-known poets as well. Identifying the sources of poetry in the *Razmnāmah* remains an unfinished project.
94. Meisami discusses how premodern readers would have been expected to recognize the sources of interpolated poetry ("Historian and the Poet," 119). That readers met such expectations is demonstrated when they added further lines onto the quoted verses (e.g., bracketed verses in *Razmnāmah*, 4:220; also see British Library, Or. 12076, fol. 2b).

95. On the weight of verse in Persian literature and how it functions when mixed with prose, see Meisami, "Mixed Prose and Verse."
96. *Panchākhyānah*, e.g., 24 for Ḥāfiẓ and 19 for Saʿdī. Akbar's *Rāmāyan* also quotes at least a half line of poetry (ms. Freer *Rāmāyan*, fol. 39a, and ms. Qatar *Rāmāyan*, p. 88).
97. Boucher, "Gāndhārī and the Early Chinese Buddhist Translations Reconsidered," 497–98.
98. *Razmnāmah*, 2:198.
99. Compare *Razmnāmah*, 2:172, and *Dīvān* of Sanāʾī, 485–86. There are also several lines of poetry given in footnotes on the following page of the *Razmnāmah* that may have been included in the original translation (2:173).
100. *Razmnāmah*, 4:219–20.
101. Ibid., 4:220; *Dīvān* of Muʿizzī, 597.
102. *Muntakhab al-Tavārīkh*, 2:399 (for a full translation of this passage, see Haider, "Translating Texts," 121–22). Badāʾūnī also incurred questions from Akbar regarding his contribution to the *Tārīkh-i Alfī* (Rizvi, *Religious and Intellectual History*, 256).
103. Alam, "Debate Within," 144–45.
104. *Muntakhab al-Tavārīkh*, 2:399.
105. Pasha Khan discusses this *naqlī* approach to history in "Marvellous Histories," 550–53.
106. *Muntakhab al-Tavārīkh*, 2:399. Also see *Razmnāmah*, 1:478, and *Safīnah-i Ḥāfiẓ*, 192.
107. Nonetheless, other specific Islamic concepts seem to have slipped into the *Razmnāmah*, such as the *kaʿba* (1:464) and the "angel of death" (*malak al-mawt*, 2:467).
108. *Muntakhab al-Tavārīkh*, 2:400.
109. *Razmnāmah*, 1:478.
110. "Muqaddamah," 19–20.
111. Ibid., 40.
112. In contrast, the *Śānti* and *Anuśāsana parvans* together make up just under 25 percent of the Sanskrit *Mahābhārata* (Fitzgerald, *Mahābhārata*, 7:82).
113. The Mughals also translated the third and final part on the ethics of spiritual liberation (*mokṣadharma*), but they do not adorn this section with many verses.
114. *Razmnāmah*, 1:462–547.
115. *Rawẓat al-Ṭāhirīn* of Ṭāhir Muḥammad Sabzavārī. Book 5 description: ms. Bodleian Elliot 314, fol. 435b, and ms. Aligarh Muslim University, Sir Suleman Collection 15/2(b), fol. 147b. Book 12 description: ms. Bodleian Elliot 314, fol. 447b, and ms. Aligarh Muslim University, Sir Suleman Collection 15/2(b), fol. 182a.
116. "Muqaddamah," 21. In his *Āʾīn-i Akbarī*, Abū al-Faẓl argues that these two *parvans* ought to be considered as one because of their shared focus on Bhishma's advice (1:517).
117. For an analysis of the framing of book 12, see Fitzgerald, *Mahābhārata*, 7:81–94.
118. The following description is a brief summary of *Razmnāmah*, 3:2–5.
119. The *Razmnāmah* explains that, before the war, Barbarik approached Krishna and promised to win the upcoming battle with only three arrows. Krishna tested Barbarik's archery abilities and was awed by his unparalleled skills. Because Krishna knew that the Pandavas would win the conflict anyway, he decided to spare the world Barbarik's destructive power. Krishna first prevailed upon Barbarik to grant any wish that Krishna desired and then requested no less than his head. Barbarik complied

on the condition that he be allowed to watch the full battle, and so Krishna put an immortal leaf in his mouth, chopped off his head, and placed it in a tree; ibid., 3:3–4.

120. Hendley, *Memorials of the Jeypore Exhibition*, plate LXXI (Barbarik's head also appears in plate LXIV).
121. *Razmnāmah*, 3:5–11; compare with *Mahābhārata* 12.1.20–5.15.
122. See Faruqui, "Forgotten Prince."
123. *Akbarnāmah*, 1:12; pp. 43–45 in Thackston's translation. Abū al-Faẓl changes this story slightly from earlier Timurid tellings in having the light not manifest itself in most of Akbar's predecessors (Lefèvre, "Mughal Genealogical Strategies," 420–21).
124. *Razmnāmah*, 1:117–18; the parallel section in Sanskrit is *Mahābhārata* 1.104. Also see the discussion of this passage in Ruby Lal, *Domesticity and Power*, 148.
125. E.g., plate LXI in Hendley, *Memorials of the Jeypore Exhibition*.
126. *Razmnāmah*, 3:11–13.
127. *Mahābhārata* 12.6–38.
128. *Razmnāmah*, 3:12.
129. *Mahābhārata* 12.65–66, and *Razmnāmah*, 3:42–44.
130. *Razmnāmah*, 3:45.
131. Ibid., 3:44.
132. Ibid., 3:45. The first four lines are from the *Būstān-i Saʿdī* (18, lines 4–5). I am unclear about the origin of the last two lines. Note that lines 3 and 4 are missing in many manuscripts of the *Razmnāmah*. Nonetheless, I do not think their addition or subtraction significantly alters the meaning or tone of the passage.
133. Scholars have previously made this point, e.g., Ernst ("Muslim Studies of Hinduism?").
134. On the date, see "Muqaddamah," 22. Later manuscripts do not always carry Abū al-Faẓl's preface, but early copies generally include it.
135. For previous translations and discussions of this passage, see Ernst, "Muslim Studies of Hinduism?" 180–82, and Shaikh Chand Husain, "Translations of the *Mahābhārata*," 278–80. Alam also translates part of this section in *Languages of Political Islam*, 65–66.
136. "Muqaddamah," 18. I follow Ernst in amending *juhūd ū hunūd* (Jews and Hindus) to read *juḥūd-i hunūd* (denials of the Hindus; "Muslim Studies of Hinduism?" 182n27). This emendation is supported by the reference to *dū farīq* later in the same passage. The manuscript tradition is confused on this point, and, in addition to the two variations already mentioned, several copies read *junūd-i hunūd* (Hindu troops) or *junūd ū hunūd* (soldiers and Hindus). Regardless of the correct reading, the use of *juhūd*, *juḥūd*, or *junūd* appears to be aimed primarily at creating a rhyme rather than adding substantive content and does not significantly alter the meaning of the passage. Note that scholars have adduced evidence for a Jewish presence at Akbar's court (Walter Fischel, "Jews and Judaism at the Court of the Moghul Emperors," 145–48). For translations of the passage that retain *juhūd ū hunūd*, see Alam, *Languages of Political Islam*, 65, and Husain, "Translations of the *Mahābhārata*," 278. Alam interprets *juhūd* as infidels in "*Akẖlāqī* Norms and Mughal Governance," 85.
137. E.g., Rizvi, "Dimensions of *Ṣulḥ-i Kul*," 15.
138. "Handling Diversity," 261.
139. "Muqaddamah," 3.
140. Ibid.

141. For overviews of some of these tensions, see Alam, "Akbari Dispensation," 154–59; MacLean, "Real Men and False Men"; Richards, *Mughal Empire*, 36–41; Rizvi, "Dimensions of *Ṣulḥ-i Kul*."
142. On some of these activities, see Rizvi, *Religious and Intellectual History*, 141–74.
143. For an in-depth discussion of Akbar's ideology in the second half of his reign, designed primarily by Abū al-Faẕl, see ibid., particularly 339–73. Also note Abū al-Faẕl's treatment of the ulama in his *Āʾīn-i Akbarī* (Hardy, "Perfect Padshah," 122).
144. "Muqaddamah," 3–4.
145. Rizvi, *Religious and Intellectual History*, 341.
146. Najaf Haider notes that, based on their titles, translations of the *Pañcatantra* and other story works done under Akbar appear to emphasize the intellect ("Translating Texts," 117).
147. This letter is contained in an earlier version of Abū al-Faẕl's *Akbarnāmah* (ms. British Library, Persian Add. 27,247, fols. 403a–403b). Also see I. A. Khan's translation in Moosvi, *Episodes in the Life of Akbar*, 94.
148. Abū al-Faẕl also employs the language of *taqlīd* versus *taḥqīq* when discussing Brahmanical leaders ("Muqaddamah," 19).
149. Ibid., 17–18; see p. 9 for the mention of carpentry and other arts.
150. On the role of *insān-i kāmil* in Akbar's political image, see Rizvi, *Religious and Intellectual History*, 356–71, and Asher, "Ray from the Sun," particularly 170–71.
151. "Muqaddamah," 13.
152. E.g., Badāʾūnī's *Najāt al-Rashīd*, 113–15.
153. "Muqaddamah," 19. My translation is closely based on Ernst, "Muslim Studies of Hinduism?" 181–82.
154. Alam, "Mughal Sufi Story of Creation," 181–85. Not all Indo-Islamic thinkers agreed that Hindu and Islamic ideas were compatible, however. E.g., Badāʾūnī condemns cyclical time in reference to Hindu ideas but seemingly endorses the idea when rooted in Sufi thought (Moin, "Peering through the Cracks," 515–16).
155. "Muqaddamah," 20–21.
156. Ibid., 21. The emphasis on inner and outer rulership also arises elsewhere in the Mughal dispensation, such as in the verses inscribed on the well-known painting of Jahangir preferring a Sufi to kings (Freer Gallery of Art F1942.15).
157. "Muqaddamah," 34.
158. In his court history, Abū al-Faẕl similarly uses *gūyand* (they say) when he repeats potentially unreliable information (Alam, "Akbari Dispensation," 164).
159. E.g., *Muntakhab al-Tavārīkh*, 2:322.
160. "Muqaddamah," 18.
161. Ibid., 19.
162. Ibid.
163. Ibid.; translation from Ernst, "Muslim Studies of Hinduism?" 181. Abū al-Faẕl does not specify which Mughal translation projects will provide Brahmans greater access to Islamic learning. Despite his attestation that Akbar wished "to translate the canonical books of each group into other tongues," Akbar did not sponsor renderings of Persian or Arabic works into Sanskrit.
164. Whether the *Razmnāmah* ever actually prompted Brahmanical introspection is another question. While knowledge of Persian was not especially widespread among Brahmans in the late sixteenth century, Hindus were beginning to learn Persian in

substantial numbers and enter into Mughal service. Manuscript evidence attests that Hindus read the *Razmnāmah* widely, even those who also had access to the Sanskrit tradition, but mainly in the mid-seventeenth century and later.

165. *Najāt al-Rashīd*, quoted and translated in Moin, "Challenging the Mughal Emperor," 397.
166. "Ecology of Hindi," 54.
167. E.g., Asher and Talbot, *India Before Europe*, 140.
168. Quoted in Rizvi, *Religious and Intellectual History*, 254–55.
169. *zabān-dānāyān-i har dū ṭā'ifah muslimānān ū hunūd bā ittifāq-i shaykh abū al-faẕl taṣnīf-i mahābhārat mī nimāyand* (Free Library of Philadelphia, Lewis m18).
170. In particular, later translators follow Abū al-Faẕl en masse in detailing the nature of cyclical time in much Indic thought and the theory of the four eras (*yugas*).
171. *Ā'īn-i Akbarī*, 1:515–17.
172. For a brief biography of Fayẕī, see Alam and Subrahmanyam, "Travels with Faiẓî in the Deccan," 272–75, and Grobbel, *Der Dichter Faiḍī*, 18–21.
173. *bipāyān baram hizhdah daftar tamām* / (ms. British Library, IO Islamic 761, fol. 186b; ms. British Library, IO Islamic 3014, fol. 171a).
174. *dar īn hizhdah hangāmah-i gīr ū dār / nimāyam tamāshā-yi hizhdah hazār // kunam garm hangāmah-i pāstān / bigūyam sukhan dāstān dāstān* // (ms. British Library, IO Islamic 761, fol. 186b; ms. British Library, IO Islamic 3014, fols. 171a–b).
175. The two *parvans* of Fayẕī's *Mahābhārat* survive today in numerous manuscript copies. I have viewed manuscripts in the following collections: Asiatic Society of Mumbai, Bibliothèque nationale de France (Paris), Bodleian Library (Oxford), British Library (London), Maulana Azad Library (Aligarh), Khuda Bakhsh Library (Patna), Oriental Research Library (Srinagar), and Raza Library (Rampur). Fayẕī's text is often miscataloged as the *Razmnāmah*. I have seen no dated manuscripts of Fayẕī's *Mahābhārat* before the eighteenth century, manuscripts are often incomplete, and variant readings abound. As a result, I rely here on several manuscripts and cite multiple copies wherever possible. Badā'ūnī confirms that Fayẕī completed only the first two books (*Muntakhab al-Tavārīkh*, 2:321). Fayẕī also left other projects unfinished, such as his set of five poems (*khamsah*) in imitation of Niẓāmī (Sunil Sharma, "Genre of Historical Narratives," 115).
176. See Sunil Sharma's comments on Fayẕī's emphasis on originality in multiple poems ("Nauʿī's *Sūz u Gudāz*," 256). On newness in Indo-Persian poetry more broadly, see Kinra, "Fresh Words," and "Make It Fresh." Losensky talks about trends toward innovation across the broader Persianate world (*Welcoming Fighānī*, 193–249).
177. *kuhannāmah bā ṣad afsūngarī / zi hindī biram dar zabān-i dar // zadam gām-i naẓārah bā dūstān / bih butkhānah-i dayr-i hindūstān* // (ms. British Library, IO Islamic 761, fol. 186b; ms. British Library, IO Islamic 3014, fol. 171b).
178. *bar ātashgah-i fārs māndam asās* / (ms. British Library, IO Islamic 761, fol. 186b; ms. British Library, IO Islamic 3014, fol. 171b).
179. *Kulliyāt-i Fayẕī*, 57. In calling himself an Indian parrot, Fayẕī echoes Amīr Khusraw, who was known as *tūtī-yi hind*.
180. *kih awṣāfash nagunjad dar ʿibārat // banāmīzad ay fikrat-i tīz raw / kih dādī sukhan rā saranjām-i naw* // (ms. British Library, IO Islamic 761, fol. 235a). Fayẕī made grandiose claims about his poetic skills with some regularity. E.g., see his poetry quoted in the *Ā'īn-i Akbarī*, 1:235–42.

181. *qalam rā bikhūn-i dil āghashtah'am / kih nas̱rash kam az naẓm nanivishtah'am //* (ms. British Library, IO Islamic 761, fol. 186b; ms. British Library, IO Islamic 3014, fol. 171b).
182. *Razmnāmah*, 1:210.
183. *nakhlbandān-i būstān-i sukhan va ramzdānān-i īn dāstān-i kuhan chunīn āvardah'and* . . . (ms. British Library, IO Islamic 761, fol. 189b; ms. Srinagar ORL Persian 211, fol. 83b, which reads . . . *īn asrār-i kuhan chunīn rivāyat kardah'and*). Ms. BNF Supplément Persan 1038 has *dayr-i kuhan* in lieu of *dāstān-i kuhan* (fol. 86a).
184. On prosimetrum in histories and stories, see Meisami, "Mixed Prose and Verse," 303–15.
185. Ms. British Library, IO Islamic 761, fol. 2a; ms. Srinagar ORL Persian 211, fol. 2a.
186. *sitāyish bar ān maʿdan-i āb ū khāk / kih zāyad chunīn gawhar-i tābnāk // bar ān āsitān bād farkhundah rūz / kih dārad chunīn akhtarī shab furūz // chih farrukh havā būd ān būstān / kih bigushāyad az vay dil-i dūstān // tū ān gūft ū rā pisar-i arjmand / kih nām-i pidar gardad az vay buland //* (ms. British Library, IO Islamic 761, fol. 2a; ms. Srinagar ORL Persian 211, fol. 2a, reads *āsmān* for *āsitān*).
187. *sukhan az man ū himmat az shāh būd* (ms. British Library, IO Islamic 761, fol. 186b).
188. Ms. British Library, IO Islamic 761, fol. 105a; ms. Srinagar ORL Persian 175, fol. 61b. These lines may also allude to Akbar's well-documented practice of sun veneration.
189. *s̱anākhvan-i awrang-i shāhinshaham* (ms. British Library, IO Islamic 761, fol. 187a; ms. Aligarh Muslim University, University Collection No. Persian/Ikhbar 129, fol. 269b).
190. There are a few later prose reworkings of individual chapters of the *Mahābhārata* in Persian (including books 4, 5, and 14) and some prose abridgements of the entire epic. Fathullah Mujtabai lists some of the alternative adaptations in *Aspects of Hindu Muslim Cultural Relations*, 73–74.
191. Mujtabai, *Aspects of Hindu Muslim Cultural Relations*, 68–71.
192. E.g., *Razmnāmah*, ms. Asiatic Society of Bombay A.N. 143693 contains Fayẓī's *Ādi Parvan*, and ms. BNF Supplément Persan 1038 contains his *Sabhā Parvan*.
193. E.g., ms. Srinagar ORL Persian 211 and ms. Asiatic Society of Bombay A.N. 143693 (*Ādi Parvan*) omit many of the verses within the text. Of the manuscripts I have consulted, British Library, IO Islamic 761 offers the fullest set of both opening and closing verses, although some of the final verses in the *Sabhā Parvan* have been damaged.
194. On Fayẓī's *Nal-Daman*, see Alam and Subrahmanyam, "Faizi's *Nal-Daman* and Its Long Afterlife" in *Writing the Mughal World*, 204–48, originally printed as "Love, Passion and Reason in Faizi's *Nal-Daman*" in *Love in South Asia: A Cultural History*, ed. Francesca Orsini (Cambridge: Cambridge University Press, 2006).
195. As Deven Patel has discussed, the twelfth-century Sanskrit *Naiṣadhīyacarita* in particular proved fertile material for poets to comment upon in Sanskrit and retell in vernacular languages ("Source, Exegesis, and Translation").
196. *īn nashā' az ān ziyādah dāram / kaz shikarr-i hind bādah dāram // chūn jurʿah fashān shavam bar ayyām / aḥsant bar āyad az may ū jām //* (*Dāstān-i Nal va Daman*, 39). Kinra quotes a similar sentiment from Fayẓī that hundreds of nightingales will sing of an Iraqi rose blossoming in India ("Make It Fresh," 24).
197. Many scholars have noted Fayẓī's debt to Niẓāmī (e.g., Alam and Subrahmanyam, *Writing the Mughal World*, 211).
198. Abū al-Faẓl lists the *Nal-Daman* among the illustrated manuscripts in Akbar's court (*Ā'īn-i Akbarī*, 1:118). Alam and Subrahmanyam note numerous retellings of the *Nal-Daman* in *Writing the Mughal World* (205) and also discuss one later rewriting in more detail (241–48).

199. The start date of the *Rawẕat al-Ṭāhirīn*, 1602–1603, is recorded in the title's chronogram (Beveridge, "Rauẕat-uṭ-Tāhirīn," 269).
200. On the date that Ṭāhir Muḥammad entered Akbar's service, see *Rawẕat al-Ṭāhirīn*, ms. Bodleian Elliot 314, fol. 626a. For some highlights of his employment with the Mughals, see Marshall, *Mughals in India*, 1, no. 1768, and Zaidi, *Hinduism in Aligarh Manuscripts*, 11.
201. Muzaffar Alam gives an overview of the *Rawẕat al-Ṭāhirīn*'s contents in *Languages of Political Islam*, 67. On Ṭāhir Muḥammad's treatment of the Portuguese and non-Indian lands, see Alam and Subrahmanyam, *Writing the Mughal World*, 97–122.
202. Subrahmanyam, "Taking Stock of the Franks," 87.
203. A 1759 manuscript names *śrī bhāgavat* as Ṭāhir Muḥammad's source (ms. British Library, IO Islamic 753, fol. 118b). But modern scholars have yet to confirm this connection, and Ṭāhir Muḥammad is silent about his source(s) for information about Vishnu's incarnations. While the *Bhāgavata Purāṇa* was rendered into Persian multiple times, we lack evidence that any translations were completed as early as Akbar's reign (for an overview of *Bhāgavata* translations, see Shukla, "Persian Translations of Sanskrit Works," 182). Much confusion surrounds the Persian *Bhāgavatas*, not least because manuscript catalogues often mislabel translations as *Bhagavadgītās*. There was at least one partial Braj adaptation of the *Bhāgavata Purāṇa* available by the end of the sixteenth century (McGregor, *Hindi Literature*, 156).
204. *ẕikr-i aḥvāl-i farmān-farmāyān-i hindūstān kih qabl az ẓuhūr-i islām būdah'and brahmanān mīgūyand . . .* (*Rawẕat al-Ṭāhirīn*, ms. Bodleian Elliot 314, fol. 11b). Ṭāhir Muḥammad describes the *Mahābhārata* in a similar fashion (fol. 421b).
205. Ms. Bodleian Elliot 314, fol. 421b.
206. Compare ms. Bodleian Elliot 314, fols. 423b–24b, and "Muqaddamah," 37–40.
207. Ms. Bodleian Elliot 314, fol. 422a.
208. Ibid., fols. 458b–59a.
209. See Ṭāhir Muḥammad's table of contents ibid., fols. 12b–13a.
210. E.g., see the beginning of the three major sections: ibid., fols. 388a, 422a, and 459a.
211. Ibid., fols. 387b.
212. *Muntakhab al-Tavārīkh*, 2:366.
213. Ibid.
214. E.g., see the section on "Reproaching the Envious" (Dar Maẕammat-i Ḥussād) in Masīḥ Pānīpatī's *Rāmāyan-i Masīḥī* (24–27).
215. Alam and Subrahmanyam note the diverse locations of manuscripts of the *Rawẕat al-Ṭāhirīn*, including a copy at the Asiatic Society of Bengal that may have belonged to Tipu Sultan of Mysore (*Writing the Mughal World*, 98).
216. E.g., after briefly noting a series of unnamed sovereigns, the *Tārīkh-i Rājhā-yi Dilhī* (dated 1657) begins with the reign of Yudhishthira (ms. Gujarat Vidya Sabha 46, fol. 2b), and Banvālī Dās does likewise in his *Rājāvalī* (ms. Hyderabad Salar Jung Tarikh 244, fol. 10a). Curiously, one author combines excerpts from the summary of the *Mahābhārata* given in Abū al-Faẕl's preface with an account of Indo-Islamic kings, which is altogether appended to a copy of Giridhardās's *Rāmāyan* (ms. BNF Supplément Persan 18, fols. 231–52).
217. E.g., Firishtah's *Tārīkh-i Firishtah*, ʿAbd al-Raḥmān Chishtī's *Mir'āt al-Makhlūqāt* (Alam, "Mughal Sufi Story of Creation"), and Sujān Rāī Bhandārī's *Khulāṣat al-Tavārīkh* (Alam and Subrahmanyam, "Witnesses and Agents of Empire," 403–4). Also the anonymous *Bahāristān-i Shāhī* written in the early seventeenth century

begins with an account of pre-Muslim kings drawn from the *Rājataraṅgiṇī*s (I am indebted to Dean Accardi for this information). Other Persian histories of Kashmir continued to propagate Sanskrit-derived information well into the nineteenth century (Zutshi, "Translating the Past," 10).

218. Independent manuscript copies of Ṭāhir Muḥammad's *Mahābhārat* include Aligarh Muslim University, Sir Suleman Collection 15/2(b) and British Library, IO Islamic 753. There is also a copy in a private collection in Pune (Chaghatai, "Illustrated Edition of the Razm Nama," 323, no. 41). Ms. British Library, Or. 2016 contains, in order, *ʿIyār-i Dānish*, Ṭāhir Muḥammad's *Mahābhārat*, and a Persian translation of the *Prabodhacandrodaya*.
219. "Muqaddamah," 18.
220. Pollock, *Language of the Gods*, 223–37.
221. Ricci, *Islam Translated*, 65.
222. *Promise of the Foreign*, 15
223. Early illuminated copies of the *Razmnāmah* include the master imperial copy in Jaipur, the 1598–1599 copy (five books are ms. British Library, Persian Or. 12076 and the rest are dispersed), the dispersed ca. 1600 manuscript (on this work, see Seyller, "Model and Copy," 65n3), the Birla *Razmnāmah* (dated 1605), and the dispersed 1616–1617 *Razmnāmah* (for a reconstruction of the paintings, see Seyller, "Model and Copy," appendix B, 62–65).
224. Several more simply and sparsely illustrated later manuscripts of the *Razmnāmah* (largely nineteenth century) are extant in the Srinagar Oriental Research Library, Asiatic Society of Mumbai, Delhi National Archives, and Delhi National Museum.
225. See ms. British Library, Persian Add. 5641, fols. 7b–14b; ms. British Library, IO Islamic 2517, fols. 1b–8b. The table of contents is dated 1686–1687 (1688 in ms. British Library, IO Islamic 2517) and does not include the *Harivaṃśa*.

4. ABŪ AL-FAẔL REDEFINES INDO-PERSIAN KNOWLEDGE AND AKBAR'S SOVEREIGNTY

1. On the unity of the *Āʾīn-i Akbarī* and the *Akbarnāmah*, see Hardy, "Perfect Padshah," 114.
2. Most obviously, Moosvi relies extensively on the *Āʾīn-i Akbarī* in her *Economy of the Mughal Empire*. In addition to the issue of mining texts for data, scholars have convincingly criticized Moosvi's overuse of the *Āʾīn-i Akbarī* and pointed out that this concern preceded the publication of her *Economy of the Mughal Empire* by a decade (Subrahmanyam, "Review of *The Economy of the Mughal Empire*," 104).
3. *Religious and Intellectual History* (Rizvi also has several later articles on Abū al-Faẕl and his formulation of Akbar's political agendas). Other authors have also fruitfully explored Abū al-Faẕl's imperial contributions: e.g., Hardy, "Perfect Padshah"; Mukhia, *Historians and Historiography*, 58–88; Nizami, *History and Historians*, 141–60; O'Hanlon, "Kingdom, Household and Body"; Richards, "Formulation of Imperial Authority." More recently, Alam discusses Abū al-Faẕl at various places in his *Languages of Political Islam*.
4. E.g., M. Athar Ali, "Evolution of the Perception of India"; M. S. Khan, "Al-Bīrūnī and Abul Fazl."
5. In 1800, Francis Gladwin published a translation of the *Āʾīn-i Akbarī* (titled *Ayeen Akbery*). In the late nineteenth century, Henry Blochmann translated the first two

books of the *Āʾīn-i Akbarī* and H. S. Jarrett the final three (available online at http://persian.packhum.org/persian/). D.C. Phillott revised Blochmann's work, and Jadunath Sarkar reworked Jarrett's text.

6. Blochmann and Jarrett use "Hindu" to translate several Persian words, including *hind*, *hindī*, and *hindī-nizhād*. They even occasionally insert the word "Hindu" when there is no equivalent term in the Persian text.
7. Recent examples of citing translations instead of Persian texts, particularly for the Mughal period, include Asher and Talbot's *India Before Europe* (2006) and Richards's *Mughal Empire* (1993). The *Āʾīn-i Akbarī* is available in several Persian printed editions, and the Persian text of two versions of the *Account of India* are out of copyright and available online. Here I cite the Calcutta edition unless otherwise noted.
8. On court conflicts during the 1570s–1580s, see chapter 3. Abū al-Faẓl began the *Akbarnāmah* in 1589 and completed it in 1598.
9. E.g., see Moin's analysis of Akbar as a "saint king" (*Millennial Sovereign*, 138–46).
10. I draw here on the work of O'Hanlon, who discusses the Mughal political philosophy of different spheres all revolving around Akbar in her analysis of *akhlāq* texts ("Kingdom, Household and Body," particularly 892–93).
11. For a more elaborate description of books 1–3, see Blake, "Patrimonial-Bureaucratic Empire," 82–90.
12. Abū al-Faẓl also includes a few shorter references to Sanskrit knowledge earlier in his *Āʾīn-i Akbarī* (e.g., his mention in book 2 of four genres of Sanskrit works that students should study, 1:202).
13. ʿArīf Qandahārī praises Akbar for supporting the construction of mosques, sponsoring *hajj* groups, and sending money to Mecca and Medina. But he rarely mentions the induction of Rajputs into the imperial nobility and omits altogether Akbar's strategic marriages to Indian women. See, respectively, Pirbhai, *Reconsidering Islam*, 71–72; Faruqui, *Princes of the Mughal Empire*, 141.
14. Moin, *Millennial Sovereign*, 133–34.
15. Meisami, "History as Literature," 15–16.
16. On Abū al-Faẓl's praise of Akbar as God-like, see Hardy, "Perfect Padshah," 114–18, and Blake, "Patrimonial-Bureaucratic Empire," 82–83.
17. *Āʾīn-i Akbarī*, 1:1. Throughout his *Akbarnāmah*, Abū al-Faẓl develops the argument that he honors God by praising Akbar. Hardy discusses some of the theological and political implications of this logic in "Perfect Padshah," 114–16.
18. *Āʾīn-i Akbarī*, 1:1.
19. Ibid., 1:2.
20. Hardy, "Perfect Padshah," 130–31.
21. E.g., Ahmed, "Long Thirteenth Century of the *Chachnama*," 462–64; Pasha M. Khan, "Marvellous Histories," 528–29; Moin, "Peering through the Cracks," 497–98.
22. Rao, Shulman, and Subrahmanyam, *Textures of Time*, 4–5.
23. Many scholars have convincingly criticized the theoretical framework of *Textures of Time*. E.g., Pollock, "Pretextures of Time"; Guha, "Speaking Historically," 1090–91.
24. *Āʾīn-i Akbarī*, 2:245.
25. *Languages of Political Islam*, 46–80. Other scholars have also drawn attention to Abū al-Faẓl's use of the *Nasirean Ethics* (Rizvi, *Religious and Intellectual History*, chapter 9; O'Hanlon, "Kingdom, Household and Body").
26. O'Hanlon, "Kingdom, Household and Body."

27. Sunil Sharma, *Amir Khusraw*, 87.
28. Busch, "Poetry in Motion," 204.
29. Dale, *Garden of the Eight Paradises*, 43.
30. On Islamicate texts that predate al-Bīrūnī and address Indian religious beliefs, see Habibullah, "Early Arab Report on Indian Religious Sects." Al-Bīrūnī also authored an Arabic translation of the *Yogasūtras*. On this work, see the series of four articles of the 1960s–1980s by Shlomo Pines and Tuvia Gelblum in the *Bulletin of the School of Oriental and African Studies* (all are titled "Al-Bīrūnī's Arabic Version of Patañjali's *Yogasūtra*"). On the relationship of al-Bīrūnī's *Yogasūtras* and his *India*, see Lawrence, "Use of Hindu Religious Texts."
31. Scholars have long posited a connection between al-Bīrūnī and Abū al-Faẓl (e.g., Jarrett, preface to the *Āʾīn-i Akbarī* [English translation], 3:8–9; Khan, "Al-Bīrūnī and Abul Fazl," 42–43).
32. Halbfass discusses some of the major features of al-Bīrūnī's *India* (*India and Europe*, 25–28). Also see Ernst, "Muslim Studies of Hinduism?" 176–78, and Lawrence, "Use of Hindu Religious Texts."
33. Al-Bīrūnī wrote under the larger auspices of the Ghaznavid court, but we lack evidence of direct patronage for his *India* (Halbfass, *India and Europe*, 25).
34. Abū al-Faẓl names the following core texts of Sanskrit astronomy, of which he attributes the first four to divine origin and the latter five to earthly authorship (I have reconstructed the Sanskrit titles): *Brahmasiddhānta*, *Sūryasiddhānta*, *Somasiddhānta*, *Bṛhaspatisiddhānta*, *Gargasiddhānta*, *Nāradasiddhānta*, *Parāśarasiddhānta*, *Pauliśasiddhānta*, and *Vāsiṣṭhasiddhānta* (*Āʾīn-i Akbarī*, 1:267–68).
35. Ibid., 1:268.
36. Chase Robinson, *Islamic Historiography*, 15–17.
37. Ernst, "Sufism and Yoga," 11.
38. *Āʾīn-i Akbarī*, 1:269.
39. Ms. Staatsbibliothek zu Berlin, Preußischer Kulturbesitz, no. 117, fol. 25a. Also see Beach's discussion of this image in "Mughal Painter Kesu Dās," 49.
40. Ms. British Library, Persian Or. 1251, fol. 242a. Also see my discussion in chapter 6 about how to resolve the slight discrepancy between the two dates.
41. Sreeramula Rajeswara Sarma, "Jyotiṣarāja at the Mughal Court," 369–70. Excerpts printed in Bendrey, *Tārīkh-i Ilāhī*, appendixes A and B.
42. *Āʾīn-i Akbarī*, 1:388.
43. Ibid., 1:389. Stainton notes the popularity of *stotras* to the Ganges, including in the early modern period ("Stotras").
44. *Āʾīn-i Akbarī*, 1:515–17.
45. Ibid., 1:423.
46. Ibid., 1:538. Versions of this story are found in many Sanskrit texts. Typically Sati throws herself into the sacrificial fire and then her body falls apart as Shiva carries it across the subcontinent in mourning (Eck, *India*, 287–92). In some versions, Vishnu dismembers Sati's body (Doniger, *Hindus*, 415–16).
47. *Āʾīn-i Akbarī*, 1:538.
48. Ibid., 1:574–78 (he mentions the *Rājataraṅgiṇī* on 1:578). As I note in chapter 3, Abū al-Faẓl depicts the *Rājataraṅgiṇī* here as a single text, although Akbar's translators appear to have rendered a combination of the works of Kalhaṇa, Jonarāja, and Śrīvara into Persian.

49. *Āʾīn-i Akbarī*, 1:583. For Sanskrit works that discuss Akbar's cancellation of the jizya and other taxes and bans on harming animals, see chapter 1.
50. Ibid., 1:584.
51. Ibid. Earlier in the *Āʾīn-i Akbarī* Abū al-Faẓl underscores that Akbar ordered translations from multiple languages (1:115).
52. Ibid., 2:1; read *guzārī* with the Aligarh edition of the *Āʾīn-i Akbarī* (360).
53. On these works, see, respectively, Jackson, "Banākatī," and Subtelny and Melville, "Ḥâfeẓ-e Abru."
54. Rizvi, *Religious and Intellectual History*, 204n1, on Ḥāfiẓ-i Abrū. Jahn notes the similarity of the sections on Buddhism in all three texts (*Rashīd al-Dīn's History of India*, lxxvii).
55. Halbfass discusses a few examples in *India and Europe*, 28–30. Also, see Lawrence, *Shahrastānī on the Indian Religions*, 17–29.
56. E.g., writing in the Deccan around 1600, Firishtah uses Banākatī in part of his section on pre-Islamic India (Alam and Subrahmanyam, "Witnesses and Agents of Empire," 403n11).
57. *Āʾīn-i Akbarī*, 2:2.
58. Scholars have suggested specific sources for parts of the *Āʾīn-i Akbarī*, generally inconclusively. E.g., Rizvi posits Mādhava's *Sarvadarśanasaṅgraha* as a potential basis (*Religious and Intellectual History*, 273). Mukhia sees the *Manusmṛti* reflected in a few passages (*Historians and Historiography*, 68). Halbfass notes that Abū al-Faẓl's list of eighteen *vidyās* follows the pattern of Madhusūdana Sarasvatī's *Prasthānabheda* (*India and Europe*, 33).
59. E.g., *Āʾīn-i Akbarī*, 2:115–17. Most of these Sanskrit texts were not translated into Persian, at least so far as we know. Abū al-Faẓl is likely cataloging relevant works rather than listing specific sources here.
60. Ibid., 2:61. Compare with al-Bīrūnī's comments (*Alberuni's India*, 1:171).
61. Respectively, Pollock, "New Intellectuals," 20, and *Bhānucandragaṇicarita* 2.58–60. It is unclear whether Siddhicandra intends to refer to Haribhadra's *Ṣaḍdarśanasamuccaya* or Rājaśekhara's later work of the same name. In any case, the two share certain portions of text (Folkert, *Scripture and Community*, 359–60).
62. See chapter 3.
63. *Āʾīn-i Akbarī*, 2:1–2.
64. No doubt many definitions of tolerance are at work in modernity, but noninterference is generally a crucial component (e.g., see Talal Asad's analysis in *Formations of the Secular*).
65. I elaborate on the idea that enlightened men ought to criticize some of their own precepts and adopt superior positions in my analysis of Abū al-Faẓl's preface to the *Razmnāmah* in chapter 3. For an overview of *ṣulḥ-i kull* as invoked in Akbar's political philosophy, see Rizvi, "Dimensions of *Ṣulḥ-i Kul*."
66. E.g., Rizvi, "Dimensions of *Ṣulḥ-i Kul*."
67. *Āʾīn-i Akbarī*, 2:111.
68. Firoze, "Abul Fazl's Account of Hindu Mythology," 114–15.
69. *Āʾīn-i Akbarī*, 2:2–4.
70. Ibid., 2:2. The *Āʾīn-i Akbarī*'s later section on Buzurjmihr is 2:201.
71. Shamma, "Translating into the Empire," 74–75.
72. *Āʾīn-i Akbarī*, 2:5.

73. Ibid.
74. As I discuss in chapters 1 and 5, Mughal elites were generally willing to tolerate theological diversity but only within a spectrum of monotheistic religions. Jains incurred serious questioning regarding their theological precepts on several occasions before Akbar and avoided severing their imperial ties by professing unwavering commitment to monotheism. Jahangir likewise probed Brahmans about whether they professed belief in a single, supreme deity.
75. *Āʾīn-i Akbarī*, 2:5.
76. Later Mughal thinkers, such as Dara Shikuh, drew a clear distinction between a small group of sophisticated monotheist Hindus and the unwashed masses of infidels (Gandhi, "Mughal Engagements with Vedānta," 70–71).
77. *Āʾīn-i Akbarī*, 2:6.
78. Ibid.
79. E.g., Firoze, "Abul Fazl's Account of Hindu Mythology," 113–14.
80. *Āʾīn-i Akbarī*, 2:61.
81. Ibid., 2:113.
82. Ibid., 2:114.
83. The *nyāya* section is nearly as long as the Jainism account, but *nyāya* also covers much of the *vaiśeṣika* perspective ([*bayshīkhik*] *bā nukhustīn* [*nyāy*] *yiktāʾī dārad*, ibid., 2:76).
84. Ibid., 2:62. The *ṣaḍdarśana* (six schools) given are *nyāya*, *vaiśeṣika*, *mīmāṃsā*, *vedānta*, *saṅkhyā*, and *pātañjala*.
85. For Gautama, see ibid. and, for Kapila, 2:84.
86. Ibid., 2:76.
87. Ibid., 2:78.
88. Ibid., 2:111.
89. Ibid., 2:110. Akbar's court was not familiar with Digambara monks, although they may very well have met members of the Digambara laity given the prevalence of this community in Agra from the late sixteenth to mid-seventeenth centuries (Cort, "Tale of Two Cities," 40–50).
90. E.g., see the discussion of the names of the four overarching castes (*Āʾīn-i Akbarī*, 2:54). Nonetheless, like nearly all Mughal intellectuals, Abū al-Faẕl spells Sanskrit terms in ways that reflect vernacular pronunciation to some degree.
91. Jarrett frequently adds his own glosses of Sanskrit terms in his translation, which obscures the original effect in Persian but has the virtue of making the text intelligible to non-Sanskritists. Contrast Abū al-Faẕl's approach with that of Dara Shikuh's *Sirr-i Akbar*, which contains a glossary (Mahesh Prasad, "Upanishads by Prince Dara Shikoh," 628–29).
92. *Āʾīn-i Akbarī*, 2:78–79. I have reconstructed the Sanskrit terms here.
93. Ibid., 2:77. The Aligarh edition omits this particular spelling (447).
94. Ibid., 2:117–19. Jarrett's translation somewhat misleadingly publishes the Sanskrit letters here in Devanagari. In the original, e.g., the Sanskrit vowels *a* and *ā* read *a hamzah-yi maftūḥ* and *ā hamzah-yi maftūḥ va alif.*
95. I am grateful to Fabrizio Speziale for this point.
96. On the popularity of *nāyikā-bheda* in Sanskrit, see Pollock, introduction to *Bouquet of Rasa*, xxxiii–xxxv and on its elaboration in Braj Bhasha, see Busch, *Poetry of Kings*, 79–87.

97. *Āʾīn-i Akbarī*, 2:131.
98. Scholars have identified several direct quotations from Bhānudatta's *Rasamañjarī* in Abū al-Faẓl's account of *sāhitya* (Pollock, introduction to *Bouquet of Rasa*, xix and xl–xli, n. 1).
99. Compare *Āʾīn-i Akbarī*, 2:130, and *Sāhityadarpaṇa*, 64–69. Jarrett recognized Abū al-Faẓl's use of Viśvanātha in his translation of the *Āʾīn-i Akbarī*, 3:255n2.
100. *Bouquet of Rasa*, p. 39, v. 40 (Pollock's translation).
101. *Āʾīn-i Akbarī*, 2:132.
102. Quoted in Sunil Sharma, "Translating Gender," 98; my translation is indebted to Sharma's rendering of these lines.
103. *Bouquet of Rasa*, pp. 24–25, v. 22 (Pollock's translation).
104. *Āʾīn-i Akbarī*, 2:132.
105. Ibid., 2:134.
106. "Hidden in Plain View," 284. Bilingual Hindi-Persian texts from shortly after Abū al-Faẓl's time further confirm that Persianate readers were interested in Hindi poetry and aesthetics (Phukan, "Ecology of Hindi," 38–43).
107. On the *Rasikpriyā*, see Busch, *Poetry of Kings*, 32–40 and 109–16.
108. *Dabistān-i Maẕāhib*, 1:121–212. On this work, see Behl, "Pages from the Book of Religions."
109. On the contents of the *Tuḥfat al-Hind*, see Ziauddin, *Grammar of the Braj Bhakha*, 13–32.
110. Busch, "Poetry in Motion," 209–10.
111. *Āʾīn-i Akbarī*, 2:193.
112. E.g., he specifically mentions that Sanskrit texts (*hindī nām-hā*) do not refer to Adam (ibid.).
113. Ibid., 2:207.
114. Ibid., 2:223–25.
115. Ibid., 2:207.
116. On different formulations of Khizr's relationship with Alexander, see Wensinck, "Al-Khaḍir."
117. *Culture and Imperialism*, 100.
118. E.g., Appadurai, "Number in the Colonial Imagination"; Cohn, *Colonialism*, 16–56.
119. Sharma, "Translating Gender," 98–100; Ernst, "Āzād Bilgrāmī's Depiction of *Nāyikas*," 39.
120. Juan Cole estimates that India housed seven times more people literate in Persian than Iran in 1700 ("Iranian Culture and South Asia," 18). The ratio was likely lower ca. 1600 but still skewed heavily in India's favor.

5. WRITING ABOUT THE MUGHAL WORLD IN SANSKRIT

1. The *Jagadgurukāvya* and the *Hīrasaubhāgya* eulogize Hīravijaya (d. 1596). The *Vijayapraśastimahākāvya* details the life of Vijayasena (d. 1615). The *Vijayadevamāhātmya* is devoted to Vijayadeva (d. 1656–1657).
2. Siddhicandra's *Bhānucandragaṇicarita*.
3. Jayasoma's *Mantrikarmacandravaṃśāvalīprabandha*.
4. Kharataras authored the *Mantrikarmacandravaṃśāvalīprabandha* and the *Vijayadevamāhātmya* (even though the latter details the life of a Tapa Gaccha figure),

and Tapa Gaccha affiliates wrote the remaining four texts. Paul Dundas dispels the surprisingly resilient myth that the *Hīrasaubhāgya* was intended for consumption at the Mughal court (*History, Scripture and Controversy*, 60–61).

5. The genre of *prabandhas* is fairly malleable and has been defined in different ways by scholars. E.g., Granoff divides sectarian (*paṭṭāvalī*, *gurvāvalī*) and nonsectarian (*prabandha*) biographies rather strictly ("Biographies of Siddhasena," 331). Many of the *prabandhas* I discuss here are indeed sectarian.
6. E.g., Meghavijaya's (ca. 1653–1704) *Devānandamahākāvya* and *Digvijayamahākāvya* (pp. 30–31 on the Mughals).
7. Chattopadhyaya outlines the favored approaches for representing Islam and Islamic figures in Sanskrit (*Representing the Other?*). Also see my discussion in chapter 2.
8. Quoted in Granoff, "Jinaprabhasūri and Jinadattasūri," 36 (her translation).
9. *Cultures of History*, 8.
10. E.g., Pollock proposes Persianate influences in the poetry of Jagannātha Paṇḍitarāja ("Death of Sanskrit," 408–12), and Bronner and Tubb submit that awareness of Persian may also have informed Jagannātha's poetic theory ("Blaming the Messenger," 87). Minkowski suggests that Persian writing partly inspired the practice of bidirectional Sanskrit poetry ("On Sūryadāsa").
11. Sumit Guha has recently pointed out the importance of forgetting in Maratha history ("Frontiers of Memory"). Speaking in the modern context of nationhood, Ernest Renan emphasized forgetting in attempts to assimilate people into a shared community ("What Is a Nation?" 11).
12. The Sanskrit translation of the *Akbarnāmah* has been edited and printed by Subhadra Jha under the title *Sarvadeśavṛttāntasaṅgraha*. The edition is based on two manuscripts: one in the British Library (Sans. 2775) and a recent copy of a lost manuscript in Calcutta (on both manuscripts, see Jha's introduction to the *Sarvadeśavṛttāntasaṅgraha*, ii–viii).
13. E.g., cf. *Bhānucandragaṇicarita* 1.111.
14. *saphārākurānapramukhāṇi tāny evāmbudhir bahutvāt samudras . . .* (*Hīrasaubhāgya*, comm. on 13.120). I am reading *saphārā* as *tafsīr*. Although this may be a stretch, Devavimala intends to refer to some set of Islamic religious texts here.
15. *niḥśeṣaśāstropaniṣady adhītī* (ibid.), glossed in the commentary as *niḥśeṣāṇāṃ sarveṣāṃ śāstrāṇām kurānādiyavanāgamānām upaniṣadi rahasye adhītam adhyayanam asyāstīti*.
16. *hiṃsādaye nirdiśatī virodhidharme mithaḥ svīyatadīyaśāstre* (ibid.). *Svīyatadīyaśāstre* is glossed in the commentary as *yavanajātisaṃbandhi* and *sūriśāsanasaṃbandhi*. Abū al-Faẕl is described as *vineyāyitavṛtti* (13.136). The mention of Islam promoting violence likely refers to Muslims being meat eaters, whereas Jains are vegetarians as part of a larger commitment to avoid harming all life forms.
17. *Hīrasaubhāgya* 13.137–43. Dundas translates the same passage in "Jain Perceptions of Islam," 38. This passage is also found in Devavimala's *Hīrasundaramahākāvya*, a shortened and likely earlier version of the *Hīrasaubhāgya* with the variant reading *avabodha* instead of *anurodha* in the third verse (*Hīrasundaramahākāvya* 13.136–42; on this text, see Dundas, *History, Scripture and Controversy*, 59).
18. E.g., Madhusūdana's *Prasthānabheda*, a catalog of numerous religious and philosophical perspectives, does not mention Islam (Nicholson, *Unifying Hinduism*, 190).

19. *ayaṃ nijaḥ paro veti gaṇanā laghucetasām / udāracaritānāṃ tu vasudhaiva kuṭumbakaṃ //* (*Hīrasaubhāgya*, p. 619, comm. on v. 139).
20. Hatcher discusses the provenance of this verse and its modern resonances in "Problematic Mantra of Hindu Humanism."
21. *Hīrasaubhāgya*, p. 620, comm. on v. 142. Raghavan establishes this date for the *Vidagdhamukhamaṇḍana* based on citations in Bhoja's *Śṛṅgāraprakāśa* ("Vidagdhamukhamaṇḍana of Dharmadāsa").
22. *Hīrasaubhāgya* 13.145–50 (also see *Hīrasundaramahākāvya* 13.144–49).
23. Dundas, *Jains*, 90; also see Guṇaratna's elaborate arguments on vv. 45–46 of Haribhadra's *Ṣaḍdarśanasamuccaya*, pp. 112–36.
24. *Hīrasaubhāgya*, p. 621, comm. on v. 145.
25. Ibid. 13.151 and commentary. For a full translation of the passage, see Dundas, "Jain Perceptions of Islam," 39.
26. Granoff, "Authority and Innovation," 53–55.
27. Padmasāgara's *Jagadgurukāvya* (vv. 122–89), Devavimala's *Hīrasaubhāgya* (*sargas* 10–14), Hemavijaya's *Vijayapraśastimahākāvya* (chapter 9), and Siddhicandra's *Bhānucandragaṇicarita* (1.78–128). The Adishvara inscription also relays this initial meeting between Hīravijaya and Akbar, although in less detail (*Epigraphia Indica*, 2, no. 12).
28. Dundas, "Jain Perceptions of Islam," 41.
29. *Unifying Hinduism*, 196.
30. See Mughal criticisms of atheism in the *Āʾīn-i Akbarī* (2:113–14). The *Majālis-i Jahāngīrī* records the imprisonment of Naqīb Khān's son (Alam and Subrahmanyam, "Frank Disputations," 488).
31. Siddhicandra's *Bhānucandragaṇicarita* is undated but ends in the mid-1610s. Hemavijaya completed sixteen chapters of his twenty-one-chapter work in the early seventeenth century; Guṇavijaya wrote the remaining five chapters in addition to a full commentary, which he completed in 1632 (introduction to the *Vijayapraśastimahākāvya*, 2–3).
32. *Vijayapraśastimahākāvya* 12.142–45; *darśana*, here translated as "sight," is likely a *śleṣa*, also meaning Jain philosophy.
33. Ibid. 12.148–49.
34. Ibid. 12.178.
35. E.g., Haribhadra's *Ṣaḍdarśanasamuccaya* vv. 45–46 (the Jain *devatā* is *jinendra*); Merutuṅga's *Ṣaḍdarśananirṇaya*, p. 7 (the Jain *deva* is *jina*). On Haribhadra's use of the term *devatā*, see Nicholson, *Unifying Hinduism*, 157–58.
36. Nicholson discusses different understandings of the *āstika-nāstika* distinction in Indian intellectual history ("Doxography and Boundary-Formation"). On Jain uses of this dichotomy, he notes that Maṇibhadra, a commentator on Haribhadra's *Ṣaḍdarśanasamuccaya*, defines *āstika* as those who affirm "the existence of another world (*para-loka*), transmigration (*gati*), virtue (*puṇya*), and vice (*pāpa*)" (108). For Haribhadra's description of the Lokāyatas, a *nāstika* school, see his *Ṣaḍdarśanasamuccaya* vv. 80–87.
37. Akbar's court had ties with Vaishnava communities dating back to the 1560s and even issued *farmāns* related to temple land grants for Chaitanya communities (Mukherjee and Habib, "Akbar and the Temples of Mathura," 235–36).

38. Compare Hemavijaya's verse to a similar approach used by Samayasundara in his *Artharatnāvalī* (*The String of Jewels of Meaning*), where he interprets a single sentence to have many meanings, the final of which praises Akbar (*Artharatnāvalī*, 65–66).
39. *Vijayapraśastimahākāvya* 12.174a.
40. Ibid. 12.211.
41. See Phillip Wagoner's discussion of "essential ambiguities" and "fortuitous convergences" that had long characterized cross-cultural relations in India and beyond ("Fortuitous Convergences and Essential Ambiguities").
42. *Jahāngīrnāmah*, 19.
43. *Vijayapraśastimahākāvya* 12.180–210.
44. Ibid. 12.186–87. Compare with the *samavasaraṇa* imagery described in the *Āvaśyakaniryukti* (cited in Dundas, *Jains*, 35).
45. Compare *Vijayapraśastimahākāvya* 12.182–83 and *Āʾīn-i Akbarī*, 2:108.
46. *Āʾīn-i Akbarī*, 2:99.
47. *Vijayapraśastimahākāvya* 12.212.
48. Ibid. 12.216.
49. Ibid. 12.219–20.
50. *Bhānucandragaṇicarita* 4.20; the full debate is 4.19–47. Ramdas Kachhwaha is here called Rāmadāsa Mahārāja. For more details on Ramdas Kachhwaha's relationship to the Mughal court, see Desai, "Introduction," 39n54, and *Maʾāṣir al-Umarā*, 2:155–57. He also appears later in the *Bhānucandragaṇicarita* as serving Jahangir (4.218).
51. Ramdas Kachhwaha was involved with procuring imperial orders (*farmāns*) to give tax-free lands to Vaishnava temples (Chatterjee, "Cultural Flows," 155). Mukherjee and Habib note mentions of Ramdas Kachhwaha in several such *farmāns* ("Akbar and the Temples of Mathura," 240–41).
52. Writing in 1652, Vallabha Pāṭhaka also contextualizes this debate in terms of Jain-Brahmanical disputes and characterizes Akbar as asking Vijayasena, "Why do you not believe in Rama and mother Ganga?" (*Vijayadevamāhātmya* 6.28a).
53. I am grateful to Daniele Cuneo for this suggestion. Note that Siddhicandra avoids Perso-Arabic vocabulary throughout his *Bhānucandragaṇicarita*. Thus it is unsurprising that he declined to employ a less ambiguous phrase here, such as *ahl-i kitāb*. The use of "Veda" to refer to the scriptures of people of the book is also attested in a seventeenth-century Tamil text (Narayanan, "Religious Vocabulary and Regional Identity," 80–81).
54. *Bhānucandragaṇicarita* 4.23b.
55. Ibid. 1.68–71.
56. Ibid. 4.35. Note the similarity of some arguments here to Kumārila's *Ślokavārttika*.
57. Also see *Bhānucandragaṇicarita* 4.37 ("all beings are creators," *sarvabhāveṣu kartṛtvam*).
58. Ibid. 4.39–41.
59. Ibid. 4.42.
60. Ibid. 4.43–47.
61. See Granoff, "Jinaprabhasūri and Jinadattasūri."
62. At the end of the fifteenth century, the Tapa Gaccha numbered 428 members (Darśanavijaya, quoted in Flügel, "Demographic Trends," 317).
63. Jain thinkers also pursued other options, such as arguing for the Tapa Gaccha's authority in relation to other Jain sects on detailed theological grounds (Dundas, *History, Scripture and Controversy*, chapter 4).

64. Cort, "Genres of Jain History," 487–88.
65. *Jagadgurukāvya* vv. 138–39. Other Jain texts describe Hīravijaya as "like an image of God" but use the Sanskrit term *parameśvara* (e.g., *Hīrasaubhāgya* 13.125a).
66. *Ẓill-i allāh* or *ẓill-i khudā* was a common epithet for Persianate kings, and the phrase comes up several times in Abū al-Faẓl's writings, including in his recorded sayings of Akbar in the *Āʾīn-i Akbarī*.
67. *Jagadgurukāvya* v. 174.
68. Ibid. v. 189.
69. Ibid. v. 191.
70. *History, Scripture and Controversy*, 188–89n29.
71. *Hīrasaubhāgya* 17.90.
72. Dundas, *History, Scripture and Controversy*, 24. Also see *Digvijayamahākāvya*.
73. Sheikh, *Forging a Region*, 162–64.
74. E.g., on rejecting money: *Jagadgurukāvya* vv. 175–76. On the perils of carpets: *Hīrasaubhāgya* 14.6–7 and *Jagadgurukāvya* vv. 169–70.
75. *Bhānucandragaṇicarita* 4.90. Siddhicandra also refers to his Persian skills in his commentary on the *Kādambarī*, p. 483, v. 5 of *ṭīkā*. Moreover, he attests that he was employed by Akbar to read Persian books to the royal princes and even the king himself on a daily basis (*Bhānucandragaṇicarita* 4.104). Siddhicandra's teacher, Bhānucandra, also lauds his pupil as famous for knowing all virtuous Persian books (*Vasantarājaśākuna*, p. 1, v. 9 of *ṭīkā*).
76. *Bhānucandragaṇicarita* 4.238–39.
77. Ibid. 4.247–48.
78. Despite Siddhicandra's exaggerations, Kharatara inscriptions and texts about interceding in the aftermath of this event confirm that the argument and exile (see later in this chapter) actually occurred (Azad, *Religion and Politics in India*, 119). Later vernacular texts also corroborate the episode (Desai, "Introduction," 57n88).
79. *Bhānucandragaṇicarita* 4.269.
80. Rūmī famously relays this tale in his *Maṡnavī*. Oddly, Niccolao Manucci, a traveler to India during Shah Jahan's reign, seems to have picked up a quite different version of this tale (*Storia do Mogor*, 2:469–70).
81. *Bhānucandragaṇicarita* 4.271.
82. Ibid. 4.275–79.
83. Ibid. 4.280–83.
84. Ibid. 4.289.
85. . . . *arhanmatajñena śāhinā* (ibid. 4.306).
86. Ibid. 4.301–5. In 4.304a, read *syādvāda eva sarvatra*.
87. See ibid. 4.311, on *syādvāda* in particular and 4.307–13 for Siddhicandra's full response.
88. Ibid. 4.316–17a.
89. Ibid. 4.326.
90. Here I summarize ibid. 4.317b–33.
91. Ibid. 4.334.
92. Ibid. 4.313b.
93. Here Siddhicandra likely refers to the imperial order that Jahangir issued in 1616 promising Jains freedom to travel and worship (the *farmān* is reproduced and

translated in Commissariat, "Imperial Mughal Farmans in Gujarat," plate 1 and pp. 26–27).

94. *Bhānucandragaṇicarita* 4.352–53.
95. *Jahāngīrnāmah*, 250.
96. E.g., see Sheldon Pollock's analysis in *Language of the Gods*, particularly chapters 1, 3, and 6.
97. Granoff, "Visible and Invisible Sacred Realms," 147.
98. Balbir, "Mount Śatruñjaya."
99. Granoff, "Mountains of Eternity," 44–45.
100. The Adishvara inscription is printed in *Epigraphia Indica*, 2:50–59.
101. Ibid., 2:52–55, vv. 14–34. Vv. 1–34 are translated by A. B. Orlebar in Jacob, "Inscriptions from Palitana," 59–63. Also see the brief discussion of this passage in Vincent Smith, "Jain Teachers of Akbar," 272–73.
102. *Epigraphia Indica*, 2:52–53, vv. 17–21.
103. Ibid., 2:59–60, lines 2–4. Jains also frequently enumerated the benefits gained from their imperial alliances in written texts, such as Śānticandra in the conclusion of his Sanskrit work on compassion written for Akbar (*Kṛpārasakośa* vv. 126–27).
104. E.g., *Epigraphia Indica*, 2:52, v. 17; *Kṛpārasakośa* v. 125; *Kalpapradīpikā* of Saṅghavijaya, as quoted in *Catalogue of the Sanskrit Manuscripts in the Library of the India Office*, vol. 2, part 2, p. 1257, no. 7474.
105. *Epigraphia Indica*, 2:53, vv. 19–21 and 18, respectively.
106. Ibid., 2:53, v. 22. Also see the similar comparison in Hemavijaya's *Vijayapraśastimahākāvya* 9.55.
107. *Epigraphia Indica*, 2:53, v. 21a.
108. Devavimala tells the story at some length of how Akbar wished to grant Hīravijaya the books that had been left at court by Padmasundara. Hīravijaya initially refused the king's offer owing to his eradication of any material desires but was eventually persuaded by the joint effort of Abū al-Faẓl and Thānasiṃha (also known as Sthānasiṃha). Hīravijaya then established a Jain library with Thānasiṃha as its head (*Hīrasaubhāgya* 14.93–128). Also see the brief narration of this episode by Vidyavijayji, who uses vernacular sources (*Monk and a Monarch*, 36).
109. *Epigraphia Indica*, 2:59, line 2.
110. Ibid., 2:54, v. 29, reading the suggested alternative of *pratyakṣa* (n. 10).
111. Ibid., 2:54–55, vv. 31–32.
112. Ibid., 2:55, v. 34.
113. Printed and discussed ibid., 1:319–24.
114. Ibid., 1:324, lines 33–35. These *farmān*s are confirmed by Jayasoma (although the precise terms of prohibiting animal slaughter are different) in *Mantrikarmacandravaṃśāvalīprabandha* vv. 446–47.
115. *Epigraphia Indica*, 1:324, lines 25–26.
116. *suratāṇanūradījahāṅgīrasavāīvijayirājye* (ibid., 2:60–67, nos. 15, 17, 18, 19, 20, 23, and 24; the spelling of some words vary slightly in no. 15). The title *savāī* means "One and One-Quarter" and honors a person considered greater than any single man.
117. Ibid., 2:72, no. 30.
118. . . . *hindūkaturuṣkādhipatiśrīakabara* . . . (ibid., 2:62, no. 18).
119. "Jina Bleeds," 129.

120. "Making of a Medieval Jain Monk," 410. For Kharatara texts and inscriptions on the Tughluqs, see, e.g., Granoff, "Jinaprabhasūri and Jinadattasūri," and Nahar, "Rajgir Jain Inscription."
121. Many of the verses in the *Kavīndracandrodaya* mention this political context. E.g., see the following penned by the work's compiler, Kṛṣṇa Upādhyāya: vv. 15, 21, and 23 mention rescinding taxes, and v. 15 specifies that the taxes previously applied to Kashi and Prayag. For more on the *Kavīndracandrodaya*, see Truschke, "Contested History."
122. *Kavīndracandrodaya* v. 9.
123. O'Hanlon, "Letters Home," 231–32. Sharma and Patkar have tentatively identified twenty-four of the sixty-nine named authors of the *Kavīndracandrodaya* (introduction to the *Kavīndracandrodaya*, v–ix). Also see Har Dutt Sharma's earlier comments on roughly twenty of the sixty-one authors named in one manuscript of the *Kavīndracandrodaya* ("Forgotten Event of Shah Jehan's Reign," 56–60). One contributor, Vrajabhūṣaṇa, also engaged with the Persianate world by composing the *Pārasīprakāśavinoda* (*Play of the Light on Persian*, 1659), an abridgement of Vedāṅgarāya's Sanskrit-Persian astronomical lexicon authored for Shah Jahan, *Pārasīprakāśa* (Sreeramula Rajeswara Sarma, "Persian-Sanskrit Lexica," 144–46).
124. The precise number of verses differs depending on the manuscript. The printed edition is based on three manuscripts, two from the Asiatic Society of Bengal and one from the Asiatic Society of Mumbai. The later two copies both contain an additional thirty-five verses omitted from the older manuscript (printed in *Kavīndracandrodaya*, 59–64).
125. Pollock, "Death of Sanskrit," 407.
126. *Kavīndracandrodaya* v. 2.
127. E.g., *Kavīndracandrodaya* v. 39 and vv. 52 and 310, respectively.
128. E.g., *Kavīndracandrodaya* vv. 96 and 136. Also note similar comparisons to Karna (among other figures) in vv. 275 and 172.
129. Ibid., p. 25. Sharma and Patkar also point out this overlap in their introduction to the *Kavīndracandrodaya*, iv.
130. E.g., ibid. vv. 39, 115, 116, and 118. The title is also mentioned in the majority of prose contributions to the *Kavīndracandrodaya*.
131. Ibid. v. 115.
132. *Kavīndracandrodaya* v. 269 mentions all three sages. Several other verses also favorably compare Kavīndra to Kālidāsa or other poets (e.g., *Kavīndracandrodaya* vv. 183, 304, 305, and 306).
133. Ibid. v. 92. The verse depends upon a *śleṣa* (double entendre), which I have translated both ways by introducing a simile ("just as") for clarity. Cf. Raghavan's interpretation of this verse ("Kavīndrācārya Sarasvatī," 161). Whether the author is the same Nīlakaṇṭha Bhaṭṭa who wrote the legal treatise *Vyavahāramayūkha* remains unclear (Sharma and Patkar tentatively make this identification in their introduction to the *Kavīndracandrodaya*, vii).
134. *Kavīndracandrodaya* v. 58.
135. E.g., on Hīravijaya's rejection of the wealth offered by Akbar, see *Jagadgurukāvya* vv. 175–76.
136. For Persian sources, see *ʿAmal-i Ṣāliḥ*, 3:122, and *Pādshāhnāmah* of Vāriṣ as cited in Chand, "Rāfi'-ul-Khilāf," 8–9. For a European source, see Bernier, *Travels in the Mogul Empire*, 341.
137. *Kavīndracandrodaya* v. 126.

138. Introduction to the *Kavīndracandrodaya*, v.
139. The Karaskaras served in Yudhishthira's household in the *Mahābhārata* (2.46.21), and later literature identifies their origins as near the Narmada River valley (Olivelle, *Dharmasūtras*, appendix 2, 343). However, the listing of Karaskara here surrounded by areas outside the subcontinent or on its northern fringes suggests that Hīrārāma may have had another location in mind.
140. Darada is near Kashmir, and the Darada people appear in many Sanskrit texts, including *Kalhaṇa's Rājataraṅgiṇī* (e.g., 1.312 and 7.911).
141. *Kavīndracandrodaya* v. 170. I translate *rūṃmaśāmāḥ* as "Ottomans," literally the "Empire of Rome." See a similar usage of the term a few decades later in Marathi (quoted in Guha, "Westerners and Knowledge of the West").
142. The Daradas and Shakas are frequently listed among the warriors in the Great War (e.g., *Mahābhārata* 7.19.7–8). Elsewhere the Shakas and Daradas are said to have been born from the wishing cow through Vasishtha's power (1.165.35–36).
143. Raghavan takes *phiraṅga* here as meaning the Portuguese ("Kavīndrācārya Sarasvatī," 161). Given the range of Westerners who visited Shah Jahan's court, I think it is more likely that Hīrārāma meant Europeans generally.
144. *Kavīndracandrodaya* v. 95.
145. The *Kavīndracandrikā* contains 122 verses (no prose) and contributions from thirty-one named authors (the contributors are listed in the introduction to the *Kavīndracandrikā*, 44–45).
146. Divarkar lists several dual contributors in his introduction to the *Kavīndracandrikā*, such as Viśvanātha, Vrajabhūṣaṇa, Tvarita Kavirāja, Viśvaṃbhara Maithila, and Harīrāma Kavi (given as Hīrārāma Kavi in the *Kavīndracandrodaya*) (44–45).
147. *Kavīndracandrikā* v. 24 and *Kavīndracandrodaya* v. 170. In the Hindi verse, people from particular regions are not at Shah Jahan's court; rather, Hīrārāma enumerates the places to which Kavīndra's fame has traveled. Interestingly, the *Kavīndracandrikā* verse includes Tibet (*tibbata*).
148. I discuss this work in more detail in Truschke, "Setting the Record Wrong."
149. *Jagadgurukāvya* vv. 41–42.
150. E.g., *Kṛpārasakośa* of Śānticandra vv. 8–17. However, Hindu merchants, particularly from Multan, maintained villages and rest houses further north than Kabul during the sixteenth century and even earlier (Alam, "Trade, State Policy and Regional Change," 203–5 and 211–12; Levi, "Indian Merchant Diaspora," 485–88).
151. Babur sets the tone for understanding India and Central Asia as discrete places in his memoir, which is divided according to place and quite explicitly frames the first Mughal king as a foreign conqueror of Hindustan (Dale, *Garden of the Eight Paradises*, 149 and chapter 6). Historians writing early in Akbar's reign likewise conceived of Kabul as distinct from Hindustan (Faruqui, "Forgotten Prince," 490n8). On how their ancestral lands played vividly in the minds of Mughal rulers through Shah Jahan, see Foltz, *Mughal India and Central Asia*, 127–47.
152. The omission of Babur was not a standard strategy in Sanskrit. For Sanskrit texts that include praise of Babur, see, e.g., *Kṛpārasakośa* vv. 18–20; *Akbarasāhiśṛṅgāradarpaṇa* v. 2.
153. Akbar's age is given in *Jagadgurukāvya* vv. 44 and 82, respectively.
154. For a more detailed discussion of Padmasāgara's rewriting of the timeline of early Mughal history in the *Jagadgurukāvya*, see Truschke, "Setting the Record Wrong," 376–78.

155. *Jagadgurukāvya* v. 59.
156. Sheikh, *Forging a Region*, 139–43 and 153–54, respectively.
157. *Jagadgurukāvya* v. 74.
158. *Rāṣṭrauḍhavaṃśamahākāvya*, chapter 6; in addition, see de Bruyne's discussion in *Rudrakavi's Great Poem*, 45–46.
159. On Jahangir's unreal painting of Malik Ambar, see Moin, *Millennial Sovereign*, 193–96.
160. Ms. British Library, Sans. 2775, fol. 228. Also see the discussion of this final page in the introduction to the *Sarvadeśavṛttāntasaṅgraha*, v–vi.
161. Jha, introduction to the *Sarvadeśavṛttāntasaṅgraha*, viii–ix. Vincent A. Smith suggested a Maheśadāsa of the Rathor clan as the author, but his reasons for this attribution are unclear (Smith, *Akbar the Great Moghul*, as quoted by Jha, introduction to the *Sarvadeśavṛttāntasaṅgraha*, ix).
162. See the discussion in Jha, introduction to the *Sarvadeśavṛttāntasaṅgraha*, xii–xiii.
163. E.g., in the early nineteenth century, Buchanan recorded the tradition that Akbar granted Tirhut to Maheśa Ṭhakkura after being impressed by the learning of a Brahman whom Maheśa had sent to the royal court (*Account of the District of Purnea*, 506–7).
164. *Akbarnāmah*, 1:1; also see Thackston's translation (p. 3).
165. *Sarvadeśavṛttāntasaṅgraha* vv. 11–12a.
166. *Akbarnāmah*, 1:226; *Sarvadeśavṛttāntasaṅgraha*, p. 167 (the text breaks off on p. 168).
167. These works are titled *Nṛpatinītigarbhitavṛtta* and *Ābdullacarita*; both have been printed.
168. *Bhaviṣyapurāṇa*, 2:269–83. Also see Naim's comments in "Popular Jokes and Political History," 1460.
169. *Bhaviṣyapurāṇa*, 2:271, v. 22. Seven sages are listed along with their original and reincarnated names on pp. 271–72, vv. 20–26.
170. E.g., Pushpa Prasad cites an inscription that mentions the rulers of Hariyana beginning with the Tomaras and Chauhanas and continuing through Ghiyas al-Din Balban in the thirteenth century (*Sanskrit Inscriptions of Delhi Sultanate*, 3–15, no. 4).
171. *Rājavaṃsavarṇana*, fol. 9a, vv. 3–4.
172. Busch suggests that the Hindi turn toward political topics was itself informed by the Indo-Persian tradition ("Poetry in Motion," 191).
173. As Sheldon Pollock has pointed out, early modern Sanskrit thinkers were incredibly dynamic in terms of discursive style and methods but generally remained focused on the same topics ("New Intellectuals," 11–14). Also see Bronner and Tubb's analysis of new methods in Jagannātha Paṇḍitarāja's poetic analysis ("New School of Sanskrit Poetics").
174. Jain-authored Gujarati works on the Mughals include Ṛṣabhadās's *Hīravijayasūrirāsa*, Dayākuśala's *Lābhodayarāsa*, and Darśanavijaya's *Vijayatilakasūrirāsa* (1622–1623). Vidyavijayji draws on the *Hīravijayasūrirāsa* in his *Monk and a Monarch*.
175. Allison Busch has written about Braj works on the Mughals in several of her articles and book.
176. E.g., see Ashis Nandy's discussion of religion as a "way of life" versus as an ideology ("Politics of Secularism," 322–23).
177. Kaviraj, "Thick and Thin Religion."

6. INCORPORATING SANSKRIT INTO THE PERSIANATE WORLD

1. See, respectively, Kinra, "Fresh Words," and Faruqi, "Stranger in the City," 30–59 (Faruqi thinks we can emphasize new themes within the framework of *sabk-i hindī*).
2. "Society, Space, and the State in the Deccan Sultanates," 248–67.
3. *Muntakhab al-Tavārīkh*, 2:326.
4. See discussion in Adamjee and Truschke, "Reimagining the 'Idol-Temple of Hindustan.'"
5. The master imperial copy of Akbar's *Rāmāyan* is held in the royal collection of the Maharaja of Jaipur. Asok Das has written several short articles about this manuscript (see the bibliography).
6. I discuss the translation's contested authorship in some detail in my dissertation. In brief, Badāʾūnī claims that he worked alone to render the *Rāmāyan* into Persian over the span of four years (*Muntakhab al-Tavārīkh*, 2:366). Abū al-Faẕl names as cotranslators of the work Naqīb Khān, Badāʾūnī, and Sultan Thānīsarī (*Āʾīn-i Akbarī*, 1:115; Sujān Rāī also repeats this information in the late seventeenth-century *Khulāṣat al-Tavārīkh*, 6). ʿAbd al-Raḥīm Khān-i Khānān credits the full Persian text to Naqīb Khān (flyleaf printed and translated in Seyller, *Workshop and Patron*, 73–74). In addition to these differing claims, Badāʾūnī attests that he wrote his translation as a versified *maṡnavī* while the extant translation is in prose. I find it unlikely that there were two simultaneous copies made, and Badāʾūnī's versified one was conveniently lost (for the view that Badāʾūnī's *Rāmāyan* has been lost, see Dihlavi, "Introduction," 39). It seems more likely that there was one prose translation done by Naqīb Khān and Badāʾūnī (likely with the assistance of others), and Badāʾūnī somehow misremembers (or, for reasons that remain opaque to me, misrepresents) the details of the translation in his unofficial history. I readily admit that this issue remains unresolved. In the interest of leaving room for further work on the topic, I break with the scholarly precedent of speaking about Badāʾūnī's *Rāmāyan* and refer to the initial Persian translation as Akbar's *Rāmāyan*.
7. The most complete listing of distinct Persian *Rāmāyans* to date remains Mujtabai, *Aspects of Hindu Muslim Cultural Relations*, 68–71.
8. *Muntakhab al-Tavārīkh*, 2:366. For the portions in Arabic (italicized), I borrow from Lowe's translation.
9. Badāʾūnī is often characterized as orthodox or conservative (in contrast to the heterodox or liberal Akbar). Azfar Moin discusses why such categorizations are unhelpful and details some of Badāʾūnī's complex theological views and sympathies (*Millennial Sovereign*, 155–61).
10. *Muntakhab al-Tavārīkh*, 2:399.
11. In addition to the *Rāmāyaṇa*, Badāʾūnī's translation oeuvre includes portions of the *Mahābhārata*, *Siṃhāsana-dvātriṃśikā*, and *Rājataraṅgiṇī*. Additionally, Badāʾūnī was asked to translate the *Atharva Veda* but failed to complete the work.
12. See my discussion of Abū al-Faẕl's preface in chapter 3.
13. Other prefaces to Persian translations of Sanskrit texts also skipped praise of Muhammad, such as the *Sharīq al-Maʿrīfat* attributed to Fayẕī (Ernst, "Fayzi's Illuminationist Interpretation of Vedanta," 358).
14. *Muntakhab al-Tavārīkh*, 2:320.
15. "Muqaddamah," 1.

16. E.g., *Intikhāb-i Mahābhārat*, ms. Srinagar ORL Persian 176, fol. 1b. A Persian translation of the *Bhāgavata Purāṇa* also cites these verses (ms. BNF Supplément Persan 20, fol. 130b).
17. *Muntakhab al-Tavārīkh*, 2:321 (translation Lowe, *Muntakhab al-Tawarikh*, 2:331).
18. Ricci, "Citing as a Site," 333–40.
19. In the Freer *Rāmāyan*, such invocations occur at the end of books 1, 3, 4, and 5. Currently I have no way of knowing whether these phrases occur in the master imperial copy.
20. *Najāt al-Rashīd*, 114–15.
21. Ibid., 115; also see Rizvi, *Religious and Intellectual History*, 450–51.
22. "Mughal Historians," 290–94.
23. Ibid., 289–90 and 293.
24. *Muntakhab al-Tavārīkh*, 2:326.
25. Das, "Akbar's Manuscript of the Persian Ramayana," 146.
26. The bulk of this copy is now held in the Museum of Islamic Art in Doha, Qatar. There are two inscriptions that mention Maryam Makānī, the honorific name of Hamida Banu Begum (discussed in Leach, *Paintings from India*, 40–49). Some of the illustrations of this manuscript have been dispersed; many have been tracked and printed in Diane de Selliers, *Rāmāyaṇa* of Vālmīki (Paris: Diane de Selliers, 2011).
27. This image is held in the National Museum of India in Delhi.
28. Note on flyleaf of the Jaipur *Rāmāyan*. I borrow heavily here from Seyller's translation of this note ("Inspection and Valuation," 308).
29. Niẓām al-Dīn Pānīpatī made a translation of Abhinanda's *Laghuyogavāsiṣṭha* for Jahangir while he was still a prince (Mujtabai, "Persian Translations of Hindu Religious Literature," 20–21). As emperor, two translations of the *Rāmāyaṇa* and one of the *Yogavāsiṣṭha* (by Ṣūfī Sharīf Qutbjahānī) were dedicated to Jahangir (I discuss the *Rāmāyan*s later in this chapter). Additionally, Bhāramal produced a translation of the *Siṃhāsana-dvātriṃśikā* during Jahangir's reign, although whether it was patronized by or dedicated to the royal court remains unclear (Ethe, *Catalogue of Persian Manuscripts in the Library of the India Office*, vol. 1, no. 1988).
30. *Millennial Sovereign*, 202–3.
31. Lefèvre, "Recovering a Missing Voice," 480–81.
32. Seyller, "Inspection and Valuation," 270–72.
33. Ten illustrations from the Jaipur *Rāmāyan* are published in Das, "Introductory Note on the Emperor Akbar's *Ramayana*" and another eight in "Akbar's Imperial Ramayana." Seyller prints several additional illustrations in his *Workshop and Patron* and also lists the subjects and artists of all the Jaipur *Rāmāyan* illustrations in appendix A. Some of these images and a few additional illustrations from the Jaipur *Rāmāyan* have been published recently in de Selliers's *Rāmāyaṇa*.
34. Das, "Introductory Note on the Emperor Akbar's *Ramayana*," 94.
35. Seyller, "Inspection and Valuation," 274–76 (based on Seyller's suggested muhrs to rupees ratio of 1:10, p. 256).
36. According to Seyller, the Freer *Rāmāyan*'s 130 extant illustrations are "remarkably congruent in subject to the 176 paintings in the Jaipur manuscript" (*Workshop and Patron*, 81).
37. Freer *Rāmāyan*, fol. 1a; the translation is taken from Seyller with a few emendations (*Workshop and Patron*, 73–74).

38. *Workshop and Patron*, 74. Rama's relationship to Vishnu is clearly laid out in the first book of Akbar's *Rāmāyan* (ms. Freer *Rāmāyan*, fols. 25a–25b).
39. *Āʾīn-i Akbarī*, 2:168.
40. One could understand Raḥīm as saying that Shiva is the creator of all people and gods, including Rama, but this is a significant stretch. I think it is most honest to the text to take Raḥīm rather literally here.
41. Kinra, "Handling Diversity," 276.
42. Seyller discusses the paucity of highly illustrated subimperial manuscripts in Mughal India (*Workshop and Patron*, 29–32).
43. The *Jahāngīrnāmah* relates that Raḥīm vacillated in and out of Jahangir's favor a few times and was often tempted to pit his own formidable resources against the imperial center.
44. *Rāmāyan-i Masīḥī*, 24. For another translation of this passage, see Phillips, "Garden of Endless Blossoms," 81 (on the final two lines, cf. Aggarwal, "Rama Story of Brij Narain Chakbast," 153). The Persian of the final line is ambiguous, but the context supports Phillips's reading.
45. *Rāmāyan-i Masīḥī*, 26.
46. Aggarwal, "Rama Story of Brij Narain Chakbast," 154.
47. See Meisami's discussion in *Medieval Persian Court Poetry*, chapters 3–5.
48. Phillips identifies a moral edge in Masīḥ's poem ("Garden of Endless Blossoms," 82–84).
49. There has been some confusion on the date of Giridhardās's *Rāmāyan* because, while Giridhardās dates his text according to both the *hijri* and *vikrama saṃvat* systems, the two dates are a few years apart in some manuscripts (see ms. British Library, Persian Or. 1251, fol. 242a). This discrepancy may be the result of a scribal error (Sri Ram Sharma, "Little Known Persian Version of the Ramayan," 674–75). For Giridhardās's characterization of the text as *nāmah-i rām*, see ms. British Library, Persian Or. 1251, fol. 6b.
50. Sharma discusses some details of Giridhardās's narration in the only article I have found to date that contains substantial analysis of this *Rāmāyan* ("Little Known Persian Version of the Ramayan").
51. *Rāmāyan* of Giridhardās, ms. British Library, Persian Or. 1251, fol. 5a.
52. Ibid., fol. 5b.
53. Ibid., fol. 6b.
54. Ms. Freer *Rāmāyan*, fol. 1b.
55. On the sixth-century Pahlavi version of the *Pañcatantra* and its subsequent translation into Arabic in the eighth century, see Shamma, "Arabic Version of *Kalila wa Dimna*." For a brief account of later Persian redactions, see Riedel, "Kalila wa Demna I."
56. In addition to projecting a royal audience, Masīḥ Pānīpatī's poem was quite well liked by Indo-Persian readers according to the extant manuscript evidence. The popularity of Giridhardās's *Rāmāyan* is hard to gauge, but far fewer manuscript copies appear to survive today.
57. Firishtah completed the first draft of his history in 1606, produced a second version in the following years, and continued to adjust the text until his death in 1623 (Subrahmanyam, *Courtly Encounters*, 46).
58. *Tārīkh-i Firishtah*, 1:4.

59. Ibid., 1:6.
60. General John Briggs translated the bulk of Firishtah's history into English in the early nineteenth century, and this remains the version Indologists most frequently cite today. Briggs excised several portions of Firishtah's text as he saw fit and accordingly heavily abbreviated the introductory chapter on India's pre-Islamic past without overtly noting the abridgement. Elliot and Dowson later offered a nearly full translation of this section, deleting only the verses and the introductory praise of God (*History of India*, vol. 6, n. E).
61. *Tārīkh-i Firishtah*, 1:6.
62. Ibid., 1:6.
63. Here I summarize *Tārīkh-i Firishtah*, 1:6–14.
64. E.g., compare *Tārīkh-i Firishtah*, 1:7, and "Muqaddamah," 21; *Tārīkh-i Firishtah*, 1:8, and "Muqaddamah," 23. Beveridge also notes Firishtah's reliance on Abū al-Faẓl (*Akbarnāmah*, 1:151–52n3).
65. *Tārīkh-i Firishtah*, 1:13–14.
66. Ibid., 1:15.
67. Ibid.
68. E.g., Khvāndamīr's *Ḥabīb al-Siyar* (Bashir, "Perso-Islamic Universal Chronicle").
69. Other Persianate authors in the late sixteenth and seventeenth centuries also dealt with similar issues of how to write the pre-Islamic history of Iran. See Tavakoli-Targhi's discussion in "Contested Memories."
70. Savant, "Genealogy and Ethnicity in Islam."
71. Trautmann, *Aryans and British India*, 41–61; Raj, *Relocating Modern Science*, 129–30.
72. *Tārīkh-i Firishtah*, 1:16. Firishtah also articulates this vision of Islamic history in respect to the rest of the known world and says that Noah's other sons and their offspring gave rise to the Persians, Turks, Chinese, etc.
73. *Tārīkh-i Firishtah*, 1:19.
74. Rizvi, *History of Sufism*, 2:398.
75. Yücesoy, "Translation as Self-Consciousness," 538–45.
76. *Tārīkh-i Firishtah*, 1:22.
77. Ibid., 1:19.
78. Lefèvre, "Mughal Genealogical Strategies."
79. Rice, "Mughal Interventions," 157.
80. "Mughal Genealogical Strategies," 415.
81. *Tārīkh-i Rājhā-yi Dilhī*, ms. Gujarat Vidya Sabha 46, fol. 1a. The copy is dated 1851 (fol. 19b).
82. Rajeev Kinra has written at length about the literary, imperial, and historical contexts of Chandar Bhān in his book, *Writing Self, Writing Empire*.
83. Kinra calls the *Tārīkh-i Rājhā-yi Dilhī* "one of Chandar Bhan's apocryphal texts" (ibid., 263).
84. The author pays increasing attention to events beginning with the reign of Raja Vikramaditya, who seized power from a minister who had defeated Rajapala (*Tārīkh-i Rājhā-yi Dilhī*, ms. Gujarat Vidya Sabha 46, fol. 7a).
85. Ibid., fol. 11b.
86. Ibid., fols. 18b–19a. For modern accounts of these events, see Richards, *Mughal Empire*, 116–18; Faruqui, *Princes of the Mughal Empire*, 36–37.
87. 1:529–37.

88. *Tārīkh-i Rājhā-yi Dilhī*, ms. Gujarat Vidya Sabha 46, fol. 2a.
89. Banvālī Dās's *Rājāvalī* is extant in many manuscript copies today.
90. Alam and Subrahmanyam, "Witnesses and Agents of Empire," 405.
91. Ernst, *Eternal Garden*, 297n228.
92. Munis Faruqui lists several ways that Shah Jahan favored Dara Shikuh above his other sons (*Princes of the Mughal Empire*, 38–39).
93. Dara Shikuh's seal appears on an order from Shah Jahan (Jhaveri, *Imperial Farmans*, nos. 6–8).
94. On the literary records of these conversations, see Kinra, "Infantilizing Bābā Dārā," and Gandhi, "Mughal Engagements with Vedānta," 73–84.
95. D'Onofrio, "Persian Commentary to the Upaniṣads," 541–45.
96. Kunhan Raja published this letter in 1940 ("Sanskrit Letter of Mohamed Dara Shukoh"). A few years later, Gode showed that the letter was addressed to Brahmendra Sarasvatī ("Identification of Gosvāmi Nṛsiṁhāśrama").
97. Gandhi, "Mughal Engagements with Vedānta," 65–67.
98. Ernst, "Muslim Studies of Hinduism?" 184.
99. Ibid., 184–85. The *Ātmavilāsa* translation is attributed to Chandar Bhān Brahman, although there is little supporting evidence (Kinra, "Secretary-Poets in Mughal India," 165n7).
100. Ernst, "Muslim Studies of Hinduism?"185.
101. Gandhi, "Mughal Engagements with Vedānta," 75–76.
102. While the *Sirr-i Akbar* records the author as Dara himself, most likely a group of intellectuals in the prince's employ carried out this translation (D'Onofrio, "Persian Commentary to the Upaniṣads," 536–40).
103. Quoted ibid., 541n37.
104. The *Samudrasaṅgama* was edited and published in 1954 by J. B. Chaudhuri along with a critical study by Roma Chaudhuri. Also, see Gode, "Samudra-Saṅgama," and Filliozat, "Dara Shikoh's *Samudrasangama*." Carl Ernst notes that there are later translations of the text into Arabic and Urdu ("Muslim Studies of Hinduism?" 186n49).
105. "Mughal Engagements with Vedānta."
106. Ganeri, *Lost Age of Reason*, 13.
107. Supriya Gandhi makes this point in her unpublished dissertation (unavailable at the time of writing).
108. *Princes of the Mughal Empire*, 164–68.
109. "Mughal Engagements with Vedānta," 77.
110. Faruqui, *Princes of the Mughal Empire*, 166–68.
111. "Mughal Sufi Story of Creation."

CONCLUSION

1. In this sense, it seems to me that Foucault speaks too narrowly when he emphasizes that power circulates through networks of individuals but is necessarily directed toward a larger audience (*Discipline and Punish*, 26–27).
2. "Frontier in the Imperial Imagination," 61.
3. "How to Do Multilingual Literary History?" 242.

4. Some scholars have asserted without a substantial basis that members of the Mughal elite knew Sanskrit (e.g., on Fayẓī, Alam and Subrahmanyam in *Writing the Mughal World*, 209, and Rahman, "Fayżī, Abu'l Fayż"). More frequently scholars simply dismiss that Sanskrit could have played any meaningful role in Mughal court life.
5. *Argumentative Indian*, 288.
6. Habib, "Commemorating Akbar," xii.
7. See Kruijtzer's brief but insightful discussion of the tension between the desire for scholarly accuracy and the knowledge that people often view the past as their direct heritage (*Xenophobia in Seventeenth-Century India*, 10–11). On some of the historical problems with Sen's arguments in particular, see Khilnani, "Democracy and Its Indian Pasts."
8. Richards details politics in the Deccan and Aurangzeb's expansion southward (*Mughal Empire*, 205–52).
9. Alavi, introduction to *Eighteenth Century in India*.
10. Vinay Lal provides a good overview of standard Mughal historiography on Aurangzeb ("Aurangzeb, Akbar, and the Communalization of History").
11. As Satish Chandra notes, some modern scholars have moved away from discussing religion and culture under Aurangzeb altogether and are focusing on socioeconomic and political concerns instead (*State, Society, and Culture in Indian History*, 129–37).
12. E.g., see Carvalho's closing sentence in *Mirʾāt al-Quds*, 40.
13. "Did Aurangzeb Ban Music?"
14. *Millennial Sovereign*, 233–34.
15. Although this story line is not altogether satisfying, because, in certain ways, Aurangzeb centered authority on the king more than his predecessors. E.g., see Faruqui's discussion of Aurangzeb's greater control over the Mughal princes (*Princes of the Mughal Empire*, 274–308).
16. The Persian word *hindī* was frequently used for both Sanskrit and Old Hindi.
17. Peter van der Veer raises the point for Sanskrit knowledge systems generally that emphasizing the linguistic medium may be more of a modern concern ("Does Sanskrit Knowledge Exist?" 634).
18. See ms. British Library, Persian Add. 5641, fols. 7b–14b; ms. British Library, IO Islamic 2517, fols. 1b–8b.
19. Caturbhuja expresses his intention to gratify Shaystah Khan in *Rasakalpadruma*, p. 4, v. 10. In previous scholarship, Harkare quotes from the work ("Sanskrit Under Mohammedan Patronage," 61–62).
20. E.g., *Rasakalpadruma*, p. 216, v. 44, and p. 211, v. 32 by Caturbhuja; p. 218, v. 52 by Vācaspati.
21. *Rasakalpadruma*, pp. 294 (*śāntarasa*), 311 (*saṃkīrṇa*), and the rest *anyokti*: pp. 330, 332, 343 (two verses), and 345. ʿAbd al-Raḥīm provides a possible precedent for Mughal figures writing in Sanskrit. As I discuss in chapter 2, we ought to treat claims that Raḥīm wrote in Sanskrit with caution.
22. Azad, *Religion and Politics in India*, 236.
23. *Travels in the Mogul Empire*, 341.
24. Minkowski, "Learned Brahmins and the Mughal Court," 121. On this work, also see Patkar, "Muhūrtaratna."

25. Minkowski discusses Keśava Śarma ("Learned Brahmins and the Mughal Court," 151 and 120). The suggestion that Īśvaradāsa wanted to gain Mughal support is mine.
26. Scheurleer and Kruijtzer, "Camping with the Mughal Emperor," 55–56.
27. E.g., the Sanskrit Knowledge-Systems Project, which "investigates the structure and social context of Sanskrit science and knowledge from 1550 to 1750" (http://www.columbia.edu/itc/mealac/pollock/sks/).
28. On Sanskrit's formative role concerning Braj Bhasha's intellectual structures, particularly in *alaṅkāraśāstra*, see Busch, "Anxiety of Innovation," and *Poetry of Kings*. Aditya Behl's *Love's Subtle Magic* analyzes Hindavi Sufi romances.
29. Also see the Perso-Indica project and affiliated scholars (www.perso-indica.net).
30. Starn traces the use of "early modern" ("Early Modern Muddle").
31. "Early Modern India and World History."
32. *Ends of Man*, 83–84.
33. "Death of Sanskrit," 417.
34. See, e.g., Chattopadhyaya, *Representing the Other?*; Cort, "Genres of Jain History"; Granoff, "Jinaprabhasūri and Jinadattasūri"; Thapar, *Somanatha*.
35. Sheldon Pollock provocatively outlined the death of Sanskrit theory ("Death of Sanskrit"). For subsequent criticisms, see Hanneder, "On 'The Death of Sanskrit,'" and Bronner and Shulman, "Sanskrit in the Vernacular Millennium." There is also the more heavy-handed condemnation by Hatcher ("Sanskrit and the Morning After").
36. E.g., see the history development of *āyurveda* sketched out by Wujastyk and Smith in their introduction to *Modern and Global Ayurveda*.
37. Sudipta Kaviraj raises the possibility of multiple breaks in India's path to modernity ("Sudden Death of Sanskrit," 138–39).
38. "Muddle of Modernity," 674.
39. "Revisioning Modernity," 285.
40. Chakrabarty, "Muddle of Modernity," 672. Washbrook has raised similar queries concerning the values embedded in "modernity" ("Intimations of Modernity," 125).
41. Thackston, introduction to the *Baburnama*, xliii.
42. "Contours of Persianate Community," particularly 34–44.
43. Francis Robinson, "Perso-Islamic Culture in India," 113.
44. On the relationship between Persian and Urdu poetics, see Faruqi, *Early Urdu Literary Culture and History*.
45. Ernst details some of this history and also notes that early colonialists frequently sponsored new Persian works on Indian religions ("Muslim Studies of Hinduism?" 187–91).
46. Von Hirschhausen and Leonhard suggest a few political reasons behind this shift in "Beyond Rise, Decline and Fall," 10–11.
47. Howe, *Empire*, 10–11.
48. *Empires in World History*, 3–4. Nonetheless, see Roy Fischel's compelling and important discussion about the potentially narrowing focus of the framework of empire and the need to analyze some dynasties, such as the Deccan Sultanates, according to "a different concept of statehood" ("Society, Space, and the State in the Deccan Sultanates," 245–52).

49. J. N. Farquhar first recorded this legend in the early twentieth century. For a more recent recounting and discussion based on Farquhar, see Pinch, *Warrior Ascetics*, 30–32.
50. Pinch discusses this event and other references to yogis in Mughal texts ibid., 28–58.
51. Bhattacharyya, "Sanskrit Scholars of Akbar's Time," 31–32.
52. Jack Hawley notes similar difficulties in connecting vernacular poets and singers, such as Sūrdās, with brief mentions in Persian texts (*Memory of Love*, 21–23).
53. Since most Mughal historians do not know Sanskrit, this blanket condemnation alleviates the fear that they may lack access to a crucial archive.
54. "Portrait of a Raja in a Badshah's World," 290.
55. "Pretextures of Time," 377.
56. *Courtly Culture*, 14.
57. *Westminster Abbey*, 9.

APPENDIX 2

1. *Razmnāmah*, 1:54. The editors of the *Razmnāmah* also transliterate the verses into Roman script, but they appear to follow an unidentified Sanskrit version of the epic, not the Persian text. These verses are all available with slight variations in the Sanskrit critical edition. The first verse is 1.53.23. The first two lines of the second verse are 1.53.22, and the final line is the first line quoted in note 463*(Vol.1). The third verse offers the second and third lines in note 463*. The first two lines of the final verse correspond to lines 4 and 5 in note 463*, and the final line repeats line 3 of note 463*.
2. This name is unclear; the Persian reads Astīn, whereas the Sanskrit reads Asita or, in a variant, Astīka. I have used Asita in my reconstruction.

BIBLIOGRAPHY

MANUSCRIPT SOURCES

Akbarasāhiśṛṅgāradarpaṇa of Padmasundara. Rajasthan Oriental Research Institute, Jodhpur, Sanskrit 19607.

Akbarnāmah of Abū al-Faẕl ibn Mubārak. British Library, London, Persian Additional 27,247.

Āsaphavilāsa of Jagannātha Paṇḍitarāja. Bhandarkar Oriental Research Institute, Pune, 732.iii of 1886–92.

Bhagavadgītā. British Library, London, India Office Sanskrit 2244.

Bhagavadgītā. British Library, London, India Office Sanskrit 2387.

Bhāgavata Purāṇa (Persian). Bibliothèque nationale de France, Paris, Supplément Persan 20.

Intikhāb-i Mahābhārat. Oriental Research Library, Srinagar, Persian 176. (All Srinagar manuscripts accessed at the Indira Gandhi National Centre for the Arts, Delhi.)

Jahāṅgīracarita of Rudrakavi. Oriental Institute at the Maharaja Sayajirao University of Baroda, Vadodara, No. 5761.

Kalpasūtrāntravākya of Ratnacandragaṇi. LD Institute of Indology, Ahmedabad, No. 11654.

Khānakhānācarita, *Kīrtisamullāsa*, and *Dānaśāhacarita* of Rudrakavi. British Library, London, Buhler 70.

Kṛpārasakośa of Śānticandra. LD Institute of Indology, Ahmedabad, No. 11878.

Mahābhārat (Persian, book 1 by Fayẕī and rest *Razmnāmah*). Asiatic Society of Mumbai, Mumbai, A.N. 143693.

Mahābhārat (Persian, book 2 by Fayẕī and rest *Razmnāmah*). Bibliothèque nationale de France, Paris, Supplément Persan 1038.

Mahābhārat (Persian, books 1 and 2 by Fayẕī and rest *Razmnāmah*). Oriental Research Library, Srinagar, Persian 175.

Mahābhārat (Persian, books 1 and 2 by Fayẕī and rest *Razmnāmah*). Oriental Research Library, Srinagar, Persian 211.

Mahābhārat of Fayẕī (Persian, books 1 and 2). British Library, London, India Office Islamic 761.

Mahābhārat of Fayẕī (Persian, books 1 and 2). British Library, London, India Office Islamic 3014.

Mahābhārat of Fayẓī (Persian, books 1 and 2). Maulana Azad Library at Aligarh Muslim University, Aligarh, University Collection No. Persian/Ikhbar 129.

Pañcatattvaprakāśa of Veṇīdatta. Biblioteca Nazionale, Rome, Orientali 172. Facsimile printed in *The Sanskrit Grammar and Manuscripts of Father Heinrich Roth S.J. (1620–1668)*, edited by Arnulf Camps and Jean-Claude Muller. Leiden: Brill, 1988.

Pārasīprakāśa of Kṛṣṇadāsa. Man Singh Pustak Prakash, Jodhpur, No. 626(c).

Rājāvalī of Banvālī Dās. Salar Jung Museum, Hyderabad, Tarikh 244.

Rājavaṃsavarṇana. Sastra Bhandar of the Digambara Jain Bada Terapanthi Mandir, Jaipur, No. 1751.

Rāmāyan (Akbari Persian Translation). Freer Gallery of Art, Smithsonian Institution, Washington, D.C., No. 07.271.

Rāmāyan (Akbari Persian Translation), Museum of Islamic Art, Doha, Qatar.

Rāmāyan of Giridhardās (Persian). Bibliothèque nationale de France, Paris, Supplément Persan 18.

Rāmāyan of Giridhardās (Persian). British Library, London, Persian Oriental 1251.

Rāmāyan of Sumīr Chand (Persian). Raza Library, Rampur, Persian 5008.

Rawẓat al-Ṭāhirīn of Ṭāhir Muḥammad Sabzavārī. Bodleian Library, Oxford, Elliot 314.

Rawẓat al-Ṭāhirīn of Ṭāhir Muḥammad Sabzavārī (chapter 4). British Library, London, India Office Islamic 753.

Rawẓat al-Ṭāhirīn of Ṭāhir Muḥammad Sabzavārī (*Mahābhārat* section). Maulana Azad Library at Aligarh Muslim University, Aligarh, Sir Suleman Collection 15/2(b).

Razmnāmah. Birla Family's Private Collection, Calcutta, bound in three volumes.

Razmnāmah. Bodleian Library, Oxford, Ouseley 239.

Razmnamah. Bodleian Library, Oxford, Ouseley 326.

Razmnamah. Bodleian Library, Oxford, Wilson 422b.

Razmnāmah. British Library, London, India Office Islamic 1702.

Razmnāmah. British Library, London, Persian Oriental 12076.

Razmnāmah. Khuda Bakhsh Oriental Public Library, Patna, Persian 2714

Razmnāmah. Khuda Bakhsh Oriental Public Library, Patna, Persian 2718–2719.

Razmnāmah. Maulana Azad Library at Aligarh Muslim University, Aligarh, University Collection No. Persian/Ikhbar 2.

Razmnāmah. National Museum, Delhi, Persian 63.47.

Razmnāmah. Oriental Research Library, Srinagar, Persian 188.

Razmnāmah. Oriental Research Library, Srinagar, Persian 1294.

Razmnāmah (with table of contents by Basant Rae). British Library, London, India Office Islamic 2517.

Razmnāmah (with table of contents by Basant Rae). British Library, London, Persian Additional 5641–5642.

Śabdavilāsa of Salakṣa. Hemacandra Jnana Mandir, Patan, No. 995.

Saṃskṛtapārasīkapadaprakāśa of Karṇapūra. Asiatic Society of Bengal, Calcutta, No. 24327.

Sarvadeśavṛttāntasaṅgraha. British Library, Sanskrit 2775.

Tārīkh-i Rājhā-yi Dilhī of Chandar Bhān Brahman. Gujarat Vidya Sabha, Ahmedabad, No. 46.

Tarjumah-i Barāhī. British Library, London, India Office Islamic 1262.

Tarjumah-i Razmnāmah. Oriental Manuscript Library at Osmania University, Hyderabad, Tarikh 266.

PRIMARY SOURCES

Āʾīn-i Akbarī of Abū al-Faẕl ibn Mubārak. Edited by Sir Sayyid Ahmad. Aligarh: Sir Sayyid Academy, Aligarh Muslim University, 2005. Original edition, 1855.

Āʾīn-i Akbarī of Abū al-Faẕl ibn Mubārak. Edited by H. Blochmann. 2 vols. Calcutta: Asiatic Society of Bengal, 1867–1877.

Āʾīn-i Akbarī of Abū al-Faẕl ibn Mubārak. Translated by H. Blochmann, Colonel H. S. Jarrett, P. C. Phillott, and Jadunath Sarkar. 3 vols. Calcutta: Royal Asiatic Society of Bengal, 1927–1949.

Aitihasik Jain Kavya Samgraha. Edited by Agarchand Nahata. Calcutta: Shankardan Shubhairaj Nahata, 1937.

Akbar and the Jesuits: An Account of the Jesuit Missions to the Court of Akbar of Pierre du Jarric. Translated by C. H. Payne. New York: Harper, 1926.

Akbarasāhiśṛṅgāradarpaṇa of Padmasundara. Edited by K. Madhava Krishna Sarma. Bikaner: Anup Sanskrit Library, 1943.

Akbarnāmah of Abū al-Faẕl ibn Mubārak. Edited by Maulawi Abd-ur-Rahim. 3 vols. Calcutta: Asiatic Society, 1873–1887.

Akbarnāmah of Abū al-Faẕl ibn Mubārak. Translated by Henry Beveridge. 3 vols. Delhi: Low Price Publications, 2010. Original edition, 1902–1939.

Alberuni's India: An Account of the Religion, Philosophy, Literature, Geography, Chronology, Astronomy, Customs, Laws and Astrology of India, about A.D. *1030*. Translated and edited by Edward C. Sachau. 2 vols. London: Trübner, 1888. Reprint, Boston: Elibron Classics, 2005.

ʿAmal-i Ṣāliḥ or Shah Jahan Namah of Muḥammad Ṣāliḥ Kambūh Lāhawrī. Edited by Ghulam Yazdani. 3 vols. Bibliotheca Indica. Calcutta: Asiatic Society of Bengal, 1923–1939.

Ardhakathanaka: Half a Tale of Banārasīdās. Edited by Mukund Lath. New Delhi: Rupa and Co., 2005.

Artharatnāvalī [also called *Aṣṭalakṣārthī*] of Samayasundara. In *Anekārtharatnamañjūṣā*, edited by Hiralal Rasikdas Kapadia. Bombay: Jivanchand Sakerchand Javeri, 1933.

Āsaphavilāsa of Jagannātha Paṇḍitarāja. In *Pandita Raja Kavya Samgraha: Complete Poetical Works of Panditaraja Jagannatha*, edited by K. Kamala. Hyderabad: Sanskrit Academy, Osmania University, 2002.

The Baburnama: Memoirs of Babur, Prince and Emperor. Translated by Wheeler M. Thackston. New York: Modern Library, 2002.

Bādshāhnāmah of ʿAbd al-Ḥamīd Lāhawrī. Edited by Mawlawi Kabir al-Din Ahmad, Mawlawi Abd al-Rahim, and W. N. Lees. 3 vols. Calcutta: Bibliotheca Indica, 1867–1872. Reprint, Osnabruck: Biblio Verlag, 1983.

Bhāminīvilāsa of Jagannātha Paṇḍitarāja. Edited by Lakshman Ramachandra Vaidya. Bombay: Bharati Press, 1887.

Bhānucandragaṇicarita of Siddhicandra. Edited by Mohanlal Dalichand Desai. Ahmedabad-Calcutta: Sanchalaka Singhi Jain Granthamala, 1941.

Bhaviṣyapurāṇa. Edited by Shriram Sharma. 2 vols. Bareli: Sanskriti Samsthan, 1968–1969.

Bouquet of Rasa and River of Rasa of Bhānudatta. Translated by Sheldon Pollock. New York: New York University Press, 2009.

Būstān-i Saʿdī. Edited by Nur Allah Iranparast. Tehran: Danish, 1973.

The Commentary of Father Monserrate, S. J., on His Journey to the Court of Akbar of Antoni Montserrat. Translated by John S. Hoyland and S. N. Banerjee. London: Humphrey Milford, Oxford University Press, 1922.

Dabistān-i Maẕāhib. Edited by Rahim Rizazadah Malik. 2 vols. Tehran: Kitabkhanah-i Tahuri, 1983.

Dānaśāhacarita. See *Works of Rudra Kavi*.

Dāstān-i Nal va Daman of Abū al-Fayẓ ibn Mubārak Fayẓī. Tehran: Fardin, 1956.

Devānandamahākāvya of Meghavijaya. Edited by Pandit Bechardas J. Doshi. Ahmedabad-Calcutta: Sanchalaka Singhi Jain Granthamala, 1937.

Digvijayamahākāvya of Meghavijaya. Edited by Ambalal Premchand Shah. Bombay: Bharatiya Vidya Bhavan, 1945.

Dīvān of Muʿizzī. Edited by ʿAbbas Iqbal. Tehran: Kitabfurushi-i Islamiyah, 1940.

Dīvān of Sanāʾī. Edited by Mudarris Razavi. Tehran: Shirkat-i Tabʿ-i Kitab, 1941.

Early Travels in India, 1583–1619. Edited by William Foster. London: H. Milford, Oxford University Press, 1921.

The Embassy of Sir Thomas Roe to the Court of the Great Mogul, 1615–1619, as Narrated in His Journal and Correspondence. Edited by William Foster. 2 vols. London: Bedford Press, printed for the Hakluyt Society, 1899.

Epigraphia Indica. Calcutta/Delhi: Archaeological Survey of India, 1892–.

Epigraphia Indo-Moslemica. 19 vols. Calcutta: Government of India, 1909–1950.

The Hawkins' Voyages During the Reigns of Henry VIII, Queen Elizabeth, and James I. Edited by Clements R. Markham. London: Printed for the Hakluyt Society, 1878.

Hīrasaubhāgya of Devavimalagaṇi with his own gloss. Edited by Mahamahopadhyaya Pandit Sivadatta and Kashinath Pandurang Parab. Bombay: Tukaram Javaji, 1900.

Hīrasundaramahākāvya of Devavimala. Edited by Muni Ratnakirtivijaya. Khambhat: Shri Jain Granthaprakashan Samiti, 1996.

The History of Akbar of Abu'l Fazl. Edited and Translated by Wheeler M. Thackston. Vol. 1. Cambridge, Mass.: Harvard University Press, 2015.

Jagadgurukāvya of Padmasāgara. Edited by Hargovinddas and Becardas. Benares: Harakhchand Bhurabhai, 1910.

Jagadvijayacchandas of Kavīndrācārya Sarasvatī. Edited by C. Kunhan Raja. Bikaner: Anup Sanskrit Library, 1945.

Jahāṅgīravirudāvalī of Harideva Miśra. Edited by Jagannath Pathak. Allahabad: Ganganatha Jha Kendriya Sanskrit Vidyapithan, 1978.

The Jahangirnama: Memoirs of Jahangir, Emperor of India. Translated and edited by Wheeler M. Thackston. Washington, D.C.: Freer Gallery of Art, Arthur M. Sackler Gallery; New York: Oxford University Press, 1999.

Jahāngīrnāmah yā Tūzuk-i Jahāngīrī. Edited by Muhammad Hashim. Tehran: Bunyad-i Farhang-i Iran, 1980.

Jambūsvāmicarita of Rājamalla. Edited by Jagdish Chandra Shastri. Bombay: Manikchandra Digambar Jain Granthamala Samiti, 1936.

The Kādambarī of Bāṇabhaṭṭa and His Son (Bhuṣaṇabhaṭṭa) with the Commentaries of Bhānuchandra and His Disciple Siddhichandra. Edited by Kashinath Pandurang Parab. Bombay: Pandurang Jawaji, 1940.

Kalhaṇa's Rājataraṅgiṇī: A Chronicle of the Kings of Kaśmīr. Edited by Marc Aurel Stein. Westminster, 1900. Reprint, Delhi: Motilal Banarsidass, 1989.

Kavīndracandrikā. Edited by Krishna Divakar. Pune: Maharashtra Rashtrabhasha Sabha, 1966.

Kavīndracandrodaya. Edited by M. M. Patkar and Har Dutt Sharma. Poona: Oriental Book Agency, 1939.

Kavīndrakalpadruma of Kavīndrācārya Sarasvatī. Edited by R. B. Athavale. Bombay: Asiatic Society of Bombay, 1981.

Kavīndrakalpalatā of Kavīndrācārya Sarasvatī. Edited by Lakshmikumari Cundavat. Jaipur: Rajasthan Oriental Research Institute, 1958.

Kāvyaprakāśakhaṇḍana of Siddhicandra. Edited by Rasikalal Chotalal Parikh. Bombay: Bharatiya Vidya Bhavan, 1953.

Khānakhānācarita. See *Works of Rudra Kavi*.

Khulāṣat al-Tavārīkh of Sujān Rāī Bhandārī. Edited by M. Zafar Hasan. Delhi: J. and Sons Press, 1918.

Kīrtisamullāsa. See *Works of Rudra Kavi*.

Kṛpārasakośa of Śānticandra. Edited by Muni Jinavijaya. Bhavnagar: Sri Jain Atmanand Sabha, 1917.

Kulliyāt-i Fayẓī. Edited by A. D. Arshad and Vazir al-Hasan Abidi. Lahore: Idarah-ʾi Tahqiqat-i Pakistan, 1967.

Light of Truth; or, An English Translation of the Satyarth Prakash: The Well-Known Work of Swami Dayananda Saraswati. 4th ed. Edited by Chiranjiva Bharadwaja. New Delhi: Sarvadeshik Arya Pratinidhi Sabha, 1994.

Maʾāsir al-Umarā of Shāhnavāz Khān. Edited by Maulavi ʿAbdur Rahim and Maulavi Mirza Ashraf ʿAli. 3 vols. Calcutta: Asiatic Society of Bengal, 1888–1891.

[*Mahābhārata*]. *The Mahābhārata, for the First Time Critically Edited*. Edited by Vishnu S. Sukthankar, S. K. Belvalkar, P. L. Vaidya, et al. 19 vols. Poona: Bhandarkar Oriental Research Institute, 1933–1966.

Mahābhārat-i Fārsī: Bhīkham Parb. Lucknow: Nawal Kishore, 1880–1910.

Majālis-i Jahāngīrī of ʿAbd al-Sattār ibn Qāsim Lāhawrī. Edited by ʿArif Nawshahi and Muʿin Nizami. Tehran: Miras-i Maktub, 2006.

Mantrikarmacandravaṃśāvalīprabandha of Jayasoma, with the commentary of Guṇavinaya. Edited by Acharya Muni Jinavijaya. Bombay: Bharatiya Vidya Bhavan, 1980.

Muntakhab al-Tavārīkh of ʿAbd al-Qādir Badāʾūnī. Edited by Ahmad ʿAli and Tawfiq Subhani. Vols. 2–3. Tehran: Anjuman-i Asar va Mafakhir-i Farhangi, 2000.

Muntakhab al-Tavārīkh of ʿAbd al-Qādir Badāʾūnī. Edited by Captain W. N. Lees and Munshi Ahmad Ali. Vol. 2. Calcutta: College Press, 1865.

Muntakhab al-Tawarikh of ʿAbd al-Qādir Badāʾūnī. Translated by George S. A. Ranking, Sir Wolseley Haig, and W. H. Lowe. 3 vols. Calcutta: Asiatic Society of Bengal, 1884–1925. Reprinted with revisions by Brahmadeva Prasad Ambashthya, Delhi: Renaissance, 1986.

"Muqaddamah" of Abū al-Faẓl ibn Mubārak. In *Mahabharata: The Oldest and Longest Sanskrit Epic. Translated by Mir Ghayasuddin Ali Qazvini Known as Naqib Khan (D. 1023 AH)*, edited by Sayyid Muhammad Reza Jalali Naini and Dr. N. S. Shukla. 4 vols. Tehran: Kitabkhanah-i Tahuri, 1979–1981.

Najāt al-Rashīd of ʿAbd al-Qādir Badāʾūnī. Edited by Sayyid Muʿin al-Haqq. Lahore: Idarah-ʾi Tahqiqat-i Pakistan, Danishgah-i Panjab, 1972.

Nartananirṇaya of Puṇḍarīkaviṭṭhala. Edited by R. Sathyanarayana. 3 vols. New Delhi: Indira Gandhi National Centre for the Arts and Motilal Banarsidass, 1994.

Padyaveṇī of Veṇīdatta. Edited by Jatindra Bimal Chaudhuri. Calcutta: Pracyavani, 1944.

Panchākhyānah of Muṣṭafá Khāliqdād Hāshimī ʿAbbāsī. Edited by Tara Chand, Jalali Naini, and Dr. Abidi. Tehran: Eqbal, 1984.

Pandita Raja Kavya Samgraha: Complete Poetical Works of Panditaraja Jagannatha. Edited by K. Kamala. Hyderabad: Sanskrit Academy, Osmania University, 2002.

Pārasīprakāśa of Kṛṣṇadāsa. Edited by Vibhuti Bhushan Bhattacharya. Varanasi: Varanaseya Sanskrit Vishvavidyalaya, 1965.

Princess Kādambarī of Bāṇa. Edited and translated by David Smith. New York: New York University Press, 2009.

Rahīmgranthāvalī. Edited by Vidyanivas Mishra and Govind Rajnish. New Delhi: Vani Prakashan, 1994.

Rāmāyan-i Masīḥī of Saᶜd Allāh Masīḥ Pānīpatī. Lucknow: Nawal Kishore, 1899.

Rasagaṅgādhara of Jagannātha Paṇḍitarāja. Edited by Kedaranath Ojha. 2 vols. Varanasi: Sampurnanand Sanskrit Vishvavidyalaya, 1977–1981.

Rasakalpadruma of Caturbhujamiśra. Edited by Bhaskara Mishra. New Delhi: Eastern Book Linkers, 1991.

Rasikajīvana of Gadādharabhaṭṭa. Edited by Trilokanatha Jha. Darbhanga: Mithila Sanskrit Research Institute, 2010.

Rasikpriyā of Keśavdās. In *Keśavgranthāvalī*, edited by Vishvanathprasad Mishra. Vol. 1. Allahabad: Hindustani Academy, 1954.

Rāṣṭrauḍhavaṃśamahākāvya of Rudrakavi. Edited by Embar Krishnamacharya. Baroda: Central Library, 1917.

[*Razmnāmah*] *Mahabharata: The Oldest and Longest Sanskrit Epic. Translated by Mir Ghayasuddin Ali Qazvini Known as Naqib Khan (D. 1023 AH)*. Edited by Sayyid Muhammad Reza Jalali Naini and Dr. N. S. Shukla. 4 vols. Tehran: Kitabkhanah-i Tahuri, 1979–1981.

River of Rasa. See *Bouquet of Rasa*.

Rudrakavi's Great Poem of the Dynasty of Rāṣṭrauḍha: Cantos 1–13 and 18–20. Edited and translated by J. L. de Bruyne. Leiden: Brill, 1968.

Śabdakalpadruma. Edited by Varadaprasad Vasu and Haricaran Vasu. 5 vols. Delhi: Naga, 1988.

Ṣaḍdarśananirṇaya of Merutuṅga. In *Jainadārśanikaprakaraṇasaṅgraha*, edited by Nagin J. Shah. Ahmedabad: LD Institute of Indology, 1973.

Ṣaḍdarśanasamuccaya of Haribhadra with *Tarkarahasyadīpikā* Commentary of Guṇaratna. Edited by Luigi Suali. Calcutta: Asiatic Society, 1905.

Safīnah-i Ḥāfiẓ. Edited by Masᶜud Janati ᶜAtaʾi. Tehran: Chapkhanah-i Haydari, 1968.

Sāhityadarpaṇa of Viśvanātha. Edited by Durga Prasad Dvivedi. 1922. Reprint, New Delhi: Panini, 1982.

Saṃskṛtapārasīkapadaprakāśa of Karṇapūra. Kashi: Yogapracarini, 1952.

Sarvadeśavṛttāntasaṅgraha; or, Akbarnāmā: Being an Abridged Sanskrit Rendering of the Persian Akbarnāmā of Maheśa Ṭhaskkura. Edited by Subhadra Jha. Patna: Patna University, 1962/1963.

Shāhnāmah of Abū al-Qāsim Firdawsī. Edited by Jalal Khaleghi Motlagh. 8 vols. New York: Bibliotheca Persica, 1987–2008.

Śṛṅgāradarpaṇa of Padmasundara. Edited by Shiv Shanker Tripathi. Allahabad: Bharatiya Manisha-Sutram, 2006.

Śṛṅgāratilaka of Rudraṭa with *Sahṛdayalīlā* of Ruyyaka. Edited by Richard Pischel. Varanasi: Prachya Prakashan, 1968.

Storia do Mogor; or, Mogul India 1653–1708 of Niccolao Manucci. Translated by William Irvine. 4 vols. London: J. Murray, 1907–1908.

Ṭabaqāt-i Akbarī of Khvājah Niẓām al-Dīn Aḥmad. Edited by Brajendranath De. 2 vols. Calcutta: Asiatic Society of Bengal, 1927–1931.

Tārīkh-i Firishtah of Muḥammad Qāsim Firishtah. 2 vols. Pune: Dar al-Imarah, 1832.

Travels in the Mogul Empire, A.D. *1656–1668* of François Bernier. Edited by Vincent A. Smith. Translated by Archibald Constable. London: Oxford University Press, 1914.

Vasantarājaśākuna with *Ṭīkā* of Bhānucandra. Mumbai: Khemraj Sri Krishnadasa Sreshthina, 1987.

Vijayadevamāhātmya of Vallabha Pāṭhaka. Edited by Bhikshu Jinavijaya. Ahmedabad: Modi, 1928.

Vijayapraśastimahākāvya of Hemavijaya with the Commentary of Guṇavijaya. Mumbai: Shri Jinashasan Aradhana Trust, 1988.

Virudāvalī of Raghudeva Miśra. Edited by Jagannath Pathak. Prayag: Ganganatha Jha Kendriya Sanskrit Vidyapithan, 1979.

Vividhatīrthakalpa of Jinaprabhasūri. Edited by Jina Vijaya. Shantiniketan: Adhisthat, Singhi Jain Jnanapitha, 1934.

Works of Rudra Kavi [including *Dānaśāhacarita*, *Khānakhānācarita*, and *Kīrtisamullāsa*]. Edited by Jatindra Bimal Chaudhuri. Calcutta: Pracyavani, 1959.

SECONDARY SOURCES

Adamjee, Qamar, and Audrey Truschke. "Reimagining the 'Idol-Temple of Hindustan': Textual and Visual Translation of Sanskrit Texts in Mughal India." In *Pearls on a String: Artists, Patrons, and Poets at the Great Islamic Courts*, edited by Amy Landau. Baltimore: Walters Art Museum; Seattle: University of Washington Press, 2015.

Aggarwal, Neil Krishan. "The Rama Story of Brij Narain Chakbast." *Annual of Urdu Studies* 22 (2007): 146–61.

Ahmed, Manan. "Adam's Mirror: The Frontier in the Imperial Imagination." *Economic and Political Weekly* 46, no. 13 (2011): 60–65.

——. "The Long Thirteenth Century of the *Chachnama*." *Indian Economic and Social History Review* 49, no. 4 (2012): 459–91.

Ahuja, Y. D. "Some Aspects of the Persian Prose Translation of the Gita Ascribed to Abu'l-Fazl." *Indo-Iranica* 13, no. 3 (1960): 20–27.

Alam, Muzaffar. "*Akẖlāqī* Norms and Mughal Governance." In *The Making of Indo-Persian Culture: Indian and French Studies*, edited by Muzaffar Alam, Françoise "Nalini" Delvoye, and Marc Gaborieau, 67–95. New Delhi: Manohar, 2000.

——. "Competition and Co-existence: Indo-Islamic Interaction in Medieval North India." Special issue, *Itinerario* 13, no. 1 (1989): 37–60.

——. "The Culture and Politics of Persian in Precolonial Hindustan." In *Literary Cultures in History: Reconstructions from South Asia*, edited by Sheldon Pollock, 131–98. Berkeley: University of California Press, 2003.

——. "The Debate Within: A Sufi Critique of Religious Law, *Tasawwuf* and Politics in Mughal India." *South Asian History and Culture* 2, no. 2 (2011): 138–59.

——. *The Languages of Political Islam: India, 1200–1800*. Chicago: University of Chicago Press, 2004.

——. "The Mughals, the Sufi Shaikhs and the Formation of the Akbari Dispensation." *Modern Asian Studies* 43, no. 1 (2009): 135–74.

——. "Strategy and Imagination in a Mughal Sufi Story of Creation." *Indian Economic and Social History Review* 49, no. 2 (2012): 151–95.

——. "Trade, State Policy and Regional Change: Aspects of Mughal-Uzbek Commercial Relations, c. 1550–1750." *Journal of the Economic and Social History of the Orient* 37, no. 3 (1994): 202–27.

Alam, Muzaffar, and Sanjay Subrahmanyam. "Frank Disputations: Catholics and Muslims in the Court of Jahangir (1608–11)." *Indian Economic and Social History Review* 46, no. 4 (2009): 457–511.

———. "A Place in the Sun: Travels with Faiẓî in the Deccan, 1591–1593." In *Les sources et le temps, Sources and Time: A Colloquium*, edited by François Grimal, 265–307. Pondicherry: Institut Français de Pondichery, École Française d'Extrême-Orient, 2001.

———. "Witnesses and Agents of Empire: Eighteenth-Century Historiography and the World of the Mughal *Munshī*." *Journal of the Economic and Social History of the Orient* 53, nos. 1–2 (2009): 393–423.

———. *Writing the Mughal World: Studies on Culture and Politics*. New York: Columbia University Press, 2012.

Alavi, Seema, ed. *The Eighteenth Century in India*. New Delhi: Oxford University Press, 2002.

———. "Siddiq Hasan Khan (1832–90) and the Creation of a Muslim Cosmopolitanism in the 19th Century." *Journal of the Economic and Social History of the Orient* 54, no. 1 (2011): 1–38.

Ali, Daud. *Courtly Culture and Political Life in Early Medieval India*. Cambridge: Cambridge University Press, 2004.

Ali, M. Athar. *The Apparatus of Empire: Awards of Ranks, Offices and Titles to the Mughal Nobility, 1574–1658*. Aligarh: Centre of Advanced Study in History, Aligarh Muslim University and Oxford University Press, 1985.

———. "The Evolution of the Perception of India: Akbar and Abu'l Fazl." *Social Scientist* 24, no. 1/3 (1996): 80–88.

———. "Pursuing an Elusive Seeker of Universal Truth: The Identity and Environment of the Author of the *Dabistān-i Mazāhib*." *Journal of the Royal Asiatic Society*, 3rd ser., 9, no. 3 (1999): 365–73.

———. "Translations of Sanskrit Works at Akbar's Court." *Social Scientist* 20, no. 9/10 (1992): 38–45.

Allsen, Thomas T. *Culture and Conquest in Mongol Eurasia*. Cambridge: Cambridge University Press, 2001.

Alvi, Sajida S. "Religion and State During the Reign of Mughal Emperor Jahăngīr (1605–27): Nonjuristical Perspectives." *Studia Islamica* 69 (1989): 95–119.

Amin, Shahid. "Retelling the Muslim Conquest of North India." In *History and the Present*, edited by Partha Chatterjee and Anjan Ghosh, 24–43. Delhi: Permanent Black, 2002.

Andhare, Shridhar. "Imperial Mughal Tolerance of Jainism and Jain Painting Activity in Gujarat." In *Arts of Mughal India: Studies in Honour of Robert Skelton*, edited by Rosemary Crill, Susan Stronge, and Andrew Topsfield, 223–33. London: Victoria and Albert Museum; Ahmedabad: Mapin, 2004.

Anooshahr, Ali. "Author of One's Fate: Fatalism and Agency in Indo-Persian Histories." *Indian Economic and Social History Review* 49, no. 2 (2012): 197–224.

———. "Mughal Historians and the Memory of the Islamic Conquest of India." *Indian Economic and Social History Review* 43, no. 3 (2006): 275–300.

Ansari, Mohammad Azhar. *Administrative Documents of Mughal India*. New Delhi: B. R. Publishing, 1984.

Appadurai, Arjun. "Number in the Colonial Imagination." In *Orientalism and the Postcolonial Predicament: Perspectives on South Asia*, edited by Carol A. Breckenridge and Peter van der Veer, 314–40. Philadelphia: University of Pennsylvania Press, 1993.

Appiah, Kwame Anthony. "Thick Translation." *Callaloo* 16, no. 4 (1993): 808–19.

Apte, Prabhakar. "The Empire of Polysemy as Evidenced in Artharatnavali of Samaya Sundaragani." In *Kośa Vijñāna: Siddhānta Evaṃ Mūlyāṅkana*, edited by Satish Kumar Rohra and D. Pitambar, 89–91. Agra: Kendriya Hindi Samsthan, 1989.

Asad, Talal. *Formations of the Secular: Christianity, Islam, Modernity*. Stanford: Stanford University Press, 2003.

Asher, Catherine B. "A Ray from the Sun: Mughal Ideology and the Visual Construction of the Divine." In *The Presence of Light: Divine Radiance and Religious Experience*, edited by Matthew T. Kapstein, 161–94. Chicago: University of Chicago Press, 2004.

Asher, Catherine B., and Cynthia Talbot. *India Before Europe*. Cambridge: Cambridge University Press, 2006.

Athavale, R. B. "New Light on the Life of Paṇḍitarāja Jagannātha." *Annals of the Bhandarkar Oriental Research Institute* 48/49 (1968): 415–20.

Azad, Mohammad Akram Lari. *Religion and Politics in India During the Seventeenth Century*. New Delhi: Criterion, 1990.

Balabanlilar, Lisa. *Imperial Identity in the Mughal Empire: Memory and Dynastic Politics in Early Modern South and Central Asia*. London: Tauris, 2012.

Balbir, Nalini. "Mount Śatruñjaya." *Jainpedia* (2012), http://www.jainpedia.org/themes/places/jain-holy-places/mount-satrunjaya.html.

——. "Samayasundara's *Sāmācārī-śataka* and Jain Sectarian Divisions in the Seventeenth Century." In *Essays in Jaina Philosophy and Religion*, edited by Piotr Balcerowicz, 253–77. Delhi: Motilal Banarsidass, 2003.

Barker, Rodney. *Legitimating Identities: The Self-Presentations of Rulers and Subjects*. Cambridge: Cambridge University Press, 2001.

Bashir, Shahzad. "A Perso-Islamic Universal Chronicle in Its Historical Context: Ghiyās̱ al-Dīn Khwāndamīr's *Ḥabīb al-siyar*." In *History and Religion: Narrating a Religious Past*, edited by Bernd-Christian Otto, Susanne Rau, and Jörg Rüpke, 209–25. Berlin: De Gruyter, 2015.

Bauer, Jerome. "Dohada (Pregnancy Cravings)." In *South Asian Folklore: An Encyclopedia*, edited by Margaret A. Mills, Peter J. Claus, and Sarah Diamond, 163. New York: Routledge, 2003.

Beach, Milo Cleveland. *The Imperial Image: Paintings for the Mughal Court*. Rev. and expanded ed. Washington, D.C: Freer Gallery of Art, Arthur M. Sackler Gallery; Ahmedabad: Mapin, 2012.

——. *Mughal and Rajput Painting*. Cambridge: Cambridge University Press, 1992.

——. "The Mughal Painter Kesu Dās." *Archives of Asian Art* 30 (1976): 34–52.

Behl, Aditya. *Love's Subtle Magic: An Indian Islamic Literary Tradition, 1379–1545*. Edited by Wendy Doniger. New York: Oxford University Press, 2012.

——. "The Magic Doe: Desire and Narrative in a Hindavi Sufi Romance, Circa 1503." In *India's Islamic Traditions, 711–1750*, edited by Richard M. Eaton, 180–208. New Delhi: Oxford University Press, 2003.

——. "Pages from the Book of Religions, Encountering Difference in Mughal India." In *Forms of Knowledge in Early Modern Asia: Explorations in the Intellectual History of India and Tibet, 1500–1800*, edited by Sheldon Pollock, 210–39. Durham: Duke University Press, 2011.

Bendrey, Vasudeo Sitaram. *Tārīkh-i-Ilāhī*. Poona: Nare, 1933.

Berlekamp, Persis. *Wonder, Image, and Cosmos in Medieval Islam*. New Haven: Yale University Press, 2011.

Beveridge, H. "The Rauẓat-uṭ-Tāhirīn." *Journal and Proceedings of the Asiatic Society of Bengal* 14 (1918): 269–77.

Bhandarkar, R. G. *Report on the Search for Sanskrit Mss. in the Bombay Presidency During the Year 1882–83*. Bombay: Government Central Press, 1884.

Bhattacharyya, Dineshchandra. "Sanskrit Scholars of Akbar's Time." *Indian Historical Quarterly* 13 (1937): 31–36.

Binski, Paul. *Westminster Abbey and the Plantagenets: Kingship and the Representation of Power, 1200–1400*. New Haven: Yale University Press, 1995.

Blair, Sheila S. *A Compendium of Chronicles: Rashid al-Din's Illustrated History of the World*. London: Nour Foundation in association with Azimuth Editions and Oxford University Press, 1995.

Blake, Stephen P. "*Nau Ruz* in Mughal India." In *Rethinking a Millennium: Perspectives on Indian History from the Eighth to the Eighteenth Century; Essays for Harbans Mukhia*, edited by Rajat Datta, 121–35. Delhi: Aakar Books, 2008.

—. "The Patrimonial-Bureaucratic Empire of the Mughals." *Journal of Asian Studies* 39, no. 1 (1979): 77–94.

Boucher, Daniel. "Gāndhārī and the Early Chinese Buddhist Translations Reconsidered: The Case of the *Saddharmapuṇḍarīkasūtra*." *Journal of the American Oriental Society* 118, no. 4 (1998): 471–506.

Brand, Michael, and Glenn D. Lowry, eds. *Fatehpur-Sikri*. Bombay: Marg, 1987.

Bronkhorst, Johannes. "Bhaṭṭoji Dīkṣita on Sphoṭa." *Journal of Indian Philosophy* 33, no. 1 (2005): 3–41.

Bronner, Yigal. "Change in Disguise: The Early Discourse on *Vyājastuti*." *Journal of the American Oriental Society* 129, no. 2 (2009): 179–98.

Bronner, Yigal, and David Shulman. "'A Cloud Turned Goose': Sanskrit in the Vernacular Millennium." *Indian Economic and Social History Review* 43, no. 1 (2006): 1–30.

Bronner, Yigal, and Gary Tubb. "Blaming the Messenger: A Controversy in Late Sanskrit Poetics and Its Implications." *Bulletin of the School of Oriental and African Studies* 71, no. 1 (2008): 75–91.

—. "*Vastutas tu*: Methodology and the New School of Sanskrit Poetics." *Journal of Indian Philosophy* 36, nos. 5–6 (2008): 619–32.

Brown, Katherine Butler. "Did Aurangzeb Ban Music? Questions for the Historiography of His Reign." *Modern Asian Studies* 41, no. 1 (2007): 77–120.

—. "Evidence of Indo-Persian Musical Synthesis? The *Tanbur* and *Rudra Vina* in Seventeenth-Century Indo-Persian Treatises." *Journal of the Indian Musicological Society* 36–37 (2006): 89–103.

Buchanan, Francis. *An Account of the District of Purnea in 1809–10*. Patna: Bihar and Orissa Research Society, 1928.

Burbank, Jane, and Frederick Cooper. *Empires in World History: Power and the Politics of Difference*. Princeton: Princeton University Press, 2010.

Busch, Allison. "The Anxiety of Innovation: The Practice of Literary Science in the Hindi/*Riti* Tradition." *Comparative Studies of South Asia, Africa and the Middle East* 24, no. 2 (2004): 45–59.

—. "Hidden in Plain View: Brajbhasha Poets at the Mughal Court." *Modern Asian Studies* 44, no. 2 (2010): 267–309.

—. "Poetry in Motion: Literary Circulation in Mughal India." and *Culture and Circulation: Literature in Motion in Early Modern India*, edited by Thomas de Bruijn and Allison Busch, 186–221. Leiden: Brill, 2014.

———. *Poetry of Kings: The Classical Hindi Literature of Mughal India*. New York: Oxford University Press, 2011.
———. "Portrait of a Raja in a Badshah's World: Amrit Rai's Biography of Man Singh (1585)." *Journal of the Economic and Social History of the Orient* 55, nos. 2–3 (2012): 287–328.
———. "Riti and Register: Lexical Variation in Courtly Braj Bhasha Texts." In *Before the Divide: Hindi and Urdu Literary Culture*, edited by Francesca Orsini, 84–120. Delhi: Orient Blackswan, 2010.
Carvalho, Pedro Moura. *Mirʾāt al-Quds (Mirror of Holiness): A Life of Christ for Emperor Akbar; A Commentary on Father Jerome Xavier's Text and the Miniatures of Cleveland Museum of Art, Acc. No. 2005.145*. With a translation and annotated transcription of the text by Wheeler M. Thackston. Leiden: Brill, 2012.
Chaghatai, M. A. "The Illustrated Edition of the Razm Nama (Persian Version of the Mahābhārata) at Akbar's Court." In *Bulletin of the Deccan College Research Institute: V. S. Sukthankar Memorial Volume*, edited by V. M. Apte and H. D. Sankalia, 281–329. Poona: Deccan College, 1944.
Chakrabarty, Dipesh. "The Muddle of Modernity." *American Historical Review* 116, no. 3 (2011): 663–75.
Chakravarti, Chintaharan. "Muslim Patronage to Sanskrit Learning." In *B.C. Law Volume*, edited by D. R. Bhandarkar, K. A. Nilakanta Sastri, B. M. Barua, B. K. Ghosh, and P. K. Gode, 2:176–82. Poona: Bhandarkar Oriental Research Institute, 1946.
———. "Review of *Jagadvijayacchandas* ed. Raja." *Indian Historical Quarterly* 22 (1946): 320–22.
Chand, Tara. "Rāfiʾ-ul-Khilāf of Sita Ram Kayastha Saksena, of Lucknow (Kavīndrācārya's Jñānasāra and Its Persian Translation)." *Journal of the Ganganatha Jha Research Institute* 2, no. 1 (1944): 7–12.
Chandra, Jnan. "ʿAlamgir's Tolerance in the Light of Contemporary Jain Literature." *Journal of the Pakistan Historical Society* 6, no. 1 (1958): 269–72.
Chandra, Pramod. "Ustād Sālivāhana and the Development of Popular Mughal Art." *Lalit Kala* 8 (1960): 25–46.
Chandra, Satish. *State, Society, and Culture in Indian History*. New Delhi: Oxford University Press, 2012.
Chatterjee, Kumkum. "Cultural Flows and Cosmopolitanism in Mughal India: The Bishnupur Kingdom." *Indian Economic and Social History Review* 46, no. 2 (2009): 147–82.
———. *The Cultures of History in Early Modern India: Persianization and Mughal Culture in Bengal*. New Delhi: Oxford University Press, 2009.
Chattopadhyaya, Brajadulal. *Representing the Other? Sanskrit Sources and the Muslims (Eighth to Fourteenth Century)*. New Delhi: Manohar, 1998.
Chaudhuri, Jatindra Bimal. *Contributions of Muslims to Sanskrit Learning: Khān Khānān Abdur Rahim (1557 A.D.–1605 A.D.) and Contemporary Sanskrit Learning (1551–1650 A.D.)*. Calcutta: Pracyavani, 1954.
———. *Muslim Patronage to Sanskritic Learning*. Calcutta: Pracyavani, 1954.
Cohn, Bernard S. *Colonialism and Its Forms of Knowledge: The British in India*. Princeton: Princeton University Press, 1996.
Cole, Juan R. I. "Iranian Culture and South Asia, 1500–1900." In *Iran and the Surrounding World: Interactions in Culture and Cultural Politics*, edited by Nikki R. Keddie and Rudi Matthee, 15–35. Seattle: University of Washington Press, 2002.
Commissariat, M. S. "Imperial Mughal Farmans in Gujarat." *Journal of the University of Bombay* 9, no. 1 (1940): 1–56.

Cort, John E. "Genres of Jain History." *Journal of Indian Philosophy* 23, no. 4 (1995): 469–506.
——. "Making It Vernacular in Agra: The Practice of Translation by Seventeenth-Century Jains." In *Tellings and Texts: Music, Literature and Performance Cultures in North India*, edited by Francesca Orsini and Katherine Butler Schofield. Cambridge: Open Book, 2015.
——. "A Tale of Two Cities: On the Origins of Digambar Sectarianism in North India." In *Multiple Histories: Culture and Society in the Study of Rajasthan*, edited by Lawrence A. Babb, Varsha Joshi, and Michael W. Meister, 39–83. Jaipur: Rawat, 2002.
——. "Who Is a King? Jain Narratives of Kingship in Medieval Western India." In *Open Boundaries: Jain Communities and Culture in Indian History*, edited by John E. Cort, 85–110. Albany: SUNY Press, 1998.
Dale, Stephen F. *The Garden of the Eight Paradises: Bābur and the Culture of Empire in Central Asia, Afghanistan and India (1483-1530)*. Leiden: Brill, 2004.
Danner, Victor. "Arabic Literature in Iran." In *The Cambridge History of Iran, Volume 4: The Period from the Arab Invasion to the Saljuqs*, edited by R. N. Frye, 566–94. Cambridge: Cambridge University Press, 1975.
Das, Asok Kumar. "Akbar's Imperial Ramayana: A Mughal Persian Manuscript." In *The Legend of Rama: Artistic Visions*, edited by Vidya Dehejia, 73–84. Bombay: Marg, 1994.
——. "Daswant: His Last Drawings in the *Razmnama*." In *Mughal Masters: Further Studies*, edited by Asok Kumar Das, 52–67. Mumbai: Marg, 1998.
——. "An Introductory Note on the Emperor Akbar's *Ramayana* and Its Miniatures." In *Facets of Indian Art: A Symposium Held at the Victoria and Albert Museum on 26, 27, 28 April and 1 May 1982*, edited by Robert Skelton, Andrew Topsfield, Susan Stronge, and Rosemary Crill, 94–104. London: Victoria and Albert Museum, 1986.
——. "Notes on the Emperor Akbar's Manuscript of the Persian Ramayana." In *Asian Variations in Ramayana: Papers Presented at the International Seminar on "Variations in Ramayana in Asia: Their Cultural, Social, and Anthropological Significance," New Delhi, January 1981*, edited by K. R. Srinivasa Iyengar, 144–53. New Delhi: Sahitya Akademi, 1983.
——. "Notes on Four Illustrations of the Birla *Razmnama* and Their Counterparts in Other *Razmnama* Manuscripts." In *Arts of Mughal India: Studies in Honour of Robert Skelton*, edited by Rosemary Crill, Andrew Topsfield, and Susan Stronge, 67–79. London: Victoria and Albert Museum; Ahmedabad: Mapin, 2004.
——. *Paintings of the Razmnama: The Book of War*. Ahmedabad: Mapin, 2005.
Dayal, Parmeshwar, ed. and trans. *Gita in Persian*. Lucknow: Prakashan Kendra, 1995.
de Bruijn, Thomas. "Shifting Semantics in Early Modern North Indian Poetry: Circulation of Culture and Meaning." In *Culture and Circulation: Literature in Motion in Early Modern India*, edited by Thomas de Bruijn and Allison Busch, 139–59. Leiden: Brill, 2014.
Delvoye, Françoise "Nalini." "Indo-Persian Accounts on Music Patronage in the Sultanate of Gujarat." In *The Making of Indo-Persian Culture: Indian and French Studies*, edited by Muzaffar Alam, Françoise "Nalini" Delvoye, and Marc Gaborieau, 253–80. New Delhi: Manohar, 2000.
——. "Indo-Persian Literature on Art-Music: Some Historical and Technical Aspects." In *Confluence of Cultures: French Contributions to Indo-Persian Studies*, edited by Françoise "Nalini" Delvoye, 93–130. New Delhi: Manohar; Tehran: Institut Français de Recherche en Iran, 1995.
——. "Les chants *dhrupad* en langue Braj des poètes-musiciens de l'Inde Moghole." In *Littératures médiévales de l'Inde du nord*, edited by Françoise Mallison, 139–85. Paris: École Française d'Extrême-Orient, 1991.

Derrett, J. Duncan M. "Greece and India Again: The Jaimini-Aśvamedha, the Alexander-Romance and the Gospels." *Zeitschrift für Religions- und Geistesgeschichte* 22 (1970): 19–44.

Desai, Mohanlal Dalichand. "Introduction." In *Bhānucandragaṇicarita*, 1–102. Ahmedabad-Calcutta: Sanchalaka-Singhi Jain Granthamala, 1941.

Deshpande, Madhav M. *Sanskrit and Prakrit: Sociolinguistic Issues*. Delhi: Motilal Banarsidass, 1993.

Deshpande, Prachi. *Creative Pasts: Historical Memory and Identity in Western India, 1700–1960*. New York: Columbia University Press, 2007.

Dihlavi, Abd al-Vadud Azhar. "Introduction." In *Rāmāyan: Kitāb-i Muqaddas-i Hindū'ān*. Tehran: Intisharat-i Bunyad-i Farhang-i Iran, 1971.

Dirlik, Arif. "Revisioning Modernity: Modernity in Eurasian Perspectives." *Inter-Asia Cultural Studies* 12, no. 2 (2011): 284–305.

Doniger, Wendy. *The Hindus: An Alternative History*. New York: Penguin, 2009.

D'Onofrio, Svevo. "A Persian Commentary to the Upaniṣads: Dārā Šikōh's *Sirr-i Akbar*." In *Muslim Cultures in the Indo-Iranian World during the Early-Modern and Modern Periods*, edited by Fabrizio Speziale and Denis Hermann, 533–63. Berlin: Klaus Schwarz Verlag, 2010.

Dundas, Paul. *History, Scripture and Controversy in a Medieval Jain Sect*. London: Routledge, 2007.

—. "Jain Perceptions of Islam in the Early Modern Period." *Indo-Iranian Journal* 42, no. 1 (1999): 35–46.

—. *The Jains*. 2nd ed. London: Routledge, 2002.

Eaton, Richard M., ed. *India's Islamic Traditions, 711–1750*. New Delhi: Oxford University Press, 2003.

—. "Temple Desecration and Indo-Muslim States." In *Beyond Turk and Hindu: Rethinking Religious Identities in Islamicate South Asia*, edited by David Gilmartin and Bruce B. Lawrence, 246–81. Gainesville: University Press of Florida, 2000.

Eaton, Richard M., and Phillip B. Wagoner. *Power, Memory, Architecture: Contested Sites on India's Deccan Plateau, 1300–1600*. New Delhi: Oxford University Press, 2014.

Eck, Diana L. *India: A Sacred Geography*. New York: Harmony Books, 2012.

Edgerton, Franklin. "Introduction." In *The Mahābhārata, for the First Time Critically Edited*, edited by Vishnu S. Sukthankar et. al. Vol. 2. Poona: Bhandarkar Oriental Research Institute, 1944.

Eggeling, Julius, Ernst Windisch, Ernst Anton Max Haas, Arthur Berriedale Keith, and Frederick William Thomas, eds. *Catalogue of the Sanskrit Manuscripts in the Library of the India Office*. 4 vols. London: Printed by order of the secretary of state for India in council, 1887–1935.

Elliot, H. M., and John Dowson. *The History of India, as Told by Its Own Historians*. London: Trübner, 1867–1877.

Ernst, Carl W. *Eternal Garden: Mysticism, History, and Politics at a South Asian Sufi Center*. Albany: SUNY Press, 1992.

—. "Fayzi's Illuminationist Interpretation of Vedanta: The *Shariq al-ma'rifa*." *Comparative Studies of South Asia, Africa and the Middle East* 30, no. 3 (2010): 356–64.

—. "Indian Lovers in Arabic and Persian Guise: Āzād Bilgrāmī's Depiction of *Nāyikas*." *Journal of Hindu Studies* 6, no. 1 (2013): 37–51.

—. "The Islamization of Yoga in the *Amrtakunda* Translations." *Journal of the Royal Asiatic Society* 13, no. 2 (2003): 199–226.

——. "The Limits of Universalism in Islamic Thought: The Case of Indian Religions." *Muslim World* 101, no. 1 (2011): 1–19.

——. "Muslim Studies of Hinduism? A Reconsideration of Arabic and Persian Translations from Indian Languages." *Iranian Studies* 36, no. 2 (2003): 173–95.

——. "Sufism and Yoga According to Muhammad Ghawth." *Sufi* 29 (1996): 9–13.

Ethe, Hermann. *Catalogue of Persian Manuscripts in the Library of the India Office*. Vol 1. Oxford: India Office, 1903.

Faruqi, Shamsur Rahman. *Early Urdu Literary Culture and History*. New Delhi: Oxford University Press, 2001.

——. "A Stranger in the City: The Poetics of *Sabk-e Hindi*." *Annual of Urdu Studies* 19 (2004): 1–93.

Faruqui, Munis D. "The Forgotten Prince: Mirza Hakim and the Formation of the Mughal Empire in India." *Journal of the Economic and Social History of the Orient* 48, no. 4 (2005): 487–523.

——. *The Princes of the Mughal Empire, 1504–1719*. New York: Cambridge University Press, 2012.

Filliozat, Jean. "Dara Shikoh's *Samudrasangama*." In *On Becoming an Indian Muslim: French Essays on Aspects of Syncretism*, edited by M. Waseem, 131–44. New Delhi: Oxford University Press, 2003.

Findly, Ellison B. *From the Courts of India: Indian Miniatures in the Collection of the Worcester Art Museum*. Worcester: Worcester Art Museum, 1981.

——. "Jahāngīr's Vow of Non-Violence." *Journal of the American Oriental Society* 107, no. 2 (1987): 245–56.

Firoze, M. "A Note on Abul Fazl's Account of Hindu Mythology." *Indo-Iranica* 39, nos. 1–4 (1986): 100–119.

Fischel, Roy S. "Society, Space, and the State in the Deccan Sultanates, 1565–1636." Ph.D. diss., University of Chicago, 2012.

Fischel, Walter J. "Jews and Judaism at the Court of the Moghul Emperors in Medieval India." *Proceedings of the American Academy for Jewish Research* 18 (1948–1949): 137–77.

Fitzgerald, James L., ed. and trans. *The Mahābhārata: Book 11, The Book of the Women, Book 12, The Book of Peace, Part One*. Vol. 7. Chicago: University of Chicago Press, 2004.

Flood, Finbarr B. *Objects of Translation: Material Culture and Medieval "Hindu-Muslim" Encounter*. Princeton: Princeton University Press, 2009.

Flores, Jorge. "How Cosmopolitan Were the Hindu Interpreters of Early Modern Goa?" Paper presented at Cosmopolitanism in the Early Modern World: The Case of South Asia (16th–18th centuries), Paris, May 24–25, 2012.

Flores, Jorge, and Sanjay Subrahmanyam. "The Shadow Sultan: Succession and Imposture in the Mughal Empire, 1628–1640." *Journal of the Economic and Social History of the Orient* 47, no. 1 (2004): 80–121.

Flügel, Peter. "Demographic Trends in Jaina Monasticism." In *Studies in Jaina History and Culture: Disputes and Dialogues*, edited by Peter Flügel, 312–98. London: Routledge, 2006.

Folkert, Kendall W. *Scripture and Community: Collected Essays on the Jains*. Edited by John E. Cort. Atlanta: Scholars Press, 1993.

Foltz, Richard C. *Mughal India and Central Asia*. Karachi: Oxford University Press, 1998.

Foucault, Michel. *Discipline and Punish: The Birth of the Prison*. New York: Random House, 1977.

Friedmann, Yohanan. "Medieval Muslim Views of Indian Religions." *Journal of the American Oriental Society* 95, no. 2 (1975): 214–21.

Gabbay, Alyssa. *Islamic Tolerance: Amīr Khusraw and Pluralism*. New York: Routledge, 2010.

Gadon, Elinor W. "Note on the Frontispiece." In *The Sants: Studies in a Devotional Tradition of India*, edited by Karine Schomer and W. H. McLeod, 415–21. Delhi: Motilal Banarsidass; Berkeley: Berkeley Religious Studies Series, 1987.

Gallego, María Angeles. "The Languages of Medieval Iberia and Their Religious Dimension." *Medieval Encounters* 9, no. 1 (2003): 107–39.

Gandhi, Supriya. "The Prince and the *Muvaḥḥid*: Dārā Shikoh and Mughal Engagements with Vedānta." In *Religious Interactions in Mughal India*, edited by Vasudha Dalmia and Munis D. Faruqui, 65–101. New Delhi: Oxford University Press, 2014.

Ganeri, Jonardon. "Dārā Shukoh and the Transmission of the Upaniṣads to Islam." In *Migrating Texts and Traditions*, edited by William Sweet, 150–61. Ottawa: University of Ottawa Press, 2012.

——. *The Lost Age of Reason: Philosophy in Early Modern India 1450–1700*. Oxford: Oxford University Press, 2011.

Gode, P. K. "Bernier and Kavīndrācārya Sarasvatī at the Mughal Court." In *Studies in Indian Literary History*, 2:364–79. Bombay: Singhi Jain Sastra Sikshapith, 1954.

——. "The Chronology of the Works of Puṇḍarīkaviṭṭhala of Karṇāṭak." *Journal of the Music Academy, Madras* 6–8 (1935–1937): 119–26.

——. "The Historical Background of the Cimani-carita." In *Cīmanicarita*, edited by Prabhat Shastri, 67–80. Allahabad: Devabhasha Prakashanam, 1976.

——. "The Identification of Gosvāmi Nṛsiṁhāśrama of Dara Shukoh's Sanskrit Letter with Brahmendra Sarasvatī of the Kavīndra-Candrodaya—Between A.D. 1628 and 1658." In *Studies in Indian Literary History*, 2:447–51. Bombay: Singhi Jain Sastra Sikshapith, 1954.

——. "Quotations from the Śṛṅgāra-Sañjīvinī of Harideva Miśra in the Śloka-Saṁgraha of Maṇirāma—Between A.D. 1650 and 1700." In *Studies in Indian Literary History*, 2:211–15. Bombay: Singhi Jain Sastra Sikshapith, 1954.

——. "Samudra-Saṅgama, a Philosophical Work by Dara Shukoh, Son of Shah Jahan, Composed in A.D. 1655." In *Studies in Indian Literary History*, 2:435–46. Bombay: Singhi Jain Sastra Sikshapith, 1954.

——. "Some Evidence about the Location of the Manuscript Library of Kavindracharya Sarasvati at Benares in A.D. 1665." In *Jagadvijayacchandas*, edited by C. Kunhan Raja, 47–57. Bikaner: Anup Sanskrit Library, 1945.

Gopal, Surendra. "The Jain Community and Akbar." In *Akbar and His Age*, edited by Iqtidar Alam Khan, 160–67. New Delhi: Northern Book Centre, 1999.

Gordon, Stewart, ed. *Robes of Honour:* Khil'at *in Pre-colonial and Colonial India*. New Delhi: Oxford University Press, 2003.

Granoff, Phyllis. "Authority and Innovation: A Study of the Use of Similes in the Biography of Hiravijaya to Provide Sanction for the Monk at Court." *Jinamanjari* 1 (1990): 48–60.

——. "The Biographies of Siddhasena: A Study in the Texture of Allusion and the Weaving of a Group-Image (Part 1)." *Journal of Indian Philosophy* 17, no. 4 (1989): 329–84.

——. "The Jina Bleeds: Threats to the Faith and the Rescue of the Faithful in Medieval Jain Stories." In *Images, Miracles, and Authority in Asian Religious Traditions*, edited by Richard H. Davis, 121–39. Boulder: Westview Press, 1998.

——. "Jinaprabhasūri and Jinadattasūri: Two Studies from the Śvetāmbara Jain Tradition." In *Speaking of Monks: Religious Biography in India and China*, edited by Phyllis Granoff and Koichi Shinohara, 1–96. Oakville, Ont.: Mosaic Press, 1992.

—. "Medieval Jain Accounts of Mt. Girnar and Śatruñjaya: Visible and Invisible Sacred Realms." *Journal of the Oriental Institute* 49 (1999): 143–70.

—. "Mountains of Eternity: Raidhū and the Colossal Jinas of Gwalior." *Rivista di Studi Sudasiatici* 1 (2006): 31–50.

—. "The Politics of Religious Biography: The Biography of Balibhadra the Usurper." *Bulletin d'Études Indiennes* 9 (1991): 75–91.

Grobbel, Gerald. *Der Dichter Faiḍī und die Religion Akbars*. Berlin: Klaus Schwarz Verlag, 2001.

Guha, Sumit. "Westerners and Knowledge of the West at the Maratha Courts c.1670–1820." Paper presented at Cosmopolitanism in the Early Modern World: The Case of South Asia (16th–18th centuries), Paris, May 24–25, 2012.

—. *Environment and Ethnicity in India, 1200–1991*. Cambridge: Cambridge University Press, 1999.

—. "The Frontiers of Memory: What the Marathas Remembered of Vijayanagara." *Modern Asian Studies* 43, no. 1 (2009): 269–88.

—. "Speaking Historically: The Changing Voices of Historical Narration in Western India, 1400–1900." *American Historical Review* 109, no. 4 (2004): 1084–1103.

Guy, John, and Jorrit Britschgi. *Wonder of the Age: Master Painters of India, 1100–1900*. New York: Metropolitan Museum of Art, 2011.

Habib, Irfan. *An Atlas of the Mughal Empire: Political and Economic Maps with Detailed Notes, Bibliography and Index*. Reprinted with corrections. Delhi: Oxford University Press, 1986.

—. "Introduction: Commemorating Akbar." In *Akbar and His Age*, edited by Iqtidar Alam Khan, xi–xvi. New Delhi: Northern Book Centre, 1999.

Habibullah, A. B. M. "An Early Arab Report on Indian Religious Sects." In *History and Society: Essays in Honour of Professor Niharranjan Ray*, edited by Debiprasad Chattopadhyaya. Calcutta: Bagchi, 1978.

—. "Medieval Indo-Persian Literature Relating to Hindu Science and Philosophy, 1000–1800 A.D." *Indian Historical Quarterly* 14, no. 1 (1938): 167–81.

Haider, Najaf. "The Monarch and the Millennium: A New Interpretation of the *Alf* Coins of Akbar." In *Coins in India: Power and Communication*, edited by Himanshu Prabha Ray, 76–83. Mumbai: Marg, 2006.

—. "Translating Texts and Straddling Worlds: Intercultural Communication in Mughal India." In *The Varied Facets of History: Essays in Honour of Aniruddha Ray*, edited by Ishrat Alam and Syed Ejaz Hussain, 115–24. Delhi: Primus Books, 2011.

Hakala, Walter Nils. "Diction and Dictionaries: Language, Literature, and Learning in Persianate South Asia." Ph.D. diss., University of Pennsylvania, 2010.

Halbfass, Wilhelm. *India and Europe: An Essay in Understanding*. Albany: SUNY Press, 1988.

Hanneder, J. "On 'The Death of Sanskrit.'" *Indo-Iranian Journal* 45, no. 4 (2002): 293–310.

Hardy, Peter. "Abul Fazl's Portrait of the Perfect Padshah: A Political Philosophy for Mughal India—or a Personal Puff for a Pal?" In *Islam in India: Studies and Commentaries*, edited by Christian W. Troll, 114–37. New Delhi: Vikas, 1985.

Harkare, Gunde Rao. "Sanskrit Under Mohammedan Patronage." *Islamic Culture* 26 (1952): 54–62.

Hatcher, Brian A. "'The Cosmos is One Family' (*Vasudhaiva Kuṭumbakam*): Problematic Mantra of Hindu Humanism." *Contributions to Indian Sociology*, n.s., 28, no. 1 (1994): 149–62.

———. "Sanskrit and the Morning After: The Metaphorics and Theory of Intellectual Change." *Indian Economic and Social History Review* 44, no. 3 (2007): 333–61.

Hawley, John Stratton. *The Memory of Love: Sūrdās Sings to Krishna*. Oxford: Oxford University Press, 2009.

Hendley, Thomas Holbein. *Memorials of the Jeypore Exhibition 1883*. Vol. 4. London: Griggs, 1884.

Hiltebeitel, Alf. *Rethinking India's Oral and Classical Epics: Draupadī Among Rajputs, Muslims, and Dalits*. Chicago: University of Chicago Press, 1999.

Hodgson, Marshall G. S. *The Venture of Islam: The Classical Age of Islam*. Vol. 1. Chicago: University of Chicago Press, 1974.

Hodivala, Shahpurshah Hormasji. *Studies in Indo-Muslim History: A Critical Commentary on Elliot and Dowson's "History of India as Told by Its Own Historians."* Vol. 1. Bombay: De Sousa, 1939.

Howe, Stephen. *Empire: A Very Short Introduction*. Oxford: Oxford University Press, 2002.

Hunsberger, Alice C. "Marvels." In *Encyclopaedia of the Qurʾān*, edited by Jane Dammen McAuliffe. Brill, 2009, http://www.brillonline.nl/entries/encyclopaedia-of-the-quran/marvels-EQSIM_00274.

Husain, Afzal. *The Nobility Under Akbar and Jahāngīr: A Study of Family Groups*. New Delhi: Manohar, 1999.

Husain, Shaikh Chand. "Translations of the *Mahābhārata* into Arabic and Persian." In *Bulletin of the Deccan College Research Institute: V. S. Sukthankar Memorial Volume*, edited by V. M. Apte and H. D. Sankalia, 267–80. Poona: Deccan College, 1944.

Ikegami, Eiko. *Bonds of Civility: Aesthetic Networks and the Political Origins of Japanese Culture*. Cambridge: Cambridge University Press, 2005.

Jackson, P. "Banākatī, Abū Solaymān Dāwūd B. Abi'l-Fażl Moḥammad (d. 1329–30), Poet and Historian." *Encyclopaedia Iranica* (1988), http://www.iranicaonline.org/articles/banakati-abu-solayman-dawud-b.

Jacob, Captain LeGrand. "Inscriptions from Palitana." *Journal of the Bombay Branch of the Royal Asiatic Society* 1 (1841–1844): 56–66.

Jahn, Karl, ed. *Rashīd al-Dīn's History of India: Collected Essays with Facsimiles and Indices*. The Hague: Mouton, 1965.

Jain, Shalin. "Interaction of the 'Lords': The Jain Community and the Mughal Royalty under Akbar." *Social Scientist* 40, nos. 3–4 (2012): 33–57.

———. "Piety, Laity and Royalty: Jains under the Mughals in the First Half of the Seventeenth Century." *Indian Historical Review* 20, no. 1 (2013): 67–92.

Jalali, S. Farrukh Ali, and S. M. Razaullah Ansari. "Persian Translation of Varāhamihira's Bṛhatsaṃhitā." *Studies in History of Medicine and Science* 9, nos. 3–4 (1985): 161–69.

Jeremiás, Éva M. "Tradition and Innovation in the Native Grammatical Literature of Persian." *Histoire épistémologie langage* 15, no. 2 (1993): 51–68.

Jhaveri, Krishnalal Mohanlal. *Imperial Farmans (*A.D. *1577 to* A.D. *1805) Granted to the Ancestors of His Holiness the Tikayat Maharaj, Translated into English, Hindi and Gujarati, with Notes*. Bombay: News Printing Press, 1928.

Kahrs, Eivind. *Indian Semantic Analysis: The* Nirvacana *Tradition*. Cambridge: Cambridge University Press, 1998.

Kapadia, Aparna. "The Last Cakravartin? The Gujarat Sultan as 'Universal King' in Fifteenth Century Sanskrit Poetry." *Medieval History Journal* 16, no. 1 (2013): 63–88.

Karambelkar, V. W. "Nabābakhānakhānācaritam." *Indian Historical Quarterly* 28 (1952): 240–48.

Karmarkar, Raghunath Damodar. "Introduction." In *The Mahābhārata, for the First Time Critically Edited*, edited by Vishnu S. Sukthankar et. al. Vol. 18. Poona: Bhandarkar Oriental Research Institute, 1960.

Kaviraj, Sudipta. *The Imaginary Institution of India: Politics and Ideas*. New York: Columbia University Press, 2010.

——. "On Thick and Thin Religion: Some Critical Reflections on Secularisation Theory." In *Religion and the Political Imagination*, edited by Ira Katznelson and Gareth Stedman Jones, 336–55. Cambridge: Cambridge University Press, 2010.

——. "The Sudden Death of Sanskrit Knowledge." *Journal of Indian Philosophy* 33 (2005): 119–42.

——. "The Two Histories of Literary Culture in Bengal." In *Literary Cultures in History: Reconstructions from South Asia*, edited by Sheldon Pollock, 503–66. Berkeley: University of California Press, 2003.

Khan, M. S. "Al-Bīrūnī and Abul Fazl: A Comparative Study of the Two Humanists and Historians." *Indo-Iranica* 38, nos. 3–4 (1985): 36–50.

Khan, Pasha M. "Marvellous Histories: Reading the *Shāhnāmah* in India." *Indian Economic and Social History Review* 49, no. 4 (2012): 527–56.

Khandalavala, Karl, and Kalpana Desai. "Indian Illustrated Manuscripts of the *Kalilah wa Dimnah*, *Anvar-i Suhayli*, and *Iyar-i Danish*." In *A Mirror for Princes from India*, edited by Ernst J. Grube, 128–44. Bombay: Marg, 1991.

Khilnani, Sunil. "Democracy and Its Indian Pasts." In *Arguments for a Better World: Essays in Honor of Amartya Sen*, vol. 2, edited by Kaushik Basu and Ravi Kanbur, 488–502. Oxford: Oxford University Press, 2009.

Kia, Mana. "Contours of Persianate Community, 1722–1835." Ph.D. diss., Harvard University, 2011.

Kinra, Rajeev. "Fresh Words for a Fresh World: *Tāza-Gūʾī* and the Poetics of Newness in Early Modern Indo-Persian Poetry." *Sikh Formations* 3, no. 2 (2007): 125–49.

——. "Handling Diversity with Absolute Civility: The Global Historical Legacy of Mughal *Ṣulḥ-i Kull*." *Medieval History Journal* 16, no. 2 (2013): 251–95.

——. "Infantilizing Bābā Dārā: The Cultural Memory of Dārā Shekuh and the Mughal Public Sphere." *Journal of Persianate Studies* 2, no. 2 (2009): 165–93.

——. "Make It Fresh: Time, Tradition, and Indo-Persian Literary Modernity." In *Time, History and the Religious Imaginary in South Asia*, edited by Anne Murphy, 12–39. London: Routledge, 2011.

——. "Secretary-Poets in Mughal India and the Ethos of Persian: The Case of Chandar Bhān Brahman." Ph.D. diss., University of Chicago, 2008.

——. *Writing Self, Writing Empire: Chandar Bhar Brahman and the Cultural World of the Indo-Persian State Secretary*. Oakland: University of California Press, 2015.

Koch, Ebba. *The Complete Taj Mahal and the Riverfront Gardens of Agra*. London: Thames and Hudson, 2006.

——. "The Mughal Emperor as Solomon, Majnun, and Orpheus, or the Album as a Think Tank for Allegory." *Muqarnas* 27 (2010): 277–311.

Kosambi, D. D. "Introduction." In *The Subhāṣitaratnakoṣa*, compiled by Vidyākara, edited by D. D. Kosambi and V. V. Gokhale, xiii–cvi. Cambridge, Mass.: Harvard University Press, 1957.

Koskikallio, Petteri, and Christophe Vielle. "Epic and Puranic Texts Attributed to Jaimini." *Indologica Taurinensia* 27 (2001): 67–93.

Krishnamurthi, R. "Jains at the Court of Akbar." *Journal of Indian History* 23 (1944): 137–43.

Kruijtzer, Gijs. *Xenophobia in Seventeenth-Century India*. Leiden: Leiden University Press, 2009.

Kugle, Scott Alan. *Sufis and Saints' Bodies: Mysticism, Corporeality, and Sacred Power in Islam*. Chapel Hill: University of North Carolina Press, 2007.

Kumar, Sunil. "Qutb and Modern Memory" In *The Partitions of Memory: The Afterlife of the Division of India*, edited by Suvir Kaul, 140–82. New Delhi: Permanent Black, 2001.

Lal, Ruby. *Domesticity and Power in the Early Mughal World*. Cambridge: Cambridge University Press, 2005.

Lal, Vinay. "Aurangzeb, Akbar, and the Communalization of History." *Manas* (1998), http://www.sscnet.ucla.edu/southasia/History/Mughals/Aurang3.html.

Lawrence, Bruce B. *Shahrastānī on the Indian Religions*. The Hague: Mouton, 1976.

—. "The Use of Hindu Religious Texts in al-Bīrūnī's *India* with Special Reference to Patanjali's Yoga-Sutras." In *The Scholar and the Saint: Studies in Commemoration of Abu'l-Rayhan al-Bīrūni and Jalal al-Din al-Rūmī*, edited by Peter J. Chelkowski, 29–48. New York: New York University Press, 1975.

Leach, Linda York. *Paintings from India*. London: Nour Foundation in association with Azimuth Editions and Oxford University Press, 1998.

Lefevere, André. "Composing the Other." In *Post-colonial Translation: Theory and Practice*, edited by Susan Bassnett and Harish Trivedi, 75–94. London: Routledge, 1999.

Lefèvre, Corinne. "The Court of ʿAbd-ur-Raḥīm Ḵẖān-i Ḵẖānān as a Bridge between Iranian and Indian Cultural Traditions." In *Culture in Circulation: Literature in Motion in Early Modern India*, edited by Thomas de Bruijn and Allison Busch, 75–106. Leiden: Brill, 2014.

—. "Europe–Mughal India–Muslim Asia: Circulation of Political Ideas and Instruments in Early Modern Times." In *Structures on the Move: Technologies of Governance in Transcultural Encounter*, edited by Antje Flüchter and Susan Richter, 127–45. Berlin: Springer, 2012.

—. "In the Name of the Fathers: Mughal Genealogical Strategies from Bābur to Shāh Jahān." *Religions of South Asia* 5, no. 1/2 (2011): 409–42.

—. "Recovering a Missing Voice from Mughal India: The Imperial Discourse of Jahāngīr (r. 1605–1627) in his Memoirs." *Journal of the Economic and Social History of the Orient* 50, no. 4 (2007): 452–89.

Levi, Scott. "The Indian Merchant Diaspora in Early Modern Central Asia and Iran." *Iranian Studies* 32, no. 4 (1999): 483–512.

Loomba, Ania. "Of Gifts, Ambassadors, and Copy-cats: Diplomacy, Exchange, and Difference in Early Modern India." In *Emissaries in Early Modern Literature and Culture: Mediation, Transmission, Traffic, 1550-1700*, edited by Brinda Charry and Gitanjali Shahani, 41–75. Farnham, Surrey, U.K.: Ashgate, 2009.

Losensky, Paul E. *Welcoming Fighānī: Imitation and Poetic Individuality in the Safavid-Mughal Ghazal*. Costa Mesa: Mazda, 1998.

Maclagan, E. D. "Jesuit Missions to the Emperor Akbar." *Journal of the Asiatic Society of Bengal* 65 (1896): 38–113.

MacLean, Derryl N. "Real Men and False Men at the Court of Akbar: The *Majalis* of Shaykh Mustafa Gujarati." In *Beyond Turk and Hindu: Rethinking Religious Identities in Islamicate South Asia*, edited by David Gilmartin and Bruce B. Lawrence, 199–215. Gainesville: University Press of Florida, 2000.

Mahapatra, Sri Kedarnath. "Some Forgotten Smṛti-Writers of Orissa: (2) Narasiṃha Vājapeyī." *Orissa Historical Research Journal* 2, no. 1 (1953): 1–16.

Malcolm, Sir John. *A Memoir of Central India, Including Malwa, and Adjoining Provinces*. 2 vols. London: Parbury and Allen, 1832.

Maneck, Susan Stiles. *The Death of Ahriman: Culture, Identity, and Theological Change Among the Parsis of India*. Bombay: K. R. Cama Oriental Institute, 1997.

Marroum, Marianne. "*Kalila wa Dimna*: Inception, Appropriation, and Transmimesis." *Comparative Literature Studies* 48, no. 4 (2011): 512–40.

Marshall, D. N. *Mughals in India: A Bibliographical Survey*. Vol. 1. Bombay: Asia Publishing House, 1967.

McGregor, Ronald Stuart. *Hindi Literature from Its Beginnings to the Nineteenth Century*. Wiesbaden: Harrassowitz, 1984.

Mehta, Makrand. *Indian Merchants and Entrepreneurs in Historical Perspective with Special Reference to Shroffs of Gujarat: 17th to 19th Centuries*. Delhi: Academic Foundation, 1991.

Meisami, Julie Scott. "The Historian and the Poet: Rāvandī, Nizami, and the Rhetoric of History." In *The Poetry of Nizami Ganjavi: Knowledge, Love, and Rhetoric*, edited by Kamran Talattof and Jerome W. Clinton, 97–128. New York: Palgrave, 2000.

—. "History as Literature." *Iranian Studies* 33, no. 1/2 (2000): 15–30.

—. *Medieval Persian Court Poetry*. Princeton: Princeton University Press, 1987.

—. "Mixed Prose and Verse in Medieval Persian Literature." In *Prosimetrum: Crosscultural Perspectives on Narrative in Prose and Verse*, edited by Joseph Harris and Karl Reichl, 295–319. Cambridge: Brewer, 1997.

Meredith-Owens, G., and R. H. Pinder-Wilson. "A Persian Translation of the *Mahābhārata*, with a Note on the Miniatures." *British Museum Quarterly* 20, no. 3 (1956): 62–65.

Minkowski, Christopher. "Advaita Vedānta in Early Modern History." *South Asian History and Culture* 2, no. 2 (2011): 205–31.

—. "Learned Brahmins and the Mughal Court: *The Jyotiṣas*." In *Religious Interactions in Mughal India*, edited by Vasudha Dalmia and Munis D. Faruqui, 102–34. New Delhi: Oxford University Press, 2014.

—. "On Sūryadāsa and the Invention of Bidirectional Poetry (*Vilomakāvya*)." *Journal of the American Oriental Society* 124, no. 2 (2004): 325–33.

Mitra, Babu Rajendralala. "The Alla Upanishad, a Spurious Chapter of the Atharva Veda—Text, Translation, and Notes." *Journal of the Asiatic Society of Bengal* 40 (1871): 170–76.

Mitra, Kalipada. "Jain Influence at Mughul Court." *Proceedings of the Indian History Congress* (1939): 1061–72.

Mohanty, Pramod Kumar. *Colonialism and South Asia: Cuttack, 1803–1947*. Kolkata: Bhattacharya, 2007.

Moin, A. Azfar. "Challenging the Mughal Emperor: The Islamic Millennium According to ʿAbd al-Qadir Badayuni." In *Islam in South Asia in Practice*, edited by Barbara D. Metcalf, 390–402. Princeton: Princeton University Press, 2009.

—. *The Millennial Sovereign: Sacred Kingship and Sainthood in Islam*. New York: Columbia University Press, 2012.

—. "Peering through the Cracks in the *Baburnama*: The Textured Lives of Mughal Sovereigns." *Indian Economic and Social History Review* 49, no. 4 (2012): 493–526.

Moosvi, Shireen. *The Economy of the Mughal Empire, c. 1595: A Statistical Study*. Delhi: Oxford University Press, 1987.

—, ed. and trans. *Episodes in the Life of Akbar: Contemporary Records and Reminiscences*. New Delhi: National Book Trust, 1994.

—. "The Mughal Encounter with Vedanta: Recovering the Biography of 'Jadrup.'" *Social Scientist* 30, no. 7/8 (2002): 13–23.

Mujtabai, Fatullah. *Aspects of Hindu Muslim Cultural Relations*. New Delhi: National Book Bureau, 1978.

——. "Persian Translations of Hindu Religious Literature." In *Anquetil Duperron Bicentenary Memorial Volume*, 13–24. Tehran: Anjuman-i Farhang-i Iran-i Bastan, 1973.

Mukherjee, Tarapada, and Irfan Habib. "Akbar and the Temples of Mathura and Its Environs." *Proceedings of the Indian History Congress* 48 (1987): 234–50.

——. "The Mughal Administration and the Temples of Vrindavan During the Reigns of Jahangir and Shahjahan." *Proceedings of the Indian History Congress* 49 (1988): 287–99.

Mukhia, Harbans. *Historians and Historiography During the Reign of Akbar*. New Delhi: Vikas, 1976.

Nahar, Puran Chand. "Rajgir Jain Inscription." *Journal of the Bihar and Orissa Research Society* 5 (1919): 331–43.

Nahar, Puran Chand, and Krishnachandra Ghosh. *An Epitome of Jainism, Being a Critical Study of Its Metaphysics, Ethics, and History in Relation to Modern Thought*. Calcutta: Duby, 1917.

Naik, Chhotubhai Ranchhodji. *'Abduʾr-Raḥīm Khān-i-Khānān and His Literary Circle*. Ahmedabad: Gujarat University, 1966.

Naim, C. M. "Popular Jokes and Political History: The Case of Akbar, Birbal and Mulla Do-Piyaza." *Economic and Political Weekly* 30, no. 24 (1995): 1456–64.

Nair, Shankar. "Sufism as Medium and Method of Translation: Mughal Translations of Hindu Texts Reconsidered." *Studies in Religion* 43, no. 3 (2014): 390–410.

Nandy, Ashis. "The Politics of Secularism and the Recovery of Religious Tolerance." In *Secularism and Its Critics*, edited by Rajeev Bhargava, 321–44. Oxford: Oxford University Press, 1998.

Naravane, M. S. *A Short History of Baglan*. Pune: Palomi, 1997.

Narayanan, Vasudha. "Religious Vocabulary and Regional Identity: A Study of the Tamil *Cirappuranam*." In *Beyond Turk and Hindu: Rethinking Religious Identities in Islamicate South Asia*, edited by David Gilmartin and Bruce B. Lawrence, 74–97. Gainesville: University Press of Florida, 2000.

Nicholson, Andrew J. "Doxography and Boundary-Formation in Late Medieval India." In *World View and Theory in Indian Philosophy*, edited by Piotr Balcerowicz, 103–18. Delhi: Manohar, 2012.

——. *Unifying Hinduism: Philosophy and Identity in Indian Intellectual History*. New York: Columbia University Press, 2010.

Nizami, Khaliq Ahmad. *On History and Historians of Medieval India*. New Delhi: Munshiram Manoharlal, 1983.

Nongbri, Brent. *Before Religion: A History of a Modern Concept*. New Haven: Yale University Press, 2013.

O'Hanlon, Rosalind. "Kingdom, Household and Body: History, Gender and Imperial Service Under Akbar." *Modern Asian Studies* 41, no. 5 (2007): 889–923.

——. "Letters Home: Banaras Pandits and the Maratha Regions in Early Modern India." *Modern Asian Studies* 44, no. 2 (2010): 201–40.

——. "Speaking from Siva's Temple: Banaras Scholar Households and the Brahman 'Ecumene' of Mughal India." *South Asian History and Culture* 2, no. 2 (2011): 253–77.

Olivelle, Patrick, ed. and trans. *The Dharmasūtras: The Law Codes of Ancient India*. Oxford: Oxford University Press, 1999.

Orsini, Francesca. "How to Do Multilingual Literary History? Lessons from Fifteenth- and Sixteenth-Century North India." *Indian Economic and Social History Review* 49, no. 2 (2012): 225–46.

Orthmann, Eva. "Court Culture and Cosmology in the Mughal Empire: Humāyūn and the Foundations of the *Dīn-i ilāhī*." In *Court Cultures in the Muslim World: Seventh to Nineteenth Centuries*, edited by Albrecht Fuess and Jan-Peter Hartung, 202–20. London: Routledge, 2011.

Patel, Alka, and Karen Leonard, eds. *Indo-Muslim Cultures in Transition*. Leiden: Brill, 2012.

Patel, Deven M. "Source, Exegesis, and Translation: Sanskrit Commentary and Regional Language Translation in South Asia." *Journal of the American Oriental Society* 131, no. 2 (2011): 245–66.

——. *Text to Tradition: The "Naiṣadhīyacarita" and Literary Community in South Asia*. New York: Columbia University Press, 2014.

Patkar, M. M. *History of Sanskrit Lexicography*. New Delhi: Munshiram Manoharlal, 1981.

——. "Moghul Patronage to Sanskrit Learning." *Poona Orientalist* 3 (1938): 164–75.

——. "Muhūrtaratna: A Religio-Astrological Treatise, Composed in the Reign of Aurangzeb." *Poona Orientalist* 3 (1938): 82–85.

Peterson, Peter. *A Fifth Report of Operations in Search of Sanscrit Mss. in the Bombay Circle, April 1892–March 1895*. Bombay: Government Central Press, 1896.

Phillips, Robert Lowell. "Garden of Endless Blossoms: Urdu *Rāmāyans* of the 19th and Early 20th Century." Ph.D. diss., University of Wisconsin–Madison, 2010.

Phukan, Shantanu. " 'Through Throats Where Many Rivers Meet': The Ecology of Hindi in the World of Persian." *Indian Economic and Social History Review* 38, no. 1 (2001): 33–58.

Pinch, William R. *Warrior Ascetics and Indian Empires*. New Delhi: Cambridge University Press, 2006.

Pingree, David. *Census of the Exact Sciences in Sanskrit: Series A*. 5 vols. Philadelphia: American Philosophical Society, 1970–1995.

——. *From Astral Omens to Astrology: From Babylon to Bīkāner*. Rome: Istituto Italiano per l'Africa e l'Oriente, 1997.

——. "The *Sarvasiddhāntarāja* of Nityānanda." In *The Enterprise of Science in Islam: New Perspectives*, edited by Jan P. Hogendijk and Abdelhamid I. Sabra, 269–84. Cambridge, Mass.: MIT Press, 2003.

Pirbhai, M. Reza. *Reconsidering Islam in a South Asian Context*. Leiden: Brill, 2009.

Pollock, Sheldon. "Comparison Without Hegemony." In *The Benefit of Broad Horizons: Intellectual and Institutional Preconditions for a Global Social Science; Festschrift for Björn Wittrock on the Occasion of his 65th Birthday*, edited by Hans Joas and Barbro Klein, 185–204. Leiden: Brill, 2010.

——. "The Death of Sanskrit." *Comparative Studies in Society and History* 43, no. 2 (2001): 392–426.

——. *The Ends of Man at the End of Premodernity*. 2004 Gonda Lecture. Amsterdam: Royal Netherlands Academy of Arts and Sciences, 2005.

——. *The Language of the Gods in the World of Men: Sanskrit, Culture, and Power in Premodern India*. Berkeley: University of California Press, 2006.

——. "The Languages of Science in Early Modern India." In *Forms of Knowledge in Early Modern Asia: Explorations in the Intellectual History of India and Tibet, 1500–1800*, edited by Sheldon Pollock, 19–48. Durham: Duke University Press, 2011.

——. "Mīmāṃsā and the Problem of History in Traditional India." *Journal of the American Oriental Society* 109, no. 4 (1989): 603–10.

——. "New Intellectuals in Seventeenth-Century India." *Indian Economic and Social History Review* 38, no. 1 (2001): 3–31.

———. "Pretextures of Time." *History and Theory* 46, no. 3 (2007): 364–81.
———. "Sanskrit Literary Culture from the Inside Out." In *Literary Cultures in History: Reconstructions from South Asia*, edited by Sheldon Pollock, 39–130. Berkeley: University of California Press, 2003.
Prasad, Mahesh. "The Unpublished Translation of the Upanishads by Prince Dara Shikoh." In *Dr. Modi Memorial Volume: Papers on Indo-Iranian and Other Subjects*, edited by Dr. Modi Memorial Volume Editorial Board, 622–38. Bombay: Fort Printing Press, 1930.
Prasad, Pushpa. "Akbar and the Jains." In *Akbar and His India*, edited by Irfan Habib, 97–108. Delhi: Oxford University Press, 1997.
———. *Sanskrit Inscriptions of Delhi Sultanate, 1191-1526*. Delhi: Centre of Advanced Study in History, Aligarh Muslim University; New York: Oxford University Press, 1990.
Qanungo, K. R. "Some Side-Lights on the Character and Court-Life of Shah Jahan." *Journal of Indian History* 8 (1929): 45–52.
Rafael, Vicente L. *The Promise of the Foreign: Nationalism and the Technics of Translation in the Spanish Philippines*. Durham: Duke University Press, 2005.
Raghavacharya, E. V. Vira. "Akbarīya-Kālidāsa Alias Govindabhaṭṭa (16th Century)." In *Bhārata-Kaumudī: Studies in Indology in Honour of Dr. Radha Kumud Mookerji*, 565–73. Allahabad: Indian Press, 1945.
Raghavan, V. "Kavīndrācārya Sarasvatī." In *D. R. Bhandarkar Volume*, edited by B. C. Law, 159–65. Calcutta: Indian Research Institute, 1940.
———. "The Vidagdhamukhamaṇḍana of Dharmadāsa." In *Professor P. K. Gode Commemoration Volume*, edited by H. L. Hariyappa and M. M. Patkar. Poona: Oriental Book Agency, 1960.
Raghavan, V., K. Kunjunni Raja, T. Aufrecht, et. al. eds. *New Catalogus Catalogorum: An Alphabetical Register of Sanskrit and Allied Works and Authors*. Madras: University of Madras, 1949–.
Rahman, Munibur. "Fayżī, Abu'l Fayż." In *Encyclopaedia Iranica* (1999, updated 2012), http://www.iranicaonline.org/articles/fayzi-abul-fayz.
Rahurkar, V. G. "The Bhāṣā-yogavāsiṣṭhasāra of Kavīndrācārya Sarasvatī." *Poona Orientalist* 21 (1956): 95–108.
Raj, Kapil. *Relocating Modern Science: Circulation and the Construction of Knowledge in South Asia and Europe, 1650-1900*. Basingstoke, U.K.: Palgrave Macmillan, 2007.
Raja, Kunhan. "A Sanskrit Letter of Mohamed Dara Shukoh." *Adyar Library Bulletin* 4, no. 3 (1940): 87–94.
Rao, Velcheru Narayana, David Shulman, and Sanjay Subrahmanyam. *Textures of Time: Writing History in South India 1600-1800*. New York: Other Press, 2003.
Renan, Ernest. "What Is a Nation?" In *Nation and Narration*, edited by Homi K. Bhabha, 8–22. London: Routledge, 1990.
Rezavi, Syed Ali Nadeem. "Religious Disputations and Imperial Ideology: The Purpose and Location of Akbar's *Ibadatkhana*." *Studies in History* 24, no. 2 (2008): 195–209.
Ricci, Ronit. "Citing as a Site: Translation and Circulation in Muslim South and Southeast Asia." *Modern Asian Studies* 46, no. 2 (2012): 331–53.
———. *Islam Translated: Literature, Conversion, and the Arabic Cosmopolis of South and Southeast Asia*. Chicago: University of Chicago Press, 2011.
Rice, Yael. "Mughal Interventions in the Rampur *Jāmiʿ al-Tavārīkh*." *Art Orientalis* 42 (2012): 151–64.
———. "A Persian Mahabharata: The 1598–1599 *Razmnama*." *Manoa* 22, no. 1 (2010): 125–31.

Richards, John F. "Early Modern India and World History." *Journal of World History* 8, no. 2 (1997): 197–209.

——. "The Formulation of Imperial Authority Under Akbar and Jahangir." In *The Mughal State 1526–1750*, edited by Muzaffar Alam and Sanjay Subrahmanyam, 126–67. Delhi: Oxford University Press, 1998.

——. *The Mughal Empire.* Cambridge: Cambridge University Press, 1993.

Riedel, Dagmar. "Kalila wa Demna I: Redactions and Circulation." *Encyclopaedia Iranica* (2010), http://www.iranicaonline.org/articles/kalila-demna-i.

Rieu, Charles. *Catalogue of the Persian Manuscripts in the British Museum.* 3 vols. London: British Museum, 1879–1883.

Rizvi, Saiyid Athar Abbas. "Dimensions of *Ṣulḥ-i Kul* (Universal Peace) in Akbar's Reign and the *Ṣūfī* theory of Perfect Man." In *Akbar and His Age*, edited by Iqtidar Alam Khan, 3–22. New Delhi: Northern Book Centre, 1999.

——. *A History of Sufism in India.* Vol. 2. New Delhi: Munshiram Manoharlal, 1983.

——. *Religious and Intellectual History of the Muslims in Akbar's Reign, with Special Reference to Abu'l Fazl, 1556–1605.* New Delhi: Munshiram Manoharlal, 1975.

Robinson, Chase F. *Islamic Historiography.* Cambridge: Cambridge University Press, 2003.

Robinson, Francis. "Perso-Islamic Culture in India from the Seventeenth to the Early Twentieth Century." In *Turko-Persia in Historical Perspective*, edited by Robert L. Canfield, 104–31. Cambridge: Cambridge University Press, 1991.

Roxburgh, David J. *Prefacing the Image: The Writing of Art History in Sixteenth-Century Iran.* Leiden: Brill, 2001.

Sachau, Ed, and Hermann Ethe. *Catalogue of the Persian, Turkish, Hindustani, and Pushtu Manuscripts in the Bodleian Library.* Vol 1. Oxford: Clarendon Press, 1889.

Said, Edward W. *Culture and Imperialism.* New York: Vintage, 1994.

——. *Humanism and Democratic Criticism.* New York: Columbia University Press, 2004.

Sarma, D. D. "Saṃskṛtapārasīkapadaprakāśa: Ek viśleṣaṇātmak paricay." In *Saṃskṛta Sāhitya ko Islām-Paramparā kā Yogadāna*, edited by Radhavallabh Tripathi, 187–200. Sagara: Sanskrit Parishad, 1986.

Sarma, Sreeramula Rajeswara. "A Bilingual Astrolabe from the Court of Jahāngīr." *Indian Historical Review* 38, no. 1 (2011): 77–117.

——. "From Yāvanī to Saṃskṛtam: Sanskrit Writings Inspired by Persian Works." *Studies in the History of Indian Thought* 14 (2002): 71–88.

——. "Jyotiṣarāja at the Mughal Court." In *Studies on Indian Culture, Science and Literature: Being Prof. K. V. Sarma Felicitation Volume Presented to Him on His 81st Birthday*, edited by N. Gangadharan, S. A. S. Sarma, and S. S. R. Sarma, 363–71. Chennai: Sree Sarada Education Society Research Centre, 2000.

——. "Persian-Sanskrit Lexica and the Dissemination of Islamic Astronomy and Astrology in India." In *Kayd: Studies in History of Mathematics, Astronomy and Astrology in Memory of David Pingree*, edited by Gherardo Gnoli and Antonio Panaino, 129–50. Rome: Istituto Italiano per l'Africa e l'Oriente, 2009.

——. "Sanskrit Manuals for Learning Persian." In *Adab Shenasi*, edited by Azarmi Dukht Safavi, 1–12. Aligarh: Aligarh Muslim University, 1996.

——. "Sulṭān, Sūri and the Astrolabe." *Indian Journal of History of Science* 35, no. 2 (2000): 129–47.

——. "Translation of Scientific Texts into Sanskrit under Sawai Jai Singh." *Sri Venkateswara University Oriental Journal* 41 (1998): 67–87.

Sastri, Hirananda. *Ancient Vijñaptipatras*. Baroda: Baroda State Press, 1942.
Savant, Sarah. "Finding Our Place in the Past: Genealogy and Ethnicity in Islam." Ph.D. diss., Harvard University, 2006.
Scharfe, Hartmut. *Grammatical Literature*. Wiesbaden: Harrassowitz, 1977.
Scheurleer, Pauline Lunsingh, and Gijs Kruijtzer. "Camping with the Mughal Emperor: A Golkonda Artist Portrays a Dutch Ambassador in 1689." *Arts of Asia* 35, no. 3 (2005): 48–60.
Schimmel, Annemarie. "A Dervish in the Guise of a Prince: Khān-i Khānān Abdur Rahīm as a Patron." In *The Powers of Art: Patronage in Indian Culture*, edited by Barbara Stoler Miller, 202–23. Delhi: Oxford University Press, 1992.
Schofield, Katherine Butler. "Reviving the Golden Age Again: 'Classicization,' Hindustani Music, and the Mughals." *Ethnomusicology* 54, no. 3 (2010): 484–517.
Schrader, F. Otto. *A Descriptive Catalogue of the Sanskrit Manuscripts in the Adyar Library (Theosophical Society)*. Vol. 1, Upaniṣads. Madras: Oriental, 1908.
Sen, Amartya. *The Argumentative Indian: Writings on Indian History, Culture and Identity*. New York: Farrar, Straus and Giroux, 2005.
Sen, Shekhar Kumar. "Introduction." In *Jaiminiya Ashvamedha Parvan*, edited by Pradip Bhattacharya. Calcutta: Writers Workshop, 2008.
Seyller, John. "The Inspection and Valuation of Manuscripts in the Imperial Mughal Library." *Artibus Asiae* 57, no. 3/4 (1997): 243–349.
———. "Model and Copy: The Illustration of Three *Razmnāma* Manuscripts." *Archives of Asian Art* 38 (1985): 37–66.
———. *Workshop and Patron in Mughal India: The Freer Rāmāyaṇa and Other Illustrated Manuscripts of ʿAbd al-Raḥīm*. Washington, D.C.: Artibus Asiae, 1999.
Shah, Umakant P. "Śabda-vilāsa or Pārasīnāmamālā of Mantrī Salakṣa of Gujarat." *Vimarśa: A Half-Yearly Research Bulletin of Rashtriya Sanskrit Samsthan* 1, no. 1 (1972): 31–36.
Shamma, Tarek. "Translating into the Empire: The Arabic Version of *Kalila wa Dimna*." *Translator* 15, no. 1 (2009): 65–86.
Sharma, Dasharatha. "The Three Earliest Jain Influencers of Mughal Religious Policy: Padmasundara, Ānandarāja, and Ajayarāja." *Annals of the Bhandarkar Oriental Research Institute 1944* (1945): 145–46.
Sharma, Har Dutt. "A Forgotten Event of Shah Jehan's Reign." In *Mahamahopadhyaya Kuppuswami Sastri Commemoration Volume*, 53–60. Madras: G.S. Press, 1936.
———. "The Poet Rudra and His Works." In *Woolner Commemoration Volume*, edited by Mohammad Shafi, 241–44. Lahore: Mehar Chand Lachhman Das, 1940.
Sharma, Sri Ram. "A Little Known Persian Version of the Ramayan." *Islamic Culture* 7 (1933): 673–78.
Sharma, Sunil. "Amir Khusraw and the Genre of Historical Narratives in Verse." *Comparative Studies of South Asia, Africa and the Middle East* 22, nos. 1–2 (2002): 112–18.
———. *Amir Khusraw: The Poet of Sufis and Sultans*. Oxford: Oneworld, 2005.
———. "The Nizamshahi Persianate Garden in Zuhūrī's *Sāqīnāma*." In *Garden and Landscape Practices in Pre-colonial India: Histories from the Deccan*, edited by Daud Ali and Emma J. Flatt, 159–71. New Delhi: Routledge, 2012.
———. "Novelty, Tradition and Mughal Politics in Nauʿī's *Sūz u Gudāz*." In *The Necklace of the Pleiades: Studies in Persian Literature Presented to Heshmat Moayyad on His 80th Birthday; 24 Essays on Persian Literature, Culture and Religion*, edited by Franklin Lewis and Sunil Sharma, 251–65. Leiden: Leiden University Press, 2010.

——. "The Production of Mughal *Shāhnāmas*: Imperial, Sub-Imperial, and Provincial Manuscripts." In *Ferdowsi's Shāhnāma: Millennial Perspectives*, edited by Olga M. Davidson and Marianna Shreve Simpson, 86–107. Cambridge, Mass.: Harvard University Press, 2013.

——. "Translating Gender: Āzād Bilgrāmī on the Poetics of the Love Lyric and Cultural Synthesis." *Translator* 15, no. 1 (2009): 87–103.

Shastri, Mahamahopadhyaya Haraprasad. *A Descriptive Catalogue of Sanskrit Manuscripts in the Government Collection Under the Care of the Asiatic Society*. 2nd ed. Vol. 4. Kolkata: Asiatic Society, 2005.

Sheikh, Samira. *Forging a Region: Sultans, Traders, and Pilgrims in Gujarat, 1200–1500*. Delhi: Oxford University Press, 2010.

Sheth, Chimanlal Bhailal. *Jainism in Gujarat (A.D. 1100 to 1600)*. Bombay: Shree Vijaydevsur Sangh Gnan Samity, 1953.

Shukla, N. S. "Persian Translations of Sanskrit Works." *Indological Studies* 3, nos. 1–2 (1974): 175–91.

Sircar, Dineschandra. *Studies in Indian Coins*. Delhi: Motilal Banarsidass, 1968.

Skelton, Robert. "Mughal Paintings from Harivaṃśa Manuscript." *Victoria and Albert Museum Yearbook* 2 (1970): 41–54.

Slaje, Walter. "Der Pārasīprakāśa: Über das indische Modell für Kṛṣṇadāsas persische Grammatik aus der Moġulzeit." In *Akten des Melzer-Symposiums 1991: Veranstaltet aus Anlass der Hundertjahrfeier indo-iranistischer Forschung in Graz (13.–14. November 1991)*, edited by Walter Slaje and Christian Zinko, 243–73. Graz: Leykam, 1992.

——. *Medieval Kashmir and the Science of History*. Madden Lecture 2003–04. Austin: South Asia Institute, University of Texas at Austin, 2004.

——. "A Note on the Genesis and Character of Śrīvara's So-Called '*Jaina-Rājataraṅgiṇī*.'" *Journal of the American Oriental Society* 125, no. 3 (2005): 379–88.

Smith, Vincent A. "The Confusion Between Hamida Bano Begam (Maryam-Makani), Akbar's Mother, and Haji Begam or Bega Begam, the Senior Widow of Humayun: Humayun's Tomb." *Journal of the Royal Asiatic Society of Great Britain and Ireland* (1917): 551–60.

——. "The Jain Teachers of Akbar." In *Commemorative Essays Presented to Sir Ramkrishna Gopal Bhandarkar*, 265–76. Poona: Bhandarkar Oriental Research Institute, 1917.

Smith, W. L. "Strīrājya: Indian Accounts of Kingdoms of Women." *Studia Orientalia* 94 (2001): 465–77.

Sreenivasan, Ramya. *The Many Lives of a Rajput Queen: Heroic Pasts in India c. 1500–1900*. Seattle: University of Washington Press, 2007.

Stainton, Hamsa. "Stotras, Sanskrit Hymns." In *Brill's Encyclopedia of Hinduism, Volume Two: Sacred Texts, Ritual Traditions, Arts, Concepts*, edited by Knut A. Jacobsen et al., 193–207. Leiden: Brill, 2010.

Starn, Randolph. "The Early Modern Muddle." *Journal of Early Modern History* 6, no. 3 (2002): 296–307.

Stewart, Tony K. "In Search of Equivalence: Conceiving Muslim-Hindu Encounter Through Translation Theory." *History of Religions* 40, no. 3 (2001): 260–87.

Subrahmanyam, Sanjay. *Courtly Encounters: Translating Courtliness and Violence in Early Modern Eurasia*. Cambridge, Mass.: Harvard University Press, 2012.

——. *Mughals and Franks: Explorations in Connected History*. New Delhi: Oxford University Press, 2005.

——. "Review of *The Economy of the Mughal Empire, c. 1595: A Statistical Study*." *Indian Economic and Social History Review* 25, no. 1 (1988): 103–7.

——. "Taking Stock of the Franks: South Asian Views of Europeans and Europe, 1500–1800." *Indian Economic and Social History Review* 42, no. 1 (2005): 69–100.

Subtelny, Maria Eva, and Charles Melville. "Ḥāfeẓ-e Abru." In *Encyclopaedia Iranica* (2012), http://www.iranicaonline.org/articles/hafez-e-abru.

Sukthankar, Vishnu S. "Prolegomena." In *The Mahābhārata, for the First Time Critically Edited*, edited by Vishnu S. Sukthankar et. al. Vol. 1. Poona: Bhandarkar Oriental Research Institute, 1933.

Taft, Frances H. "Honor and Alliance: Reconsidering Mughal-Rajput Marriages." In *The Idea of Rajasthan: Explorations in Regional Identity*, edited by Karine Schomer, Joan L. Erdman, Deryck O. Lodrick, and Lloyd I. Rudolph, 2:217–41. New Delhi: South Asia Publications, 1994.

Talbot, Cynthia. "Inscribing the Other, Inscribing the Self: Hindu-Muslim Identities in Pre-Colonial India." *Comparative Studies in Society and History* 37, no. 4 (1995): 692–722.

——. "Justifying Defeat: A Rajput Perspective on the Age of Akbar." *Journal of the Economic and Social History of the Orient* 55, nos. 2–3 (2012): 329–68.

Tavakoli-Targhi, Mohamad. "Contested Memories: Narrative Structures and Allegorical Meanings of Iran's Pre-Islamic History." *Iranian Studies* 29, nos. 1–2 (1996): 149–75.

——. *Refashioning Iran: Orientalism, Occidentalism, and Historiography*. Basingstoke, U.K.: Palgrave, 2001.

Thackston, Wheeler M. "Literature." In *The Magnificent Mughals*, edited by Zeenut Ziad, 83–111. Oxford: Oxford University Press, 2002.

Thapar, Romila. *Somanatha: The Many Voices of a History*. New Delhi: Penguin, 2004.

——. "The Tyranny of Labels." *Social Scientist* 24, no. 9/10 (1996): 3–23.

Trautmann, Thomas R. *Aryans and British India*. Berkeley: University of California Press, 1997.

Truschke, Audrey. "Contested History: Brahmanical Memories of Relations with the Mughals." *Journal of the Economic and Social History of the Orient* 58, no. 4 (2015): 419–52.

——. "Dangerous Debates: Jain Responses to Theological Challenges at the Mughal Court." *Modern Asian Studies* 49, no. 5 (2015): 1311–1344. First published online February 27, 2015.

——. "Defining the Other: An Intellectual History of Sanskrit Lexicons and Grammars of Persian." *Journal of Indian Philosophy* 40, no. 6 (2012): 635–68.

——. "The Mughal *Book of War*: A Persian Translation of the Sanskrit *Mahabharata*." *Comparative Studies of South Asia, Africa and the Middle East* 31, no. 2 (2011): 506–20.

——. "Setting the Record Wrong: A Sanskrit Vision of Mughal Conquests." *South Asian History and Culture* 3, no. 3 (2012): 373–96.

van der Kuijp, Leonard W. J. "The Earliest Indian Reference to Muslims in a Buddhist Philosophical Text of *Circa* 700." *Journal of Indian Philosophy* 34, no. 3 (2006): 169–202.

van der Veer, Peter. "Does Sanskrit Knowledge Exist?" *Journal of Indian Philosophy* 36, nos. 5–6 (2008): 633–41.

Vassie, Roderic. "ʿAbd al-Raḥman Chishtī and the Bhagavadgita: 'Unity of Religion' Theory in Practice." In *The Legacy of Medieval Persian Sufism*, edited by Leonard Lewisohn, 367–77. London: Khaniqahi-Nimatullahi, 1992.

——. "Persian Interpretations of the *Bhagavadgītā* in the Mughal Period: With Special Reference to the Sufi Version of ʿAbd al-Raḥmān Chishtī." Ph.D. diss., School of Oriental and African Studies, University of London, 1988.

Versteegh, Kees. *Landmarks in Linguistic Thought III: The Arabic Linguistic Tradition*. London: Routledge, 1997.

Vidyavijayji, Muniraj. *A Monk and a Monarch*. Translated by Dolarrai R. Mankad. Baroda: Deepchandji Banthia, 1944.

von Hees, Syrinx. "The Astonishing: A Critique and Re-reading of ʿAǧāʾib Literature." *Middle Eastern Literatures* 8, no. 2 (2005): 101–20.

von Hirschhausen, Ulrike, and Jörn Leonhard. "Beyond Rise, Decline and Fall: Comparing Multi-Ethnic Empires in the Long Nineteenth Century." In *Comparing Empires: Encounters and Transfers in the Long Nineteenth Century*, edited by Jörn Leonhard and Ulrike von Hirschhausen, 9–36. Göttingen: Vandenhoeck and Ruprecht, 2011.

Vose, Steven M. "The Making of a Medieval Jain Monk: Language, Power, and Authority in the Works of Jinaprabhasūri (c. 1261–1333)." Ph.D. diss., University of Pennsylvania, 2013.

Vrat, Satya. *Glimpses of Jaina Sanskrit Mahākāvyas*. Jaipur: Raj Publishing House, 2003.

——. *Studies in Jaina Sanskrit Literature*. Delhi: Eastern Book Linkers, 1994.

Wade, Bonnie C. *Imaging Sound: An Ethnomusicological Study of Music, Art, and Culture in Mughal India*. Chicago: University of Chicago Press, 1998.

Wagoner, Phillip B. "Fortuitous Convergences and Essential Ambiguities: Transcultural Political Elites in the Medieval Deccan." *International Journal of Hindu Studies* 3, no. 3 (1999): 241–64.

Washbrook, David. "Intimations of Modernity in South India." *South Asian History and Culture* 1, no. 1 (2009): 125–48.

Weber, Albrecht. "Über den Pârasîprakâçades Kṛishṇadâsa." In *Abhandlungen der Königlichen Akademie der Wissenschaften zu Berlin*. Berlin: Verlag der Königlichen Akademie der Wissenschaften, 1887.

Wensinck, A. J. "Al-Ḵh̲aḍir." In *Encyclopaedia of Islam Online*, 2nd ed., edited by P. Bearman, Th. Bianquis, C. E. Bosworth, E. van Donzel, W. P. Heinrichs. Brill, 2012.

Wink, André. *Akbar*. Oxford: Oneworld, 2009.

Winter, H. J. J., and Arshad Mirza. "Concerning the Persian Version of Līlāvatī." *Journal of the Asiatic Society. Science* 18, no. 1 (1952): 1–10.

Wujastyk, Dagmar, and Frederick M. Smith, eds. *Modern and Global Ayurveda: Pluralism and Paradigms*. Albany: SUNY Press, 2008.

Wujastyk, Dominik. "Contrasting Examples of Ayurvedic Creativity Around 1700." In *Mathematics and Medicine in Sanskrit*, edited by Dominik Wujastyk, 139–53. Delhi: Motilal Banarsidass, 2009.

Yashaschandra, Sitamshu. "From Hemacandra to *Hind Svarāj*: Religion and Power in Gujarati Literary Culture." In *Literary Cultures in History: Reconstructions from South Asia*, edited by Sheldon Pollock, 567–611. Berkeley: University of California Press, 2003.

Yücesoy, Hayrettín. "Translation as Self-Consciousness: Ancient Sciences, Antediluvian Wisdom, and the ʿAbbāsid Translation Movement." *Journal of World History* 20, no. 4 (2009): 523–57.

Zadeh, Travis. "The Wiles of Creation: Philosophy, Fiction, and the *ʿAjāʾib* Tradition." *Middle Eastern Literatures* 13, no. 1 (2010): 21–48.

Zaidi, Shailesh, ed. *Hinduism in Aligarh Manuscripts: Descriptive Catalogue of Persian Mss. of Maulana Azad Library, A.M. U., Aligarh; On Hindu Legends, Philosophy and Faith*. Patna: Khuda Bakhsh Oriental Public Library, 1994.

Ziauddin, M. *A Grammar of the Braj Bhakha by Mīrzā Ḵh̲ān (1676 A.D.)*. Calcutta: Visva-Bharati Book-Shop, 1935.

Zutshi, Chitralekha. *Languages of Belonging: Islam, Regional Identity, and the Making of Kashmir*. New York: Oxford University Press, 2004.

——. "Past as Tradition, Past as History: The *Rajatarangini* Narratives in Kashmir's Persian Historical Tradition." *Indian Economic and Social History Review* 50, no. 2 (2013): 201–19.

——. "Translating the Past: Rethinking *Rajatarangini* Narratives in Colonial India." *Journal of Asian Studies* 70, no. 1 (2011): 5–27.

INDEX

Abbasid translation movement, ix, 220
'Abd al-Azīz Shams Bahā-yi Nūrī, 285n91
'Abd al-Raḥīm Khān-i Khānān, 81–86, 227;
  and Akbari *Rāmāyan*, 211–14, 307n36,
  308nn40, 43; Hindi authorship, 84,
  274n93; and imperial reception of
  Sanskrit texts, 83–85, 274nn93, 94,
  275n102; military prowess, 84, 274n96;
  Sanskrit authorship, 84, 274n94,
  311n21; and Sultan Thānīsarī, 281n26.
  See also Khānakhānācarita
'Abd al-Sattār, 280n21
Abhinanda, 279n11, 307n29
Abū al-Faẓl: on Akbar's Hindi fluency,
  271n14; and atheism vs. monotheism,
  178, 179; *Bhagavadgītā* translations
  attributed to, 285n86; and al-Bīrūnī,
  147, 294n31; on cyclical time, 130,
  148–49, 289n170; Hīravijaya debate,
  42, 170–74, 183, 298nn14, 16, 17;
  and Mughal political concessions
  to Jains, 302n108; and *Rājataraṅgiṇī*
  translations, 279n9; on Sanskrit
  literary conventions, 274n87; and sun
  veneration, 122, 287n123; and titling,
  56, 59, 269n197. *See also Abū al-Faẓl's*
  Razmnāmah preface; Āʾīn-i Akbarī
Abū al-Faẓl's *Razmnāmah* preface, 102,
  103, 126–33, 279n1; on *ʿajāʾib*, 110; and
  Akbari *Rāmāyan*, 207–8; and Akbar's
  imperial image, 121, 122, 128; on

Brahmans, 131–32, 288–89nn163, 164;
  on credibility of *Mahābhārata*, 130–31,
  140; Firishtah's reliance on, 218–19;
  on *Harivaṃśa*, 282n37; on importance
  of *Mahābhārata*, 139; influence of,
  132–33, 208, 289n170, 307n16; on
  inner/outer rulership, 131, 288n156;
  limited audience for, 214; and *rājāvalīs*,
  291n216; Ṭāhir Muḥammad Sabzavārī's
  use of, 138; on *taqlīd* vs. *taḥqīq*, 128–29,
  287n136, 288n148. *See also Abū al-Faẓl's*
  Razmnāmah preface on Islam
Abū al-Faẓl's *Razmnāmah* preface on
  Islam: and Akbar's conflicts with
  ulama, 120, 127–28, 263n74; and
  Akbar's imperial image, 129–30;
  Badāʾūnī on, 208, 209, 306n13; and
  Brahmanical attitudes toward Islam,
  131–32, 288–89nn163, 164; and
  Firishtah, 219; and intrareligious
  tensions, 126–27, 287n136; and *taqlīd*
  vs. *taḥqīq*, 128–29, 287n136
Abū Maʿshar, 263n84
Account of India. See Āʾīn-i Akbarī
Adam, 128, 162, 219
Ādi Parvan (Fayżī's *Mahābhārata* retelling),
  133, 136
Ādi Parvan (*Razmnāmah*), 107, 112
Advaita Vedanta, 224, 225, 244
Agra, 13, 36, 88, 256n89
Ahmed, Manan, 231

SOUTH ASIA ACROSS THE DISCIPLINES

◈ ◈ ◈

Extreme Poetry: The South Asian Movement of Simultaneous Narration by Yigal Bronner (Columbia)

The Social Space of Language: Vernacular Culture in British Colonial Punjab by Farina Mir (California)

Unifying Hinduism: Philosophy and Identity in Indian Intellectual History by Andrew J. Nicholson (Columbia)

The Powerful Ephemeral: Everyday Healing in an Ambiguously Islamic Place by Carla Bellamy (California)

Secularizing Islamists? Jama'at-e-Islami and Jama'at-ud-Da'wa in Urban Pakistan by Humeira Iqtidar (Chicago)

Islam Translated: Literature, Conversion, and the Arabic Cosmopolis of South and Southeast Asia by Ronit Ricci (Chicago)

Conjugations: Marriage and Form in New Bollywood Cinema by Sangita Gopal (Chicago)

Unfinished Gestures: Devadāsīs, Memory, and Modernity in South India by Davesh Soneji (Chicago)

Document Raj: Writing and Scribes in Early Colonial South India by Bhavani Raman (Chicago)

The Millennial Sovereign: Sacred Kingship and Sainthood in Islam by A. Azfar Moin (Columbia)

Making Sense of Tantric Buddhism: History, Semiology, and Transgression in the Indian Traditions by Christian K. Wedemeyer (Columbia)

The Yogin and the Madman: Reading the Biographical Corpus of Tibet's Great Saint Milarepa by Andrew Quintman (Columbia)

Body of Victim, Body of Warrior: Refugee Families and the Making of Kashmiri Jihadists by Cabeiri deBergh Robinson (California)

Receptacle of the Sacred: Illustrated Manuscripts and the Buddhist Book Cult in South Asia by Jinah Kim (California)

Cut-Pieces: Celluloid Obscenity and Popular Cinema in Bangladesh by Lotte Hoek (Columbia)

From Text to Tradition: The Naisadhīyacarita *and Literary Community in South Asia* by Deven M. Patel (Columbia)

Democracy against Development: Lower Caste Politics and Political Modernity in Postcolonial India by Jeffrey Witsoe (Chicago)

Writing Resistance: The Rhetorical Imagination of Hindi Dalit Literature by Laura R. Brueck (Columbia)

Wombs in Labor: Transnational Commercial Surrogacy in India by Amrita Pande (Columbia)

I Too Have Some Dreams: N. M. Rashed and Modernism in Urdu Poetry by A. Sean Pue (California)

We Were Adivasis: Aspiration in an Indian Scheduled Tribe by Megan Moodie (Chicago)

The Place of Devotion: Siting and Experiencing Divinity in Bengal-Vaishnavism by Sukanya Sarabadhikary (California)

Writing Self, Writing Empire: Chandar Bhan Brahman and the Cultural World of the Early Modern Indo-Persian State by Rajeev Kinra (California)

CPSIA information can be obtained
at www.ICGtesting.com
Printed in the USA
JSHW081556241022
32060JS00001B/17

9 780231 173636